Monetary Theory

To my mother Claire
and brother Larry

Monetary Theory

Alan A. Rabin

The University of Tennessee at Chattanooga

Edward Elgar

Cheltenham, UK • Northampton, MA, USA

Published by
Edward Elgar Publishing Limited
Glensanda House
Montpellier Parade
Cheltenham
Glos GL50 1UA
UK

Edward Elgar Publishing, Inc.
136 West Street
Suite 202
Northampton
Massachusetts 01060
USA

A catalogue record for this book
is available from the British Library

Library of Congress Cataloguing in Publication Data
Rabin, Alan A.
   Monetary theory / Alan A. Rabin.
       p. cm.
   Includes bibliographical references.
   1. Money. I. Title.

   HG220.A2R33 2004
   339.5'3—dc22

                                                        2003066006

ISBN 1 84064 744 2

Printed and bound in Great Britain by MPG Books Ltd, Bodmin, Cornwall

Contents

Figures

Preface

Leland Yeager is probably best known for his contributions to international economics and monetary reform. While he has written highly regarded work in the area of trade theory (for example, Yeager and Tuerck, 1966, 1976), he is most famous for his *International Monetary Relations* (1966, 1976b), a landmark book that became the standard reference in the field. Both editions of that volume are divided into theory and historical narrative. (Friedman and Schwartz's (1963) purely historical narrative was published just three years earlier.) Some economists have recently 'rediscovered' many of the ideas, theories and evidence found in Leland's books of over a quarter of a century ago. In the area of monetary reform, he and Robert Greenfield developed the much discussed 'BFH system'.

I believe his legacy, however, will be in the entire arena of monetary theory. When I first arrived at the University of Tennessee at Chattanooga in 1977, students would ask me whether I was a 'Keynesian' or a 'monetarist'. I would reply: 'Neither, I am a Yeagerite'. Since then labels have changed and schools of thought have come and gone, but the one constant is that I still regard myself as a 'Yeagerite', albeit a little wiser and a lot older. I view this book as a tribute to Leland's enormous contributions to monetary theory, especially his development of monetary-disequilibrium theory.

Years ago I joined Leland's efforts to produce this work, which is a hybrid of treatise and graduate textbook. Toward what I hoped was the end of what we both recognized as an excessively long-drawn-out process, Leland felt obliged to withdraw his name as co-author of the book. Nevertheless, the bulk of the material contained in it (both published and unpublished) is his. Leland has provided draft chapters as well as numerous notes and other materials. We have had voluminous correspondence and have exchanged many drafts. I have copious notes taken during our many visits together. He has been kind and patient in answering literally thousands of questions.

As sole author of this book, I accept responsibility for any errors. On the other hand, the theories presented are Leland's, and he should receive full credit for them. The Acknowledgements section lists his published articles and books, from which passages appear in part here. In no case was an article or manuscript reproduced in its entirety. I have edited this material, which includes passages from articles that we wrote together. In most cases I have tried to stay as close as possible to the original wording, sometimes repeating it verbatim, sometimes not.

I have chosen to focus on what I consider to be the timeless, enduring fundamentals of monetary-disequilibrium theory. The book does not examine the empirical evidence which supports this theory. Nor does it need to do so. I believe that Clark Warburton, Milton Friedman, Anna Schwartz, Karl Brunner, Allan Meltzer, Phillip Cagan, David Laidler, Leland Yeager, and many others already have provided ample evidence in support of orthodox monetarism. This book provides the theory – with special emphasis on the processes involved – which underlies the monetarist evidence. It specifically sheds light on the so-called 'black box' of the monetarists (see pages 129–30 below).

Two schools of thought dominate the textbook market. First is the new Keynesian economics. Second is the fashionable exaggeration of monetarism into the so-called new classical macroeconomics. These two schools, reviewed in chapters 6, 7 and 8, have crowded the monetary-disequilibrium hypothesis, or orthodox monetarism, off the intellectual stage. Because this work tries to remedy this imbalance, I feel no obligation to give equal space to doctrines and pieces of apparatus already receiving ample exposure. Instead of reproducing whatever may be considered (rightly or wrongly) to be standard fare, I concentrate on what I judge to be the essentials of the topic.

Alan Rabin

Acknowledgements

When I joined Professor Yeager's efforts to produce this book many years ago, little did I realize how much theory I still needed to learn. Fortunately Leland's great devotion to learning, teaching and economics was highly contagious. I appreciate the numerous hours he spent with me discussing monetary theory and responding to my thousands of inquiries. I shall always be grateful for his unparalleled patience and generosity. Writing this book has been a once-in-a-lifetime experience; it truly has been a labor of love.

So many people have helped me over the years that trying to list them all would be a formidable task. Moreover, I fear leaving some of them out. However, I do want to single out Tom Humphrey of the Federal Reserve Bank of Richmond. Although he came aboard the project at the tail end, I could not have completed it without his help. He provided the encouragement, 'sounding board' and 'third voice' that I sorely needed.

Parts of the book include extracts from material that Leland has previously published. I want to thank the editors and publishers who have granted permission to use the following:

Birch, D.E., A.A. Rabin and L.B. Yeager (1982), 'Inflation, output, and employment: some clarifications', *Economic Inquiry*, April, 209–21, material is reproduced by permission of the Western Economic Association.

Rabin, A.A. and L.B. Yeager (1982), *Monetary Approaches to the Balance of Payments and Exchange Rates*, Essays in International Finance No. 148, November, copyright *c*. 1982 by the International Finance Section of Princeton University, permission granted by publisher.

Rabin, A.A. and L.B. Yeager (1997), 'The monetary transmission mechanism', *Eastern Economic Journal*, Summer, 293–9, permission granted by the Eastern Economic Association.

Yeager, L.B. (1956), 'A cash-balance interpretation of depression', *Southern Economic Journal*, April, 438–47, appearing with permission of the Southern Economic Association.

Excerpts from *The International Monetary Mechanism* by Yeager, L.B. copyright *c*. 1968 by Holt, Rinehart and Winston, reprinted by permission of the publisher.

Yeager, L.B. (1968), 'Essential properties of the medium of exchange', *Kyklos*, **21** (1), 45–69, permission granted by Helbing & Lichtenhahn Verlag AG.

Yeager, L.B. (1973), 'The Keynesian diversion', *Western Economic Journal*, June, 150–63, material is reproduced by permission of the Western Economic Association.

Yeager, L.B. (1976), *International Monetary Relations Theory History and Policy*, 2nd edition, New York: Harper & Row, permission granted by Pearson Education, Inc.

Yeager, L.B. (1978), 'What are banks?', *Atlantic Economic Journal*, December, 1–14, permission granted by the *Atlantic Economic Journal*.

Yeager, L.B. (1979), 'Capital paradoxes and the concept of waiting', in Mario J. Rizzo (ed.), *Time, Uncertainty and Disequilibrium: Exploration of Austrian Themes*, Lexington, MA: Lexington Books, pp. 187–214, permission granted by Mario J. Rizzo.

Yeager, L.B. and associates (1981), *Experiences with Stopping Inflation*, Washington, D.C.: American Enterprise Institute for Public Policy Research, permission granted by publisher.

Yeager, L.B. (1982), 'Individual and overall viewpoints in monetary theory', in Israel M. Kirzner (ed.), *Method, Process, and Austrian Economics: Essays in Honor of Ludwig von Mises*, Lexington, MA: Lexington Books, pp. 225–46, permission granted by Israel M. Kirzner.

Yeager, L.B. (1986), 'The significance of monetary disequilibrium', *Cato Journal*, Fall, 369–99, permission granted by the *Cato Journal*.

Yeager, L.B. and A.A. Rabin (1997), 'Monetary aspects of Walras's Law and the stock-flow problem', *Atlantic Economic Journal*, March, 18–36, permission granted by the *Atlantic Economic Journal*.

Several of the above articles are reprinted in Yeager, L.B. (1997), *The Fluttering Veil: Essays on Monetary Disequilibrium*, edited and with an introduction by George Selgin, Indianapolis: Liberty Fund.

1. Money in macroeconomics: frameworks of analysis

TWO APPROACHES TO MACROECONOMICS – SPENDING AND GOODS-AGAINST-GOODS

Monetary (or money/macro) theory investigates the services and disorders of money and the relations between money, production, employment and the level of prices. We define money 'narrowly' as media of exchange, including currency and all transaction deposits. Reasons for this definition will become clear as we move through the book. In addition to this narrow money, 'broad money' includes nearmoneys that do not circulate in payments. Examples include certificates of deposit, time deposits, and in some contexts, treasury bills and commercial paper.

Two approaches tackle the central questions of macroeconomics. One we call the *spending* approach. A second, the *goods-against-goods* (or Say's Law) approach, goes further back to the fundamentals of production and the exchange of goods against goods. These two approaches reconcile. No issue arises of a right one versus a wrong one. The spending approach is potentially misleading, however, unless grounded in the fundamentals of production and exchange.

Admittedly one can raise objections to the concept of total spending. According to Hutt (1979, Chapter 11), spending is an ex post notion, a money measure of exchanges accomplished, and so cannot be a determinant of nominal income or prices or anything else. (Other things being equal, the higher the prices at which a given volume of exchanges is measured, the greater the 'spending' observed.) This, however, is not the meaning we adopt. We stick closer to the ordinary dictionary meaning, according to which it makes sense to say that someone has gone on a spending spree. Total spending is the same as what is commonly called 'aggregate demand' for goods and services, expressed in money or nominal terms. Usually we mean spending on final output or nominal income. Spending that includes transactions in intermediate goods and services is much larger.

Concern with total spending, though misleading by itself, becomes more meaningful if linked to a disaggregated view of market transactions. Fundamentally, 'behind the veil of money', goods and services exchange against other

1

goods and services. The key question of macroeconomics boils down to how well or how poorly the market process facilitates these exchanges by coordinating the decentralized decisions of millions of people, making use of the specialized knowledge each possesses with respect to his own situation, and transmitting appropriate signals and incentives. A sufficiently disaggregated analysis considers how imbalance between desired and actual quantities of money can frustrate exchanges and discourage production, how such imbalance can arise, how appropriate price adjustments could cure or forestall it, and what circumstances impede the curative price adjustments.

It is not enough to consider how prices affect the demand for and supply of goods and services. It is also necessary to consider the *processes* whereby people determine prices and adjust them, readily or sluggishly, to clear markets under changed conditions. One price whose decentralized and piecemeal manner of determination requires special attention is the purchasing power of the money unit, the reciprocal of some sort of average price level. It is hardly a price in the ordinary, straightforward sense. Nevertheless, the relation between it and the nominal quantity of money in existence has much to do with the adequacy of total spending and with the economy's macroeconomic performance.

OUTPUT AND SPENDING

It is convenient to begin with questions that are *not* fundamental ones. Why they are not becomes clear later in this chapter. Figure 1.1 charts the growth and fluctuations over time of a country's total real income, both actual and potential. Because of the logarithmic vertical scale, a straight line would represent a constant growth rate. Total real income is the sum of the physical outputs of goods and services newly produced in the country (in a year, say). We need not be precise here about how different things are added up or just which of the national income and product concepts we mean. Potential (or full-employment) real income is the total output that could be produced in virtue of the economy's *real factors* – the population or labor force and its size, health and strength, skills, alertness to opportunities, orientation toward work and risk-bearing and other traditions and attitudes; natural resources; the state of technology; accumulated capital equipment (roads, harbors, buildings, machines and so forth), as well as the attitudes that influence saving and investment. Another real factor is the tightness of resource allocation or degree of efficiency of economic *coordination*, as influenced in part by legal and other institutions. The figure shows 'potential output' growing over time as the labor force grows in size and abilities, technology advances and capital equipment accumulates.

Figure 1.1 is consistent with Friedman's (1964, 1993) 'plucking model' of business fluctuations. Potential output acts as a ceiling against which actual

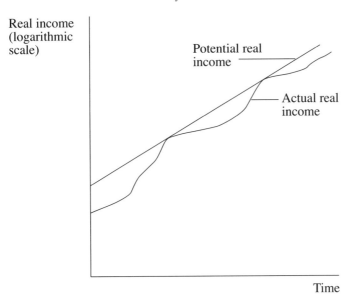

Figure 1.1   Growth of real income, actual and potential

output may bump after first being 'plucked downward' by economic forces. An asymmetry arises: a fall in output below the ceiling is followed by a rise in output of similar magnitude (that is, back to the ceiling), but a rise in output is not correlated with the subsequent contraction that occurs.[1] In contrast to self-generating business cycles, business fluctuations consist of recessions followed by recoveries. (Chapter 6 and Birch, Rabin and Yeager, 1982, explore the possible case of output temporarily expanding beyond its full-employment level.)

At least two other versions of Figure 1.1 appear in the literature. According to De Long (2000, p. 84), new Keynesian economists view business cycles as fluctuations in actual output around the sustainable long-run trend.[2] Advocates of real business cycle theory argue that the economy is always in equilibrium and that actual and potential output are equivalent. Output changes in response to random changes in technology (supply shocks), in which case both actual and potential output can permanently change (see pages 208–209 below).

Whether actual output fully meets the potential determined by real factors or instead sometimes falls short depends largely on *monetary factors*. Business firms produce in hope of selling their output – for money, and at a profit. They will not persist in producing things that they cannot expect to sell profitably. If total spending falls short of what is necessary to buy the potential output of a fully employed economy, output will fall short and workers will be unemployed. It hardly follows, however, that policy should always aim at pumping up the quantity of money and the flow of spending. Why that does not follow is one of the lessons of this book.

The distinction between monetary and real factors is not sharp. Monetary factors can influence real ones. Depression and unemployment due to too little money and spending will hold down income, saving and investment, and so the stock of productive equipment existing thereafter. This is just one example of how monetary instability can interfere with establishment of market-clearing prices and wages and so can undermine the coordination of different sectors of the economy. (We have listed the tightness of coordination among the real factors.) Conversely, real factors can influence monetary factors. Under a gold standard, improvements in gold mining will tend to expand the money supply. Under a passively managed and passively responding money and banking system, innovations that improve investment prospects will tend to expand the money supply. Still, the distinction between real and monetary factors, though fuzzy at the fringes, is useful.

To keep actual output growing over time along with potential output, spending must be adequate to buy that potential output and to buy the necessary labor and other inputs. Abstractly considered, any flow of spending would be adequate no matter how small in dollars if prices (including wages) were flexible enough. Prices could go down enough – the purchasing power of the dollar could rise enough – to make any nominal flow of spending suffice to buy full-employment output.

Reality though poses difficulties. First, prices and wages do not adjust instantly to market-clearing levels, and good reasons exist for their stickiness. Later chapters will examine these reasons. They will show why the term 'stickiness', though traditional, labels a complex condition and must not be taken too literally. Second, prices and wages are not all equally sticky, so a general decline would distort relative prices and wages during the process, and these distortions would also hamper transactions. A third difficulty concerns expectations. As people perceived rigidities gradually dissolving and the price level sagging, they would postpone purchases and hang onto money and claims expressed in money to gain from the expected further rise in its purchasing power. Fourth, price deflation spells a rise in the real burden of existing debt. The gains of creditors would not fully offset the losses of debtors. Creditors do not gain from an increase in the apparent real value of their claims if the debtors go bankrupt and the claims become uncollectible (Fisher, 1933).

As a practical matter then, price flexibility alone cannot be counted on to maintain full employment. To keep actual real income near its potential level total spending must be adequate to buy the output of a fully employed economy at approximately the *existing* general level of prices and wages. Spending must grow over time approximately in step with the growth in potential output due to real factors. History and theory suggest that markets can cope with a slightly slower growth of spending, requiring a mild and foreseeable downtrend of prices, but they cannot cope with sudden or gross deficiencies of spending. At the other extreme, too much spending causes inflation and associated disorders. Spending and its basis in the quantity of money – after all, spending is spending of money – are crucial to the economy's macroeconomic performance.

It is sometimes said that, in the long run, money and spending affect only the general price level and not the volume and pattern of real activity. Abstractly this may be true. Over a span of decades, say, prices are flexible and can adjust to monetary conditions and keep markets cleared. Over the long run, policy-makers cannot reasonably hope to stimulate economic activity through activist monetary manipulations. In the short run though, an erratically behaving money supply can disrupt economic activity. And the long run is a series of short runs. A depression caused by monetary deficiency, for example, can impair capital formation and so impair productive capacity for the longer run. Monetary forces can thus have long-run consequences for potential output itself. Avoiding disorders of money and spending can be important not only for the price level but also for real activity even over the long run.

TYPES OF 'SPENDING' ANALYSIS – KEYNESIAN AND MONETARIST SUBAPPROACHES

Still postponing attention to more fundamental questions, let us persist with what we have called the spending approach. This approach investigates whether total spending is deficient or excessive or just right for buying the output of a fully employed economy, and for buying it at the level of prices and wages so far prevailing. It investigates what determines total spending. It conceives of aggregate supply or potential output being confronted by aggregate demand, moneyed demand, demand backed up by readiness, willingness and ability to spend money on goods and services.

The spending approach divides into two subapproaches, conveniently called *Keynesian* and *monetarist*. These labels serve convenience only. What follows is not meant to characterize the views of particular economists.

The *Keynesian* subapproach tries to explain total spending or aggregate demand as the sum of its components: consumption, *intended* investment, government purchases and exports in excess of imports. For this reason, we sometimes call it the 'sum-of-components' approach. The components may be further broken down. Consumption includes spending on durable goods, nondurable goods and services. Intended investment includes construction of buildings and of equipment and intended inventory accumulation. Exports appear as a component because they correspond to spending by foreigners on current output of domestic factors of production. Imports appear as a subtracted item because they have already been counted in consumption, intended investment, government spending and perhaps in parts of exports. (Here we follow the typical textbook treatment where imports are first included in the components and then removed at the end, since they do not belong in the demand for domestic output.)

The Keynesian subapproach tries to distinguish strategic components of total spending, such as investment, from other components that supposedly behave in a more passive way. The notion of a consumption function relating consumption to income, together with the notion of investment's strategic role, gives rise to the Keynesian doctrine of the multiplier.

Total income is commonly described as consumption plus *actual* (or total) investment plus government spending plus exports minus imports. Actual or total investment is taken to include unintended or unplanned inventory changes as well as intended changes. In the simple textbook version the condition for equilibrium is that aggregate demand equals total income. Changes in aggregate demand lead to changes in income, and demand may just as well be deemed excessive as deficient.

An autonomous increase in intended private investment or in government deficit spending – which Sir Dennis Robertson (1963, p. 350) called 'honorary investment' – can supposedly have a multiplier effect on income. Such notions depend on an assumption of rigid or at least sticky prices. Decades of empirical work have successively reduced the estimated magnitude of the multiplier so that today it probably is not a whole lot larger than one.

The Keynesian subapproach is conducive to emphasis on supposed 'real factors' governing aggregate demand, such as the marginal propensity to consume (itself perhaps affected by income distribution), the general level of income and wealth, saving gaps possibly not fully filled by investment spending, the availability of investment outlets and other factors affecting incentives to invest. The version formerly popular in the textbooks accorded only a rather backdoor influence to money (the quantity of money affected investment spending, perhaps only feebly, by affecting the interest rate). Concerned as it is with the summation and interrelation of components of total spending, especially if these components are minutely subdivided, the Keynesian subapproach invites the construction of large, detailed macroeconomic models.

The *monetarist* subapproach reverses the emphasis. It is also concerned with spending on goods and services. But instead of focusing on what is being bought, it focuses on the money being spent. It recognizes that demanding goods and services means offering money for them (or offering claims denominated in money and ultimately to be settled in money). It investigates the flow of offers of money and, in particular, the relation between the stock of money and the flow of spending of it. Its reversal of emphasis makes the monetarist subapproach less concerned than the Keynesian with the details of spending patterns, and its econometric models tend to be smaller and simpler.

Relations Among the Subapproaches

The Keynesian and monetarist approaches to the analysis of spending need not conflict. If each is correctly formulated, they can be reconciled. There is no need to analyze a given set of real world phenomena in one way only. Analytical concepts are not imposed by the very structure of reality. On the contrary, the human mind devises concepts to use in seeking an organized understanding of what happens. For some purposes one set of concepts may be more convenient than another. Or using two or more sets may be more productive of insight than using one set alone, much as viewing an object from several different angles will yield more familiarity with it than one point of view alone. As the physicist David Bohm (1957, pp. 165–6) has written:

> ... the same natural laws can often be treated with the aid of a series of very different kinds of conceptual abstractions...[T]he different possible conceptual abstrac-tions...play the role of various views of different aspects of the same basic reality. *To the extent that these different abstractions have a common domain of validity,* they must lead to the same consequences (just as different views must be consistent with each other in their domain of overlap).

We are distinguishing between a *theory* and an *approach* or framework as Harvey Leibenstein does, in a more general context, in Chapter 2 of his *Beyond Economic Man* (1976). A theory makes assertions, conceivably falsifiable, about correspondences or interdependencies or cause-and-effect relations in the real world. A framework or approach merely focuses attention on particular aspects of reality in the hope of developing warranted assertions. Approaches to understanding reality that superficially seem quite different, such as the Keynesian and monetarist (sub)approaches under discussion here, may be compatible and indeed complementary. Each may furnish distinctive views of reality. We are not necessarily saying the same thing about both Keynesian and monetarist theories of income determination.

Contradictory propositions that appear when using the Keynesian and monetarist approaches invite re-examining them for internal inconsistency or for inconsistency with the body of economic theory or with observable fact. In searching for contradictions and trying to eliminate them, it is useful to try to translate propositions formulated in the concepts of one approach into those of the other. We shall say more later about this 'translation test'.[3]

We reiterate that approaches are not causal theories but rather ways of organizing discussion. Unlike theories, the question of 'right' or 'wrong' does not arise. For example, Rabin and Yeager (1982) distinguish between a 'weak version' of the monetary approach to the balance of payments and a 'strong version', which is a theory that happens not to be generally valid (see pages 264–5 below). The weak version is an approach or framework and therefore can*not* be tested, although theories or propositions derived from it certainly can be. The three approaches to balance-of-payments analysis that used to dominate the literature – monetary, elasticities and absorption – reconcile with one another (Mundell, 1968, pp. 150–51; Yeager 1976b and see pages 264–5 below).

Figure 1.2 classifies approaches to the central money/macro questions. It shows two subcategories of the monetarist approach – quantity-velocity and money-supply-and-demand (see the next section). It also shows the Keynesian approach as well as an alternative to either spending approach, the goods-against-goods view, that penetrates more deeply to the heart of macroeconomics. Each of the two dotted lines represents a particularly close affinity between the indicated sets of concepts.

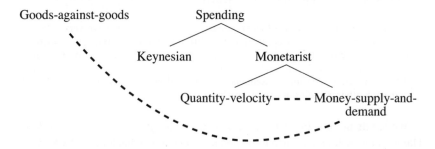

Figure 1.2   Classification of approaches and subapproaches to the central questions of money/macro theory

VARIETIES OF THE MONETARIST APPROACH

The monetarist (sub)approach subdivides further into two categories. One speaks of money's quantity and velocity, the other of its supply and demand. For demonstrating the close affinity between these two subcategories, it is convenient to recall the familiar identity: MV = PQ. Here M is the average nominal quantity of money existing in the country over a period of time. V for velocity, specifically income or circular velocity, is the average number of times a unit of money changes ownership in purchases of final goods and services produced during the period. P is the average price level of those goods and services. Q, quantity, is a measure of their physical volume produced. If each of its terms is defined with suitable care (with more precision than our purpose here requires), the equation is true as an identity, that is, true as a matter of interlocking definitions. In that respect its two sides are equal for broadly the same reason as why the two sides of a company's balance sheet sum to the same amount. In effect the equation says that the volume of payments for goods and services produced and *bought* during a period is equal to the aggregate value of goods and services produced and *sold*. On both sides of the equation the units are dollars per time period. The left side analyzes this dollar volume into a quantity of money and its rate of turnover, the right side into a physical rate of production and its average price.

The equation is a tautology, but tautologies are far from useless. A tautology can serve as a filing system or as a device for organizing theoretical and factual inquiry, such as inquiry into how money affects production and the price level. Combined with the translation test, tautologies can aid in pinpointing and correcting error. Any proposition that contradicts $MV = PQ$ must be wrong (compare Yeager, 1994a and pages 210–12 below).

$MV = PQ$ is a modification of Irving Fisher's equation of exchange, $MV = PT$. There T expresses the physical volume of transactions in goods and services and securities, both currently produced ones and already existing ones. An item counts in T each time it changes ownership, so T far exceeds Q. Correspondingly, Fisher's MV, being the total flow of payments in all transactions, is much larger than the MV that expresses payments for final outputs only. Also correspondingly, Fisher's V or transactions velocity is much larger than the so-called income or circular velocity in $MV = PQ$. Finally, P expresses the average price of a far broader range of goods and services (and securities) in Fisher's equation than in $MV = PQ$.

To begin sliding from the quantity-velocity to the money-supply-and-demand formulation, we rearrange $MV = PQ$ as: $M = (1/V) PQ$. For contact with the history of doctrine, we replace $1/V$ with k ('Cambridge k')[4] and recognize that PQ or the value of current production is the same thing as Y, nominal income. Then: $M = kPQ = kY$. So rearranged the equation refers not to 'flows' but rather to 'stocks' at an instant of time. Y or PQ does still refer to a period, being the rate per year (say) of nominal income. But multiplication by k converts this flow into a stock. Cambridge k has the dimension of years (realistically, k is a fraction of a year), and Y or PQ has the dimension of dollars or dollars-worths *per year*, so kPQ or kY has the dimension of simply dollars and like the M on the left side of the equation refers simply to a stock measured in dollars.

Next we interpret the equation no longer as an identity but as a genuine equation whose satisfaction is a condition of equilibrium. We interpret the M on left side, henceforth written MS for the 'money supply', as the actual nominal quantity of money, while kY or kPQ on the right side represents the nominal quantity of money that people demand. Monetary equilibrium or disequilibrium prevails accordingly as the actual quantity of money and total desired holdings of money are or are not equal. (This is a preliminary definition.

More detail comes in Chapters 3 and 4.) We are interpreting Cambridge k as a desired magnitude, so it is not the reciprocal of actual velocity out of equilibrium. Accordingly, k is an indicator of intensity of demand for money, expressed as the length of the time span (fraction of a year) over which the value of the flow of income would be equal to desired holdings. Commonly but loosely, k is called the fraction of a year's income over which people desire to hold command in the form of cash balances.

Using k to express the quantity of money demanded in relation to income in no way supposes that this quantity depends only on income. Alfred Marshall (1924 [1973], p. 86), one of the founders of the money-supply-and-demand or cash-balance approach, explicitly supposed in an example that desired money holdings depend on both income and wealth (see below). The approach can recognize k as a variable that depends on wealth, interest rates, the perceived or expected rate of price inflation, and anything else reasonably believed to influence desired money holdings.

To emphasize how open-ended our view of influences on the demand for money can be and to complete our slide between the quantity-velocity and money-supply-and-demand approaches, we can replace the right side of our equation with a general symbol for the demand-for-money function, $M^d(\ )$. Terms appear inside the parentheses for all influences on the demand for money that deserve recognition, notably nominal income – that is to say, both real income and the price level. The monetary equilibrium condition becomes simply that money supply equals money demanded or: $MS = M^d(\ )$.

Usually we adopt the money-supply-and-demand terminology in expounding the monetarist version of the spending approach. Focusing on supply of and demand for money alerts us to implications of the fact that money, alone among all goods, lacks a specific market of its own where supply and demand meet and determine a specific price. This circumstance obstructs quick restoration of equilibrium, once disturbed, between supply and demand. The money-supply-and-demand terminology helps build bridges between the spending approach and the goods-against-goods approach that goes further back to the fundamentals of production and exchange.

MONEY AND INCOME

Figure 1.3 illuminates the money-supply-and-demand approach. The dollar amounts of money demanded and actually in existence are measured horizontally. Gross domestic product, the Y or PQ of the equation of exchange, is also expressed in nominal or dollar terms and is measured vertically. The line 0L, which slopes northeastward from the origin, relates money holdings demanded to the level of income. Its slope shows the ratio of income to money demanded, that is, desired velocity or the reciprocal of k. Changes in money demanded resulting from changes in income are represented by movements along 0L. Changes in other influences on the demand for money are reflected in shifts or rotations of the line. A clockwise rotation shows strengthening of the taste to hold cash balances. The money supply is represented by a vertical MS line at the quantity set (or acquiesced in) by the monetary authority.

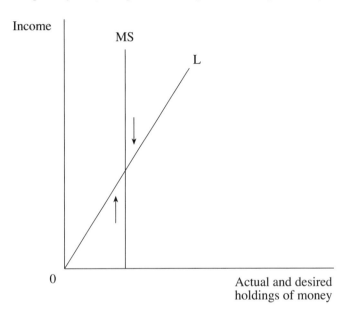

Figure 1.3   Relations among money supply, money demand and nominal income

We can distinguish between actual and desired velocity. *Actual velocity*, the velocity in MV = PQ interpreted as a tautology, is represented by the slope of a straight line from the origin to the point on the MS line at the height representing the actual level of money income, whatever it may be. *Desired velocity*, the reciprocal of k in the equation for monetary equilibrium, is represented by the slope of the straight line 0L. In equilibrium desired and actual velocity coincide. (A curved rather than straight line 0L would represent a distinction between average and marginal desired velocity, each in general varying from point to point on the line. Present purposes do not require elaborating on this distinction.)

Actual velocity tends to adjust to equilibrium or desired velocity for the same reason that the desired nominal quantity of money tends to adjust to the actual nominal quantity. The two adjustments are aspects of the same process. Income tends to adjust to the level at which the actual quantity of money is just desired. This process appears on the diagram as arrows representing pressures toward the intersection of the money supply and money demand lines. In the region of the downward arrow, an excess demand for money is pressing income down. In the region of the upward arrow, an excess supply of money is raising income. Using the money-supply-and-demand approach, we have obviously now entered the realm of theory.

Later we examine the foregoing process closely.[5] Here we are more concerned with showing how the key concepts of monetary theory relate to each other. Briefly, when people are holding less money than they desire, they try to build up their cash balances by curtailing their spending and by trying to push their sales by, for example, cutting prices. The result shows up on the macro scene as a fall in nominal spending and in the value of nominal income. In the opposite case, attempts to spend down excessive cash balances raise nominal income enough to make the actual money holdings desired after all.

Starting from equilibrium, an excess demand for money could be created by a supply or demand change represented by a leftward shift of the MS line or a rightward rotation of the OL line. An excess supply of money could be created in a way represented by an opposite shift or rotation. In either case nominal income would respond. How this response would be split between changes in prices and in real economic activity – how the Y change would be split between P change and Q change – does not appear in the diagram. In the imaginary world of completely flexible prices and wages, monetary changes would affect these alone and leave real activity unaffected. The price-quantity split in the real world must be examined at length as in Chapters 6, 7, and 8.

As an example of the translation test, we use the money-supply-and-demand framework to portray the Keynesian liquidity preference theory in which the interest rate would quickly adjust to maintain equilibrium between money supply and money demand. In terms of Figure 1.3 an increase in the money supply would shift the MS line to the right. The interest rate would fall immediately to increase money demand and thus preserve monetary equilibrium. It would show up in the figure as a rotation of the OL line to the right. We ignore the rest of the Keynesian adjustment process.

OBJECTIONS TO MONETARY ANALYSIS

Noting some conceivable objections may further clarify the quantity-velocity or money-supply-and-demand analysis of total spending. Some appear in the *Radcliffe Report* published in England in 1959.[6] One of its recurrent themes is that anything can be said in monetary terms and therefore the demand for and supply of money and related concepts are plastic, all-purpose, and meaningless. If one can say anything in monetary terms, then one can*not* say anything *in particular* in those terms. Velocity in this view is just an arithmetical ratio. One can take a country's GDP figure for one year, divide it by the year's average money stock, and get a number. One may call that result 'income velocity', but it tells nothing about reality. The *Radcliffe Report* also stigmatizes definitions of the money supply as arbitrary, makes fun of different economists' rival conceptions, and stresses difficulties of measurement. (We do not deny that the time may come when distinctions between what does and what does not serve as the medium of exchange will have been entirely blurred, making it no longer even conceptually possible to say what the quantity of money is. Such institutional changes are another matter, however, and are noted elsewhere in this book.)

Besides dwelling on the supposed meaninglessness of the velocity calculation and the fuzzy definition of the quantity involved, one might object that people and firms are nearly indifferent, within wide limits, to the sizes of their cash balances and to ratios between them and their flows of income and expenditure. Willingness to spend, instead of depending on cash balances, depends primarily on households' incomes and on business firms' profit prospects, and probably also on the terms on which loans are available. According to this line of objection, the money holder can behave rather passively and allow his cash balance to fluctuate widely without needing to revise his plans for buying and selling goods and services.

When we apply the translation test to the notion that velocity is meaningless or passive and when we consider what that notion would imply about the decisions and behavior of individual people and firms to hold money, we find the objection unpersuasive. It would be unreasonable for individuals to exhibit near-indifference to the sizes of their money holdings in dollar terms and in relation to their incomes and expenditure and holdings of other portfolio assets. As for the notion that 'anything can be said in monetary terms', that is just not true. One cannot sensibly discuss diagnosing and treating pneumonia or preparing Southern fried chicken in terms of money's supply and demand or velocity. The fact that a concept like nominal income *can* sensibly be discussed in such terms says at least something about the concept itself.

As for the contention that each household's or firm's spending decisions depend more on its actual or expected income or sales receipts than on its cash balance, that may well be true from its individual point of view. But it hardly settles the macroeconomic issue. One must beware of the fallacy of composition: illegitimate generalization from what is true from the individual point of view to what is supposedly true from the overall point of view. To be sure, the individual person (or firm) does not regard his cash balance as determining the flows of his receipts and expenditures. It by no means follows from the overall point of view that the total of cash balances or money supply is unimportant in

influencing those flows. Yet Tobin (1952, p. 115) did make such an inference
in a passage quoted with approval by Meier (1954, p. 936):[7]

> A variable is not useful in explaining the behavior of an individual if its magnitude
> is just as much subject to his discretion as the behavior which it is supposed to explain.
> An explanation of spending decisions must relate the spending of a household to
> determinants outside its control. This is the fatal objection to the hypothesis...that the
> spending of an individual unit depends on the size of its cash balances, and to the
> macroeconomic hypothesis [that total spending will, other things being equal, vary
> directly with the quantity of money] derived from it. By exchanging cash for other
> assets, or vice versa, a household or firm can control the size of its cash balance
> extremely rapidly.

According to the 'fundamental proposition of monetary theory', already
introduced in a preliminary way but still to be explained in detail, the nominal
supply of money creates its own demand. If the money supply affects total
spending as the proposition indicates and if total spending influences the income
or sales receipts that the individual (or firm) can expect to receive and so
influences his own spending decisions, then indirectly the money supply is
influencing his spending decisions. This is true even though the individual may
not regard the size of his cash balance as an important influence on his income
and spending.

It is not true, furthermore, that individuals and firms are indifferent to their
cash balances and how they relate to income and expenditure. Demand-for-
money studies, both theoretical and statistical, presuppose otherwise. They are
based on the understanding that something exists to be investigated, that some
systematic relation exists between the quantity of money demanded and other
economic variables.[8] The typical individual is not indifferent to how much
money he holds. Rather, he is concerned to hold enough money in his checking
account to prevent his checks from bouncing if his expenditures become unexpectedly bunched. On the other hand, he becomes uneasy if his account grows
much larger than convenience recommends. Not only the academic literature
but also business periodicals explain how corporate treasurers manage their
cash balances alertly and how, in times of tight credit and high interest rates,
they try to protect their cash positions by delaying payments to creditors and
pressing for faster payments from customers.

Nevertheless the objection sometimes surfaces that a mechanical or objective
aspect of velocity or the demand for money overrides any aspect amenable to
ordinary economic analysis. (Hicks, 1967 suggests that ordinary notions of
demand do not apply to money.)[9] People do not really demand money, they
just need holdings of certain sizes in relation to their incomes and expenditures.
The need for money or money's velocity supposedly hinges on mechanical
factors such as the frequency of wage and salary payments, institutional factors

affecting use of currency and checking deposits, the degree of integration of business enterprises and the banking system, the number of bank offices in relation to population, the number of banking hours per week, and the speed of the check-clearing system (which depends, among other things, on the speed of airplanes).[10]

Actually, objective and subjective determinants need not conflict. The latter embrace personal tastes. A particularly cautious or worrisome person would be likely to hold a larger cash balance than a bolder person in otherwise similar circumstances. Besides, 'need' is a concept rather foreign to economics. People do not inexorably need the money they hold or the goods they buy. One might say that people do not simply want or demand shoes but need them, or that a diabetic does not simply want or demand insulin but needs it. But for supposed needs to count on the market, they must be perceived and interpreted by actual people, who must decide what importance they attach to their various needs and must be able to pay for having them satisfied. There are many things besides cash balances for which it is more nearly plausible to speak, not of demand, but of a quasi-mechanical need. The demands for such things may be quite intense and inflexible, yet supply and demand analysis still is useful in dealing with them. The same is true of money.

Even the demand to hold money for transactions purposes is not determined by purely objective, mechanical factors. This is the theme of well known articles by William Baumol and James Tobin (1952 and 1956, respectively, reviewed in Chapter 2). In deciding how much money to hold for transactions purposes, people at least implicitly consider the expense and time and trouble involved in switching otherwise temporarily idle cash into interest-bearing securities and then switching the funds out again in time to make a payment. Time and trouble are subjective factors that different people appraise differently. Such considerations indicate that the demand for money and therefore the velocity of money, far from being something either passive and meaningless on the one hand or purely objective or mechanical on the other, is subject to economic analysis in broadly the same way as the demand for anything else.

Important differences do exist, however, between the demands for money and for other things. People do not conceive of an exact quantity of money that they desire to hold at each instant. Rather, they conceive of some approximate level to which they would like their cash balances to average out over time. The very purposes for which people hold them explain why cash balances fluctuate up and down as inward and outward payments flow through them in amounts and at times that are not entirely predictable. Furthermore, the way that people satisfy or implement their demands for cash balances (that is, how they adjust them to the average sizes that they desire) is different from the way that they implement their demand for, say, cornflakes (see pages 17–18 below). Nevertheless, in having a subjective rather than purely mechanical aspect and in being amenable to economic analysis, the demand for money resembles the demand for anything else.

THE GOODS-AGAINST-GOODS (OR SAY'S LAW) APPROACH

Earlier we noted that population and productivity and so aggregate output producible at full employment generally grow over time. We then asked whether spending would grow enough to buy that output. Any flow of spending would be adequate in real terms, no matter how small in nominal terms, at low enough prices. Because of difficulties of rapidly adjusting the general price level, a concern for the adequacy of real aggregate demand entails concern with nominal spending after all. Keynesian and monetarist analyses focus on different aspects of what determines spending, but they share a concern with it.

By itself, that concern poses too sharp a contrast between aggregate demand and aggregate supply, supposedly confronting each other and needing to be matched somehow. It hints at the existence of definite quantitative relations to be discovered and employed by policymakers and experts responsible for this matching. It forgets that questions of successful or impaired coordination of activities do not admit of precise quantitative answers.

Yet the criticized formulation can be made useful if given microeconomic underpinnings. The chief modification required is to recognize that demand and output are not distinct magnitudes. On the contrary, outputs constitute demand. Millions of people specialize in producing their own particular goods and services because they expect to exchange them for what other specialists are producing. Say's Law, rightly understood, maintains that fundamentally no problem exists of aggregate demand as such. Supply of some goods and services constitutes demand for other (noncompeting) ones sooner or later, and demand constitutes supply.

No mindless optimism, however, follows from this observation. The exchange of goods and services for other goods and services can be disrupted, and whatever disrupts this process discourages the production of goods and services destined for exchange. Loss of production means loss of real buying power and thus further loss of production, so the disruption can snowball. To understand the nature and sources of disruption, one must first understand how the process ideally does work. Say's Law, rightly understood, directs attention to production for the purpose of exchange, to the process of exchange, to whatever automatic market-clearing tendencies may be at work, and to how they may be disrupted.

This approach recognizes the role of money in facilitating or impeding the exchange of goods against goods and, by so doing, in encouraging or discouraging the production of goods destined for exchange. Goods exchange for goods indirectly through the intermediary of money. Money serves as a device for keeping track of people's contributions to and withdrawals from the total stock or flow of goods and services and so for tending to keep each person's contributions and withdrawals equal in value (with obvious qualifications about transfers of entitlements). Money performs in a decentralized and relatively impersonal and economical way the function that could conceivably be performed by detailed, centralized record-keeping instead.[11] It accomplishes the multilateral clearing of claims and obligations required by the fact that the typical economic agent supplies goods or services to trading partners quite different from those who supply him. A monetary disorder that impedes this clearing function therefore impedes exchanges and production. To adopt a familiar metaphor, money *lubricates* exchanges. Spending is the monetary measure of the volume being lubricated. If the lubricant goes awry, so do the processes being lubricated.

BRIDGING THE SPENDING AND GOODS-AGAINST-GOODS APPROACHES

Now that we have introduced the fundamentals of goods exchanging for goods and the role of money in lubricating yet possibly disrupting these exchanges, we can build bridges to the spending approach. (The long dashed line in Figure 1.2 represents some of those bridges.) We can make sense of talk about whether spending is adequate or deficient or excessive, and we can move on to consider (in Chapters 6, 7 and 8) how changes in spending and nominal income are split between quantity and price changes.

The two frameworks of analysis obviously overlap. In accomplishing exchanges, people are routinely receiving payments into and making payments from holdings of money, whose desired sizes are related to the sizes of these inward and outward flows, among other things. If desired holdings of money exceed or fall short of the quantity actually in existence, people try to adjust their holdings. How? They cannot respond in the same straightforward way in which they would adjust deficient or excessive holdings of cement or household furnishings. They cannot buy or sell money on a specific market at a specific price. Instead, they must try to adjust their cash balances by adjusting their inward and outward flows of payments, which means by modifying their selling and buying behavior on the markets for goods and services and securities. Thus, spending and the volume of exchanges are affected. Too little actual money and too little spending ('too little' for macroeconomic health) imply each other. Similarly, too much money and too much spending imply each other. Imbalances on the side of money imply opposite imbalances on the side of goods and services (and securities). We examine these propositions in Chapters 3 and 4.

In the analytical framework that focuses on exchanges intermediated by money, concern with the processes that may be at work, more or less effectively, to correct or forestall monetary disequilibrium takes the place of concern for the adequacy of spending or aggregate demand. This framework ties in better than the spending framework with recognition that the economic problem involves somehow *coordinating* decisions made in a decentralized and piecemeal way under conditions of dispersed knowledge. It takes fuller account of market processes and makes fuller use of what we know about the incentives and decisions and actions of individual persons. It conduces to a less activist conception of macroeconomic policy. On the other hand, the spending terminology is sometimes more convenient, as when we are talking about how a change in nominal income is split between price change and quantity change. We look into this split when, for example, we investigate in Chapter 8 the difficulties of stopping inflation.

Still, as mentioned, the two frameworks do reconcile. Both can recognize the role of moderate growth of money in a growing economy. This moderate growth is appropriate, however, not only to support aggregate demand or spending but also – which is practically the same thing – to satisfy a growing demand for real cash balances, which are nominal balances deflated by the price level. This demand for money is related (though not related exclusively) to the growing volume of goods and services produced or producible and destined for exchange against each other. Recognition of this relation is the counterpart of concern in the spending framework with whether aggregate demand for goods suffices to absorb aggregate supply.

Say's Law: Where It Can Go Wrong

We are now prepared to see exactly where Say's Law can go wrong and to comment on Keynes's criticism of the law. Say's Law as generally summarized in textbooks states that 'supply creates its own demand'. 'Fundamentally', 'behind the veil of money', people specialize in producing particular goods and services to exchange them for the specialized outputs of other people. However, anything that impairs the process of exchange also impairs production. Here is where money comes into the story and where Say's view of supply constituting demand can go wrong. Goods and services exchange for each other through the intermediary of money, and an imbalance between its supply and demand can cause trouble.

When agreeing with J.B. Say that supply creates its own demand, we hedged with the words 'fundamentally' and 'behind the veil of money'. These qualifications refer to what is only a detail relative to the supply-side truths that Say directed attention to, but it is a detail of great significance.

In rejecting Say's Law in his *General Theory* (1936), Keynes rejected not only its erroneous aspect but its central core of truth. Keynes really did believe in a deep-seated problem of deficiency of demand. He did not interpret that problem as a merely monetary disorder. And Keynes (1936, p. 18), in quoting John Stuart Mill's agreement with Say's Law, failed to acknowledge that Mill did indeed explain what was wrong with it. For Mill (1848 [1965], p. 574) states in a passage a few paragraphs after the one quoted by Keynes:

> I have already described the state of the markets for commodities which accompanies what is termed a commercial crisis. At such times there is really an excess of all commodities above the money demand: in other words, there is an under-supply of money. From the sudden annihilation of a great mass of credit, every one dislikes to part with ready money, and many are anxious to procure it at any sacrifice. Almost everybody therefore is a seller, and there are scarcely any buyers; so that there may really be, though only while the crisis lasts, an extreme depression of general prices, from what may be indiscriminately called a glut of commodities or a dearth of money.

Mill clearly recognized the possibility of recessions and depressions, with an apparent excess supply of goods and services, in consequence of monetary disequilibrium. (Mill makes the point even more clearly in 1844 [1874] [1967], p. 277.)

In some passages (1836, pp. 133–4), Say explicitly denied that an apparent general glut of goods could be due to a shortage of money:

> There is always money enough to conduct the circulation and mutual interchange of other values, when those values really exist. Should the increase of traffic require more money to facilitate it, the want is easily supplied, and is a strong indication of prosperity – a proof that a great abundance of values has been created, which it is wished to exchange for other values. In such cases, merchants know well enough how to find substitutes for the product serving as the medium of exchange or money [by bills at sight, or after date, bank-notes, running-credits, write-offs, & c. as at London and Amsterdam]: and money itself soon pours in, for this reason, that all produce naturally gravitates to that place where it is most in demand. It is a good sign when the business is too great for the money; just in the same way as it is a good sign when the goods are too plentiful for the warehouses.[12]

CONCLUSION

The key question of money/macro theory is not: what determines whether aggregate demand for goods and services confronting their aggregate supply is deficient or excessive or just right? Rather it is: what determines whether or not the market process of exchange and coordination in an economy of decentralized decisionmaking works smoothly? Or, how can monetary disequilibrium impede exchanges of goods against goods, the mobilization of scattered knowledge, and the coordination of decentralized activities?

These questions have policy implications. The question about aggregate demand invites attempts to fine-tune the macroeconomy. Questions about exchange and coordination direct attention, instead, to what background of economic institutions and policies can best help market processes work. For money is potentially a 'loose joint' (Hayek, 1941, p. 408) between decisions to produce and sell things on the one hand and decisions to buy things on the other hand. Elaborating on this point will occupy us at length in this book.

The close affinity between the goods-against-goods approach and money-supply-and-demand analysis is represented by the long dashed line in Figure 1.2. Goods exchange against goods through the intermediary of money, and whether or not money's supply and demand are in equilibrium has much to do with whether this exchange proceeds smoothly or meets obstacles. Focusing on the monetary lubricant invites attention to a familiar but nevertheless momentous fact. Money as the medium of exchange is the one thing routinely traded on *all* markets, yet its supply and demand do not confront each other on *one* particular market and are not equilibrated with each other through adjustment of *one* particular price. This circumstance helps explain how monetary disequilibrium can produce painful consequences that last months and even years. The implications of this circumstance require much attention.

Keynes believed in real obstacles to reaching full employment, real obstacles to fully filling a supposed saving gap with investment, obstacles more serious for rich than poor communities. He saw a deep-seated real problem of deficiency of demand and did not interpret the problem as a merely monetary disorder.[13] Yet Say's Law expresses a profound truth: no *real* obstacles bar achieving sufficient demand for output as long as nothing else impairs the process of exchange. Say's Law goes wrong in neglecting the full implications of the fact that some outputs constitute demand for other outputs not directly but only through the intermediary of money.

NOTES

1. Friedman (1993) provides empirical evidence supporting the plucking model. In a much-cited article on asymmetry, Cover (1992) finds that negative money supply shocks have a greater effect on output than positive shocks. Kim and Nelson (1999) formally test Friedman's model. Their results support it and find no role for symmetric cycles.
2. Some new Keynesian economists conceive of long-run 'hysteresis' effects in which potential output itself would change following a major shock to the economy.

3. The translation test is so named in a broader context by Flew (1971, p. 359), who quotes Thomas Hobbes's advocacy of it in *Leviathan*, Chapters 8 and 46.

4. Strictly speaking, k is not precisely the reciprocal of V. As becomes clear from the text that follows, k pertains to money at an instant of time, V to money over an interval of time.

5. Chapter 3 presents the Wicksell Process and the closely related fundamental proposition of monetary theory. The latter presupposes a closed economy or one with a freely floating exchange rate. Things are different, as explained in Chapters 3 and 9, in an economy open to international transactions at a fixed exchange rate.

6. Here and elsewhere, confronting errors can be an expository device. The purpose is not simply to flog dead horses, blow down straw men, or discredit other economists. Errors can be instructive by revealing points requiring clearer or fuller exposition and by making the correct doctrines stand out in contrast.

7. The words in brackets are not Tobin's but Meier's.

8. We realize that velocity became unstable for a period in the 1970s and then from the early 1980s onward. Chapter 2 investigates these phenomena.

9. Hicks (1935 [1967]) recognizes the subjective nature of money demand. Indeed, he argues (p. 63) that money must have a marginal utility. However, he later (1967, especially pp. 14, 16) repudiates that analysis and argues that no *transactions* demand for money could be analyzed with marginal utility theory. However, he does recognize a subjective precautionary and speculative demand for money.

10. Fisher (1911, 1922) pays predominant attention to mechanical determinants of velocity of the sorts mentioned in the text, but he does not deny or ignore the subjective determinants, as is evident from his surveys among Yale students and professors (1922, pp. 379–82).

11. See references to Kuenne and Schumpeter on pages 26–30 below. Chapter 2 elaborates on this paragraph.

12. The words in brackets were a footnote. Clark Warburton in an unpublished book-length manuscript argues that this passage does not fully describe Say's view. Warburton quotes other passages in which, according to his interpretation, Say recognizes that money can have an important influence on business conditions.

13. For documentation, see Yeager (1973, 1985, 1986, 1988, 1991 [1997]).

2. The services of money

INTRODUCTION

This chapter investigates (1) how money promotes economic coordination; (2) how ill-functioning money can impair coordination and (3) what services individuals derive from their holdings of money. The third topic is fundamental to understanding the demand for money and to the money-supply-and-demand analysis of total spending.

THE SERVICES AND FUNCTIONS OF MONEY

We gain insight into the damage monetary disorder does by reviewing what services a well functioning monetary system renders to the community as a whole. The traditional list includes money's functions as: (1) medium of exchange; (2) unit of account; (3) store of value and (4) standard of deferred payments.

Money overcomes the familiar difficulties of barter. It facilitates exchange not only between people working in different lines of production but also over time. By using money and claims denominated in it, people can arrange to receive what other people produce either before or after delivering their own outputs. Because people receive their incomes in generalized purchasing power rather than in the specific goods they help to produce, they enjoy enhanced freedom of choice and greater consumer sovereignty. Because money can be stored more cheaply than the goods received as income under barter, consumers have wider options about when as well as what to consume. By facilitating exchange over time, money promotes the pooling and mobilization of savings through financial intermediation and the securities markets. It thereby promotes construction of capital-intensive and specialized production facilities, which, like the division of labor, enhances productivity.

In our existing system, money is not only the medium of exchange but also the unit of account. It reduces the number of value ratios to be considered. A barter economy with n goods and services would have $n(n-1)/2$ ratios to consider; money reduces the number to just n prices. Money as the measure of value facilitates economic calculation and informed choices. The benefits expected from various goods and the costs of acquiring or producing them can be estimated in money. Contributions of inputs to the value of various kinds of output can similarly be estimated and compared. Accounting in terms of money is almost essential to budgetary control in business firms and other organizations. Higher-level executives can apply profit-and-loss tests to their subordinates in lieu of detailed bureaucratic supervision. In a way loosely similar to business budgeting, consumers can also compare costs and benefits. When the consumer compares the desirability of a contemplated purchase with its price in money, he is at least subconsciously weighing the item against other things known from experience to be obtainable for a similar sum of money.[1] (Inflation hastens the obsolescence of this sort of information.) Efficient allocation of resources and patterning of production would hardly be possible in a highly developed economy unless firms had a unit available in which to measure and compare revenues, costs and profits and unless firms, workers, resource-owners and consumers had such a unit for comparing alternative opportunities to buy and sell.

Money is almost essential to the signals with which a price system operates. The price system permits decentralized decisionmaking – decisions by 'the man on the spot' – yet coordinates these decisions by conveying to each decisionmaker, in the form of prices, information about conditions in other parts of the economy, together with incentives to take those conditions into account. The decisionmaker does not need to know the details of those other conditions. This is the message of F.A. Hayek (1945).

Supply and demand can rule markets more readily and traders can more straightforwardly compare the terms offered by rival prospective trading partners, which sharpens competition, when prices are quoted and payments made in a homogeneous thing – money. Money provides not only an economical but also an impersonal mechanism for keeping track of and for balancing the values of what each person (and his property) contributes to and draws from the flows of goods and services throughout society. This point refers either to a person's own productive contribution or to the contributions of other people who have transferred to him, perhaps by gift, some of the entitlements received for their own contributions. Here we are merely describing the process of matching withdrawals and contributions and are not now judging whether people *ought* to receive income in accordance with the marginal productivities of themselves and their property.

With money, ties of personal interdependence are fewer and looser than in a barter world, and the scope for extraneous personal discrimination is narrower. With the clear-cut motive of profit in money at work, each consumer's dollar is as good as anyone else's. Money, especially hand-to-hand currency, also contributes to anonymity and privacy. Pondering roughly the opposite arrangements helps make this last point clear. (See a review by Darby, 1973, pp. 870–71, of a book whose author advocated replacing cash by one centralized credit card system, enabling the authorities to monitor all transactions, legal as well as criminal.)

In short, money promotes efficient production responsive to people's wants. It does so by facilitating all of these: exchange and fine-grained specialization in production; the credit system, financial markets and real capital formation; the transmission and use of knowledge; and economic calculation and informed choice through comparisons of revenues and expenses, of prospective profits in different lines and scales of production, of costs and expected satisfactions, and of the offers of rival potential trading partners. By helping make markets work smoothly, money fosters impersonal cooperation among people unknown to each other; it contributes to anonymity and privacy and so even to freedom.

To summarize in another way, money helps markets work by cutting transactions costs and information costs and requirements of many kinds (compare Brunner and Meltzer, 1971 and Alchian, 1977). In 'indirect barter', for example, information would be necessary about the qualities, values and marketability of the intermediate goods that one accepted in exchange in hopes of being able to trade them away for the goods really wanted. Using money as the universal intermediate good avoids these extra information requirements and costs. These cost and information aspects of money are reflected in the traditional list of desirable characteristics of an ideal money material: portability, durability, homogeneity, cognizability, divisibility and stability of value.

Money's functions as store of value and standard of deferred payments seem less fundamental than the first two, deriving from them. Many physical and financial assets are stores of value, not just money, and money is not a good store of value in times of inflation. Money could not serve as a medium of exchange unless it could be stored between transactions. Being a standard of deferred payments – the unit in which debts and payments in long-term contracts, such as leases, are expressed – is part of the unit-of-account function.

The services of money to society as a whole, notably as an aid to economic calculation, are emphasized by considering how inflation and other monetary disorders undercut them.

THE ORIGIN OF MONEY

Considering how money probably evolved in the first place gives further insight into its services (Menger 1871 [1981], Chapter VIII and Appendix J; 1892; compare George 1898 [1941], Book V). Menger's theory describes a process that also characterizes the unplanned evolution of other social institutions such as language, the common law and the market economy itself. Money and these other institutions are examples of what Hayek (1967, Chapter 6, following Ferguson, 1767, p. 187) has called 'the results of human action but not of human design'.[2] Menger traces what he considers the correct theory of the origin of money to John Law, better known for his involvement in French finance and currency disorder in the early eighteenth century. Law rejected the contractual theory espoused by earlier writers, the theory that money had been devised and adopted by actual agreement. He argued instead that money evolved out of the commodity whose properties made it the most suitable intermediary in exchanges.

After referring to the difficulties of direct barter, requiring the notorious 'double coincidence of wants', Menger argues that people become willing to accept certain goods in exchange for their own goods even if they themselves do not want to consume them. They accept goods that they expect to be able to trade away easily to other people. Acceptable goods have characteristics making them readily marketable, and acceptability tends to reinforce itself. Ancient Mexico when Cortez arrived, says Menger, exemplified an economy in a state of transition from barter to the use of money. No one commodity had yet become the dominant medium of exchange, but several were in use, including cocoa beans in bags, gold in goose quills, and other metals.

Before the dawn of recorded history, cattle were among the goods acceptable as money. (Menger's evidence includes names of money units.) Besides being widely prized, cattle were a medium of exchange that transported itself on its own feet. Later, with rising civilization, urbanization and the division of labor, cattle lost their relatively high acceptability of more primitive times. The precious metals tended to displace them, and the names of money units derived from units of weight form part of the evidence. The metals were durable and could be divided without loss of value, were widely used and thus readily marketable, and were cheap to transport because of high value in relation to bulk and weight. These qualities of a suitable monetary material, along with others that Menger happens not to have listed, imply that money reduces the costs of conducting transactions, the knowledge necessary for indirect exchanges, and the costs of holding the medium of exchange between transactions. (Moini, 2001, pp. 284–6, argues that in some times and places units of account may have evolved before generally employed media of exchange.)

Menger's theory of the origin of money gains support from the adoption of cigarettes as money in German camps for captured British and allied officers during World War II. Radford (1945) describes the economic organization of a POW camp. The prisoners traded among themselves the rations provided by the Germans and the contents of packages sent by the Red Cross; and some prisoners produced canteen meals, tailoring services and a few other services. Cigarettes came to be acceptable as a medium of exchange even by nonsmokers and also came to be used as the unit of account.

Other principles of monetary theory were also illustrated. Gresham's Law says, roughly, that if two or more things are fixed in relative value as money but have different values otherwise, then the one with least value in nonmonetary use will remain in circulation as money and will drive out the others into their nonmonetary uses. Since the prisoners counted any cigarette as one unit of money, they circulated the less popular brands as the medium of exchange and smoked the more popular brands.

Even the effects of the quantity of money on prices and production showed themselves. When the quantity of cigarettes shrank, as when Red Cross packages were delayed or when nearby air raids caused nervous prisoners to smoke more than usual, then with prices of other goods tending to fall but only stickily, the volume of trading shriveled. Monetary disorder even impaired what little production went on in the camps, such as restaurant and tailoring services.

Attempts have been made to model formally the evolution of money as a medium of exchange. Building on the seminal work by Jones (1976), Kiyotaki and Wright (1989, 1991, 1993) use a search-theoretic approach to the process of exchange. They illuminate one of Menger's keen insights: a particular good becomes a medium of exchange because people believe that it will be accepted by others. Kiyotaki and Wright argue that while people usually prefer to use a low-cost good as money, they might choose a high-cost one if they expect everyone else to do the same. The authors formally illustrate that fiat currency can be valued as a medium of exchange even if it is dominated in rate of return by other assets. (Pages 62–3 below discuss the issue of money as a dominated asset.)

MONEY AS A CLEARING DEVICE

The likelihood that money originally evolved from commodities useful in their own right does not mean that money has the character of a commodity even in the modern world. It is the 'genetic fallacy' to suppose that the essence of a developed institution remains specified by its origin or its most primitive form. Fundamentally, modern money is what Schumpeter (1970) has called a clearing device and Kuenne (1958) has called a device that eliminates the necessity for *centralized* clearing. Whether one calls money a clearing device or an alternative to clearing is a mere question of terminology; Schumpeter and Kuenne agree on substance. Our focus on money as a clearing device is not to deny its primary function as a medium of exchange; rather, we wish to probe that function more deeply (Shah and Yeager, 1994).

Clearing is an arrangement for using each person's (and firm's) claims on some trading partners to settle his obligations to others. In a simple example of Schumpeter's (1970, p. 227), a surgeon operates on a singer, the singer performs at a lawyer's party and the lawyer handles a case for the surgeon. If their services were equal in value, the three professionals could avoid payments to one another. Without some such actual clearing and without some substitute such as the use of money, each person would have to pay for goods or services acquired from each trading partner by supplying that same partner with goods or services of equal value. Deliveries would not necessarily be simultaneous; credit between trading partners might be possible. Even so, this bilateralism of transactions down to the level of the individual person would be terribly restrictive and inefficient. Clearing makes multilateral transactions possible.

Clearing – to make another stab at a definition – is the process of keeping track of each person's contributions to, and withdrawals from, the stock or flow of goods and services in society and monitoring these transactions to keep him from making withdrawals worth more than his contributions. Splitting hairs, we could modify the definition to take account of gifts, borrowing and lending and the like. It obviously would not work to allow each person to contribute and withdraw goods and services as he saw fit, with no monitoring and record-keeping. If gathering and transmitting information (including information about relative values), keeping records, and monitoring were much easier and cheaper than they are in fact (and if the Big Brother aspects were not ominous), centralized clearing would be a workable arrangement.

In reality, it is cheaper and more efficient to accomplish clearing in a decentralized way, through the use of money. Everyone receives money for his contributions and pays money for his withdrawals of goods and services. The mere possession of money is presumptive evidence of entitlement to withdraw goods of equal value. Schumpeter (1917–18 [1956], pp. 154–5 and *passim*) calls money a 'receipt voucher' for productive contributions and a 'claim ticket' on goods to be received in return (Shah and Yeager, 1994).[3]

Kuenne explains why (contrary to denials by some writers) money would endure even in a stationary economy. Even if all economic activity repeated itself year after year in the same old pattern, so that people knew the amounts and timing of all their receipts and payments, they would still use money if its use were cheaper than any more centralized system of monitoring their contributions and withdrawals of goods and services. Precisely to preserve the routine – to keep people from withdrawing too much in relation to their contributions – either clearing or money would be necessary. The changes and uncertainties of the real world add to the reasons for using and holding money, but the economies it affords would recommend it even in a completely routinized world.

Fundamentally, behind the veil of money, goods and services exchange for one another at prices in terms of one another. Under centralized clearing, these relative prices are all that really matter. Recording prices in one particular good chosen as numéraire or, alternatively, in some abstract unit of account would simply be a convenient way of keeping track of relative prices. Multiplying all accounting prices by 1000 would leave relative prices unchanged, such as how

many bananas are worth one wheelbarrow. 'Accounting prices' are prices
expressed in an abstract unit, say the 'macute'.[4] The macute has no meaning
until the macute price of some one good is specified arbitrarily. Then, since
market supply and demand have already determined relative prices, all goods
acquire macute prices by mere arithmetic. The unit of accounting prices is
useful only for computation and record-keeping and is not an amount of
anything existing physically or quantitatively (Patinkin, 1965, p. 15).

If clearing is decentralized, however, and goods exchange through the intermediary of money that is actually paid, received, and held, then goods must
have prices in money – 'absolute prices' – and not merely relative prices or
prices expressed in an abstract accounting unit. Money must actually exist,
furthermore, whether quantities of it take the form of tangible coins and notes
or of numbers recorded on paper or in computers.

THE 'CRITICAL FIGURE' OF A MONETARY ECONOMY

What makes the level of money or absolute prices determinate and with it the
purchasing power of the money unit?[5] Money must be linked to commodities
or be kept limited in quantity somehow or other. In Schumpeter's terminology,
some 'critical figure' must be imposed on the monetary system from the outside
in a way that is distinct from the ordinary working of markets (1970, *passim*,
especially Chapter ix, as well as pp. xxii–xxiii of the editor's introduction).[6]
Some nominal money magnitude must be set by some authority, whether a
government body or the force of custom. Schumpeter mentions two alternative
ways of setting this critical figure. The money price of a definite amount of
some commodity (or bundle of commodities) might be set. This equivalence of
the money unit and a specified amount of commodity would be made operational either by actual use of the commodity as the medium of exchange or by
unrestricted two-way convertibility between the standard commodity and the
paper and bank account money that did circulate. Although he stresses that
money is not a commodity in its essence, Schumpeter (1970, p. 224) does call
a commodity standard, specifically the gold standard, a 'trick of genius in the
history of civilization'. The logic of commodity standards, including the
proposed composite-commodity standard, will be examined below. Alternatively, the critical figure could be set by direct or indirect regulation of the
quantity of money in existence, giving determinacy to the level of prices
expressed even in a fiat money. These two ways of providing determinacy
correspond to what Leijonhufvud (1987, p. 47) calls the convertibility principle
of a commodity standard and the quantity principle of a fiat standard.

While money is in essence a device for facilitating the multilaterally balanced
exchange of goods against goods, Schumpeter argues that it cannot remain a

mere neutral clearing device. It is bound to influence real economic activity because the critical figure is specified and is either held constant or changed by a process distinct from the process whereby individual prices adjust to clear the markets for individual goods and services. Money obeys laws of its own. The two leading examples of a critical figure, we recall, are the commodity content (say, weight of gold) of the money unit on a commodity standard or the number of units of a fiat money in existence.

If the critical figure is set or changed or held unchanged inappropriately, money can cause real disturbances. No automatic process prevents them. Suppose that all people suddenly decide to charge and pay doubled prices for all goods and services. Since 'relative prices' – the real terms of exchange – are unaffected, it would seem that exchange and production can continue as before. If, however, payments are made by transfer of gold pieces or paper notes or bank deposits existing in some definite amount, then that amount has become inadequate at the increased prices. Some quantities of commodities become unsalable as the economy experiences a jerk from the monetary checkrein (Schumpeter, 1970, pp. 227–8).

A more plausible example is that population growth, capital accumulation, and technical progress keep on expanding capacities to produce goods and services in relation either to scarce gold, whose money price nevertheless remains fixed under a gold standard, or to a fixed amount of a fiat money. The monetary checkrein then restrains economic activity and frustrates the increasing abundance of goods and services that a fully employed economy would produce.

Market pressures tend to push prices down, making the *real* quantity of money adequate sooner or later for a full-employment volume of transactions and production. The point remains though that the economy must accommodate itself to the monetary situation, since the critical figure does not automatically accommodate itself to the requirements of a smoothly working economy. The accommodation can be painful as the monetary checkrein operates partly on real activity. Only in the longer run does its impact shift entirely to prices (or almost entirely; recall the qualifications in Chapter 1, page 5). In other circumstances, misspecification of money's critical figure can cause inflation or stagflation.

The idea arises of trying to devise some substitute for the nonexistent automatic process of setting the critical figure in an appropriate way. This would presumably be some institutional arrangement or some rule of monetary management. (We have now gone beyond simply summarizing what Schumpeter said and have been embroidering.)

Schumpeter's way of looking at how money affects real activity reconciles with what we have called the goods-against-goods approach and the money-supply-and-demand subapproach. Oddly though, Schumpeter (especially pp. 232–3) rejects the application of supply-and-demand analysis to money.

Nevertheless, his relatively unfamiliar concepts afford a fresh slant on old questions, and we will have occasion to mention them again.[7]

Some Austrian economists view a fractional-reserve banking system as 'fraudulent' because multiple claims exist for the same base money upon which money is pyramided. They insist instead upon 100 percent reserves (Yeager, 2000, 2001). Yet the essence of money is not as a commodity as Schumpeter emphasizes (Shah and Yeager, 1994). Nor must money be backed by commodities or other property.

THE LOGIC OF A COMMODITY STANDARD

Suppose the critical figure is set as a price of $35 per ounce of gold so the dollar is defined as 1/35 ounce. Two-way convertibility between money and gold maintains this ratio. The government stands ready, or private mints stand ready, to mint anyone's gold bullion into full-weight coins, and coins may be melted at will. Furthermore, anyone is free to issue notes and deposits denominated and redeemable in gold coin. Bankers are free of special regulation and are merely bound like anyone else to honor their contracts. What if anything would then give determinacy to the price level? What would prevent an unlimited expansion of banknote and bank deposit money and an unlimited rise of prices?

First, the individual banker faces a restraint on lending too many of his notes and deposits into circulation. If he gets too far ahead of the expansion of loans and notes and deposits by other bankers, more and more of his notes and checks written on deposits in his bank will be getting paid to customers of other banks, who, either directly or through the intermediary of their own banks, will be presenting these notes and checks to him for redemption. His gold reserves will run low. Realizing in the first place this danger of not being able to redeem his obligations and realizing the importance of a reputation for probity, the banker will restrain his issues.

What about all banks considered together? Suppose all were expanding their loans and their issue of demand obligations at a similar pace, so that each was acquiring notes issued by and checks drawn on others in about the same volume that others were acquiring its notes and checks. Each could settle claims on it held by other banks with the claims it held on others. What then could restrain the expansion?

The answer hinges on the critical figure, the fixed money price of gold. If the expansion of bank-issued money was inflating the general level of prices, other goods and services would be rising in value relative to gold. Rising costs and a fixed product price would make gold mining relatively unprofitable, and the flow of new gold into monetary use would slow down or stop. Furthermore, gold would be withdrawn from the reserves of the banks as its relative cheapness made it an increasingly attractive material in dentistry, jewelry, electronics and other industrial uses. Generally rising prices would bring gold coins more actively into hand-to-hand circulation than before. The transactions demand for them would increase and more of them would be withdrawn from the banks for that purpose. An external drain of gold through the international balance of payments would provide still another restraint on expansion.

Furthermore, people might hasten to demand redemption in view of the possibility that the gold convertibility of notes and deposits might be suspended or the gold content of the dollar cut (that is, the dollar might be devalued by raising the price of gold). The very possibility of a run on the system would restrain note and deposit issue in the first place. It would encourage individual banks to work with adequate reserve ratios, especially in a competitive system in which many banks were issuing demand obligations on the basis of fractional gold reserves. This is not to say that the individual bank would practice restraint out of altruistic concern for the fate of the system as a whole. On the contrary, a bank that tried to leave the burden of practicing restraint entirely to others would be exposing itself to the already mentioned danger of adverse balances in interbank clearings.

The ideal working of the gold standard would also prevent a reverse disorder, an unrestrained drop in the money supply and price level. If prices and costs generally fell, gold at its fixed money price would become more profitable to produce and its increased relative price would curtail its use in industry. Fearing a cut in the official price of gold, people might even hasten to bring their melted-down jewelry to the mint. Coined gold would flow into bank reserves and support the issue of additional notes and deposits.

The self-regulating properties of the gold standard admittedly work only sluggishly and feebly. Gold is not an extremely important industrial material, and its becoming cheaper or dearer provides relatively little scope for reducing or increasing its production, its industrial use, and its entry into or withdrawal from the monetary system. Furthermore, current production and industrial consumption of gold are small in relation to the large stock of gold accumulated over the centuries.

The discussion so far is not meant as a review of the arguments for and against the gold standard. Much more would need saying. Here we have been concerned only with the central economic logic of a commodity standard. We need not describe various types of gold standard – 100 percent, fractional-reserve, gold coin, gold bullion, and gold exchange standards. On these distinctions see Yeager (1976b, Chapter 4) and Friedman (1961).

Some economists (for example, B. Graham, 1933, 1937, 1944; F. Graham, 1942, pp. 94–119 and R. Hall, 1982) have proposed a composite-commodity or commodity-reserve standard to expand the scope of self-regulating properties that work only feebly and sluggishly under the gold standard. The dollar – or, more likely, $1000 – would be defined not as an amount of a single commodity but as a physically specified bundle of several or many commodities: say 50 pounds of copper plus 10 bushels of wheat of specified grade plus 70 pounds of sulfuric acid of specified concentration, and so on. The commodities chosen would be industrially important, standardizable, storable and traded on competitive markets. No single one of them but only the bundle as a whole would have a fixed money price. Because of the importance and widespread production and use of the commodities composing the bundle, stabilizing the dollar in relation to it would go some way toward stabilizing the dollar's purchasing power over goods and services in general. The government would give operational meaning to the fixed dollar price of the commodity bundle by standing ready to buy bundles with newly issued money and to redeem money in bundles on demand.

Suppose the general price level, including the prices of the individual commodities composing the bundle, should rise. Arbitrageurs would find it profitable to redeem money in bundles and sell the component commodities on their individual markets. This release of commodities from monetary reserves would tend directly to hold down their prices and tend indirectly to hold down the prices of the other goods into which they entered as materials. Withdrawal from circulation of the money being redeemed would also restrain the rise of prices.

Suppose, conversely, that the general price level should sag. Arbitrageurs would profit by putting bundles together and delivering them to the government at their fixed price. Their demands for the component commodities would shore up their prices directly and the prices of goods made from them indirectly. The new money issued against the bundles would also restrain the fall of prices.

Much has been written about ways to overcome administrative and other difficulties of the scheme. Our purpose here, however, is not to review the arguments pro and con but rather to show further the logic of setting the critical figure of a monetary system in the manner characteristic of a commodity standard.

FIAT MONEY

The logic of a fiat standard consists in part of saving the resource costs of producing and storing commodities for monetary purposes. The quantity theory of money also enters into the story. Fiat money has value because demands to hold it impinge on a limited quantity. A monetary authority would set the critical figure by regulating this quantity. One candidate for a rule of regulation is to keep the actual quantity of money always equal, as closely as can be estimated and managed, to the quantity demanded at a stable price level. Changes in demand associated with economic growth would be accommodated. With the money supply neither exceeding nor falling short of the demand for nominal cash balances, the price level would remain stable. Alternatively, with monetary disequilibrium eliminated, the process of exchanging goods for other goods would work ideally, and Say's Law could not go wrong.

Although this fiat system might seem ideal, a major problem remains: how could the monetary authority keep the money supply approximately equal to money demand? One of the lessons of this book is that under our present system such an undertaking would be extremely difficult.

THE BFH SYSTEM

Greenfield and Yeager (1983) and Yeager and Greenfield (1989) propose their 'BFH system' of monetary reform, which is another way of providing the critical figure. Their system differs markedly from the composite-commodity standard, for in the BFH system no 'base money' would exist on which bank money was pyramided and in which bank money could be redeemed. The composite-commodity standard is an example of a 'directly convertible monetary system': the government or banks would have to redeem on demand their notes and deposits in the bundle of commodities that defined the unit of account and that constituted base money. On the other hand, the BFH system is an example of an 'indirectly convertible monetary system': banks would have to redeem on demand their notes and deposits in some redemption medium (for example, gold or securities) and *not* in the bundle of commodities that defined the unit of account. (Dowd, 1996, Chapter 12, examines in detail these two monetary systems. James Buchanan first suggested the term 'indirect convertibility'.)

We illustrate how indirect convertibility would operate under the BFH system. We again suppose that the unit of account is called the dollar, which would be defined by the value of a bundle of goods and services so comprehensive that its stable value would also imply stability of the general price level. As before, most likely say $1000, rather than just one dollar, would be defined by the bundle; for expository purposes we shall stick with one dollar. Notes and deposits would be privately issued by the banking system, while government money would be abolished. Although money would be denominated in dollars, it would *not* be directly convertible into the bundle that defined the dollar. Rather, notes and deposits would be 'indirectly redeemable' at their issuing banks in gold or some other redemption medium. We assume here that it would be gold. Most redemptions would probably take place at clearing-houses, where each bank would redeem notes issued by and checks drawn on other banks.

The holder of a one-dollar note or deposit would not necessarily receive upon redemption an amount of gold valued at one dollar, although we shall argue below that would indeed be the case. Rather, a person would receive an amount of gold whose *value*, calculated at gold's current market price, equaled the current value of the bundle that defined the dollar. More precisely, the value of gold received would equal the *total value* of the goods and services composing the bundle as calculated at their current market prices. Alternatively, the holder of a one-dollar note or deposit would always receive just enough gold that would allow him to purchase all the goods and services composing the bundle (abstracting from transaction costs). But the total value of those components and hence of the gold received could conceivably diverge from one dollar. Arbitrage and other pressures, however, would ensure that the bundle's value quickly returned to one dollar – or would prevent the deviation in the first place.

For example, suppose that the total value of the goods and services composing the bundle somehow rose to $1.20. Following Yeager and Greenfield (1989), we assume that an excess demand for goods raised the price of the bundle. We assume that the matching excess supply of money was the result of a drop in money demand. We now illustrate why this scenario would be implausible. A holder of a one-dollar note or deposit would find it profitable to redeem it for gold worth $1.20, that is, the new hypothesized value of the bundle. He could sell this gold on the market for $1.20 in notes and deposits, which he could then redeem at a bank for gold worth $1.44, and so on. People in general would engage in such arbitrage, buying fewer goods and services and trying to sell more in order to obtain dollars which they could profitably convert to gold. Downward pressure would be put on prices. Moreover, the conversion of dollars to gold would shrink the money supply, quite in accordance with the hypothesized drop in money demand. Banks would also engage in arbitrage at the clearinghouse as they hurriedly redeemed, in gold worth $1.20, each dollar note issued and dollar check drawn on other banks. Again the decrease in the money supply would be appropriate under the circumstances. These and other pressures described by Yeager and Greenfield would swiftly return the value of the bundle to one dollar. An opposite story could be told in the unlikely event that the total value of the bundle's components fell to, perhaps, 80 cents.

Although the dollar would be defined by the bundle's value, that by itself would not guarantee that the total value of the bundle's components measured at current market prices remained at one dollar. And it is that total value that a person would receive in gold upon redeeming a one-dollar note or deposit. Yeager and Greenfield describe the processes and forces that would operate under indirect convertibility to ensure that the bundle's value remained at one dollar; the deviations imagined above would not occur in the first place. Accordingly, a one-dollar note or deposit would indeed be redeemable for gold worth one dollar.

The BFH system would result in a stable price level, since the total value of the components of the bundle would remain at one dollar through the operation of indirect convertibility. Another advantage of the system is that it would eliminate base money and therefore bank runs. Most importantly, it would eliminate monetary disequilibrium, as explained in the BFH literature.

THE YIELD ON MONEY HELD

Earlier we reviewed money's functions and advantages from the standpoint of society as a whole – the advantages for an individual of operating in a world of money rather than barter. We now turn to the advantages that an individual derives from holding a cash balance and to influences that affect his decision about its size.[8] This topic is central to elaborating the money-supply-and-demand approach to total spending.

Money renders services as do business equipment and consumer durables and many other assets. The principle of diminishing marginal returns holds for money and its services as for these other goods.[9] The yield of noninterest-bearing money to its individual holders is intangible, nonpecuniary and subjective to be sure, but it is genuine. We must distinguish between the utility or productivity of what money can buy and the utility or productivity of the services of a cash balance as such. Suppose we hook a person up to a utilometer that measures levels of and changes in utility. In one experiment, we give him an extra $1000 to use as he likes and measure the rise in his utility. In an alternative experiment, we measure the rise when we give him an extra $1000 with the restriction that he use it for keeping his average cash balance over time $1000 larger than it otherwise would have been. We allow him to use his enlarged cash balance normally, sometimes drawing it down provided that at other times he builds it up enough to maintain the stipulated average. His lesser rise of utility in this alternative experiment illustrates the distinction between the marginal utilities of freely allocatable wealth and of wealth earmarked for a cash balance in particular. Of course, a cash balance would yield no utility unless it had purchasing power, unless the money could be spent, but its utility or services do not arise only in the very act of spending it. The *holding* of money itself yields utility.

A holder of money forgoes the interest he could have received on bonds or the satisfactions he could have obtained from goods bought with the money, so he must consider these sacrifices justified by the services of the money held. It is easy to modify this proposition to take account of interest-bearing checking accounts nowadays. The sacrifice of the additional interest or the more valuable services otherwise obtainable must be justified by the nonpecuniary services obtained on an account bearing interest at a relatively low rate.

It is instructive to compare money held with food in kitchen cabinets, a fire extinguisher on the wall, or materials in a firm's inventory. The stock of food

yields no utility unless it can be eaten; having the fire extinguisher ready yields
no utility to a householder or productivity to a firm unless it can squirt out a fire;
and the stockpiled materials yield no productivity unless they can be embodied
in output. But these things do not afford their yields only while being, respectively, eaten, squirted, or used in production. The analogy with money will
soon prove evident.

Consumers' inventories of food, clothing and so forth, afford yields even
while being held and not just while being consumed. Years ago, Leland Yeager
was a visiting professor at another university. While there he kept some food
and drink in his apartment for entertaining guests at short notice. He thought
his acquaintances preferred bourbon, but as a precaution against the embarrassment of not being able to satisfy a request for scotch, he bought a bottle of
it also. In fact no one ever asked for scotch, and he gave the bottle away
unopened before driving his jam-packed car back to Virginia. Had his tying up
money in the bottle of scotch proved a total waste? Not at all. The scotch had
been affording him security against embarrassment. It is Monday morning quar-
terbacking to say that things would have turned out exactly the same, except
for money saved, without the bottle on hand. And it is not even true, for he
would have suffered some apprehension without it. If a householder or a
business firm holds a fire extinguisher that is not in fact squirted until time to
recharge it, the story about its services is the same in principle as the story
about the scotch. Similarly, clothes in the closet afford utility even when not
being worn, and a larger wardrobe probably cuts down the frequency of trips
to the laundry and cleaner's.

Next, consider an inventory of goods for sale held by a retailer or of materials
or semi-finished or completed goods held by a manufacturer. Why doesn't the
retailer reduce the amount of capital tied up in inventory and so reduce its
borrowing and interest costs or free funds of its own to lend or invest remu-
neratively? Why doesn't the retailer sell from samples and order goods from the
manufacturer only to fill orders taken? Because doing so would lose business.
A good inventory attracts customers.

Why doesn't the manufacturer, likewise, hold smaller inventories of
materials, parts and semi-finished and finished products? Because inventories
of the size he in fact holds contribute to a smooth flow of operations, as by
avoiding bottlenecks and interruptions from particular shortages. Confidence
in this continued flow permits firmer plans for all related activities – scheduling
production, advertising and taking and filling orders. Expensive rushes to
acquire or deliver goods are less likely. Less skilled labor is used up than tighter
inventory management would require.

Thus inventory is literally productive. Of course the businessperson will not
be able to say at the end of his fiscal year exactly how much of his profits or
revenues trace to his having held inventories. Prospective contributions to

revenue and to cost savings are what count in his decisions. He can make estimates if only rough and ready ones. He tries not to hold so large an inventory that the capital tied up in it makes a contribution to revenue clearly smaller at the margin than the contributions of other available uses of capital. He tries not to hold so small an inventory that costly disruptions do occur and that building it up would clearly be more remunerative than alternative allocations of capital. Making rough and ready allowances for risk, he tries to equate the marginal yield on capital tied up in inventory to the marginal yields of capital otherwise allocated.

These observations apply to inventories not only of commodities but also of money, as Greidanus (1932, 1950) and Hutt (1956) insist. Cash balances afford a yield only if the money can be spent, just as goods held afford a yield only if they can be used in production or consumed (or sold). But money's utility or productivity does not arise only in the act of spending it. Paying out money takes only negligible time in relation to holding it. Spending it culminates and terminates the advantages of holding it.

Why does a merchant or manufacturer tie up funds in a cash balance? Why not hold a balance only half as large and lend out the difference, or save interest by borrowing less? For one thing, holding an adequate balance saves on skilled labor and other resources required for tighter cash balance management. Like commodity inventories, furthermore, it facilitates a smooth flow of operations. It helps avoid what Hart (1953, p. 202) called a 'linkage of risks' resulting from cash deficiencies. A linkage of risks is a chain reaction in which one misfortune brings on others. Hart's example concerns a motorist carrying just enough cash to pay for gasoline and meals on the way to his destination. If he was arrested for speeding, misfortunes would multiply because of his inadequate cash. He would have to pay the fine, perhaps spend a night in jail, suffer the ignominy of having to wire his friends for money, and perhaps lose a business deal because of late arrival. An adequate balance contributes to security and financial respectability. It yields valuable services. For a manufacturer, by contributing to the smooth flow of operations it can have an actual physical productivity.

Hutt (1956) notes the similarity between money held and land in the sense of space: neither has any direct pecuniary yield, unless hired out. Neither is physically used up. And neither is sterile. The productivity of money held does not differ in any material manner from that of land. As Hutt argues, money held does multiply and like any other factor of production it yields services that may be embodied in cumulable products. Although the services of consumers' durable goods including cash balances are always consumed, the services of producers' goods including cash balances can be incorporated into products.

As Hutt says, money assets are not only subject to the same laws of value as other scarce things but are likewise productive in all intelligible senses. The ways in which supply and demand operate on money and on other goods differ in important details because money lacks a price and market of its own, but the same laws of value do apply. Kessel and Alchian (1962) treat money balances as a factor of production and even speak of more and less 'money-intensive' lines of production.

What is the nature of money's yield to consumer holders? Money, which is accepted everywhere, is a key to obtaining whatever marketable good or service we may want at some time or place. Holding money saves us from having to store up not-yet-wanted goods. It substitutes to some extent for inventories. Money gives us flexibility and convenience in transactions, the means of seizing special purchase opportunities, the means of mitigating a chain of misfortunes due to a cash squeeze (the 'linkage of risks' again), and financial respectability. Money is a bearer of options over space and time; it helps hold down storage and transactions costs and information requirements. It is also a good hedge against the risks involved in holding other assets (compare Laidler, 1993a, p. 45).

George (1898 [1941], p. 484) mentions that 'the gratification which hoarding gives is the consciousness of holding at command that with which we may readily buy anything we may wish to have'. Greidanus (1950, p. 323) says:

> ... the significance of money [to the individual holder] lies not so much in the fact that we buy with it, as in the fact that if *we wish to do so we shall be able to buy*. Our demand for money for the purpose of buying immediately is at once cancelled by our offer of money when we do buy. But our demand for money in order to be able to buy as soon as it shall prove necessary is the demand for money which actually keeps the aggregate quantity of money tied up.

To understand why we hold money and derive services from it even when not spending it, think again of the analogy of the fire extinguisher. The fact that we hold such things and money – and at a cost – shows that they do afford services to us.

What concerns monetary theory is the demand for money *to hold*, not a demand for money to spend (see chapters 3 and 4). With no demand to hold money, velocity would be infinite and the price level infinite or meaningless. The very conception of a medium of exchange that people did not want to hold is self-contradictory. (Even a nonholdable service, however, could serve as a mere numéraire or unit of account.)

Of course, people hold cash balances for the purpose of receiving payments into them and making payments from them, and the sizes of desired cash balances are related to these flows of payments through them. The services of money occur as a flow and are demanded in some relation to the flow of transactions. Still, the demanded holdings and actual quantity of money are stocks (Cannan, 1921 [1951]). This discussion is preliminary; Chapters 3 and 4 elaborate on stocks and flows.

People demand cash balances of some definite size on the average over time, rather than, say, balances half or twice as large. The holdings that yield utility or productivity are *real* cash balances, balances of definite purchasing power. Holders are interested not in numbers of money units as such but in what their money will buy. For an individual, of course, the sizes of his real and nominal cash balances are proportional to one another, since nothing that he alone does will change the purchasing power of the money unit. If he wants to change his real cash balance by some percentage, he can do so only by changing his nominal cash balance by the same percentage. Hutt suggests thinking of the nominal money unit – the ordinary dollar or yen or peso – as a 'container' of real purchasing power. A person is concerned with the total amount of purchasing power contained in his cash balance rather than with the number of nominal units required to contain that real amount.

The correspondence between real and nominal sizes of a cash balance holds true for the individual but not for the economy as a whole. If members of the economy in the aggregate decided to acquire bigger nominal cash balances to have bigger real balances, then even with the nominal money supply kept unchanged, the real total of cash balances would increase as the nominal unit rose in purchasing power. Whether this deflationary process could occur without painful side effects is another story.

The principle of diminishing marginal yield or return applies to holdings – real holdings – of money as of other things. Consider shirts. When one owns only a single shirt, acquiring a second has important advantages. It cuts out the necessity of doing a little laundry every night. But when one already owns 30 shirts, a 31st affords only slight additional convenience. Similarly with money. When a consumer is trying to get along on a cash balance (including checkable deposits) of only $100, having an additional $100 in the cash balance on the average over time would add much to convenience and security. But if the consumer already had a $5000 balance, an additional $100 would afford relatively slight additional advantages. Similar examples apply to business firms.

The principle of diminishing marginal returns is important in the portfolio-equilibrium condition, explained on pages 43–6 below, of equal marginal net returns on all assets held. The marginal return on an asset can be adjusted by adjusting the amount held. This adjustability is particularly true of money because holdings of it need not be adjusted only in lumpy amounts.

SOME SUPPOSED DIFFICULTIES WITH THE YIELD ON MONEY

One might object that money held, instead of affording services or utility, simply enables the holder to avoid certain costs, such as the expenses and time and trouble of shifting funds from money into securities and then back again to earn interest in the meanwhile.[10] Is there any difficulty with the notion that avoiding inconvenience or expense counts as reaping a yield? This question bears, for example, on how to describe an asset-holder's equilibrium. Is it legitimate to describe it, as we shall, as a position in which the estimated marginal net yields on all assets held are equal, subject to qualifications about risk, liquidity and the like?

The supposed difficulty poses no problem. In economic theory, utility means desiredness or capacity for satisfying desires; and why something is desired is ordinarily more a question of psychology, sociology or technology than of economics. We buy many things to avoid cost or unpleasantness rather than to get positive pleasure – house insulation to hold down fuel costs, medicines to cope with illness, razors to avoid untidiness. Is there any fundamental difference between the yield of a picture, which affords positive pleasure, and the yield of a fire extinguisher, which hanging ready lessens the householder's apprehensions? No; no difference between the two yields seems important for economic theory.

If one raises the doubts mentioned about the yield on money, one could raise similar doubts about the yield on a vacuum cleaner owned. Why do people keep cleaners in their closets rather than rent them before each use and return them right afterwards? It is meaningful to answer that a cleaner in the closet is rendering a service of availability, which is closely related to sparing the owner the cost and trouble of a round trip to the rental shop whenever he wants to clean his rug. This transactions-costs reason for owning rather than renting a vacuum cleaner (or any reason for not hiring a house-cleaning team instead) does not deny the reality of the machine's services, including the service of ready availability. One might raise similarly unpersuasive doubts about the yield from food in the refrigerator and cabinets – that instead of affording an actual yield, the food simply holds down the trouble and time and expense of more frequent trips to the supermarket. But describing the yield as avoidance of these transactions costs in no way demolishes the notion that the food is providing a yield even while not being eaten.

Similar considerations apply to money. Do we hold it because it provides utility or because investing and disinvesting it are costly? The question poses a false alternative. We could receive interest by holding securities instead of money, and also some services similar to those of money if the securities are readily salable. We do not get all of our liquidity services in that substitute way, however. We get some by holding money itself. The reason is the just-mentioned costs, and also perhaps risks, of financial transactions. The reality of money's services is supported by the fact that we have reasons for not getting all such services, along with interest earnings besides, in some substitute way.

The principle of 'diminishing marginal returns' still holds when the returns consist of avoidance of cost or unpleasantness or inconvenience. It holds true, for example, of insulation. Beyond some thickness, anyway, each increment of insulation affords less and less further saving on fuel costs. Beyond some number, the more fire extinguishers are hanging around a house or factory, the less additional security each additional extinguisher provides. Food on the shelf can be so abundant that having still more of it would afford little additional yield in the form of avoidance of shopping trips. The same is true of money even when we insist on interpreting its yield as avoidance of investment and disinvestment costs: beyond some point, the more that is held, the less scope remains for economizing further on such costs.

MONEY IN UTILITY AND PRODUCTION FUNCTIONS

Many writers have asked whether money properly counts as an argument in the utility function of consumers and the production function of business firms. Feige and Parkin (1971, p. 336), for example, deny 'that money yields any direct services which enter as arguments of the utility function'. Its use as an efficient medium of exchange simply 'allows the individual to economize on other real resources which would otherwise be expended in the process of exchange'.

This view is instructive. Money yields no utility. It just helps people economize on time and resources that they would otherwise use up in conducting exchanges. Yes, but the same is true of pens and pencils and computers and telephones. They too save resources and time otherwise used in doing this or that. We want such things not for their own sakes but because they help us to communicate and trade and so achieve our more fundamental objectives. Does this mean that we should exclude the tools of communication, or their services, from the utility function?

The question is not a genuine issue. It is a mere matter of convenience for the analytical purpose at hand what we include in the utility function. Do we include only the cooked food ready to enter our mouths and regard all other things as items having technological properties conducive to reaching that position? Or do we count the stove, the refrigerator and food on hand, or their services, as arguments in the utility function? The question concerns not the realities of the world but convenience in describing and analyzing those realities.

Similar remarks apply to the question of what belongs in the production function. How to conceive of that function and its arguments is a matter of convenience that may well vary from one piece of analysis to another.

Writing in the same journal issue as Feige and Parkin, Saving (1971) showed that he could derive the demand for transactions balances of money without making them an argument in the utility function. He did, however, count leisure and commodities as arguments. By using money – and using it implies holding it – we save time and resources that we would otherwise spend trying to accomplish barter transactions, so we can probably have both more leisure time and more commodities than otherwise.[11]

What Saving counts in the utility function, therefore, is not cash balances but the results of holding and using them, which is hardly an earth-shaking distinction. Similarly, we could leave automobiles out of the utility function but include the time-saving and other results of using them; we could leave out medicine but include better health; we could leave out stereos and CDs but include the music reaching our ears. Whether to count *indirect* sources of satisfaction as arguments in the function or only the satisfying experiences themselves is a matter on which the analyst has a good deal of flexibility. We find it reasonable to say that cash balances are an argument in utility functions.

Saving next considers business firms. He observes that the physical output from definite amounts of labor, machines and steel does not depend on a firm's average cash balance. The productivity of money held lies in other directions – in economizing on resources expended in bringing factors of production together and in marketing the firm's output.

Well, a company airplane also facilitates assembling manpower and materials and marketing the product. It too affords economies in transactions cost. Should we therefore rule the plane out of the production function? We are insisting not on one answer or the other but only on the similarity between the plane and the cash balance as candidates for inclusion in the production function.

The productivity and utility of cash balances are recognized in the arguments of Tolley (1957) and Friedman (1959c, pp. 71–5; 1969) for interest payments on cash balances or for a yield through price deflation. If interest on alternative assets (or interest at a higher rate than received on deposits) did not prod people to economize on cash balances, they would hold larger real balances than they now do and so would reap the utility or productivity they afford or would save on the resources consumed in tight management of cash balances. Yet in a fiat money system, those additional real balances and their services would be essentially 'costless' from society's point of view. Such considerations have led Friedman (1969) to recommend a rate of deflation equal to the real rate of interest. According to the 'Fisher effect', the nominal interest rate equals the real rate of interest plus the expected rate of inflation. Assuming a positive real rate of interest, an offsetting expected rate of deflation would leave the nominal rate equal to zero. Friedman thus refers to the amount of real cash balances that would exist in this case as 'the optimum quantity of money', since people would be 'satiated' with real balances held at the zero nominal rate floor. That is, the zero marginal yield or benefit of holding money would equal the zero marginal cost of producing it.

PORTFOLIO EQUILIBRIUM

We have already mentioned the concept of portfolio equilibrium and shall make further use of it later. Here we try to sharpen the idea. An individual holder of assets aims at a portfolio composed in such a way that, with qualifications for risk, liquidity and so forth, he receives the same estimated yield on all assets at the margin. To be comparable, marginal yields have to be expressed in common units such as an annual rate of return. The income or the value of services provided by an increment of the asset in question over the course of a year might be expressed as a percentage of the value of that increment. We shall have more to say later about the units in which to estimate and compare returns. Henceforth, MER stands for an asset's marginal expected rate of return. If an asset holder perceived that he was not receiving equal MERs, he would sell assets with relatively low MERs and switch into ones affording higher yields.

Money, other financial assets, and to some extent physical assets, are means of allocating consumption over time, so time preferences enter into portfolio decisions. Suppose the individual had arranged his current consumption and command over future consumption so that he was indifferent at the margin between 100 real units of consumption now and 105 units a year from now. In this situation he is said to have an internal rate of discount (IRD) of 5 percent.[12] Loosely speaking, he appreciates future consumption that much less than present consumption. Suppose further that an MER of 10 percent were available on portfolio assets. The discrepancy would give him reason to stint on current consumption and build up his portfolio. As current consumption accordingly became scarcer and future consumption more abundant, he would discount future consumption more heavily than before. He would move into being indifferent at the margin between 100 current consumption units and 109 future units. If the same adjustments brought the estimated marginal rate of return on his portfolio down to 9 percent, then he would have achieved a portfolio of optimum size: the IRD would equal the common MER on assets. These illustrative figures are chosen to suggest that in principle the individual has some influence, if only slight, on the yields obtainable on portfolio assets. He would hardly have an appreciable influence on such cut-and-dried rates of return as bond yields, but the principle of diminishing marginal returns would operate on the subjectively estimated intangible returns on holdings of real cash balances and physical assets. The individual can adjust the marginal yields on these by changing the quantities held. Strictly speaking, in our example the MER would be fixed by interest rates on markets in which the individual is a price-taker, so only the IRD would adjust. (Recall that we have abstracted from risk, liquidity and the like.)

Let us generalize from the example. If the holder has an IRD lower than the MER, he has reason to hold more assets, which means shifting some consumption from the present to the future and thereby raising the IRD. Conversely, if he is receiving an MER that falls short of his IRD, he has reason to pare down his portfolio and consume more, resulting in a decrease in his IRD. A portfolio is *optimal* in *size* as well as in *composition* if the marginal expected rate of return afforded in common by the assets composing it is equal to the holder's internal rate of discount.

The principle of equating marginal expected yields helps explain why the quantity of money demanded – and so the velocity of money – is not an objectively determined magnitude. It depends, rather, on circumstances and people's assessments of them, including rates of return obtainable on other assets. People tend to hold real cash balances of such size that their subjectively appraised marginal yields are roughly equal to alternative rates of return. The higher explicit interest rates are, the higher is the target and equilibrium level of marginal yield on cash balances. The smaller then in accordance with the principle of diminishing marginal yield must those balances be.

Some monetary theorists used to seem skeptical of any significant degree of interest elasticity in the demand for cash balances. However, accumulating evidence has changed their judgment. This skepticism seems odd, for the idea of equating yields at the margin on different assets ties in nicely with ordinary price theory. Still, belief that the demand for money is insensitive to the interest rate would not actually contradict the marginal equalization idea. It would just assert that an increase or decrease in the interest rate would only slightly affect the real quantity of money demanded.

Suppose people start with portfolios that they consider satisfactory and then the quantity of money increases, perhaps by a drop from airplanes. Right after picking up the extra money, holders find that their portfolios contain relatively too much money. In accordance with the principle of diminishing marginal yield, the MERs on money have fallen below the MERs on other assets. And portfolios are too large, representing too much wealth held and affording command over too much future consumption relative to present consumption. A holder's MER on money in particular is below his IRD.

Why do people pick up the dropped money if doing so will disequilibrate their portfolios? The answer is trivially obvious here, but it is worth noting for comparison with cases in which new money is injected in a different way, as by monetary authority operations. People can adjust their disrupted portfolios and be better off than before.

Shifting out of money because its MERs have been reduced below the MERs on other assets and below the IRDs constitutes what we call the 'portfolio-balance effect'. Spending more freely on current consumption because of the increased size of asset portfolios constitutes a 'wealth effect'. In short, people spend money more freely on consumption, as well as investing it more freely in other assets, because the airplane drop (1) has loaded them with what they consider relatively too much money and (2) has made them wealthier than before.

People's spending and respending of the expanded money supply on goods and services (and securities) raises prices (and perhaps transitionally reduces yields on securities) until people finally are content to hold all the money after all.[13] The initial expansion of money's real quantity is reversed by the price increases that bring the MERs on it back up into line with other MERs and with people's IRDs.

The story is not entirely different if the new money is introduced by open-market operations. Why do people sell securities to the monetary authority if doing so and being paid in money will disrupt their portfolios? The answer is that the monetary authority pays a sufficiently attractive price, and people individually know they can turn around and further adjust their portfolios.

Initially holding more money and fewer securities than before the open-market operation, people perceive that MERs on money are now below their IRDs and the MERs on other assets, including securities. (Strictly, the comparison is with securities other than those bought by the monetary authority, whose prices have been raised and yields lowered by the open-market operation itself.) People accordingly try to shift out of money into other assets and goods and services. Rises in prices, which shrink real cash balances, eventually make people content to hold the expanded nominal money supply after all.

The open-market case differs from the airplane drop case chiefly in involving no straightforward wealth effect. Instead of receiving new money free, people receive it in exchange for securities. Even so, some slight wealth effect may occur after all. People who sell securities to the monetary authority presumably consider their sales advantageous. Even people who do not sell securities may find their holdings raised in value by the authority's purchases. However, we need not insist on any such wealth effect in the open-market case. The essential point is that new money ultimately entails a rise in spending and prices to make people content to hold all of it after all. An at least transitional decline in interest rates may well figure in the process.

Our stories go into reverse for a shrinkage of the money supply that initially causes people to be holding less money than they desire. The MERs on money exceed IRDs and the MERs on other assets. People's efforts to build up their cash balances result in a decline in spending and prices until they find their real cash balances no longer deficient after all.

The portfolio-balance effect is one aspect of what we call the *Wicksell Process*, which is a broader interpretation of Patinkin's (1965) real-balance effect as we explain in Chapters 3 and 4. When the portfolio-balance effect operates, a change in the money supply can directly affect not only people's spending but also firms' investment in new capital goods – though the usual presentation of the real-balance effect focuses narrowly on consumption. Following an increase in the money supply, firms increase investment because the decreased MERs on money held by them make the MERs on *new* factories, machinery and other capital goods (as well as goods in inventory) look relatively attractive.

The foregoing analysis applies equally to new consumer durables, which have an implicit yield. An increase in the money supply may therefore directly promote consumption for a second reason as the depressed MERs on money make the MERs on consumer durables look relatively attractive.

It is necessary to differentiate our 'portfolio-balance effect', whereby changes in the money supply can *directly* affect spending and nominal income, from the 'portfolio-adjustment models' found in the literature. Almost all of these models portray changes in the money supply as affecting spending and income only *indirectly*, through changing interest rates and asset prices, including the prices of existing real (physical) assets relative to costs of producing them new.[14] For example, in these models an increase in the money supply lowers the yield on money relative to yields on other assets, both financial and real. People substitute out of money into nonmoney assets, raising their prices and lowering their yields. Specifically, the prices of existing real assets rise relative to the unchanged new-supply price (cost of producing them new), which stimulates spending on new real assets. Two features of the portfolio-adjustment model stand out: (1) it depends on sequential changes in relative prices and (2) it operates only indirectly in leading to spending on new capital goods as well as new consumer durables. On the other hand, the portfolio-balance effect can directly affect spending without first requiring changes in the prices of financial and existing real assets, although this effect can also operate indirectly as we explain below.[15] (Compare Humphrey's 1984 interpretation of the monetarist transmission mechanism.)

We mention a point alluded to earlier and discussed in Chapters 3 and 4. The fact that people part with money every day in buying goods and services and securities does *not* mean their MERs on money are necessarily below their IRDs and MERs on other assets. Because money is a medium of exchange as well as a buffer stock (Laidler, 1984, 1987), people will routinely buy goods and services and securities with money without necessarily changing their desired average cash balance over time. In contrast, following an increase in the money supply, people will attempt to rearrange their portfolios by purchasing *more* goods and services and securities. In this case people's MERs on money would be below their IRDs and MERs on nonmoney assets.

THE 'YIELD THEORY' OF THE PRICE LEVEL

The concepts of diminishing marginal returns on money and of making asset yields equal at the margin lead into the theory of what Greidanus (1950, pp. 338–9) calls the 'right' price level, the one that is right for a given nominal quantity of money (and for other relevant conditions, including the real size of the economy).[16] Prices are just so high that the total money supply is of just that real size at which the marginal yield on holdings of it equal the yield on capital or assets in general. That, in brief, is Greidanus's yield theory of the equilibrium price level.

Let us try a restatement. The equilibrium price level is the one at which the nominal money supply has a total purchasing power (real size) equaling the total of desired real cash balances. Real balances are at their desired size when the marginal yield on them is neither higher nor lower than the yield on assets in general, again with obvious qualifications for risk, liquidity and so forth.

After an increase in the money supply, people act with increased eagerness to buy goods and services and securities and reduced eagerness to sell, thereby bidding up prices. At the new equilibrium the actual real size of the money supply has shrunk back into equality again with the total of desired real money holdings; and the marginal yield on money has come back up to equality with the yields on other things.

In the converse case of the actual money supply falling short of desired cash balances, people alter their behavior in the markets for goods and services and securities in ways that make prices fall. The attendant rise in the total real size of money holdings reduces their estimated marginal yield down into line with other asset yields. People are content with their nominal money holdings at the reduced equilibrium price level. As emphasized elsewhere, however, general price deflation is likely to be a slow and painful process.

The yield theory of the price level obviously complements the portfolio-balance effect. It affords an example of what we have called the translation test, which we now illustrate. Inventions that raise the marginal productivity of capital goods – or an optimistic turn in firms' judgments about investment prospects – should increase spending on investment projects, encourage borrowing to finance them, and tend to raise the price level, even with the nominal money supply unchanged. At the old real size of the money supply, its subjectively appraised marginal yield is now lower than the prevailing general rate of return, which by hypothesis has risen. People and firms feel they are now holding too much money, which they are readier than before to lend or invest at the increased interest rates and anticipated profit rates now available. In the new equilibrium the increased velocity of the unchanged money supply helps account for the higher price level. The lower real balances imply higher MERs on money. The hypothesized underlying changes also result in a change in the composition of production – more investment goods and less consumption goods. Decreased consumption will have raised people's IRDs in line with the increased MERs (compare pages 156–8 below).

THE LIQUIDITY TRAP

The concepts of diminishing marginal returns and portfolio equilibrium discredit the Keynesian notion of a liquidity trap. On one interpretation, that notion appears as a supposed demand-for-money curve with a horizontal segment extending indefinitely to the right at the level of the supposed floor rate of interest, as in Figure 2.1. The demand is infinitely interest-elastic in this range. Another interpretation appears in Figure 2.2: the curve represents a locus of equilibria between larger and larger money supplies and the associated demand-for-money curves. Shifts in the demand-for-money curve fully match rightward shifts in the supply curve, keeping their intersections all on the horizontal portion. In either case, the interest rate cannot be pushed below its floor because at that rate all further increases in the money supply are fully absorbed as additions to desired cash balances.[17] (Figure 2.1 portrays an 'individual experiment', while Figure 2.2 portrays the result of a series of conceptual 'market experiments'; see pages 113–14 below.)

On either of these interpretations, the liquidity trap notion is untenable. It supposes that the subjectively appraised marginal yield on cash balances cannot be depressed below a certain level. The notion of a floor rate of interest may make sense on the bond or loan market, but its transfer to the demand for or

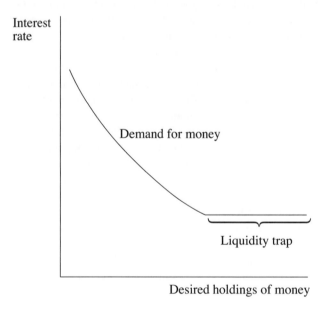

Figure 2.1   The liquidity trap

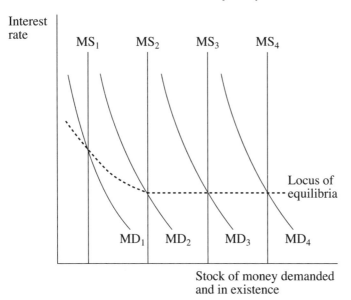

Figure 2.2   Shifts in the money supply curve matched by shifts in the demand curve

'market' for money holdings is illegitimate. Supposedly and implausibly, people know nothing better to do with additions to the money stock than passively to absorb them in full into desired cash balances. Those additions do not depress the marginal yield on cash balances below the marginal yields on other things. The version in Figure 2.1 has the further defect of supposing that people have infinite wealth that they would desire to devote to cash balances at a sufficiently low interest rate.[18]

In reality the principle of diminishing marginal yield continues to hold. For every holder there must be a cash balance so large that a further addition to it would afford him a lower marginal yield than he could expect to obtain on some other allocation of his portfolio.

INTERACTION AMONG YIELDS

Hutt and Greidanus recognize that people's tendency to hold a real quantity of money whose size makes its yield equal the economy's going rate of return undercuts the Keynesian liquidity preference theory of interest. According to that theory, the interest rate on securities falls into line with the marginal subjective yield on cash balances, which can be altered by changes in the quantity of money. One trouble with this formulation is that the yield on cash balances is not a uniquely dominant magnitude with which all other yields fall into line. Rather, people adjust their holdings of money, securities and other assets in such a way that the perceived marginal yields on all of them tend to be equal. Causation does not run in one direction only from money's yield to the interest rate. Rather, those magnitudes are just two among many rates of return in a system of mutual determination.

Thus, we cannot explain the interest rate by the liquidity yield on money when the latter is itself pulled into line with the general rate of return on assets, allowance being made for risks, liquidity and so forth. The demand for and supply of one asset, money, cannot determine the rate of return on assets in general.

To speak as we just did of money's rate of return being 'pulled into line' with other rates of return is convenient but not strictly accurate. The pulling does not go one way only. In principle the marginal yields on money and other things all affect each other. Money's yield does not just passively respond.

Although in certain cases, as we shall see in Chapter 5, the quantity of money does not affect the equilibrium rate of interest, the state of liquidity preference does. After all, people's tastes for real money holdings count among the realities of the economy. They belong to the 'wants, resources and technology' conventionally taken as given. But saying this does not rehabilitate the liquidity preference theory of interest, which says something more specific than merely that people's liquidity preferences number among the many factors affecting interest rates (see pages 116–17 below).

Allais (1947) worried that the availability of money to hold tends to divert people's propensity to save and accumulate wealth away from the construction of capital goods.[19] (Strictly speaking, Allais addressed his worry to money other than that put into circulation by way of business loans.) Under otherwise unchanged circumstances, a strengthening of the public's general propensity to save and acquire assets would presumably tend to promote real capital formation and lower the equilibrium interest rate. But given an unchanged overall propensity to save and accumulate, a shift within it toward holding money and away from other assets (or, almost equivalently, a tax or regulatory change favoring money-holding and discouraging the holding of other assets) would presumably tend to raise interest rates and divert resources from capital formation.

Allais was thus inclined to favor stamped money or a policy of chronic mild price inflation to discourage money-holding and divert propensities to save and accumulate into socially more productive directions such as real capital formation. He even suggested splitting the unit of account and medium of exchange. The 'franc', the unit of account, would be defined so as to have a stable value. The 'circul', or medium of exchange, would continuously depreciate against the stable franc discouraging holdings of circul-denominated banknotes and deposits. Use of the circul as unit of account would be 'flatly forbidden'. Allais also recognized that creation of new money in ways that tended to favor real investment, as through credit expansion for that purpose, could more or less neutralize the anti-capital-formation effect that he worried about. Allais focused on what he considered the beneficial allocation effects of mild inflation.

We mention these points not to endorse Allais's particular policy proposals but to underline the idea of *inter*dependence between propensities to hold money and other assets and between their respective yields. The subjectively appraised marginal yield on money holdings is not just passively and unidirectionally pulled into line with the general level of yields on other assets. In principle, tastes about holding money have some active influence on the general level of yields.

A line of reasoning about the benefits and costs of cash balances (for example, Tolley, 1957 and Friedman, 1959c, pp. 71–5; 1969) has roughly opposite policy implications from Allais's line about propensities to accumulate wealth. The first line we recall seems to recommend encouragements to money holding, the second discouragements. Instead of necessarily contradicting each other, however, these two strands of theory pass by each other without meeting head on. Their apparent clash illuminates a general point: one should be cautious about recommending policy interventions whenever some particular strand of theory might seem to recommend it, for that one strand might not be the whole story by far.

FURTHER QUESTIONS ABOUT YIELDS

A simple question will test the reader's understanding of the portfolio equilibrium condition that the marginal yield on money be equal to the opportunity cost of holding it. (That cost, though proxied by the interest rate, has many dimensions since it is the yield obtainable by holding all sorts of other things instead.) Consider a nominal interest rate containing an allowance for rapid inflation. Is the marginal yield on money really that high? Common sense might suggest that money's net yield is abnormally low, since its loss of purchasing power must be subtracted out. Does the idea of a high marginal yield measured by a high interest rate clash with the idea of a low net yield because of money's rapid depreciation?

No, there is no contradiction. The (gross) marginal yield on money *is* high, in accordance with the principle of diminishing marginal returns. Real balances are pared so low that the marginal yield on them is high enough to match, roughly anyway, the high cost of holding them.

This is a striking feature of hyperinflation. Some economists in Germany in the early 1920s blamed the inflation on things other than the huge and zooming nominal quantity of money – on Allied demands for reparations, the state of the balance of payments, or whatever. They emphasized that the real value or gold value of the money supply was extremely small. Businesspeople complained about a shortage of money. This argument was erroneous, but the fact cited was correct. People were holding extremely small real balances – precisely because they recognized the great cost of holding money. Workers reportedly arranged to be paid as often as twice a day so that at midday they could divide up their money among their families, who would ride off on their bicycles in all directions to buy just about anything before prices rose further. As long as German marks still served as the usual medium of exchange, however, people could hardly pare their real cash balances all the way down to zero.

We can think of the cost of holding money in such circumstances either as the loss of purchasing power or as opportunity cost. (We should also mention the real rate of interest, but in times of extreme inflation that component of the nominal rate is small relative to the inflation allowance.) In holding money, one forgoes the opportunity to preserve one's purchasing power by putting it into assets whose prices are rising or into loans or bonds bearing nominal interest rates that roughly compensate for the ongoing inflation. High interest rates, corresponding as they do to the alternative opportunity of protecting one's purchasing power, do roughly measure the high marginal yields in terms of services and convenience that people must think they are getting on the small real cash balances that they nevertheless hold. If one wants to speak of a *net* marginal yield – this subjectively appraised service yield minus loss of purchasing power – then it tends to be low, in the neighborhood of real rates of return on assets.

Whether one interprets the cost of holding money as mostly the plain loss of purchasing power or as a forgone opportunity, it is roughly equal to the sub-jectively appraised service yield obtained. Otherwise, one would adjust one's cash balance. We can describe a money-holder's equilibrium in terms different from but equivalent to those used before: his cash balance is of optimum size when the marginal return on it equals the marginal cost of holding it.

Now we must squarely face the question of what units the yield on money is supposedly measured in. We have postponed facing it because the topic may strike the reader as contrived or metaphysical.

It is plausible to imagine that a consumer subjectively estimates the services of his cash balance in dollars-worths. By holding a larger rather than smaller balance, he enjoys greater protection against unexpected contingencies, less need to monitor his balance closely, and avoidance of incurring more time and trouble and expense in dealing frequently with his securities broker. In principle he could put a dollar value on these additional services obtained from a larger rather than a smaller balance. We could ask him: 'What amount of money, given to you and designated for additional spending rather than for addition to your cash balance, would have the same significance for you – would afford you the same utility – as the yearly services from a marginal $100 of average cash balance? In other words, suppose you were required to keep your average cash balance $100 lower than you now do. What donated addition to your annual spending would just compensate you for the inconvenience of getting along on the reduced cash balance?'

Such a question is intelligible and is amenable to a meaningful if imprecise answer. 'Ten cents' would be clearly too low, 'a million dollars', too high. The dollar estimate, once made, can be expressed as a percentage per year of the capital value of the amount of the asset contemplated, in this case the marginal $100 of cash balance.

The yield on a painting could be similarly estimated. The owner could be asked what amount of additional consumption per year would just compensate him for loss of the pleasure from the painting, and his dollar estimate would be expressed as a percentage of the value of the painting. (If the painting's yield consisted not only of pleasure but also of expected capital gain, that gain would enter the calculation also.)

The marginal yield on a business cash balance can be estimated at least as straightforwardly. Adding $100 to the firm's average cash balance, like adding $100 worth of inventory, would add some dollar amount to its yearly net revenues, and this estimated amount could be expressed as a percentage of the $100.

MONEY SUBSTITUTES AND THE YIELD ON MONEY

As Greidanus recognizes, opportunities to buy on credit, the availability of loans when desired, and the availability of interest-bearing nearmoneys makes the demand for holdings of actual money weaker than it would otherwise be. He also notes that a bond or nearmoney bears a lower rate of explicit interest than it otherwise would if it also affords nonpecuniary advantages of quasi-liquidity. Its total yield, tending to equal the general rate of return on assets, has both an explicit pecuniary component and an implicit or subjective component.

In other words, the availability of credit and nearmoneys makes the velocity of circulation of a given nominal money stock greater and its real (purchasing power) size smaller than they would otherwise be. A given nominal money stock supports higher levels of nominal income and expenditure and prices than in the absence of credit and nearmoneys.

It is not correct to say that high velocity of a given nominal money supply causes low purchasing power of the money unit, nor that the low purchasing power causes the high velocity. Rather, both result from people's responses to the availability of substitutes for holding money. Furthermore, it is not how large the quantity of nearmoneys is that makes money's velocity higher and purchasing power lower than otherwise, for that quantity is determined by demand as well as supply in a way not true of the quantity of the actual medium of exchange. This remark refers to a system of our existing type in a closed economy or one with a floating exchange rate. The story about money supply determination must be modified for a fixed exchange rate as explained below. The availability and yields of nearmoneys are what induce people to hold more of them and less of real money balances than they otherwise would.

One further clarification may help. The smaller real money balances held when credit and nearmoneys are available do not bear a higher marginal yield than money would bear in the alternative case. The principle of diminishing marginal returns does not show itself in such a way. Instead of occurring along a given demand-for-money curve, the smallness of real money balances results here from a weaker demand for actual money; the demand schedule lies further to the left, as in Figure 2.3, than in the absence of credit and nearmoneys. The availability of nearmoneys makes a person's assessment of the marginal yield on a real cash balance of a given size lower than it would otherwise be, and keeping the yield from being lower after all requires a smaller real balance in

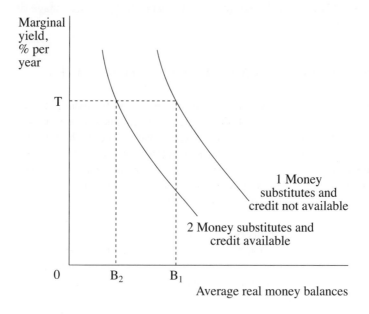

Figure 2.3   Marginal yields on a cash balance with and without the availability of money substitutes and credit

the chosen portfolio position. Nearmoneys and money are 'substitutes'. Consider an analogy: the availability and attractiveness of other meats makes a person's assessment of the marginal utility of beef at a given rate of beef consumption lower than it would otherwise be, and to keep the marginal utility per dollar's worth of beef as high as in the absence of substitutes requires a smaller consumption of beef. Similarly, to keep up the marginal yield on money balances when substitutes appear requires reducing real money balances.

An element of 'complementarity' may also exist between bonds (and even nearmoneys) and actual money, so that wealth held in the form of bonds may exert a positive wealth effect on the demand for money. That, however, is quite a different topic from the substitutability discussed here and is explored on pages 136–6 below.

CIRCULARITY AND THE REGRESSION THEOREM

We have been considering the utility and productivity of cash balances to understand the demand for such balances and prepare for considering how money's demand and supply interact in determining its purchasing power and in affecting macroeconomic performance. Before moving on, however, we should face a supposed problem of circularity sometimes thought to bedevil the application of utility concepts to cash balances. People attribute utility to real money holdings. The holder must know the purchasing power of the money unit before he can estimate his utility from cash balances of different nominal sizes. Yet the theory in question employs the concept of the utility of each cash balance to explain the total demand for cash balances, which, together with the quantity of money, determines the purchasing power of money. The theory is allegedly circular in explaining the utility of money by its purchasing power and its purchasing power by the utility that accounts for the demand for money interacting with its supply. Mises (1912 [1934] [1981], pp. 136–44) identified this apparent problem and as a solution offered the regression theorem summarized in a few paragraphs below.

The supposed circularity begins to vanish when we restate the problem. The individual's estimates of utility and the number of money units he accordingly demands to hold depend above all on the price level, yet the price level is determined by the interplay of money's supply and demand. It is easy to show, as Patinkin (1965, pp. 115–16) has done, that no vicious circularity occurs.[20] As in applying ordinary supply and demand analysis to any commodity, we must distinguish between the demand schedule and quantity demanded. For money as for bread, no inconsistency occurs in ascertaining the demand schedule by investigating how much of it people would demand at each alternative unit value or price and then confronting that schedule with a definite quantity (of money) or supply schedule (of bread) to determine the equilibrium value or price. A demand for money holdings as a function of the purchasing power of the unit together with the actual quantity of money suffices to represent determination of the price level at which demanded and actual quantities are equal.

Admittedly, bread and money are different. Bread and most other goods have physical properties that appeal to people's tastes and wants and enable people to attribute marginal utilities to various quantities of them even without regard to their prices. With money – fiat money – in contrast, its capacity to afford utility depends entirely on a nonphysical property, its purchasing power. This difference, however, is not decisive. Some other goods share (partially) in the characteristic that their capacity to afford satisfaction to their owners depends on their prices – diamonds, furs, expensive delicacies served to guests and snob goods in general. Yet no circularity vitiates supply and demand analysis on that account.

Still, Mises's regression theorem is not otiose.[21] Patinkin was content to demonstrate the mathematical or logical consistency of supply and demand analysis. Mises was mainly concerned with process, with who does what. Which one of the infinitely many alternative levels of money's purchasing power do people have in mind when they actually make their utility estimates, decide how much money to hold, and then try to conduct transactions consistent with these decisions? No one actually draws up a demand-for-money schedule by asking people about desired holdings at alternative price levels.

Could a new pure fiat money be launched without any clue to its tentative initial value? Suppose the old money was declared invalid and each person was given x units of the new money and told nothing more than to start using it. How would anyone know what prices to ask and offer for things? Fiat money, unlike bread, has no physical properties of its own for people to consider when deciding how eagerly to supply and demand it. Wouldn't the launching of the new money be facilitated by some indication of its initial value?[22]

If the answer is yes, Mises was right. According to his regression theorem, people express their demand for money, which interacts with supply to determine money's value 'today', in the light of its value 'yesterday', which was determined by supply and demand in the light of its value the day before. This process reaches back in history to the time when some commodity, valued for its own usefulness, had not quite yet evolved into money. This story is not vitiated by the fact that today's money is fiat money not redeemable in any commodity whatsoever. It became fiat money through lapse of its redeemability in the commodity previously defining the monetary standard, so that the connection still reaches back to premonetary commodities.

This theory of historical regression obviously complements Menger's theory of the origin of money. In Hicks's (1935 [1967], p. 62) capsule interpretation,

Mises identified money as 'a ghost of gold'. To say that Mises offered a valid solution to the supposed circularity problem is not to say that Patinkin was wrong, for they were dealing with subtly different questions. Perhaps Patinkin should have pointed this difference out.

STUDIES OF THE DEMAND FOR MONEY

Theoretical and statistical studies of the demand for money help illuminate the determination of nominal income. Real money demand depends positively on a scale variable like income or wealth or on both, negatively on the opportunity cost of holding money as proxied by an interest rate, negatively on expected price inflation if severe, and positively it seems on real wages. (When misunderstanding is unlikely, we often say 'demand' not only for 'demand function' but also for 'quantity demanded'.) When a change in supply disturbs equality of supply and demand, one or more of the variables affecting demand must change in the direction of restoring monetary equilibrium.

People may hold transactions balances partly in bonds or nearmoneys rather than entirely in directly spendable money. These are only imperfect substitutes for actual cash balances because of the costs of buying and selling them, broadly interpreted (and also, for bonds, because of their changeable values).

Baumol (1952) and Tobin (1956) explore the implications of holding transactions balances partly in interest-bearing money substitutes.[23] Their articles are worth reviewing as classic examples of theorizing about money's role in determining nominal income. They examine how the costs of financial transactions – switches between securities and money – influence the transactions demand for money. Recognizing this influence reconciles nicely with the notion of portfolio equilibrium presented above.

For our purposes here the relevant marginal cost of holding noninterest-bearing money is the marginal yield on other assets *net* of the costs, including trouble as well as actual expense, of shifting into and out of them. This net yield on alternative assets is likely to be higher for big than for small operators. Big operators are likely to enjoy economies of scale in financial transactions. Relative to the interest earnings at stake, they have lower costs of shifting into and out of nonmoney assets. Thanks to these smaller deductions from the gross yields available, big operators earn higher net yields on money substitutes than small operators do. (Hicks, 1935 [1967], especially parts v, vii and viii, made a similar point: thanks to greater risk-reducing diversification, big operators can receive effectively higher yields on their portfolios of earning assets than small operators.)

For these reasons, big operators come under stronger pressures of opportunity cost to keep their money holdings small relative to income and to ordinary nonfinancial transactions. Economies of scale are to be expected in cash balances held for transactions purposes.

BAUMOL'S MODEL OF THE TRANSACTIONS DEMAND FOR MONEY

In Baumol's model, the transactor periodically converts part of his transactions balance held in earning assets into actual payable money. Baumol assumes, as Tobin does not necessarily do, that the transactor invests some or all of his transactions funds in securities upon receiving his ordinary income. We shall go along with the assumption that the transactor starts each period after receiving ordinary income with his entire transactions balance in securities. More exactly, we focus attention on whatever part of his total transactions balance is initially invested in securities; his subsequent piecemeal conversions of this invested balance into money are what concern us. If, instead, we also paid attention to whatever part of income received is kept in cash from the start, then we would have to recognize that the following analysis does not apply to the initial cash part of the combined (cash-plus-invested) balance. The economy-of-scale effect being explained is diluted in the combined balance, though Baumol's analysis of the nature of the effect remains valid.

Baumol introduces the following symbols:

i = interest rate per income period.

b = 'broker's fee' for each withdrawal, each transaction converting invested funds into cash. The term is not meant literally; 'broker's fee' includes the expenses and the monetary measure of time and trouble and so forth incurred in financial transactions. Here the nominal fee is constant regardless of a transaction's size; but as we shall see, the qualitative conclusion about economies of scale in holding cash still holds as long as the fee rises less than in proportion to the withdrawal.

T = dollar volume of ordinary nonfinancial transactions or outpayments per income period, assumed to take place in a steady stream. (T is *not* the T of Irving Fisher's equation of exchange.)

C = number of dollars withdrawn (disinvested) on each occasion.

T/C = number of withdrawals per income period.

$C/2 = M$ = average nominal cash balance, here interpreted as actual and demanded cash balance. Baumol assumes that the cash withdrawn is spent down at a steady pace to zero immediately before the next withdrawal.

The *total cost* per period of holding actual noninterest-bearing money is the broker's fees of withdrawing it *plus* the interest forgone on the average holding. That combined cost is:

$$b(T/C) + i(C/2).$$

To find the conditions for minimum cost, and apologizing for using calculus when the magnitudes involved cannot vary continuously, we set the derivative of this expression with respect to C equal to zero and solve:

$$-bT/C^2 + i/2 = 0; C = (2bT/i)^{1/2}.$$

This last expression is the cost-minimizing size of each withdrawal. The average cash balance is half that much: $M = (1/2) (2bT/i)^{1/2}$. This optimal holding of transactions cash is proportional not to the volume of ordinary non-financial transactions or expenditures, T, but to its square root.

Baumol does not explicitly introduce elasticities of demand for transactions cash, but they readily suggest themselves. To simplify focusing on the response to T, we replace $(1/2) (2b/i)^{1/2}$ by a, so that $M = aT^{1/2}$. Then: $\ln M = \ln a + 1/2 \ln T$. The transactions or scale elasticity of demand for cash is +1/2: a 1 percent increase in the volume of ordinary nonfinancial transactions increases the cash balance demanded by only 1/2 of 1 percent. We should not take too seriously the apparent precision of this inelasticity result, which Baumol calls the square root rule. It depends on a specific model. The point here is the qualitative conclusion about less than full proportionality between ordinary transactions and cash balances demanded.

To focus attention on the response of money demand to the interest rate, we replace $(1/2) (2bT)^{1/2}$ by g, so that $M = gi^{-1/2}$ and $\ln M = \ln g - 1/2 \ln i$. Thus, the interest elasticity of demand for transactions cash is −1/2. The sign makes sense. The demand for money is responsive to the interest rate, but in a degree classified as inelastic.

Now suppose that the 'broker's fee' grows with the size of the withdrawal, but not in full proportion. Instead of b, it is b + kC. The number of equal-sized withdrawals per income period is still T/C. The cost of holding transactions cash on account of broker's fee and forgone interest combined is $(T/C) (b+kC) + i(C/2)$. Its derivative with respect to C is the same as the derivative of the earlier expression involving the constant broker's fee, namely $-bT/C^2 + i/2$. (Now, however, b stands for the part of the broker's fee that is independent of withdrawal size.) The solution for the optimal withdrawal and optimal average cash balance is also the same as before. So are the transactions and interest elasticities of the demand for money.

Now suppose, implausibly, that the broker's fee is strictly proportional to the withdrawal: kC. Then the combined cost of holding transactions cash is: $(T/C)kC + i(C/2) = kT + i(C/2)$. This expression has no minimum short of C becoming infinitesimally small; and its derivative, $i/2$, cannot be set equal to zero to solve for an optimal C. The smaller and more frequent the withdrawals and the larger their number, the lower the cost; the optimal cash balance is infinitesimally small. The implausibility of this case highlights, by contrast, what the economies of scale in a more realistic case do depend upon.

For a more intuitive interpretation, let us return to the general case in which $M = (1/2)(2bT/i)^{1/2}$. A doubling of all prices, including the brokers's fee, with the real volume of transactions left unchanged, would double cash balances demanded in nominal terms and leave them unchanged in real terms. In the above equation, b and T would both double, meaning their product quadrupled. The square root in the equation, and hence M, would double.

Suppose instead that the volume of ordinary nonfinancial transactions doubled in real size. What would it mean to have a fully doubled average cash balance in response? The withdrawal each time would double, since the average cash balance is half the size of a withdrawal. The number of withdrawals per income period, T/C, would remain the same as before. With the broker's fee a fixed amount per withdrawal, the total broker's fee would also be the same. But would it be reasonable to incur no additional brokerage cost yet a fully doubled cost of forgone interest? Since the balancing of interest cost against brokerage cost had previously been optimal, it would seem more reasonable to split the increased total cost of holding more cash (to support the doubled real volume of transactions) between both types of cost: a bigger forgone interest cost on a bigger average cash balance and a bigger brokerage cost on more withdrawals. More withdrawals (T/C) would mean a less than doubled size of the average cash balance (C/2), since T has doubled. Qualitatively the same result would emerge if we supposed not a fixed broker's fee but one increasing less than in full proportion to the size of withdrawals.

More briefly, it would be unreasonable for a big transactor to incur no more total brokerage cost than a small transactor and for the greater cost of holding cash for ordinary transactions to take entirely the form of interest forgone. More plausibly, the greater cost would occur partly in each of the two forms. But greater brokerage cost implies a larger number of withdrawals and less than proportionately increased sizes of each withdrawal and of the average cash balance.

It also serves intuition to consider the limiting case of a broker's fee of zero. Transactions balances would then consist entirely of earning assets. Well, the closer we approach this limit – the more nearly negligible the broker's fee becomes in relation to financial and ordinary transactions – the larger is the fraction of balances held in earning assets and the smaller the fraction held in cash.

Baumol traces economies of scale in holding cash, then, to economies of scale in the costs of shifting between earning assets and cash. He draws an implication about how increases in the money supply exert leverage. For example, suppose a depression so deep that injections of new money neither depress the interest rate nor raise the broker's fee or other prices; real activity rises instead. If doubling money no more than doubled ordinary nonfinancial transactions, then thanks to economies of scale people would still find themselves with excess cash. Their trying to get rid of it would expand real transactions further. Only when real activity had expanded in proportion to the square of the real money stock would that expanded stock all be willingly held.

Baumol's theory of the superleverage of money and a different theory of Friedman's (1959b [1969b]) illuminate each other. Both hinge on the point that cash balances demanded increase less than fully in proportion to current transactions and income. Friedman's reason is that people demand cash balances in relation to 'permanent income' – conceived, loosely speaking, as an average of current or measured income and income in recent periods. As such an average, permanent income moves more sluggishly than current measured income. To average permanent income up enough to make people content to hold an increased stock of money, current income must rise more than in proportion to that stock.

OTHER STUDIES OF THE DEMAND FOR MONEY

Tobin (1956) develops a similar analysis of both economies of scale and interest rate responsiveness in holding money. Again the economies hinge on costs of financial transactions (broker's fees) less than fully proportional to transaction sizes, together with interest forgone on money held.

Besides being classical examples of demand-for-money theorizing, studies like Baumol's and Tobin's illustrate the role of a *scale variable* – income, transactions, or wealth – in the demand-for-money function. Perhaps income and wealth are both relevant scale variables. By way of illustration, Marshall (1924 [1973], p. 86) supposed that the inhabitants of a country find it worth their while to hold on average 'ready purchasing power to the extent of a tenth part of their annual income, together with a fiftieth part of their property'. A wealth term in the demand-for-money function is relevant to the possible consequences of bond financing of government deficits as explained in Chapter 4.

Laidler (1993a, pp. 65–7) mentions additional implications of the analyses of Baumol and Tobin. First, based on an insight developed by Saving (1971), he interprets the brokerage fee to include the cost of time and trouble of going to the bank (the so-called 'shoe-leather costs'). The value of the individual's time can be proxied by the real wage, so that a higher real wage should raise the brokerage fee and hence the demand for money. Second, because of economies of scale, the aggregate demand for money should depend on the distribution as well as level of income. The more unequally a given total of income is distributed, the lower would be the demand for money. For example, one person carrying out a given volume of transactions would hold less money than two persons each carrying out half that volume.

After reviewing the empirical evidence, Laidler (1993a, p. 170) concludes that economies of scale 'have probably always been present in the demand-for-money function' if we hold institutional factors constant. Consistent with the transactions and precautionary motives for holding money, economies of scale are more important for narrowly than for broadly defined money. He (1993a, pp. 110, 168) notes that the real wage is also a significant variable in the demand function. The inverse relation between the demand for money and the interest rate is the one empirical issue in monetary economics that 'appears to have been settled most decisively' (Laidler, 1993a, p. 159). As a corollary of the principle of equal marginal yields on portfolio assets, this interest responsiveness of money demand provides one link between monetary theory and micro or value theory.

Baumol assumes in his transactions model of the demand for money that payments and receipts are known with certainty. Miller and Orr (1966) extend his model to firms whose cash balances fluctuate within a target zone because of uncertainty about payments and receipts. When cash balances hit the zone's upper limit, some are converted to securities so that cash balances return to the target level. Similarly, when cash balances hit the floor limit, some securities are converted to cash as the target level is again reached. The 'buffer stock' approach to the demand for money builds on the model of Miller and Orr and is described in detail by Laidler (1984, 1987). Beginning in Chapter 3, we focus on the buffer role of money and therefore shall postpone discussion of it here.

In the so-called 'Walrasian general-equilibrium model', every good is typically just as marketable as money, so money plays no distinctive role as the medium of exchange (see pages 171–7 below). Macroeconomists who embrace this model have thus been forced to graft money onto it. For example Wallace (1980), who is one of the leading proponents of the 'overlapping generations theory of money', introduces money into the general-equilibrium model by having it serve solely as a store of value. Tobin (1980a) and McCallum (1983) criticize his theory for ignoring money's role as a medium of exchange. Moreover, since fiat money is viewed in this theory solely as an asset that bears no interest, it is 'dominated' in rate of return by other riskless assets that do pay interest. Why then would anyone want to hold fiat money under these circumstances? Wallace (1983, 1988) responds with his legal restrictions theory of money in which people are essentially coerced by the government into holding it. He also argues (1980, pp. 49–50) that fiat money is 'intrinsically useless' and is therefore never wanted for its own sake and does not belong in anyone's utility function or firm's production function. New classical macroeconomists who share this view ignore the fact that while it may have no physical properties to give it value, fiat money is desired nevertheless because of its purchasing power which derives from the valuable services that it provides as a medium of exchange. Indeed, Wicksell (1898 [1936] [1965], p. 48) recognizes that in a country with irredeemable paper money, those '"worthless scraps of paper" can possess a value in themselves'. Some advocates of the overlapping generations theory argue, furthermore, that people hold money because it is 'well-backed' – it can be redeemed for real goods in the future (Laidler, 1993a, p. 89).

Other adherents of the Walrasian general-equilibrium model introduce money into it through a 'cash-in-advance' constraint, which stipulates that individuals must buy goods with money already held. (Remember, there is no theoretical reason for a medium of exchange to appear in that model.) This inclusion of money is thus quite arbitrary and lacks the 'microfoundations' upon which new classical macroeconomists usually insist (Laidler, 1997b, p. 1215).

INSTABILITY OF THE DEMAND FOR MONEY

The demand for money is said to be *stable* if it is a dependable function of a manageably small number of variables with only a small disturbance term. Statistical studies point to puzzling instability of this demand. In 1974–76 the demand for money grew more slowly than the standard variables would have suggested. Goldfeld (1976) writes about 'the case of the missing money'. The early 1980s brought an incompletely explained upward shift of this demand. Instability in money demand has continued since then. Several explanations suggest themselves.

First, the earlier episode can be attributed to financial innovations, such as repurchase agreements and money market funds, that facilitate economizing on transactions balances. These innovations apparently came as a response to a combination of high nominal interest rates and legal impediments to paying a market rate of return on transaction balances (Judd and Scadding, 1982, p. 1014). Economists (for example, Simpson, 1984) attribute the increase in money demand in the early 1980s to deregulation of banking and especially to the payment of interest on nonbusiness checking accounts. Bordo and Jonung (1981, 1987, 1990) find evidence of the importance of institutional change as determinants of long-run velocity in five countries including the United States and covering a century of data. The fact that the Federal Reserve has found it necessary at times to redefine the monetary aggregates also indicates the importance of institutional change. Chapter 4 considers the question of what definition of money to use for statistical purposes.

Second, both of the short periods mentioned above were turbulent. In the first period inflation accelerated. As people adjusted their expectations of inflation upwards, they decreased their demand for real balances as theory would suggest. Conversely, in the early 1980s inflation decelerated rapidly, causing people to increase their demand for real balances (see below).

Third, Laidler emphasizes in many of his writings (especially 1990b) the important distinction between the long-run and short-run demand-for-money function. Monetarists initially embraced the idea of a stable *long-run function*, as in the empirical work of Friedman (1959b [1969b]), Meltzer (1963), and Laidler (1966). According to Laidler (1990b) monetarists should have been suspicious of the short-run 'Goldfeld equation', which exhibited stability until 1974. That equation attempted to transform the long-run demand-for-money function into a short-run function by simply adding a lagged dependent variable on the right side, which supposedly captured the dynamics of the *partial adjustment* of money demand to its long-run desired level. But because monetary policy operates with 'long and variable lags' as Milton Friedman has often noted, and because the dynamics of the monetary transmission mechanism are so complex, it is therefore not surprising to observe instability in the *short-run* demand-for-money function (Laidler, 1997b, pp. 1218–19).

Fourth and most important, instability in the demand for money is not surprising for it is not actually money demand that is being estimated. The dependent variable in typical regressions is not that quantity but the actual quantity instead, the supply. Econometricians have no dependable, well-tested way to distinguish between these two quantities. They take the actual quantity as a good enough approximation to the one they want to estimate, partly on the supposition that some variables in the demand-for-money function, notably the interest rate, adjust fast enough to keep the quantity demanded approximately equal to the actual quantity. Some economists argue that as long as the monetary authority targets the interest rate, the money supply is demand-determined and monetary equilibrium *must* prevail; see pages 118–20 below. Clear empirical evidence on the issue is hard to develop, but until it is developed econometricians feel entitled to continue regarding their approximation as good enough.

Evidence should not be restricted to statistics. Theoretical considerations and qualitative observations bear on whether the actual quantity of money closely approximates the quantity demanded, which is to say, on whether the economy is always nearly in monetary equilibrium. We have our doubts and present them in later chapters. Here we sketch the argument briefly.

For an ordinary commodity, observed quantities have been both intentionally bought and intentionally sold. That fact provides some reason for regarding observed quantities as approximations to intended ones. Things are different with money. It is not intentionally bought and sold in the same way that ordinary commodities are. Instead, it functions as a medium of exchange and constitutes buffer stocks that individual holders are rather passively willing to let build up and run down within only fuzzy limits of amount and time. People are willing to *accept* additions to their cash balances brought about by the monetary authority's purchase of securities or foreign exchange without having actually *demanded* (or intended) those additions in the first place. What touches off a time-consuming process that eventually makes people demand the increased quantity of money is the monetary *dis*equilibrium caused by that increase. The following chapters elaborate on this process. These considerations warrant doubt that the actual money supply always closely approximates the quantity demanded.

NOTES

1. Compare Morgan (1965, pp. 47–8).
2. Yeager (1998) examines the close analogy between language and money and cites others who have made this observation.
3. Moini (2001) views money as an 'abstract right'. For that reason it possesses value. He distinguishes between money and the medium of exchange. The latter is the monetary instrument used to record and convey information concerning these rights. Kocherlakota (1998) recognizes the record-keeping role of money, which acts as a 'societal memory'.
4. We recognize that the macute as an abstract unit is a historical myth, not a historical fact. See Shah and Yeager (1994, p. 449), which also cites Schumpeter (1970, pp. 22–3, 35) and Sommer (1929).
5. We use the term 'determinate' in the sense of Patinkin (1965). The opposite of determinacy would leave the price level and quantity of money unanchored and adrift, with a rise or fall more likely to reinforce rather than restrain itself.
6. Swedberg (1991, pp. 81–2) recognizes the importance of the critical figure in Schumpeter's book (Shah and Yeager, 1994, p. 450n).
7. Shah and Yeager (1994) elaborate on Schumpeter's views. They apply his analysis to the unique monetary regime of Hong Kong, which prevailed from 1974 to 1983. That system lacked a critical figure and therefore ultimately collapsed.
8. Hicks (1967) makes this distinction in 'The Two Triads'. The first triad is three functions that money performs for the economy as a whole. The second is three services of a cash balance or an individual's three motives for holding money. How many functions and services a particular economist distinguishes is, of course, somewhat arbitrary.
9. Mises (1912 [1934] [1981]) was one of the pioneers in applying utility theory to analysis of the demand for money. As a pioneer he left some gaps and inconsistencies in his formulation. A fundamental contribution that has heavily influenced our exposition is Hutt (1956).
10. This notion of balancing the costs of economizing on cash balances against the earnings on funds otherwise invested is a key element in Baumol's (1952) and Tobin's (1956) theory of the demand for transactions balances.
11. Building on Saving's article, McCallum and Goodfriend (1987) present their 'shopping time' model. Like Saving, they include only consumption and leisure in the utility function. Real balances enter only indirectly.

12. The IRD can also be thought of as the 'marginal rate of time preference' (see Chapter 10). It should not be confused with the 'internal rate of return', which is the rate at which a project's net present value equals zero.

13. Pages below explain why changes in the money supply may not affect the equilibrium interest rate. For this reason we say 'transitionally'. Furthermore, we abstract from any increases in output. Our main concern is to show how an increase in the money supply can upset people's portfolios and thereby affect spending and prices. Later chapters discuss how changes in nominal income are split between changes in output and prices.

14. Trescott (1989) argues that the 'augmented portfolio balance' view typically found in the literature is different from the view in which changes in the money supply directly affect spending. He calls this latter view the 'disequilibrium real-balance effect'.

15. The portfolio-balance effect is based on Zecher (1972). In section 2 Zecher spells out the conditions for equilibrium: MER = IRD. While he does hint at the direct operation of the portfolio-balance effect, he clearly embraces the indirect portfolio-adjustment model found in the literature in section 5, which deals with how changes in the money supply affect spending and unemployment.

16. When Greidanus's *The Value of Money* first appeared in 1932, his 'yield theory' was an important contribution, tying several loose ends together. Yet the book made little splash, and even the second edition, in 1950, drew bad reviews. Readers were apparently not prepared to read the book sympathetically enough to cope with awkward writing (or an awkward translation from the Dutch).

17. Krugman (1998) helped revive interest in the liquidity trap. Mired in a decade-long stagnation, Japan allegedly fell into the trap since the nominal interest rate reached zero, its lower bound. Monetary policy – interpreted as a lowering of the interest rate – thus became impotent. Pages 137–9 below examine this episode.

18. This formulation spells out some hints provided by Patinkin (1965, pp. 225 and 349).

19. *Economie et Intérêt*. The argument is scattered over approximately pp. 300–70 of volume 1 and pp. 540–90 of volume 2. Tobin, in a better known article (1965 [1979]), developed a similar though less detailed argument. In Chapter 8 we consider some counter-effects or overriding effects of inflation that obstruct capital formation.

20. Also see Moss (1976, pp. 13–49).

21. Garrison (1981, pp. 77–81 in particular) has persuasively argued that the theorem is not otiose.

22. Selgin (1994) recognizes the issues raised here. Selgin (1987) traces various errors in monetary theory to failure to understand money's yield.

23. Baumol and Tobin (1989) credit Allais (1947) for having already spelled out the essence of their inventory-theoretic model of the transactions demand for money, although at the time their articles were published neither was familiar with Allais's model.

3. Money's demand and supply: equilibrium and disequilibrium (1)

INTRODUCTION

Monetary equilibrium and disequilibrium figure among the most important yet most misunderstood concepts of money/macro theory. Money in excess supply or demand can have momentous consequences for the economy. When the actual quantity of money exceeds or falls short of the total of cash balances demanded at existing prices, things happen that tend to restore equilibrium eventually. Instead of adjusting promptly to their new market-clearing levels, many prices and wages are 'sticky', and for reasons that make excellent sense to individual price-setters and wage-negotiators. Consequently, adjustment in the short run involves quantities (output, real income and employment) rather than prices alone.

Throughout we emphasize the *interdependence* of nonclearing markets and the role of prices and wages in achieving or obstructing *coordination*. Our analysis fills a void mentioned by Robert Gordon (1990b, pp. 1137–8) in his exposition of new Keynesian economics:

> An interesting aspect of recent U.S. new-Keynesian research is the near-total lack of interest in the general equilibrium properties of non-market-clearing models. That effort is viewed as having reached a quick dead end after the insights yielded in the pioneering work of Barro and Herschel Grossman (1971, 1976), building on the earlier contributions of Don Patinkin (1965), Clower, and Leijonhufvud...Much new-Keynesian theorizing is riddled with inconsistencies as a result of its neglect of constraints and spillovers...

For purposes of exposition we divide monetary-disequilibrium theory into two components. The first focuses on disequilibrium between the demand for and supply of money and explains money's role in determining nominal income. The second component, disequilibrium economics, explai̶   ̶d why changes in nominal income first show up as changes in quan̶ as changes in price. It builds on the contributions of Patin̶ Clower (1965 [1984], 1967 [1984]), Leijonhufvud (1968, 19̶ Grossman (1971, 1976) mentioned in the passage above. We of both components thoughout as we concentrate on processes rather than simple mechanics. Chapters 6 and 7 are specifically devoted to disequilibrium economics, while this and following chapters take up the important issue of monetary disequilibrium.

Four Assumptions

Four assumptions are crucial in this chapter. First, we suppose that the stock of money, narrowly defined as media of exchange, is under the control of the monetary authority. Admittedly, the authority might not use its power actively. It might passively allow the quantity of money to drift under the influence of production, prices and other conditions. For example, it might behave in accordance with the real-bills doctrine (reviewed on pages 239–40 below). Still, such behavior would count as money supply policy. Inappropriate use of its power would not belie the authority's power over the money supply.

Second, our analysis presupposes either a closed economy or an open economy with a floating exchange rate. An international monetary standard such as the classical gold standard or pegged exchange rates removes the money supply from the firm control of the domestic authority. The demand for nominal money can then affect the actual quantity through the balance of payments, as this chapter and Chapter 9 explain.

Third, we sharply distinguish actual money from nearmoneys that do not circulate as media of exchange. Nearmoneys include noncheckable deposits in financial intermediaries (Chapter 1 mentions some other examples). Institutional changes in the United States have made the distinction less sharp than it once was. Still, maintaining it will help the reader understand past conditions. Moreover, most of the discussion still applies to our current system.

Fourth, we assume the reader has some knowledge of the basics of money and banking, such as the money creation process.

THE UNIQUENESS OF MONEY

The actual medium of exchange is distinctive in ways seldom fully appreciated. The differences between it and other liquid assets may be unimportant to the individual holder, yet crucial to the economic system. An individual may consider certain nearmoneys to be practically the same as actual money because he can readily exchange them for it whenever he wants. But microexchangeability need not mean ready exchangeability of aggregates.

Certain assets do and others do not circulate as media of exchange. No reluctance of sellers to accept the medium of exchange hampers anyone's spending it. The medium of exchange can 'burn holes in pockets' in a way that nearmoneys do not. Supply creates its own demand, in a sense specified later, more truly for the medium of exchange than for other things. These are observed facts, or inferences from facts, not mere a priori truths or tautologies.

In comparing the medium of exchange with other financial assets, we must go beyond asking what determines the amount of each that people demand to hold. We must also consider the manner in which people acquire and dispose of each asset and implement a change in their demand for it.

EQUILIBRIUM AND DISEQUILIBRIUM

Equilibrium means balancing. Demand equals supply in the sense explained below, and no pressures are working to change prices and other variables. In the sense that markets 'clear', the plans of different people mesh. People meet no frustration in carrying out transactions they desire at the prevailing prices. Disequilibrium means imbalance, discoordination of plans, and the frustration of some desired transactions. Some variables are under pressure to change.

We say the economy is at 'full-employment equilibrium' when it is at potential output and no excess or deficiency of aggregate spending exists. Total demand equals potential output or supply and not just actual output. Patinkin (1965, p. 321), makes the crucial distinction between 'supply' and 'output'. In the depths of depression, actual output is held down to the actual amount demanded, yet an excess supply of goods prevails. Firms desire to supply more but cannot find willing buyers at the going price level. Widespread frustration persists among firms, who put downward pressure, weak though it may be, on prices. In the analogous case of an excess supply of labor in depression, the amount of labor actually carried out is limited to the amount demanded. Frustrated (unemployed) workers put downward pressure on wages, which again may be weak. Depression therefore is a *dis*equilibrium as explained on pages 94–5 below.

Full-employment equilibrium differs from the 'Walrasian general-equilibrium model' in which *all* markets are clearing simultaneously. Such a full-fledged equilibrium is of course a mere analytical concept, not a condition found in actuality. Because we recognize that most markets are not perfectly competitive and do not clear rapidly, some disequilibrium occurs on the micro level even at full-employment equilibrium. But no deficiency or excess of aggregate spending exists. Furthermore, no cyclical unemployment occurs although some structural and frictional unemployment may be present. Most importantly, at full-employment equilibrium, monetary equilibrium prevails in all the senses mentioned in this chapter.

As Clark Warburton has argued (for example, 1966, selection 1, especially pp. 26–7), a tendency toward market-clearing is inherent in the logic of market processes. Whenever, therefore, markets are generally and conspicuously failing to clear – when disequilibrium goes beyond gluts or shortages only in some particular markets – some disturbance pervasive and powerful enough to resist quick and automatic correction must have occurred. It is hard to imagine what that disturbance could be except one causing a discrepancy at the prevailing price-and-wage level between the amount of money holdings desired at full employment and the actual amount in existence. Yet monetary disequilibrium is hard for ordinary people to diagnose and remedy. Although it does entail frustration, it does not show up as frustration of buyers or sellers on any one specific market. Instead, an excess demand for money expresses itself in quite general restraint in buying things. Its pressures are obscurely diffused over myriads of individual markets and prices. This very diffusion renders any correction sluggish. Money's lacking a market of its own and any single price of its own helps explain how monetary disequilibrium can have repercussions that last for months or even years.

THE BUFFER ROLE OF MONEY

Leland Yeager once asked his graduate-school professor of monetary theory a question presupposing the distinction between actual and desired holdings of money. Astonishingly, the professor was unfamiliar with that distinction and could make no sense of it. Every existing bit of money is held by someone, and held voluntarily, he said. So actual and desired holdings not merely tend to become equal but necessarily are identical.

The professor's error lay in jumping from an aggregative fact to the supposed intentions of individuals. Of course all money belongs to somebody. Of course each holding is voluntary in the sense that the holder has accepted the money voluntarily and has not yet spent or otherwise disposed of it. But this fact does not necessarily mean that the holder is fully content with his cash balance, desiring neither to reduce or increase it. People or firms routinely accept money in exchange for whatever they sell even if they do not intend to go on holding all the money received, and they routinely pay money for whatever they buy even if they do not intend to reduce their cash balances except strictly temporarily. Not every inpayment or outpayment represents a deliberate action to increase or reduce one's cash balance.

Money serves its holder as a *buffer stock* (Laidler, 1984, 1987; and page 62 above). A person or firm receives payments into and makes payments from its cash balance in amounts and at times not precisely predetermined. Its balance is bound to fluctuate in not completely predictable ways, which is one main reason for holding money in the first place. The holder has no precise notion of just how large a cash balance it desires at each instant, no precise target size from which any departure triggers corrective action. The notion of desired cash balance applies only to some sort of average over time or to a range of fluctuation.

For holders both individually and in the aggregate then, actual holdings of money are no exact measure of desired holdings. (Whether econometricians may nevertheless justifiably use the actual quantity of money as a proxy for the demanded quantity is a question considered in Chapter 2.) It is wrong to assume that a newly accepted cash balance, merely in virtue of having been accepted voluntarily, is demanded in the fullest sense. A person may well accept money without wanting to continue holding it, intending instead to pass it along to someone else.

Notions about desired cash balances are loose, and so therefore are the very concepts of money's excess supply and demand. They are loose but not empty. Holders will sooner or later take action if they see their balances diverging markedly and persistently from desired ranges or average levels (Miller and Orr, 1966). A macroeconomic process affecting prices, and usually affecting production and employment also, does tend to bring desired holdings into line with the actual quantity of money. But understanding this process presupposes a firm grasp of the distinction between actual and desired quantities.

Laidler (1989, p. 107) argues that according to the two major schools of macroeconomic thought, monetary disequilibrium cannot occur. In the new classical school flexible prices maintain monetary equilibrium. In new Keynesian analysis changes in the interest rate 'similarly keep the supply and demand for money in perpetual equilibrium'. We also observe that some economists insist upon 'perpetual monetary equilibrium' because the monetary authority targets the interest rate (see pages 118–20 below). This chapter and those that follow elaborate on why monetary disequilibrium occurs and why it is not immediately eliminated.

THE WICKSELL PROCESS

Things happen when money's supply and demand become disequilibrated. Momentous consequences can ensue because supply and demand do not confront each other on a single 'money market' and do not impinge on a single price of money that could straightforwardly adjust to restore equilibrium. Neither the market for foreign currencies nor the market for short-term credit is a money market in the intended sense – a specific market where the demand for and supply of money confront one another. Instead, any equilibrating tendencies have to work on a great many markets and prices through a roundabout and sluggish process.

John Stuart Mill (1844 [1874] [1967], p. 277) understood the connection between monetary disequilibrium and business depression and saw how disequilibrium would make prices change. But it was Knut Wicksell (1898 [1936] [1965]) who provided one of the clearest early statements of the relation among money, prices and income. His pages 39–41 describe how people try to adjust their money holdings by altering their behavior in the markets for goods and services:

> Now let us suppose that for some reason or other commodity prices rise while the stock of money remains unchanged, or that the stock of money is diminished while prices remain temporarily unchanged. The cash balances will gradually appear to be *too small in relation to the new level of prices* (though in the first case they have not on the average altered in absolute amount. It is true that in this case I can rely on a higher level of receipts in the future. But meanwhile I run the risk of being unable to meet my obligations punctually, and at best I may easily be forced by shortage of ready money to forgo some purchase that would otherwise have been profitable.) I therefore seek to enlarge my balance. This can only be done – neglecting for the present the possibility of borrowing, etc. – through a *reduction* in my *demand* for goods and services, or through an *increase* in the *supply* of my own commodity (forthcoming either earlier or at a lower price than would otherwise have been the case), or through both together. The same is true of all other owners and consumers of commodities. But in fact nobody will succeed in realising the object at which each is aiming – to increase his cash balance; for the sum of individual cash balances is limited by the amount of the available stock of money, or rather is identical with it. On the other hand, the universal reduction in demand and increase in supply of commodities will necessarily bring about a continuous fall in all prices. This can only cease when prices have fallen to the level at which the cash balances are regarded as *adequate*. (In the first case prices will now have fallen to their original level.)

> The reverse process will take place as the result of a fortuitous fall in prices, the stock of money remaining unchanged, or of a permanent increase in the available quantity of money. But in the latter case (as in the case of a diminution in the stock of money), the nature of the effects depends to some extent upon the *route* by which the additional supply of money reaches the economic system. Eventually, however, it must become distributed in the 'channels of circulation' – at any rate this can be adopted as an assumption – and a rise in prices, if it has not already occurred, must now come about. It is not as though a man who accidentally possesses twice as many ten-mark pieces as usual would now proceed to bid double the price for every commodity. But he will probably desire to complete some purchase that he would otherwise have postponed, or he will be more hesitant in disposing of some commodity that necessity would otherwise have compelled him to sell. In short, the result of the increase in the quantity of money is a rise in the demand for commodities, and a fall in their supply, with the consequence that all prices rise continuously – until cash balances stand once again in their normal relation to the level of prices.

Wicksell is saying that an excess demand for money shows up as a weakening of demand relative to supply on the individual markets for goods and services (and securities, we would add), and an excess supply of money shows up as a strengthening of demand relative to supply on these individual markets. Prices tend to adjust until equilibrium between money's supply and demand is again restored. Wicksell is describing what we shall call the 'Wicksell Process' (not to be confused with 'Wicksell's cumulative process', discussed on pages 74–5 below). Something very similar later came to be called the 'real-balance effect'. The passages quoted from Wicksell recognize what both Keynes and Friedman separately would later call 'the fundamental proposition of monetary theory' (explained below).

Wicksell's analysis foreshadows Patinkin's (1956, 1965) exposition of the quantity theory of money.[1] Like other nominal financial assets but unlike all other goods and services, money, especially fiat money, is desired for its purchasing power and neither for its physical properties nor for its mere numerical size. Exceptions can be found – for example, the use of a coin as a part of a machine[2] – showing that we are making an empirical observation rather than stating a tautology. But the utterly fringe character of any exceptions speaks to the general validity of our proposition.

Money's value – strictly, the reciprocal of its value – is measured by the price level. A change in the quantity of money requires, somehow, an equilibrating change in that level. Note that we are not contradicting ourselves when we suggest that one can draw a graph with the quantities of money supplied and demanded on the horizontal axis and the reciprocal of the price level on the vertical. The graph does not imply a single market and price for money. Rather, the variable on the vertical axis captures the myriad prices that comprise the price level and that must adjust following a monetary disturbance.

A change in the real purchasing power quantity of money demanded (perhaps due to a fall in real income or to real economic growth) must, if not satisfied by a change in the nominal quantity of money, lead somehow to a change in the price level. Otherwise, people would be holding larger or smaller real cash balances than they desired and would try to reduce or increase them. The individual prices comprising the price level must respond to changes in supply or demand or both on the markets for individual goods and services (and securities); the Wicksell Process must operate.

Changes in supply or demand on individual markets are likely to affect quantities traded (and produced), not prices alone. Wicksell, however, did not emphasize these quantity effects. Changes in the relation between desired and actual holdings of money will affect real economic activity unless prices quickly absorb the entire impact, which is unlikely for reasons explained below.

In particular, an excess demand for money (a deficient supply) weakens demands for goods and services on their individual markets. Barring complete price flexibility, shrinkage of the flow of money routinely changing hands to accomplish the exchange of goods and services impedes that exchange and so narrows opportunities for profitable production of goods to be exchanged. Production and employment continue shrinking until people no longer consider their holdings of money inadequate in relation to the shrunken flows. (Pages 90–92 below explain why monetary *dis*equilibrium remains in one sense although *quasi*-equilibrium exists in another.) It is no doubt true that the more fully and promptly people perceive and understand and allow for the underlying monetary disturbance – and respond even to expectations of it – the more prices will fall instead of quantities. Even in the best of realistically conceivable circumstances, though, prices will not quickly absorb the entire impact. Attaining the new level of full-employment equilibrium can be a long, drawn-out and painful process.

On the other hand, with the economy starting at full-employment equilibrium, an excess supply of money strengthens demands for goods and services on their individual markets and so, under certain circumstances, may lead to an increase in quantities traded and produced *before prices have fully adjusted*. Following Birch, Rabin and Yeager (1982), Chapter 6 explores the case of real output temporarily expanding beyond the full-employment level.

WICKSELL'S CUMULATIVE PROCESS

Wicksell (1898 [1936] [1965]) applied the quoted passages above to a cash-only economy, since he did not consider demand deposits to be money (Patinkin, 1965, pp. 587–97; Laidler, 1991a, Chapter 5; Humphrey, 1997, 2002). His cumulative process – distinct from what we have called the Wicksell Process – describes the workings of a mixed economy (with cash and demand deposits) and a pure credit economy (with demand deposits but no cash).[3]

Wicksell argued that in the mixed economy prices would settle at an equilibrium level only when the actual loan or market rate of interest equaled the equilibrium or 'natural rate'. If the actual loan rate was below the natural rate, firms would borrow from banks in order to purchase investment goods. The expanded demand for goods would bid up their prices. This process is 'cumulative' since the discrepancy between the two rates, if maintained, would result in a continuous rise in prices (Patinkin, 1965, p. 590). Wicksell, however, provided an automatic equilibrating mechanism that would end the process. As prices increased, people would add to their holdings of gold coins (cash). Banks would therefore lose gold reserves, prompting them to raise their rate on loans and thereby restoring equilibrium between the actual and natural rates of interest.

Wicksell acknowledged the historical fact that rising prices were usually accompanied by higher, not lower, interest rates. His solution to this problem (what Keynes later called the 'Gibson paradox') was that a rising actual rate of interest was lagging behind an also rising natural rate, thus preserving the gap that accounted for increases in loans and prices.

In the pure credit (cashless) economy, banks would face no such constraint in the form of a limited stock of base money (gold coins for Wicksell) – hence no automatic equilibrating mechanism would exist. If banks maintained their actual loan rate below the natural rate indefinitely, prices would rise without limit through the cumulative process. No constraint would operate on the supply of loans, since banks would not have to worry about losing gold reserves. No constraint would operate on the demand for loans either, as long as the gap between the actual and natural rate were maintained.

We add that the nominal demand for loans would keep growing not only because of the interest rate gap, but also because of increased prices and expectations of further rises. Alluding to these expectations, Wicksell said (1898 [1936] [1965], p. 96): 'The upward movement of prices will in some measure "create its own draught"'.

HOW THE SUPPLY OF MONEY CREATES ITS OWN DEMAND

A further appeal to the Wicksell Process explains how money initially in excess supply can come to be fully demanded after all. The banking system as a whole can expand credit and deposits so far as reserves permit.[4] Nothing bars lending and spending new demand deposits into existence. No one need be persuaded to hold them before they can be created; no one will refuse money for fear of being stuck with too much. A person accepts money not necessarily because he chooses to continue holding it but precisely because it is the routine intermediary between his sales and his purchases or investments and because he knows he can get rid of it whenever he wants. In contrast, people will not accept noncheckable deposits or other nonmoneys that they do not desire to hold, so undesired quantities of them cannot be created in the first place. And if anyone did find himself somehow holding undesired nonmoneys, he would simply cash them in for money if they were redeemable and so make them go out of existence. He would still cash them even if he did not want to hold the money received, since money is the intermediary routinely used in buying all sorts of things.

A holder of undesired or excess money exchanges it directly for whatever he does want, without first cashing it in for something else.[5] Nothing is more ultimate, more liquid, the bearer of greater options than money. Instead of going out of existence, excess money gets passed around until through price and income changes it ceases to be undesired. (An exception concerning fixed exchange rates is developed later in this chapter and in Chapter 9.) Supply thus creates its own demand (both expressed as nominal, not real, quantities). This proposition does not apply separately, of course, to each particular type of money – to currency of each particular denomination and to deposits at each individual bank – but rather to the medium of exchange in the aggregate.

Nor does the proposition imply that a demand function for money does not exist nor that the function always shifts to keep demanded and actual quantities not merely equal but identical. Rather, an initial excess supply of money touches off a process, the Wicksell Process, that raises the nominal quantity demanded quite in accordance with the demand function. At least two of its arguments change: the money values of wealth and income rise through higher prices or fuller employment and production, and interest rates may fall during the transition process.

Initially excess cash balances 'burn holes in pockets', with direct or indirect repercussions on the flow of spending in the economy. No such process affects nearmoneys and other nonmoneys. For an ordinary asset, a discrepancy between actual and desired holdings exerts direct pressure on its price (or yield or similar terms on which it is acquired and offered). If the supply and demand for an asset are out of balance, 'something has to give'. If the something is specific and 'gives' readily, the adjustment can occur without widespread and conspicuous repercussions. But the medium of exchange has no single, explicit price of its own expressed in a good other than itself that can 'give' readily to remove an imbalance between its supply and demand. Widespread repercussions occur instead. (Chapter 4 elaborates on the way an excess demand for a nonmoney is removed or diverted, in contrast to an excess demand for money that is neither removed directly nor diverted.)

Money is unique in the further sense that its equilibrium quantity is not determined in the same way as for other goods. For most goods, like houses, cars and refrigerators, supply and demand determine equilibrium quantity and price both. However, the nominal quantity of money is determined predominantly on the supply side in the manner the textbooks describe in terms of the quantity of base money and the money-multiplier formula. Even in the case of interest rate pegging by the monetary authority, the nominal supply of money does not adjust automatically to meet the nominal demand. Pages 118–20 below explain why money demand may have to adjust to the supply in this case. Real supply does tend to meet real demand through what we have called the Wicksell Process.

Additional money can thus be thrust onto a country even without being demanded. The reasons are money's role as a medium of exchange, the lack of a specific market for money, the buffer stock role of individual money holdings, and the process whereby the nominal supply of money can create its own demand. This process is compatible with and even presupposes a fairly definite demand-for-money function.

THE FUNDAMENTAL PROPOSITION AND THE MONETARY-DISEQUILIBRIUM HYPOTHESIS

Through the Wicksell Process, incomes and prices adjust to make the total of desired nominal cash balances equal the actual money stock. This process of reconciling the demand for money with its supply is the theme of what Keynes (1936, pp. 84–5) called 'the fundamental proposition of monetary theory' and Friedman (1959a [1969], pp. 141–2) called 'the most important proposition in monetary theory'. In Keynes's words, this proposition describes what:

> harmonises the liberty, which every individual possesses, to change, whenever he chooses, the amount of money he holds, with the necessity for the total amount of money, which individual balances add up to, to be exactly equal to the amount of cash which the banking system has created. In this latter case the equality is brought about by the fact that the amount of money which people choose to hold is not independent of their incomes or of the prices of the things (primarily securities), the purchase of which is the natural alternative to holding money. Thus incomes and such prices necessarily change until the aggregate of the amounts of money which individuals choose to hold at the new level of incomes and prices thus brought about has come to equality with the amount of money created by the banking system. This, indeed, is the fundamental proposition of monetary theory.

Similarly, Friedman states:

> This essential difference between the situation as it appears to the individual, who can determine his own cash balances but must take prices and money income as beyond his control, and the situation as it is to all individuals together, whose total cash balances are outside their control but who can determine prices and money income, is perhaps the most important proposition in monetary theory...

According to the fundamental proposition, the demanded quantity of money that aligns itself with the actual stock is expressed in nominal terms. For the real (purchasing-power) quantity, the adjustment works the other way around: the desired real quantity of money pulls the actual quantity into line.

The fundamental proposition holds true of the actual medium of exchange only. Individual economic units are free to hold as much or as little of it as they see fit in view of their own circumstances; yet the total of their willingly held cash balances is identical with the money supply, which the monetary authority can make as big or small as it sees fit. The process that resolves this paradox has no counterpart for noncirculating claims on financial intermediaries; undesired holdings simply go out of existence. The proposition also fails for other nearmoneys, such as securities. But instead of shrinking in actual amount to the desired level, an initially excessive quantity shrinks in total market value.

Warburton expounds what he calls 'the monetary-disequilibrium hypothesis': '[B]usiness fluctuations are results of disturbance in the monetary system...a potent cause of disequilibrium may be a change in the quantity of money'. This hypothesis was an 'integral...part of the body of economic thought developed in the nineteenth century and the first quarter of the twentieth' (1966, pp. 26–7). When the money supply increases, prices or real income (or both) must rise. The rise in prices makes the nominal quantity of money demanded expand to absorb the increased supply. In real terms, the rise in prices arithmetically shrinks the real money supply, bringing it back into line with real demand. If real income rises instead of or along with prices, then both nominal and real quantities of money demanded increase to absorb the supply. (Real income could expand beyond the full-employment level only temporarily, as argued below.) Opposite processes occur when the nominal money supply shrinks.

THE EXCEPTION UNDER FIXED EXCHANGE RATES

The fundamental proposition, or its simplest version, presupposes either a closed economy or an open economy with a floating exchange rate. Things are different if the monetary authority intervenes on the exchange market to fix the rate of exchange between foreign and home money; for in buying and selling foreign exchange, the authority is injecting home money into and withdrawing it from circulation, much as it does when conducting open-market operations in securities. The home money supply responds to balance-of-payments developments at the fixed exchange rate, and changes in the demand for money to hold can cause supply to respond in nominal as well as real terms. This analysis applies most straightforwardly to a national currency not used as an international key currency. Because of the dollar's special international role, the US monetary system retained, even under fixed (pegged) rates, the essential domestic characteristics of a system with a floating exchange rate (see page 260 below).

Suppose, for example, that people come to desire larger money holdings than before. The Wicksell Process operates as people try to build up their cash balances by acting less eagerly to buy goods and services and securities and more eagerly to sell. This changed behavior shows up partly at the water's edge: domestic residents tend to develop an excess of sales over purchases in transactions with foreigners; the balance of payments moves into surplus; and, in the process of buying up surplus earnings of foreign exchange to keep the exchange rate fixed, the monetary authority puts additional home money into circulation. In effect, domestic residents satisfy their increased demand for money in both real and nominal terms by developing an excess of sales over purchases in transactions with foreigners. Conversely, a reduced demand or a domestically increased supply of home money gives rise to a balance-of-payments deficit at a fixed exchange rate, which tends to remove the excess money from circulation.

Although changes in a country's money supply associated with a payments surplus or deficit at a fixed exchange rate may correspond to aggregates of desired changes in individual holdings, it does not follow that the changes must so correspond. Balance-of-payments disequilibrium may also trace to some circumstance other than excess demand for or supply of cash balances. In certain circumstances, as history illustrates, foreign developments working through the balance of payments may 'impose' on a country an imbalance between its demand for and supply of money. This imbalance then must be adjusted away by the Wicksell Process, since money still lacks a market of its own on which a price of its own adjusts to equilibrate supply and demand. (The foreign exchange market and rate do not serve this function; and anyway, the exchange rate is fixed.) When the process of imported inflation imposes additional money on a country, prices and nominal income have to rise until the expanded money supply is demanded after all, and conversely with imported deflation (see Chapter 9). Thus, even under fixed rates, money is supplied and demanded in a distinctive way and still can be thrust onto or withdrawn from its holders in the aggregate in a way that does not also characterize nearmoneys.

With a freely floating exchange rate, no pegging is at work to alter the domestic money supply. The price of foreign exchange in home money is just one of the many prices that adjust to bring the nominal demand for cash balances into line with the nominal supply and the real supply into line with the real demand.

The exception to the 'fundamental proposition' that we have been noting applies not only to a country with a fixed exchange rate but especially to a locality within a country. (Here 'country' really means the area routinely using a common currency.) In using the same currency, the different parts of a country are linked together even more tightly than if they were using different currencies at fixed exchange rates. The money holdings of residents of Chicago as well as the aggregate deposits of Chicago banks, like the deposits of a single bank, are not determined by some monetary authority. For the money-multiplier analysis of the money and banking textbooks to be useful, the determinants of the multiplier must be reasonably stable and the monetary base potentially controllable, and the latter is not true of Chicago alone (compare Masera, 1973, pp. 145–6, 155–6). If Chicago banks alone should decide to expand deposit money, drainage away of reserve funds would frustrate them. If Chicago residents should act to build up their bank deposits, reserves would flow into their banks through a local balance-of-payments surplus, supporting the desired expansion of deposit money.

The fundamental proposition about how the supply of money creates its own demand in nominal terms refers, then, not to each part of a single monetary area but to the area as a whole, whose exchange rate with other moneys is floating. It is the area as a whole whose nominal money supply can be controlled.

UNINTENDED CHANGES IN THE MONEY SUPPLY

The point that changes in the nominal money supply can occur without being intended by holders is worth developing further. Money flows routinely through cash balances. People take it in and pay it out even when not intending, except passively and temporarily, to build up or run down their holdings. Fluctuations in individual money holdings can be largely unintended, and changes in the total of actual holdings can be unintended too.

When Americans fled from bank deposits into currency in 1932–3, they were acting not to reduce their money holdings but rather to shift into what they considered a safer form of money. Yet the unintended consequence was that the money supply and so total holdings fell as banks lost reserves. The situation could be similar in a country running a balance-of-payments deficit at a fixed exchange rate. The money supply is shrinking, which necessarily means that the country's residents are running down their money holdings. It could sometimes be true and may even typically be true that the payments deficit and money supply shrinkage are occurring because people are deliberately reducing what they consider to be excessive cash balances. But it is not always true: shrinkage of the money stock can be quite undesired. The payments deficit might trace, for example, to failure of an important export crop or to a collapse of foreign demand (see Chapter 9).

Similarly, suppose the monetary authority has committed itself to whatever open-market operations are necessary to hold interest rates at a target level. Now tastes change; people want to acquire more bonds by reducing current consumption (thus freeing resources for real investment), but they do not particularly want to change their money holdings. To keep interest rates from falling below the target level, the monetary authority sells bonds, with the result that money is removed from circulation, creating an excess demand for money. Or suppose an opposite change in tastes occurs that, again, does not directly involve desired money holdings. To keep interest rates from rising, the monetary authority buys bonds, incidentally creating money.

When transactors deal with the authority, they do so because they find the prices it quotes on particular bond issues attractive, not necessarily because they want to change their money holdings. They use money to make or receive payments for bonds because it is the medium of exchange used routinely in those and other transactions. More generally, people are not deliberately trying to reduce or increase their cash balances whenever they buy or sell something; engaging in a series of individual transactions does not necessarily indicate a desire to alter cash balances held on average over time. People make the purchases and sales they find attractive at the prices confronting them. If they happen to be dealing with the monetary authority, the resulting change in the money supply and thus in the total of their cash balances can be quite unintended by them (compare Greenfield and Yeager, 1986, and pages below).

Now, assuming pegged-but-adjustable exchange rates for the moment, suppose that the monetary authority revalues the home currency upward (for no reason except to provide us theorists with an experiment); it cuts in half the pegged home currency price of foreign exchange. In consequence of all the related price changes, purchases of goods and services and securities abroad become more attractive than sales abroad, the country runs a balance-of-payments deficit, and the home money supply shrinks, with painful deflationary consequences. In brief, by making foreign exchange a bargain and selling it lavishly out of its reserves, the authority takes out of circulation the home money received in payment. Yet this monetary contraction in no way represents an intentional rundown of private cash balance holdings.

Suppose instead that the monetary authority pegs the prices of foreign currencies too high. With the home currency undervalued, the balance of payments goes into surplus; and the home money supply expands with inflationary consequences as the authority absorbs all the private offers of foreign currency.

Thus, changes in a country's money supply need not correspond (though they sometimes *may* correspond) to aggregates of desired changes in individual holdings. The monetary authority's purchases or sales of bonds or foreign exchange may *create* an inflationary excess supply of money or contractionary excess demand. We elaborate on this theme throughout the book.

WALRAS'S LAW

Walras's Law is a tautology that illuminates interrelations among supplies of and demands for commodities, labor, securities and money and among supply/demand imbalances for these different things. The Law emphasizes that no one thing or group of things can be in excess supply or excess demand by itself. It thereby helps focus attention on the role in macroeconomic disorder, especially in depression, of a distinctively functioning object of market exchange – money.

Yet complications arise, and Walras's Law has itself sometimes been called into question. Yeager (1994a) and Yeager and Rabin (1997) note analogies between the Law and the equation of exchange, a firm's balance sheet, and a country's balance of payments. In our view, Walras's Law deserves broadly the same status in money/macro analysis as the balance of payments in international economics. We caution the reader not to confuse 'Walras's Law' with the 'Walrasian general-equilibrium model'. In the latter, markets always clear; the former is especially helpful in examining market disequilibrium.

Repeating what Lange (1942) and Patinkin (1965) have already done adequately anyway – translating the Law into symbols and spending time defining the symbols – would digress from our present purpose, which is not mathematical decoration. Our purpose, instead, is to clarify the very concepts that enter into the Law and into supposed difficulties. Distinctions between 'notional' and 'effective' supplies and demands and between 'stock' and 'flow' conceptions of quantities and imbalances require attention.

Our task illlustrates Harsanyi's (1976, p. 64) point that social scientists encounter not only formal or logical problems and empirical problems but also conceptual philosophical problems.[6] Impatience with conceptual problems goes far, we conjecture, to explain the current state of the literature on Walras's Law.

In discussing the Law we clear up some puzzles found in the literature and further illustrate the uniqueness, peculiarities and significance of money. We address the puzzle of what matches an excess supply of labor (and commodities) in the depths of depression. We explain why the Keynesian 'underemployment equilibrium' is in actuality a disequilibrium. We illuminate what we call the 'stock-flow problem' (Yeager and Rabin, 1997), and we shed additional light on the fundamental proposition of monetary theory.

Lange (1942) gave the name Walras's Law to the following proposition, which holds in disequilibrium as well as in equilibrium: the total value of quantities of all goods supplied equals the total value of all quantities demanded. The term 'goods' is inclusive here, covering not only commodities but also labor and other services, securities *and money*. Quantities are valued at the prices, in money or other numéraire, at which transactions are accomplished or attempted as the case may be. If some goods are in excess supply and others in excess demand, the excess supply and excess demand quantities are equal in total value. Counting excess supplies as negative excess demands, the sum of the values of all excess demands is identically zero (Lange, 1942; Patinkin, 1965, pp. 73, 229, 258–62, and *passim*, 1987; Baumol, 1965, pp. 340–42).[7]

The foregoing presents one version of Walras's Law, which might be labeled the zero-aggregate-excess-demand-value version. It straightforwardly implies another, the equation counting version. It states that if n goods exist and if supply and demand are in balance for n − 1 of them, then equilibrium must prevail for the nth good also. (Lange, 1942, p. 51n, notes that this is the version of the Law proved by Walras himself.) To the n goods correspond n equations expressing the equilibrium conditions that market excess demand for each good be zero. Mathematically, only n − 1 of these simultaneous equations are independent. Consequently, any set of prices satisfying any n − 1 equations must also necessarily satisfy the remaining equation.

Walras's Law is 'an identity,...little more than an accounting relationship'; 'it is difficult to imagine an economy in which it does not hold' (Baumol, 1965, p. 341). Where it does not hold, 'people must, by definition, be planning to exchange goods which are not equal in value – an odd assertion for any monetary economy' (Baumol, 1960, p. 30).[8] The Law holds because budget constraints operate and market transactions are two-sided. Anyone trying to acquire something is by that very token offering something in exchange of equal value at the price contemplated. Anyone trying to sell something is demanding something of equal value in return. An attempted but frustrated transaction, like a successful one, involves two goods and not just one. (In a monetary economy, one of them is ordinarily money.)

Significance yet Disregard of the Law

Identities are far from useless. They can aid in focusing analytical questions and in pinpointing and correcting error. Since Walras's Law is an identity, it has to hold. Anything that conflicts with it or contradicts it is bound to be wrong.

Most important to our present purpose is the Law's insistence on one implication of the very concept of exchange, whether accomplished or frustrated: supply/demand disequilibrium for some things necessarily entails opposite disequilibrium for other things. No single good or aggregate of goods, whether peanuts or labor or labor and commodities combined, can be the object of frustrated transactions and market disequilibrium *by itself*. When labor and commodities are in excess supply – when demand for them is inadequate to clear their markets – Keynesian 'oversaving' is too superficial a diagnosis. In particular, when labor is in excess supply in the depths of depression – when involuntary unemployment prevails – what thing or things are in matching excess demand? It is unhelpful to brush such questions aside with theories and concepts that describe markets as always in equilibrium, or practically so.

Worse, perhaps, are the implicit denials of Walras's Law often found in textbooks and the literature. Some texts assume that the money and bond markets clear quickly, unlike the remaining market, the market for commodities, which requires more time. Describing the consequences of monetary expansion, these texts wind up with an excess demand for commodities unmatched by an excess supply of anything else, thus violating Walras's Law. Such analysis is therefore logically flawed. Other texts avoid explicit violation of the Law by assuming that of the three markets into which they simplify the economy, only the 'money market' clears continuously. Acknowledging an excess demand for commodities created by monetary expansion, such texts necessarily if tacitly allow Walras's Law to imply that an excess supply of bonds is the matching imbalance. While not a logical impossibility, such a condition is to say the least empirically peculiar, as argued on pages 102–107 below.

Considering the case of monetary contraction, other texts assume that in the ensuing depression the commodities, money and bond markets are all in equilibrium. Yet violating the Law they suppose an excess supply on a separately recognized fourth market, the market for labor.

Some articles in the literature imagine two Walras's Laws, one for flows and another for stocks. For example, they refer to the condition that an excess demand for money must be exactly matched by an excess supply of bonds as 'Walras's Law for stocks'. (See Yeager and Rabin, 1997 for citations).

STOCKS, FLOWS AND TRANSACTIONS

For some goods it is convenient to think of quantities supplied and demanded as amounts per time period. Examples are food and electricity and things like haircuts that simply cannot be stockpiled. Quantities obviously must not pertain to periods of different lengths for the two sides of the same transactions.

For some stockpilable things in some contexts, it is less convenient to think of demand and supply quantities as amounts or rates over a period than as desired and actual holdings at a point in time. Examples are land, houses and cash balances (Cannan, 1921 [1951]).

In applying Walras's Law, it would be convenient to be able to speak interchangeably of the stock and flow senses of equilibrium and disequilibrium. Does disequilibrium in the one sense imply disequilibrium in the other sense as well?

Prevailing terminology causes complications. Some or most discussions of these matters identify flow demand with demand for consumption or current use and flow supply with supply from current production (for example, Bushaw and Clower, 1957, pp. 9–12, 20; Clower, 1968; Clower and Due, 1972, Chapter 3; Harrison, 1987). Other discussions use the term 'flow' more broadly to cover transactions undertaken for whatever purpose, including adjustment of holdings.[9] Things neither currently produced nor currently used up, like Old Masters, cannot be the object of flow transactions on the narrow conception of flows but can be their object on the broader conception.

For flow transactions alone, narrowly identified with consumption and production only, the sum of plus and minus excess-demand values is not necessarily zero. For example, one might attempt a flow supply without attempting a flow demand, offering current output or labor to build up one's stock of money or some other asset.

For pure flow goods like haircuts, the question of stock equilibrium or disequilibrium cannot arise. Their very existence suggests that the Law, which embraces all goods, must refer to transactions actual and attempted rather than to production and consumption alone or to stocks alone. Disequilibrium means the frustration of desired transactions. J.R. Hicks comments:

> As long as we hold to the principle of price determination by 'equilibrium of demand and supply'..., we have no call to attend to anything but transactions. We do not need to distinguish between stocks and flows...It is not the case that there is one stock equilibrium and one flow equilibrium.[10]

Building on this idea, we shall focus on transactions undertaken for whatever purpose, whether to dispose of current production, to consume currently, or to build up or run down stocks. We shall include both transactions accomplished and transactions frustrated. The Law appeals to arithmetic and not to motives.

It is possible of course to build models distinguishing two equilibrium magnitudes for each good currently produced and consumed and also stockpiled – the rate of production-and-consumption flow and the level of stocks. This distinction, while relevant to questions of inventory policy and capital formation, has no particular bearing on Walras's Law. It in no way means that each such good has one market and price for stocks and another market and price for flows of production and consumption. The good has a single market that either does or does not clear at its single price. (The section on 'fringe complications', below, notes one minor qualification concerning the price at which transactions are attempted.)

The Stock-to-Flow Questions

We continue our discussion of what we call the 'stock-flow problem'. The main purpose of this exercise is to lay the groundwork for understanding the complications concerning money. Because of money's uniqueness and peculiarities, the implications developed in this section and the next do not necessarily apply to it in any straightforward way.

Are the stock and flow senses of disequilibrium and equilibrium consonant with each other? First, does stock disequilibrium imply flow disequilibrium? For a pure flow good, like haircuts, the question cannot even arise. For a stock-and-flow good, and also for a pure stock good like a collectible item neither currently produced nor currently consumed, stock disequilibrium does imply flow disequilibrium in the same direction. Flows are disequilibrated, however, not necessarily in the narrow production-and-consumption sense but in the broader transactions sense mentioned above. An excess stock demand means that people want to hold stocks aggregating more than the stocks actually held and furthermore that they are meeting frustration as they attempt an adjustment. (If they met no frustration in building up stocks, stocks would not be in excess demand.) At the prevailing disequilibrium price, the flow of purchases attempted for consumption and stock build-ups combined exceeds the flow of sales offered from production and stock rundowns combined. The market for transactions being attempted for whatever purpose, which is the only market that the good has, fails to clear. Similarly, stock excess supply implies transactions-flow excess supply. Frustration of attempted stock reduction means frustration of attempted sales. (From here on we refer to 'transactions flows' to emphasize our broad interpretation.)

Second, does stock equilibrium imply transactions-flow equilibrium? The next section provides an example in which the implication fails to hold. But for many goods the implication holds even when people want to build up or run down their stocks over time. Divergence of future desired stocks from present desired and actual stocks no more indicates frustration than does a traveler's desire to be somewhere else next week than at his present desired and actual location (Shackle, 1961, p. 223).

This correspondence does not stand or fall according to the particular reasons why people may not be trying to adjust their stocks any faster than they actually are trying. Even if mere transactions costs are inhibiting certain transactions, these unattempted transactions are not influencing market equilibrium or disequilibrium, even though they would be influencing it if, under different circumstances, they were being attempted.

The Flow-to-Stock Questions

Third, does transactions-flow equilibrium imply stock equilibrium? For a pure flow good the question cannot arise. For pure stock goods and for stock-and-flow goods, transactions-flow equilibrium implies stock equilibrium, since desired transactions undertaken for whatever purpose are able to be carried out.

Fourth, does transactions-flow disequilibrium imply stock disequilibrium? We have argued that stock disequilibrium implies transactions-flow disequilibrium in the same direction. For pure stock goods like Old Masters, the implication runs the other way also. Since their only flows are actual and attempted stock adjustments, transactions-flow disequilibrium implies stock disequilibrium. On whether any such implication holds even for money – read on.

For stock-and-flow goods, transactions-flow disequilibrium does not necessarily imply stock disequilibrium in any straightforward sense. Consider a good whose producers would like to supply more output than is being demanded but who frustratedly hold output down to what they can sell. Since desired sales exceed quantities demanded, the good is in transactions-flow excess supply. (Page 69 above explains Patinkin's important distinction between supply and output.) Yet the good is not unambiguously in excess stock supply also, for the output restraint holds stocks down to what producers and others find appropriate to the actual situation. It is hardly worth explaining a strained sense in which the good might count as in excess stock supply after all, since transactions-flow equilibrium and disequilibrium are what are fundamental to Walras's Law, not all of their conceivable stock counterparts.

SUMMARY

We pause to review and examine some important terms and concepts. Equilibrium, disequilibrium, excess demand and excess supply all relate specifically to the market and not to any subgroups that may comprise it (see the next paragraph). Transactions-flow equilibrium implies that desired market purchases equal desired sales undertaken for whatever purpose, including adjustments of holdings. Transactions-flow disequilibrium implies frustration of market transactions. Quantity demanded exceeds or falls short of quantity supplied, both of which include desired adjustments of holdings.

We recognize that an alternative exists in the literature that interprets excess demand or excess supply as 'net purchases' or 'net sales' by a particular transactor or group of transactors. For example, under exchange rate pegging the monetary authority's sale of foreign exchange indicates that it has an excess supply of foreign exchange that is matched by the buyers' excess demand.

We eschew this interpretation in favor of the view that focuses on failure of the market to clear and the attendant frustration of some transactors' plans. Accordingly, we would not say that in depression *workers* have an excess supply of labor. Rather, excess supply refers to the labor *market* and the related frustrations of workers on that market.

We have focused thus far on money holdings or cash balances, which are stock concepts. In keeping with Walras's Law we now turn our attention to transactions flows even when discussing money. Our goal is to examine what must be true in the *depths* of depression. In Chapter 4 money holdings or cash balances regain their prominence as we shift the analysis to what must be true at the start of a depression resulting from deficient spending.

COMPLICATIONS CONCERNING MONEY

Walras's Law holds most transparently in a barter economy. Challenging questions attach to money. Does an aggregate negative (or positive) excess-demand value for all goods but money strictly entail a positive (or negative) excess demand for money itself? And even if it does do so in the transactions-flow sense appropriate to Walras's Law, does this transactions-flow imbalance imply disequilibrium between desired and actual total holdings of money?

Conversely, does imbalance between these holdings imply an opposite frustration of transactions in goods and services (and securities)?

To forestall misunderstanding of our answers, we must alert the reader to some complications tracing to money's distinctness from all other goods. We shall have to distinguish between different senses in which demand and supply of money are and are not equal (see the end of this section). The relation between supply/demand disequilibrium and perceived frustration of attempted transactions holds less straightforwardly and more loosely for money than for other goods.

This looseness derives from money's buffer stock role and in turn from its role as the general medium of exchange. Money trades against all other things but not on any one market and not at any one price specifically its own. Monetary disequilibrium does not show itself in confrontation of supply and demand on a specific market at a specific price. Instead, holders try to adjust their cash balances by altering their attempted purchases and sales of innumerable goods and services and securities. Far from being well focused, pressures of monetary disequilibrium are widely diffused with widespread consequences.

Complications arise for Walras's Law in a depression attributable to an excess demand for money. Although we take it as settled that monetary disorder can cause and has caused depression, we do not say it is the only conceivable cause.

We shall distinguish between transactions-flow demands (and excess demands) to 'acquire' money and stock demands (and excess demands) to 'hold' it. People try to acquire money as they offer their goods and labor for sale. But instead of necessarily acting to build up their cash balances (except very temporarily, in accordance with money's medium of exchange and buffer stock roles), they may well be intending promptly to respend the money received.

THE PUZZLE OF AN EXCESS SUPPLY OF LABOR (AND COMMODITIES)

When labor is in transactions-flow excess supply in a depression, what is in corresponding excess demand? Not only is labor in excess supply – so are commodities that frustrated business firms desire to produce and sell but cannot because they lack customers (recall the difference between supply and output). Again we ask: what thing or things are in transactions-flow excess demand, matching the transactions-flow excess supply of labor and commodities?

One suggested answer is 'nothing': the Law fails in a depression, which might well be described as a situation of *general* deficiency of demand. (Clower, 1965 [1984], p. 53, mentions but does not rest content with this interpretation.) Such a dismissal of Walras's Law would overlook the requirement that only demands and supplies and imbalances having the same degree of *effectiveness* be evaluated and compared.

Here we are invoking Clower's distinction between 'notional' supplies and demands and 'effective' or 'constrained' supplies and demands. Notional supply or demand in a particular market refers to transactions that suppliers or demanders would desire and be prepared to carry out if they met no frustration in carrying out their desired transactions in any other market. Effective supply or demand refers to transactions that the parties are ready and willing to carry out under actual circumstances. Note that 'effective' does not necessarily mean 'successful'. Absent frustrations elsewhere, notional supply or demand is effective also. If the parties do encounter frustrations elsewhere, then the effective supply or demand quantities in the particular market diverge from the notional quantities. They are constrained by lack of full success in accomplishing other desired transactions.

In Clower's example, his inability to find buyers for his consulting services constrains his demand for champagne. His constrained demand for champagne is effective at a lower level than his notional demand, the latter being the demand that would be effective if, contrary to fact, he were meeting no frustration in the labor (or other) markets.[11] Chapter 6 elaborates on these concepts.

With necessary distinctions made, we may return to our puzzle about what effective transactions-flow excess demand matches an effective transactions-flow excess supply of labor and commodities.[12] In a depression, labor is in effective excess supply since unemployed workers are ready and willing to sell their labor, but they cannot find employers. If workers could succeed in selling all their effectively supplied labor, they would spend their larger incomes on more commodities than they can now afford. Ultimately, they are demanding commodities (and perhaps savings assets) with their labor, but these potential demands are contingent on their sales of labor. Actually, their frustration in acquiring money in exchange for labor shields the commodities market from these more ultimate demands (Baumol, 1962, p. 53n).

Unemployed workers' demands for additional commodities are thus notional and not effective, as in the Clower champagne example. In applying Walras's Law, a merely notional demand for additional commodities cannot count as what matches an effective transactions-flow excess supply of labor.

Workers effectively but frustratedly supplying labor are by that very token effectively but frustratedly demanding money in exchange. Money then, and not commodities, is the thing in effective transactions-flow excess demand. (Leijonhufvud, 1968, p. 88, recognizes this possible interpretation.) True enough, if workers could acquire it, they would not want to add all this money to their cash balances. They would want to spend most of it on commodities. But instead of being effective, this contingent supply of money for commodities is merely notional, like Clower's supply of money for champagne.

In transactions that workers are ready and willing to carry out, money is indeed in effective excess demand. Recognizing this effective transactions-flow excess demand for money helps us understand how monetary disorder can intercept unemployed workers' signals that they wish ultimately to exchange labor for commodities.

A similar argument applies to the market for commodities. In a depression, commodities are in effective transactions-flow excess supply. Frustrated firms desire to sell more in exchange for money, but they cannot find buyers. If firms could acquire more money by producing and selling more commodities, they would hire additional factors of production, especially labor, in order to produce them. This potential demand for labor, however, is contingent on firms being able to sell more, that is, it is notional. And in applying Walras's Law a merely notional demand for labor cannot count as what matches the effective transactions-flow excess supply of commodities. Monetary then, and not labor, is the thing in effective transactions-flow excess demand. Monetary disorder intercepts firms' signals that they wish ultimately to exchange commodities for labor.

We note that the concept of notional excess demand or supply is beset with difficulties. In the depths of depression, labor is clearly in effective excess supply. But is it in notional excess supply? After all, workers are notionally *and* effectively supplying more labor than is effectively being demanded by firms. However, firms are notionally demanding more labor than they effectively demand, the latter being constrained by their inability to find buyers for their commodities. For the market as a whole we cannot say for sure whether labor is notionally in excess supply or demand. A similar argument applies to the commodity market, where consumers' notional demand for commodities exceeds their effective demand. On the other hand, the concept of just notional demand or supply (without the 'excess') is useful when referring to a particular transactor or group of transactors.

FURTHER PECULIARITIES OF MONEY

What if any *stock* aspect, pertaining to *holdings* of money, corresponds to the effective *flow* excess demand to *acquire* money in transactions? An answer must take note of the fundamental proposition of monetary theory. Each person or firm can hold as much or as little money as it sees fit in its own particular situation even if the total supply is fixed. This individual freedom reconciles with the aggregate constraint through the effects that excess supplies of or demands for money exert on incomes and prices, which in turn condition how much money individuals desire to hold. (The fundamental proposition applies most straightforwardly to a closed economy or one with a floating exchange rate; see pages 78–80.)

The fundamental proposition appeals to money's role as the medium of exchange and as buffer stocks for its individaul holders. As the proposition helps explain, the individual from his own point of view perceives *no* frustration specifically pertaining to cash balances. To build up (or run down) his balance, the individual need only curtail (or expand) his spending or lending relative to his income and other receipts. Even in the depths of depression individuals meet no frustration in holding cash balances as large as they think appropriate to their curtailed incomes, even though they do experience frustration in acquiring money by selling labor and commodities.

This is not to say that money is always in effective stock equilibrium even when in effective transactions-flow excess demand. At the *start* of depression tracing to monetary disorder, money is in excess demand in both senses (stock and transactions-flow). Suppose that some disturbance or policy blunder makes the country's money supply either shrink or fall short of a demand strengthened by real economic growth. At first individuals might see drops or shortfalls of their cash balances as nothing worse than the buffer function in operation. Sooner or later they act to rebuild or conserve their cash balances by showing reduced eagerness to buy and increased eagerness to sell things. Although any individual can succeed in this effort as the fundamental proposition states, in the aggregate they are indeed trying to hold more money than actually exists. Their effective stock excess demand for money, even if not generally identified as such, shows up as transactions-flow excess supplies – as frustrations – on myriads of markets for particular things. Since transactions are voluntary, the short side of the market prevails and transactions shrink. Under ideal conditions of pure competition and complete price and wage flexibility, transactions would shrink only in nominal terms (Wicksell, 1898 [1936] [1965], pp. 39–41). The same physical volume of transactions would occur at reduced prices and wages, and monetary disequilibrium and its frustrations would be nipped in the bud. Reality is not ideal, however, and activity does shrink and remain physically shrunken until, barring some easier remedy, price and wage cuts finally and belatedly absorb the entire nominal shrinkage. Anyway, nominal income shrinks enough so that individuals no longer effectively demand cash balances totaling more than the actual money supply.

An initial stock and transactions-flow excess demand for money thus brings about changes that indirectly and ultimately shrink the effective demand for holdings of money – the cash balances that people judge they can 'afford'. For scarcely any other good does excess demand shrink the quantity demanded itself. The familiar diagram (Figure 1.3) measuring actual and demanded stocks of money along the horizontal axis and nominal income along the vertical axis could decorate a description of this process.

Let us focus on the depths of depression, when people feel they cannot afford and so are not effectively demanding cash balances larger than their actual balances. One might try to argue that the effective transactions-flow excess demand for money, unmatched by any effective attempt to spend it (since money never received cannot be offered for commodities), itself constitutes an attempt, a frustrated attempt, to build up cash balances however temporarily. We forswear this verbal maneuver. It is more useful to explain why money, though not in effective stock excess demand, is in what might be called a 'full-employment stock excess demand'. The latter concept refers to the excess of the amount of money holdings that would be demanded at full employment and at the prevailing level of prices and wages over the actual money supply.

The depths of depression, with incomes and transactions shrunken, keeps the total of money holdings effectively demanded from exceeding the actual quantity of money. (If people were still trying to hold more than the actual money supply, transactions and incomes would still be falling as depression deepened.) Although the actual quantity of money falls short of what people would demand to hold at full employment, they are effectively demanding cash balances totaling no more than that deficient actual quantity precisely because they are not fully employed. A 'quasi-equilibrium' holds between money's effective stock demand and supply in the sense that people are holding as much money as they think appropriate in their depressed circumstances. It is not a 'full equilibrium', however, for the effective stock demand is as small as it is only in consequence of pervasive disequilibrium. (In Keynesian theory, analogously, saving and investment can be in quasi-equilibrium at less than full employment precisely because the depressed level of income holds desired saving down to what investment can absorb.)

It may seem contrived to identify the full-employment excess demand for money in the depths of depression as the stock counterpart of the effective transactions-flow excess demand for money. Still, the peculiarities distinguishing money from all ordinary goods impose our interpretation of money's stock disequilibrium, strained though it may seem. Money is the one thing that routinely changes hands in lubricating flows of incomes and transactions. Reduced transactions in money almost automatically curtail the flows of incomes and expenditures being lubricated and thereby curtail the associated effective stock demand for money itself. We are not confusing our full-employment stock excess demand for money in the depths of depression with an effective (or actual) stock excess demand, which does exist during the decline into depression but not in its depths. Nor do we forget our insistence that Walras's Law is fundamentally about transactions flows, not stocks. An effective transactions-flow excess demand for money persists in the depths of depression.

MISPERCEPTIONS OF MONETARY DISEQUILIBRIUM

In a depression when money itself is the thing whose effective transactions-flow supply and demand are out of equilibrium (with a corresponding stock disequilibrium in the 'full-employment' sense just explained), the condition that frustrates transactions is less evident than when some ordinary commodity is in excess demand or supply. First, as the medium of exchange routinely traded on all ordinary markets, money lacks a market of its own where imbalanced supply and demand squarely confront one another. As the unit of account in which all ordinary things are priced, money lacks a price specifically its own that could come under direct pressure for market-clearing adjustment. Pressures toward equilibrating adjustment in money's purchasing power operate only in piecemeal and roundabout and sluggish ways on the markets and prices of innumerable ordinary goods. These general interdependence properties pertain to money in a higher degree than to any other good. They contribute to displacement of perceptions of what it is that is out of balance. (Superficially, anyway, a depression looks more like a deficiency of demand for commodities and labor than a deficiency of money supply.)

Second, also contributing to this displacement of perceptions is the fact noted in the Keynes-Friedman fundamental proposition. Anyone can hold cash balances as small or large as he judges he can afford in his situation. No frustration exists concerning money holdings. This appearance of things from the individual's point of view in no way, of course, discredits the economist's concept of effective stock monetary disequilibrium from the overall or aggregate point of view. For example, at the start of depression, the total amount of cash balances demanded is indeed greater than the actual supply.

Third, the misperception of monetary disequilibrium also derives from the buffer stock role of cash balances. A buffer stock is supposed to fluctuate. In the very short run even an economywide excess demand for or excess supply of money may go unperceived and even be conceptually elusive. If the money supply suffers a sudden unannounced drop, individuals may initially accept the presumably temporary declines in their buffer cash balances and try to carry on their transactions as before. Macroeconomically, a temporary rise in measured velocity cushions the drop in the quantity of money. Soon, probably, individuals will recognize that their cash balances are remaining persistently too low and will try to rebuild them by restraining their purchases of commodities and by trying more eagerly to sell things. After the famous lag in its effect, the monetary policy (if that is what shrank the money supply) begins to bite on the economy.

At the start of depression money's buffer stock role may make it hard to pinpoint just when its effective stock and transactions-flow excess demand appear. Even then, this excess demand does not manifest itself to individuals as frustration specifically in holding money. It shows up instead as dispersed, generalized frustration in selling things and earning incomes, that is, in acquiring money. The people most keenly experiencing it are not necessarily those who had wanted to build up their cash balances. Conceivably, people wanting to hold more money could get it, while those parting with it are people whose shrunken incomes keep them from demanding cash balances as large as before. Anyway, flows of income and expenditure shrink until effective holdings of money no longer are inadequate *in relation to those shrunken flows*. Yet in this quasi-equilibrium the effective transactions-flow excess demand to acquire money persists, matching the effective transactions-flow excess supply of labor and commodities.

THE DIAGNOSIS OF DEPRESSION

We can now address one of our major themes: the diagnosis of the depths of depression as a disequilibrium, specifically a monetary disequilibrium. We have argued that the initial effective stock excess demand for money gets 'choked off' by the depression itself. The equality between the effective (actual) demand for cash balances and the money supply in the depths of depression represents a quasi-equilibrium. It is not a full equilibrium because money holdings fall short of what would be demanded at full employment and at the prevailing wage and price level. The situation illustrates what we call the 'centerpiece of orthodox monetarism': the nominal quantity of money is too small for the wage and price level or, equivalently, the wage and price level is too high for the nominal quantity of money.[13] This full-employment stock excess demand for money is a key aspect of pervasive disequilibrium. The effective transactions-flow excess demand for money also supports our diagnosis. Furthermore, Patinkin's (1965) analysis of the quantity theory of money, and especially his focus on the real-balance effect, shows that the 'underemployment equilibrium' envisaged by Keynes is not an equilibrium in any ordinary sense of the word.[14] It is an underemployment disequilibrium in which forces are at work, however feebly, toward restoring full employment. In the depths of depression, firms frustrated in supplying commodities and workers frustrated in supplying labor are putting downward pressure, weak though it may be, on prices and wages.

We acknowledge that falling prices can be temporarily destabilizing through the adverse effects of debt burdens and expectations of even lower prices, as explained elsewhere. Eventually, however, prices and wages would fall sufficiently to restore full-employment equilibrium. As a matter of policy, we would not recommend waiting for the self-equilibrating forces to take full effect.

But one may ask (as a graduate macro class did): 'even at full employment, wouldn't firms want to sell more at the going price if only they could find buyers?' Well, yes, since many or most of them are price-setters, facing downsloping demand curves. We have realistically been assuming that perfect competition does not prevail in most markets. Firms in the full-employment situation inquired about are in equilibrium, maximizing profits, experiencing no pressure to cut prices, and participating in no overall excess supply of commodities. Even at full employment, what almost every seller wants is a more intense demand for its output – a demand curve further to the right – in which case it would sooner or later raise its price. In the case of full employment firms are not frustrated and are not prepared to take any action. That situation is quite different from the one that mostly concerns us, a monetary disequilibrium in which prices and wages are responding only sluggishly to the downward pressure of excess supplies.

In his exposition of disequilibrium economics, Patinkin (1965, p. 323n) acknowledges a 'basic analytical problem' whose full solution is not clear to him. In disequilibrium, firms are off their demand-for-labor curves. But since he assumes perfect competition, he wonders why each individual firm does not just expand its labor input until it reaches its demand curve, as perfect competition would indicate. Here he overlooks the incompatibility of disequilibrium and perfect competition in his model. In the real world of disequilibrium and imperfect competition, firms and people may indeed be off their demand and supply curves.

WALRAS'S LAW AND RECOVERY FROM DEPRESSION

Suppose the monetary authority begins to expand the money supply to promote recovery. People spend the new money on buying more commodities and firms hire more workers. Is money therefore in overall transactions-flow excess supply and commodities and labor in excess demand? The answer to both parts of the question is 'no'. People remaining unemployed still want jobs and firms still want to produce and sell more commodities than they have customers for. Effective transactions-flow excess supplies of labor and commodities, although reduced by the monetary expansion, do persist as people and firms frustratedly demand money in exchange. Continuing expansion of money and spending would shrink these market imbalances even further.

The initial rise in spending results from an excess of the expanded money supply over total cash balances effectively demanded at the trough of depression. Until recovery is complete, however, money remains in effective transactions-flow excess demand as well as in full-employment stock excess demand. The monetary expansion reduces these excesses. Alternatively, it replaces poverty as the means of eliminating the excess demand for money that caused the depression.

We can now answer a question posed on pages 87–8: does imbalance between desired and actual total holdings of money imply an opposite frustration of transactions in goods and services (and securities)? The answer is 'it depends' because of the peculiarities of money mentioned above. At the start of depression the effective (actual) stock excess demand for money and hence transactions-flow excess demand for money imply a transactions-flow excess supply of commodities, so here the answer to the question is 'yes'. On the other hand, when recovery from depression begins, the increased money supply is greater than money holdings effectively demanded. But money remains in both full-employment stock excess demand and transactions-flow excess demand, accompanied by a transactions-flow excess supply of commodities. Here the answer to the question is 'no'.

WALRAS'S LAW AND AN EXCESS SUPPLY OF MONEY

We have not considered the case – the not completely opposite and symmetical case – of an excess supply of money, which can occur once full-employment equilibrium has been reached. Here especially, money's lack of a price and market of its own and the distinctive manner in which people acquire and dispose of the medium of exchange keep people from clearly identifying any frustration of their transactions with money itself. When trying to run down what they consider excessive cash balances, people may meet frustration in spending money on particular things at their old prices. Excess demands for those things tend to raise their prices, which is the essence of the process whereby an excess supply of money removes itself. If those particular prices somehow remain stuck at their old and currently too-low levels, people will probably succeed in finding other things to spend their money on, things whose prices do adjust readily to clear their markets (see below). Furthermore, some outputs may temporarily rise beyond sustainable levels, alleviating demand frustrations.

The more nearly complete and pervasive price flexibility is, the slighter, the more fleeting, the more nearly imperceptible, and the less evidently linked with money are any frustrations of transactions. Still, in principle, the link of an excess supply of money with frustrations does hold. That link comes closest to being obvious to everyone (not just to monetary theorists) when comprehensive controls are holding down prices in the face of a major monetary expansion, disrupting transactions, production and employment, as in Germany before the reforms of June 1948. Thinking out this suppressed-inflation case may be left to the reader, since its identification with monetary disequilibrium does not require such subtle distinctions as the depression case. (See, however, Barro and Grossman, 1971, 1976; and our discussion of their work in Chapter 6.)

Another topic we pass over quickly is discoordination due to something other than monetary disorder, for example, widespread failure of electronic data processing and communications. We do not deny the possibility of nonmonetary depression, but that has not been our topic. We have been paying attention to money in the context of Walras's Law and have been concerned with what must be true in the depths of depression caused by monetary disorder.

FRINGE COMPLICATIONS

We acknowledge setting some minor problems aside. We have been concerned with whether markets are or are not clearing over time spans that people operate in in the real world. We have set aside questions of full stationary equilibrium, in which, by definition, activities continue indefinitely in their same old ruts, with prices and stock and flow quantities all remaining unchanged. Such a state of affairs can never be reached, one obvious reason being that exhaustible natural resources exist and are exploited.

We have also left aside questions of intertemporal planning – the build-up and rundown not only of inventories but also of equipment and structures and related questions of saving, investment and economic growth. We have been concerned with stock-flow issues primarily as they relate to whether we may legitimately associate positive or negative excess demand for some things with negative or positive excess demand for other things.

Our reconsideration of Walras's Law has paid attention to nonmarket-clearing prices but not explicitly to different prices prevailing for the same good, that is, to lapses from the law of one price. We could take account of those lapses by remembering the two-sidedness of each individual transaction, whether frustrated or successful. We have not explicitly considered the role of expectations or considered situations when different transactors are trying to trade on the basis of different information or misinformation about market conditions. We have not taken international trade and capital movements and foreign currencies explicitly into account, although we could do so by stretching the concept of securities. Nor have we considered payments, like corporate dividends, that are not straightforward payments for an actual good or service or security exchanged at its particular price, though such a complication could be handled by treating owners' entitlements to shares in firms' profits as securities. We have left aside nonmarket events like gifts and theft.

PUZZLES RESOLVED: CONCLUSION

The complications mentioned do not undermine Walras's Law. The Law applies only to what count as market transactions, both actual and attempted. Every transaction considered has two aspects, since people are exchanging or trying to exchange quid pro quo. This key insight, together with justifiable stretching of the concept of the object of market exchange in some cases, suffices to rescue Walras's Law from difficulties. Actually carrying out the rescues in these cases of fringe importance would have obscured the main points of this chapter.

The sum of the positive or negative excess demand quantities of all goods (inclusively defined), each multiplied by its price, is zero. This result holds when we use effective or constrained supply and demand quantities, as defined by Clower and as reviewed above. We must avoid muddling together notional quantities of some goods and constrained quantities of other goods all in the same attempted application of Walras's Law. In analyzing multimarket disequilibrium, in which the quantities that people are trying to buy or sell of particular things are constrained by frustrations experienced in other attempted trades, constrained or effective quantities are what are relevant to the Law.

The distinction between stock and flow aspects of equilibrium and disequilibrium does not discredit Walras's Law. The Law refers to transactions accomplished or attempted. Demands and supplies of some goods, true enough, are conveniently treated in some contexts as stocks. But stock disequilibrium implies transactions-flow disequilibrium in the same direction on suitably operational interpretations of both concepts.

The reverse implication, from transactions-flow disequilibrium to stock disequilibrium, does not always hold – most obviously not for nonstockable services and not straightforwardly, anyway, for commodities whose actual output is held below desired sales because of deficient demand. Nothing much, fortunately, depends on insisting on a flow-to-stock implication in such cases.

For money, however, one can say more. Its demand and supply are conveniently conceived of as stocks. When a transactions-flow excess supply of labor and commodities has as its counterpart a transactions-flow excess demand for money, it would be convenient if this transactions-flow disequilibrium translated into a stock monetary disequilibrium as well.

With recourse to some subtleties the translation does work. The effective transactions-flow excess demand for money matching the excess supply of commodities and labor in depression translates into a 'full-employment stock excess demand'. The actual quantity of money falls short of total holdings that would be demanded at full employment, though not short of total cash balances that people are effectively demanding under their constrained circumstances in the depths of depression. In view of the special way in which money functions, distinct from that of all other goods, this interpretation is not excessively strained.

Further to dispel any suspicion of metaphysics in distinguishing between different senses of demand and excess demand for money, let us consider the situation on the labor market from the viewpoint of the unemployed workers in the depths of a depression traceable to monetary disorder. They find that lower average cash balances are more suitable to their straitened circumstances. Their *notional* demand for cash balances though is far greater, since they would hold more money if, contrary to fact, they met no frustration in the labor market. But because they are unemployed, their effective (actual) demand for money to hold is satisfied in the quasi-equilibrium.

In a different effective sense, however, the unemployed workers are trying *to acquire* money by offering their labor services. Their frustrated demand to acquire money corresponds to their frustrated supply of labor. If they should again obtain jobs, they would want to use part of their newly acquired money to build up their cash balances, but only a small part. They would want to spend most of it on consumption (and perhaps on portfolio assets). Since money is the medium of exchange, the unemployed workers can want to acquire it without necessarily desiring to hold it.

The unemployed workers' desires to acquire money is not cancelled by their turning around and supplying it for commodities. For this subsequent supply of money is merely hypothetical or notional and is kept from becoming effective by their frustration in acquiring it in the first place. One might object that workers are not really demanding money, but rather are demanding commodities with their labor. This objection is misconceived. Their merely hypothetical or notional demand for (additional) commodities is kept from becoming effective by their frustration in acquiring money. Their desire for the labor-for-money part of a *two-stage exchange* is effective though frustrated, while their money-for-commodities part is not even effective, being kept hypothetical by their frustration in the first stage. In the transactions-flow sense, the sense relevant to Walras's Law, money is indeed in effective excess demand and labor in excess supply.

Money is also in stock excess demand in the full-employment sense. Actual holdings fall short of what would be demanded at full employment and at the prevailing wage and price level.

We have four clarifications. First, one must not confuse the transactions-flow 'excess demand to acquire money' with the invalid notion of an 'excess demand for money to spend' found in the literature. The former expression does not deal with the issue of what people would do with the money *if* they acquired it, since 'excess demand' implies they are not successful in doing so. The latter expression is a self-contradiction, since 'money demand' in the literature refers to cash-balance *holdings*. One cannot demand more money *to hold* and at the same time *spend* that money when received.

Second, a colleague has attempted to rescue some textbook authors by suggesting that they mean to say that an excess supply of labor matches any excess demand for commodities. (We refer to those texts that assume the bond and money markets are in equilibrium while an excess demand for commodities exists.) But if labor were in excess supply, the unemployed workers' demand for commodities would be notional and not the effective demand portrayed in textbooks.

Third, pages 111–12 below examine the effects of a newly imposed minimum wage law, which would be an example of a nonmonetary disturbance. We argue that an excess supply of labor and an excess demand for commodities would result. Does this contradict the previous paragraph? No, because the excess supply of labor would be matched by a frustrated demand for money, while the excess demand for commodities would be matched by a frustrated supply of money. The two excesses in question would not match or offset each other.

Fourth, we summarize some of the conclusions reached in our discussion of the depression case:

1. As long as the economy is below full-employment equilibrium, an effective transactions-flow excess demand for money persists.
2. Under the same circumstances as in (1), a full-employment stock excess demand for money exists.
3. During the decline into depression, an effective stock excess demand for money is present.
4. In the depths of depression, the money supply actually equals the effective stock demand for money, which has been reduced by poverty. A quasi-equilibrium exists.
5. During recovery from depression, the increased money supply that drives the recovery is greater than the effective stock demand for money. However, we argue that the full-employment excess demand for money is the stock counterpart of the effective transactions-flow excess demand for money. Both persist until full employment is reached.

NOTES

1. As Patinkin (1956, 1965) points out, Wicksell was one of the few classical or neoclassical economists – perhaps the only one – who went to the trouble of explicitly spelling out just how the quantity of money, interacting with the demand to hold it, determines spending and prices. Wicksell was giving an early description of what Patinkin calls the 'real-balance effect' (1965, p. 19). Whether Patinkin's own conception of the effect is excessively narrow is a question discussed in Chapter 4.
2. On use of a copper penny as Part 527-GB in a hydraulic pipe bender, see *Coin World*, 11 March 1981, p. 92.
3. The 'pure credit' designation results from his not considering demand deposits to be money (compare Humphrey, 2002).
4. Compare Yeager (1978) on banks not holding large excess reserves and their paying, if not lending, excess reserves into circulation.
5. One qualification is minor in this context. When demand deposits are cashed in for currency, the drain on reserves limits banks' assets and deposits. But this limitation works on the supply-

of-money side, not the demand side. If the authority that creates high-powered money and the banks, taken together, want to expand the money supply, they can do so unhampered by any unwillingness of the public to accept or hold money. In the unlikely event that banks could not make loans, they could always buy securities on the bond market to expand the money supply.

6. Newton-Smith (1981, p. 89) and Laudan (1977, Chapter 2) make the same point, and in some detail, about conceptual problems in the natural sciences (Yeager, 1994).

7. Lange named Walras's Law, stated its rationale, contrasted Say's Law with it, and diagnosed serious inconsistencies in received theory. While he may have been wrong in interpreting what Say really meant, he furthered the doctrinal discussion by clarifying the issues.

8. In one version of Gustav Cassel's system of general-equilibrium equations, as Patinkin notes (1965, p. 36 and Supplementary Note H), Walras's Law does not apply. The reason is Cassel's assumption that total money expenditures of consumers are fixed beforehand. His model does not yet recognize these expenditures as conditioned by earnings from selling goods and factors and as related to any total quantity of money. Money is merely a unit of account. The version of Cassel's system in which Walras's Law might be said to fail is thus a crucially incomplete representation of reality. It is adequate for some purposes, but not for illuminating the aspects of economic interdependence to which Walras's Law pertains.

9. Patinkin (1958, p. 305) appears, though not quite unambiguously, to count stock adjustments as flows: 'all of economic analysis is really concerned with flows and not stocks'. Baumol (1965) clearly does not identify flow demand with consumption and flow supply with production, and he speaks (p. 56) of 'the flows by means of which the public adjusts its inventory holdings'. Lloyd (1960) calls the identification of flows with consumption and production a 'new stock-flow analysis', contrasting it with an earlier literature that he cites.

10. Hicks (1965, p. 85), a passage cited by Harrison (1987, p. 506). Hicks confines these remarks to the context of his own temporary-equilibrium condition in a 'flexprice' model, but his words apply more widely than he himself may have intended.

11. Although these distinctions are due to Clower (1965 [1984]), Grossman (1972) reminds us that Patinkin had sketched them as early as 1949. Tucker (1971, p. 62) suggests the terminology of unconstrained or notional demand on the one hand and constrained or effective demand on the other.

12. Patinkin (1965, p. 333) tries to dispose of the problem with Walras's Law in the depression case by 'attributing to workers a completely passive behavior pattern according to which they adjust their planned supply of labor to the amount demanded by employers. Hence, by definition, "equilibrium" always exists in the labor market'. Patinkin thus avoids logical error by begging a live question.

13. Gordon comes close to making this statement. He argues (1990a, p. 236) '...*both* the nominal wage rate and price level are too high in relation to the level of aggregate demand...' However he does not mention the specific monetary nature of recession or depression.

14. Patinkin (1965, Chapter 13) foreshadowed much of the disequilibrium theory developed by Clower (1965 [1984]), Leijonhufvud (1968), and Barro and Grossman (1971, 1976).

4. Money's demand and supply: equilibrium and disequilibrium (2)

EXCESS DEMAND FOR MONEY AND THE START OF DEPRESSION

We are concerned with what *must* be in excess demand at the *start* of a depression resulting from a deficiency of spending. Chapter 3 deals specifically with what must be in excess demand in the depths of depression.

By Walras's Law any transactions-flow excess supply of commodities must be matched by a transactions-flow excess demand for all other things. The way the medium of exchange functions differently from even close nearmoneys justifies a more specific assertion. Demand for commodities in general cannot be deficient unless at the same time the opposite is true of the medium of exchange in particular. At levels of income and prices not yet changed from those at which the disequilibrium first appeared, people must be desiring to hold more money than exists. We are referring here to income not yet fallen to the quasi-equilibrium level that suppresses the actual or effective stock excess demand for money.

Moreover, in the current context it is not necessary to dwell on the distinction between the stock and transactions-flow senses of disequilibrium. That distinction is crucial for understanding the depths of depression. In what follows we shall just refer to excess demands and supplies. Similarly, we are not overly concerned with the distinction between output and supply. That distinction is important in discussing the depths of depression in which actual output is kept down to equal demand, although an excess supply of commodities exists.

Exceptions to the claim that money must be in excess demand at the start of depression that hinge on excess demands for securities or other noncurrently-produced goods are conceivable but behaviorally implausible. In his *General Theory* (1936), Chapter 17, Keynes remarks that a deficiency of demand for current output might be matched by an excess demand for assets having three 'essential properties': (1) their supply from private producers responds slightly if at all to an increase in demand for them; (2) a tendency to rise in value will only to a slight extent enlist substitutes to help meet a strengthened demand for them; (3) their liquidity advantages are large relative to the costs of holding them. Another point that Keynes notes by implication belongs explicitly on the list: (4) their values are 'sticky' and do not adjust readily to remove a disequilibrium.

Money is the asset most obviously having these properties. Keynes asks, however, whether a deficiency of demand for current output might be matched by an excess demand for other things instead, perhaps land or mortgages.[1] Other writers have asked, similarly, about other securities, works of art and jewelry. Conceivably, an excess supply of commodities could be matched by an excess demand not for actual money but for land, collectibles, or other assets not currently produced. We maintain however – not as a logically airtight necessity but as an extremely plausible proposition about reality – that an excess demand for such things is not what matches a deficiency of demand for current output. Such things might be in excess demand *along with* but not *instead of* money. If money broadly defined is in excess demand, money narrowly defined must be in excess demand also (see page 1 above for this distinction).

Because a nonmoney (asset) does not have a routine flow, lubricating exchanges of other things, efforts to hold more than its actual quantity cannot cause pervasive trouble. Excess demand for a nonmoney hits its own specific market, which reacts in one of three alternative ways: (1) the amount supplied responds, as with government savings bonds and various nonmonetary deposits; (2) even if the quantity cannot expand, as with Old Masters, the thing's price may rise to the level that restores supply/demand equilibrium or (3) if for some reason (perhaps through controls or market imperfections) neither method (1) nor method (2) operates, so that the excess demand for the thing remains frustrated, then frustrated demanders may turn to demanding other things as substitutes.[2] In this case, the economic system behaves in broadly the same way as if demands had run in the first place in favor of the substitutes that people wind up buying. If those substitutes happen to be newly produced commodities, then no deficiency of aggregate demand ensues. If instead, frustrated demanders decide to hold more money in relation to income and expenditure than they otherwise would, contributing to an excess demand for money, such behavior provides an illustration of our point that a deficiency of demand for commodities must realistically be associated with an excess demand for money, whatever excess demands for other assets may also prevail.

For money, in contrast, excess demand is neither directly removed nor diverted. Because of money's peculiarity as the medium of exchange, without a single market and price of its own, its excess demand does not manifest itself to the individual as a deficiency of the total stock, as argued in Chapter 3. It shows up not as specific frustration in adding to cash balances (since demand for cash balances can be satisfied by mere restraint in spending them), but rather as an excess supply of other things in general. If the prices of these other things are not sufficiently flexible downwards, their outputs fall, and so do incomes earned in producing them.

The individual is likely to regard the scale of his income and spending flows as less readily adjustable than his cash balance. But for the economy as a whole (excluding the monetary authority), the money stock is a datum to which flows adjust. If total cash balances demanded exceed the money stock, the flow of income shrinks in the aggregate and for the typical or average economic unit. This happens as the unit shrinks its spending, thereby cutting others' receipts and spurring greater and more widespread efforts to shrink spending into line. Efforts to build up or conserve cash balances make the flow of income and expenditure shrink precisely because money is what routinely flows to accomplish the exchange of goods and services. Any interference with exchange narrows opportunities for profitable production of goods to be exchanged. The shrinkage continues until holdings of money no longer are inadequate in relation to the shrunken flows as the quasi-equilibrium described in Chapter 3 is reached. (The economy still suffers from depression and monetary disequilibrium as explained above.) An inadequate quantity of nonmoney alone could not do the same pervasive damage, since it does not share with money the simple but momentous characteristic of routine circulation in lubricating exchanges. An excess demand for a nonmoney hits its own specific market, so an excess demand for it cannot show up as deficiency of demand for other things in general *unless* it is accompanied by an excess demand for money.

In order to present these arguments more formally, we look ahead to Figure 5.2 reproduced as Figure 4.1. Here, as so often in economics, a particular point would come across better if everything else could have been said first. The reader may advantageously return to the present point after studying Chapter 5. Yet the main lines of the argument should be intelligible even now. The interest rate is measured vertically, average prices horizontally. The discussion in Chapter 5 assumes the economy remains at full employment, so only prices respond to an excess demand for or supply of commodities. Since we make no such assumption here, we can allow for either prices *or* output to respond in what follows.

We aggregate all exchangeable items into three composite goods: commodities-and-labor (called simply 'commodities'), bonds and money. In Figure 4.1, regions of excess demand are labeled XDC, XDB and XDM for commodities, bonds and money, respectively; XSC, XSB and XSM indicate excess supplies. In the southern sector of the diagram, commodities and money are both in excess demand, bonds in matching excess supply. In the northern sector, commodities and money are both in excess supply, bonds in excess demand. These associations, though abstractly conceivable, are economically implausible.

We focus on the northern sector, but a symmetrical argument applies to the opposite peculiar pattern of disequilibrium. We assume the economy starts at

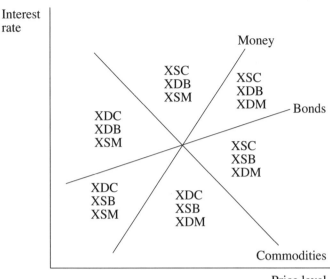

Figure 4.1   Conditions of equilibrium

full-employment equilibrium. People's preferences then change so they are holding more money than they desire. Money is therefore in excess supply. Yet in the northern sector the spending of money on commodities is inadequate for full-employment equilibrium at prevailing prices and wages. A depression is getting started. Attempts to unload excessive money holdings, far from being directed toward commodities, are directed toward bonds. Unlike money, bonds have a market of their own as well as a price that moves toward market-clearing levels. With bonds in excess demand and money in excess supply, there occurs unequivocal downward pressure on the interest rate and upward pressure on the price of bonds. This price increase tends to eliminate the excess demand for bonds. Thus any remaining excess supply of commodities must be matched by an excess demand for – no longer, if ever, an excess supply of – money.

The reader may wonder: couldn't an excess supply of commodities be matched by an excess demand for bonds, while equilibrium prevailed in the 'money market'? Again the answer is no. The reason can be made clear by supposing, for the sake of argument, that people's preferences shift away from commodities and in favor of bonds without also shifting away from commodities in favor of money. (We again assume the economy starts at full-employment equilibrium.) The shift toward bonds would raise the price of bonds and thereby eliminate the excess demand, since bonds have a market and price of their own. Any remaining deficiency of demand for commodities would therefore be accompanied by an excess demand for money. Money demand would have increased with the fall in the interest rate, which is the counterpart of the rise in the price of bonds.

The price of bonds would so rise unless official intervention prevented it. If transactions at a price above the legal maximum were simply forbidden, the situation would be essentially the same as in the type (3) response to excess demand considered above. If, on the other hand, the monetary authority used open-market sales to keep the price from rising, that very addition to the bond supply and subtraction from the money supply would prevent an excess demand for bonds and would create an excess demand for money, as explained on pages 118–20 below.

Let us rephrase our point. A deficient demand for commodities is extremely implausible unless associated with a deficient quantity of the stuff that gets spent, namely money. The medium of exchange is the one thing that routinely circulates, lubricating transactions in commodities. It is the one thing having a routine flow whose constriction by people's efforts to pay out less of it than they are acquiring can constitute a shortfall of spending on current output. An excess demand for money might conceivably be *accompanied by* an excess demand for nonmoney assets, but a deficient demand for commodities accompanied by no excess demand for money at all (let alone by an excess supply, as in the implausible northern sector of the diagram) is very nearly inconceivable as a matter of economics. In theorizing about the start of depression, therefore, it is eminently reasonable to focus attention on an excess demand for money.

We do not say, however, that only an excess demand for money could cause a depression. Conceivably, as Barro and Grossman show (1976, summarized in Chapter 6 below), coordination could be impaired and activity depressed not only by an excess demand for money, with wages and prices stuck too high, but also by an excess supply of money, with wages and prices stuck too low. Or it could be the result of widespread misalignment of sticky relative prices (real wage rates, for example, being stuck too high). Pages 111–12 below imagine the case of widespread unemployment caused by imposition of a new minimum wage law. We explain there why this *non*monetary disorder would not be characterized by a *general* deficiency of demand for commodities. Moreover, on pages 109–11 below we illustrate how a 'correct' money supply could forestall depression even when a major nonmonetary disturbance distorted the pattern of relative prices. The money supply would restrain any cumulative contraction of spending. A massive failure of all electronic communications could conceivably cause depression, but it would not be characterized by a general deficiency of aggregate demand. Historically, though, as documented by Warburton and Friedman and other monetarists, depression has been caused by excessive prices and wages in relation to the nominal quantity of money, that is, to a deficient real quantity.

In the opposite situation of an excess demand for commodities, it follows that an excess supply of money must exist. Like the northern sector, the southern sector in Figure 4.1 is implausible.

EXCESS DEMAND FOR MONEY AND OVERSAVING

What do we make of the Keynesian worry about too much saving? Well, people cannot save without acquiring some assets or other. If this process, including the associated financial transactions, results in real capital formation, there is no need to worry. Saving applied to capital formation is in no way contractionary. If, on the other hand, savers neither acquire real assets themselves nor directly nor indirectly transfer their command over resources to others, such as entrepreneurs who will use the resources to construct assets – if real investment does not fully fill the saving gap – then savers must be trying to build up their holdings of money. In such a situation, other noncurrently producible assets may be in excess demand along with money, but, for reasons explained a few pages above, not instead of money.

Keynesians might counter that attempts to save do not necessarily imply actual acquisition of assets. According to the 'paradox of thrift', a fall in income might choke off their acquisition, along with the otherwise increased volume of saving desired. True enough, but something must have matched the deficient demand for commodities, namely an excess demand for money. The attempt to hold more money than exists makes income fall. Keynes himself, in a passage quoted in part on page 77 above, went on to draw an analogy between the process that equates saving and investment and the process that equates demanded and actual quantities of money.

Suppose that the propensity to save rises or that investors' optimism wanes (their 'animal spirits' flag; Keynes, 1936, pp. 161–2). In either case, the interest rate declines, unless the change in the saving/investment relation involves a sufficient strengthening of desires to hold money at the expense of bonds, as explained in Chapter 5. Anyway, even if only in response to a reduced interest rate, the quantity of money demanded in relation to income and expenditure rises and desired velocity falls. What would have been oversaving at full employment entails what would have been an excess demand for money at full employment.

Recognizing this relation is an application of the translation test. We do not deny that full-employment oversaving can cause trouble. Rather, we insist that it must have a monetary aspect. It is theoretically quite conceivable, if not historically typical, that an excess demand for money can originate on the demand-for-money side rather than from reduced or negative growth of the quantity of money.

THE 'CURE' FOR DEPRESSION

Considering its cure reinforces our diagnosis of depression as a monetary disorder. While we do not necessarily advocate activist policies or even suppose that they could work as intended, in some contexts considering policy questions helps convey theoretical points.

An initial excess demand for money holdings results in deficient demand for commodities, bringing cutbacks in production, employment and income. The demand for cash balances responds until the quasi-equilibrium of Chapter 3 is reached. In this situation, any monetary expansion would begin to replace poverty as the means of eliminating the stock excess demand for money that caused the depression. So would an increase in the real quantity of money through a fall in prices and wages. While stickily fall*ing* prices and wages are a symptom of an excess demand for money, a sufficient *fall* in prices and wages would be a cure. A rise in the value of money would cut the number of money units demanded and so strengthen the demand for commodities.

The concept of stickiness in the value of money as an obstacle to restoring monetary equilibrium helps illuminate how depression and suppressed inflation are similar in nature, though opposite in direction. Lerner (1949) has emphasized this contrast by renaming suppressed inflation 'suppression'. Suppression is the condition of a 'sellers' market', general shortages and impairment of allocation by prices that develops when prices are kept from fully adjusting to monetary inflation. Depression, as Lerner remarks, is the name for monetary deflation with prices kept from falling.

Now we can understand the paradox that either deflation or inflation would cure depression, and that either inflation or deflation would cure suppression. The kind of deflation that would cure depression is price-and-wage deflation – a big enough rise in the value of money to cut the nominal quantity of money demanded at full employment down to the quantity in existence. The kind of inflation that would cure depression is monetary inflation – a big enough increase in the money supply to relieve the full-employment stock excess demand (or, just conceivably, a sufficient fall in the demand schedule for cash balances to bring the same relief).

The kind of inflation that would cure suppression is price-and-wage inflation – a big enough fall in the value of money to raise its nominal quantity demanded up to the quantity in existence. Here is the sense in the quip that the best cure for (suppressed) inflation is inflation. The kind of deflation that would cure suppression is monetary deflation – a big enough cut in the money supply (or rise in the demand schedule for cash balances) to wipe out the excess supply.

Confusion between price-and-wage and monetary inflation and deflation has frequently bedeviled theory and policy. The National Recovery Act (NRA), with its price-raising codes of 'fair competition' in the depressed years of 1933–35, seems to have been an example. A policy the opposite of NRA would have been superior. For in the absence of sufficient monetary inflation, which marked the period 1933–35, price-and-wage deflation is a better treatment for depression than price-and-wage inflation.

One more paradox is now understandable. Depression could conceivably be prevented either by maintaining wages and prices or – barring transitional difficulties – by cutting them. Wage-price maintenance would be salutary only if accomplished by just enough monetary expansion to avoid the excess demand for money whose symptom is a sticky sag in wages and prices. But barring monetary action, swift reduction of wages and prices to a new full-employment equilibrium level would be needed to forestall an excess demand for money. As we argue elsewhere, though, reliance on price and wage deflation is not a practical way of avoiding or curing depression.

HOW A 'CORRECT' MONEY SUPPLY CAN FORESTALL DEPRESSION

An 'adequate' nominal quantity of money is one no smaller than would be demanded at the existing level of prices and wages and at full employment. Adequacy in that sense would offer protection against the cumulativeness of nonmonetary disturbances that could, in contrast, conceivably plague a barter economy. Although failure of prices to adjust to an equilibrium pattern, structure, or composition, distorts resource allocation away from any plausible ideal, it need not unequivocally and pervasively depress aggregate economic activity.

To see this, let us suppose that a nonmonetary disturbance, such as a massive shift in the pattern of demand at the end of a war, leaves the old pattern of relative prices wrong. Prices adjusting only sluggishly leave markets disequilibrated; and since transactions are voluntary, the actual volume of transactions in each market is the smaller of quantity demanded and quantity supplied. Trading and production drop off, or so we might expect. The sectors suffering drops in demand for their outputs must curtail their demands for the products of other sectors. Suppose that these cutbacks do initially outweigh the additional purchases desired by people earning increased incomes in the sectors favored by the original shifts in demand. Even some of these latter sectors may be unable to take advantage of the shift in their favor if disequilibrium prices impede their purchases of necessary inputs. What keeps the rot from spreading?

To answer, let us tentatively suppose that real income does fall. Now, even with the demand-for-money function unchanged, the quantity of money demanded at the existing price level declines along with income. A quantity of money adequate for full employment is overabundant for underemployment. People cannot 'afford' to hold as much money as before, so they try to reduce their now excessive cash balances. The spending sustained by an adequate money supply checks the spread of rot from the sectors initially depressed by adverse shifts of demand. Money's intermediary role in the two-stage process of exchanging 'goods for goods' keeps the production of goods to be exchanged from being disrupted as badly as it might be in a barter economy. Just as a badly behaved money supply can inflict burdens on a monetary economy from which a barter economy is exempt, so a well-behaved money supply can confer benefits. (Compare our discussion of Leijonhufvud's 'corridor theory' of economic fluctuations on pages 182–3 below.)

The aspect of the Wicksell Process just alluded to is more than a wealth effect, narrowly conceived.[3] It is more nearly what might be called a Cambridge effect. People demand cash balances in relation to their flows of income and expenditure. (Pages 126–7 below elaborate on this effect.) As their incomes fall, people will not want to continue indefinitely holding absolutely unchanged and so relatively increased cash balances. The steps that households and firms take to reduce their money holdings promote the recovery of spending and aggregate income until cash balances no longer seem too large – or those steps check the decline in the first place.

None of this is to say that an adequate money supply can avoid all wastes due to a wrong and rigid pattern of prices. It cannot keep prices from conveying misinformation about wants, resources, technology and market conditions. In a monetary economy, misallocation waste – the loss of utility from a mispatterning of activity – can persist even without extensive waste through involuntary idleness. In a barter economy lacking a monetary cushion, however, misallocation waste and idleness waste would go together, idleness being an extreme form of misallocation.

With regard to these wastes, the cases of too much and too little money in relation to a wrong level and pattern of prices are not entirely symmetrical. When money is in excess supply and commodities in excess demand, nonprice rationing (probably informal, accidental rationing) shunts frustrated demands onto other commodities from commodities whose prices are furthest below market-clearing levels. But when money is in deficient supply, nothing shunts demand around so as to maintain aggregate productive activity. Nonprice rationing has no close counterpart in the opposite direction. The possibility that producers frustrated in selling some things might shift into other lines of production avails little when demand is deficient even for the latter products. Demand, to be effective, must be exercised with money.

Monetary-disequilibrium theory tells us more about depression than about inflation. It shows why nonmonetary disturbances alone, even when leaving the existing pattern of relative prices wrong, cannot cause a *general deficiency* of aggregate demand. (Extreme nonmonetary shocks – perhaps a sudden mysterious failure of all electronic communications – could conceivably cause a depression, but not one characterized by a general deficiency of demand.) Maintaining an actual quantity of money equal to the total that would be demanded at full employment at the existing level of wages and prices would restrain any cumulative contraction of demand. It follows that such troubles – though not all economic troubles – must involve an inappropriate quantity of money.

WALRAS'S LAW AND A NONMONETARY DISTURBANCE

After imagining pervasive disequilibrium not traceable to monetary disorder, we now ask whether Walras's Law would hold even in such a situation. Superficially it might seem to fail in the conceivable case of widespread involuntary unemployment caused by a new minimum wage law. (We are interested here in the initial stage of the disturbance in which Walras's Law might be called into question. We are purposely choosing this extreme or worst-case scenario in order to make our point.) The new law makes some workers no longer profitably employable, much as if disease had removed them from the labor force. With production, real incomes and the effective size of the economy shrunken, pressure on the price level is upward, for people no longer wish to hold the entire money stock at the old price level. It seems implausible, then, to maintain that money is in transactions-flow excess demand, more or less matching a transactions-flow excess supply of labor.

Yet the arithmetic of Walras's Law still holds. The workers who are frustrated in obtaining jobs exhibit a frustrated transactions-flow demand for money. Moreover, at the depressed level of income – depressed because the minimum wage thwarts transactions – people now find they cannot 'afford' to hold the existing total of cash balances. Their frustrated supply of money is reflected in an excess demand for commodities. This excess of demand over supply of commodities occurs because the minimum wage makes it unprofitable for employers to hire the labor necessary for additional production.

Taking account of both the workers' frustrated demand for money and the frustrated supply of money being offered for commodities, one might ask whether money is in *overall* transactions-flow excess demand or supply. Three comments are in order. First, no answer to this question is necessary to save the arithmetic of Walras's Law. The frustrated demand for money is matched by the excess supply of labor, while the frustrated supply of money is matched by the excess demand for commodities. Second, the frustrated demand for money and frustrated supply of money do not directly confront each other. No opportunity arises for them to neutralize each other, for the minimum wage is disrupting coordination. Third, the aggregate of them – if we insist on adding them – could be of either sign.

For an obvious example, consider how sensitive to income the demand for money might be. If the demand for money at the depressed level of income is only slightly below what it would be at full employment and if, accordingly, the attempted unloading of money onto commodities is only slight, then the workers' frustrated demand for money predominates. The overall transactions-flow excess demand for money is positive. If, on the other hand, the demand for money is highly sensitive to income, then the depressed level of income causes the frustrated supply of money to be large enough so that the overall transactions-flow excess demand is negative. At any rate, this excess demand for money must be equal to but different in sign from the total of the excess supply of labor and excess demand for commodities.

Though arithmetically unscathed, Walras's Law is not necessarily useful in every case. The minimum wage is a basically nonmonetary disturbance, as a failure of telephones, computer networks and other electronic communications would be. Coordination is impaired, markets are thrown out of equilibrium, and real incomes fall. Although its arithmetic still holds, Walras's Law is of little help in explaining such a situation.

Three further observations are worth making about the minimum wage case. First, *no* general deficiency of aggregate demand exists and hence no cumulative decline takes place. (That is one reason why we say that Walras's Law is not very helpful in explaining this situation.)

Second, as people tried to unload money onto commodities, might not prices rise enough to whittle the nominal minimum wage down to a market-clearing level in real terms? Could not employment and production revert to their full-employment levels, with all nominal prices and wages simply marked up in the same proportion as the legal minimum wage exceeded the lowest free-market wage? No; for given an unchanged nominal money supply, real balances would then be inadequate to sustain a full-employment level of activity. Monetary considerations thus enter, after all, into analyzing the effects of a minimum wage. Still, emphasis properly belongs on the nonmonetary character of the disturbance.

Third, the involuntary unemployment resulting from the minimum wage would be considered 'structural' and not 'cyclical'.

INDIVIDUAL EXPERIMENTS AND MARKET EXPERIMENTS

Patinkin (1965) introduces an illuminating distinction between two types of experiment. This distinction is important in understanding the sections that follow. An *individual experiment* involves discovering the desired behavior of an individual person, of a small or large group, or even of all people in the community, acting in certain capacities in specified circumstances. Whether these circumstances are compatible with other economic conditions and whether they can in fact prevail is beside the point. It is not the purpose of an individual experiment, all by itself, to describe what equilibrium will tend to emerge.

The demand curve for an ordinary commodity is an example of the result of a (conceptual) individual experiment. It shows how much of a particular commodity its buyers and potential buyers will demand under various specified circumstances, notably including alternative prices of the commodity. It is true that facts other than the circumstances and tastes reflected in the demand curve may rule out many and perhaps all but one of these prices as genuine possibilities. By itself, however, the demand curve is not meant to describe what prices can in fact prevail. This description becomes possible only by an analysis that takes all relevant circumstances into account, including the results of individual experiments reflecting the circumstances and attitudes of people besides buyers and potential buyers of the commodity in question. Most notably, in the present example, these other people are the suppliers and potential suppliers of the commodity.

This more comprehensive analysis consists of *market experiments*. It pulls together the results of various individual experiments, examines the conditions under which the plans of various people would and would not mesh, describes the processes at work when plans fail to mesh, and describes the equilibrium position.

In the market experiment that mainly concerns us, an initial equilibrium is disturbed by a change in the money supply. We then inquire into the nature of the new equilibrium position. The main individual experiment that concerns us is how a change in a certain variable would affect the demand for money. Chapter 2 illustrates that the demand for money is inversely related to the interest rate. Patinkin (1965, p. 372) emphasizes that this proposition does not imply that the equilibrium interest rate is inversely related to the quantity of money. The first proposition describes an individual experiment, while the latter describes a market experiment. He argues that Keynes (1936) repeatedly confused the two propositions. Chapter 5 presents Patinkin's exposition of what we call the 'strict version' of the quantity theory, in which the equilibrium interest rate is invariant with respect to changes in the quantity of money.

The discussion of the liquidity trap in Chapter 2 also invokes the above distinction. Figure 2.1 includes a demand-for-money curve portraying an individual experiment, while Figure 2.2 includes a market-equilibrium curve portraying the result of a series of conceptual market experiments. Similarly, Chapter 5 relates this distinction to the issue of the elasticity of demand for nominal money with respect to the inverse of the price level. Following Patinkin, we show the demand-for-money curve does not exhibit uniform unitary elasticity, while the market-equilibrium curve does.

SOME POSSIBLE DIFFICULTIES CONSIDERED

A Shortage of Money

One conceivable line of argument questions the dire consequences of an excess demand for money. It suggests that the demand will tend to adapt itself to the actual supply in a relatively direct and painless way, so that the quantity of money need not severely constrain transactions.[4] When faced with a shortage of coins in particular, people will cooperate to carry out their transactions anyway. (The customer will give the retailer the extra dime or two cents needed to reduce the amount of change due.) Similarly, Akerlof (1975) and Blinder and Stiglitz (1983, pp. 297–302, especially p. 299) suggest that people will cooperate to keep their transactions going when *total* money is in short supply. They may adjust payments schedules or make increased use of trade credit, or financial institutions may devise new nearmoneys.

This argument is overoptimistic but instructive. If only coins are in short supply, then even though demand for them presumably is related to income, income, of course, does not fall to whatever level would choke off the excess demand for coins. At so fallen a level, total money would be in excess supply, exerting upward pressure on income. A shortage specifically of coins is fairly easy to diagnose, and collaboration in coping with it works not only in the general interest but also in one's private interest (to keep one's own transactions going and to earn good will).

An overall shortage of money is harder for individuals to diagnose. The disequilibrium does not show up on any particular market, whereas coins do have a market of their own in the sense that they exchange against money of other denominations. Instead, monetary disequilibrium shows itself obscurely as a generalized difficulty in selling things and earning incomes. Most relevantly, the fact that it would be in the common interest of people in general to employ money-economizing instruments and practices does not mean that it is in the interest of any individual to do so even before such expedients have already been generally adopted. (Compare pages 195–6 below on divergence between what is 'collectively rational' and 'individually rational'.)

Analogy Between Money and Bonds

Alluding to a familiar thought experiment involving drops of new money from helicopters, James Tobin asks (1974, p. 87): 'Is a "rain" of Treasury bills – promises to pay currency in three months or less – of no consequence for the price level, while a "rain" of currency inflates prices proportionately?' Some members of the new classical macroeconomics school have suggested that increases in the money supply and in federal interest-bearing debt are essentially similar in causing price inflation. 'Federal bonds are nothing more than an alternative form of currency – they are promises to deliver currency in the future. Like currency, these bonds are pieces of paper backed by nothing tangible; they are fiat paper.' Since the government has no intention of ever retiring its debt, 'there is little difference between currency and bonds; both are money'. Any increase in the federal budget deficit, whether financed by issue of currency or of bonds, is therefore inflationary. 'As is well understood, government can cause inflation by printing more money. It can also cause inflation by printing more bonds. Additions to the stock of money or bonds, by increasing the total amount of nominal wealth, increase private demands for goods and services. The increased demands, in turn, push up the prices of goods.'[5]

It would seem to follow from this argument that if government deficits are not to be avoided and are inflationary in any case, they might as well be financed in the simplest and cheapest way (Bryant and Wallace, 1979, pp. 365–81). The fallacy in these ideas rests, first of all, on the tacit assumption, reflected in the next-to-last of the sentences quoted, that money affects spending only by being part of its holders' wealth. The Wicksell Process consists of nothing but a wealth effect. In this view, whether a good fairy gave a country's inhabitants $1 billion worth of blankets (say) or $1 billion of new money, spending on other goods and services would respond in the same way. Now, it is presumably true of an individual that his increased spending on goods and services would be unaffected by whether he received a gift of $1 million in cash or in blankets salable for $1 million after expenses. But it would be illegitimate to generalize from the irrelevance of the form of the gift for the individual to its supposed irrelevance for the economy as a whole. Pages 132–6 below consider the possibility that nominal income might even fall in the case of a gift of blankets.

Yet a similar fallacy is committed in practically identifying bonds and money. No matter how wealthy the holders of bonds feel and how many goods and services their perceived wealth prompts them to buy, they can buy only by spending money. Buying on credit merely delays but does not eliminate payment in money. A comprehensive system of offsetting debts against each other would make a big difference, but our discussion refers to actually existing institutions and practices (compare pages 26–8 above). Because some relation holds between the flow of income and expenditure and desired holdings of the medium of exchange, the quantity of the medium in existence does pose some restraint on the flow of spending. Replacement of much of the money supply by bonds of equal value could hardly leave total spending unaffected.

This is not to say that bond-financed deficits have no effect on spending. Pages 132–6 below explain how bond financing by itself could result in an increase or conceivably, a decrease in nominal spending and income.

Money in Credit Transactions

A possible objection to insistence on the role of money notes that many transactions take place on credit. Does this fact trivialize the question of monetary equilibrium or disequilibrium? No. First, money is the ultimate means of settlement if not always the immediate means of payment. Whether or not a prospective transaction gets carried out depends on whether or not the prospective buyer can expect to be able to make and the prospective seller can reasonably expect to receive ultimate settlement in money. Second, money is the unit of account even in credit transactions. Disequilibrium in its value can disrupt these as well as cash transactions. The microeconomic points about price stickiness, developed in Chapters 6, 7 and 8, remain valid and relevant even for things traded on credit rather than paid for immediately. It seems trivial but is profoundly significant that prices are expressed in money.

Liquidity Preference Versus Loanable Funds Theories

Chapters 2 and 10 illuminate the mutual determination of the interest rate, *broadly* interpreted. In this section we focus on the *narrow* rate on bonds or loans and its determination in a partial-equilibrium setting.

The liquidity preference theory of the rate of interest may be associated with the following five propositions. First, the rate is determined in the 'money market' by the supply of and demand for money. Second, if money supply and demand are not equal, the rate immediately adjusts to maintain what Laidler calls 'perpetual equilibrium' (see page 71 above). Third, the interest rate is the price of money. Fourth, monetary policy is to be viewed as interest rate policy. Fifth, the interest rate is a good indicator of whether policy has been 'loose' or 'tight'. Our analysis throughout this book elaborates on why each of these propositions is invalid.

The alternative loanable funds theory holds that the narrow rate is determined in the market for bonds or loans. It views these two markets as identical; they are two sides of the same coin (compare Patinkin, 1965, p. 367). For instance, an increase in the demand for loans is equivalent to an increase in the supply of bonds. From either point of view, the rate rises. Moreover, the narrow interest rate is the 'price of loans' and is inversely related to the price of bonds.

General equilibrium could not prevail, of course, unless the interest rate (along with all other variables) were at a level where not only desired lending and borrowing but also desired and actual stocks of money were equal. Outside of general equilibrium, however, it is not necessarily true that upward pressure on the interest rate corresponds to an excess demand for money and downward pressure corresponds to an excess supply. An example illustrates a conflict between the two theories. Suppose tastes shift so that money and bonds are in excess demand and commodities are in excess supply, as in the northeast sector of Figure 4.1. The liquidity preference theory indicates upward pressure on the interest rate, while the loanable funds theory indicates downward pressure. The excess demand for bonds should indeed raise their price and thus depress their yield or rate of interest. As partial-equilibrium theories, the liquidity preference and loanable funds theories of the interest rate are not equivalent, and the latter is preferable. Lutz (1968, p. 184), among others, has pointed out that 'the immediate cause of a price change has to be sought in changes of supply or demand in the market of the good in question and not in other markets' (compare Fellner and Somers, 1966).

Although the narrow rate is *determined* directly in the bond (or loan) market, this does not deny that changes in the money supply can *affect* that rate. But they do so through pressures working in the bond market, that is, by affecting the demand for and supply of bonds. The interest rate that emerges temporarily equilibrates only that market. (The next section explains why we say 'temporarily'.) Contrary to the typical liquidity preference diagram found in most money/macro textbooks, a change in the interest rate does not equilibrate the nonexistent 'money market'; it does not eliminate an excess supply of or demand for money. Only the Wicksell Process does that. (See Rabin 1993 for examples of the errors committed in textbooks.)

Patinkin (1965, pp. 270–73, p. 367) argues that the narrow interest rate is not determined by saving and investment per se. He shows that saving is not identical to demanding bonds (supplying loans) and investment is not identical to supplying bonds (demanding loans). For one could save by demanding money rather than bonds, and firms could invest out of cash balance holdings rather than by supplying bonds. Patinkin concludes that a monetary economy precludes the above two identities, which would imply a barter economy.

Money's Influence on the Interest Rate

We address the issue of how the interest rate can be influenced (distorted) in the short run by changes in the money supply. Following an increase in the money growth rate, people spend excess cash balances partly on bonds, raising their price and lowering the interest rate. We refer to this as the 'liquidity effect'. As the Wicksell Process unfolds, spending on commodities rises along with incomes and prices. Consequently, the demand for loans (supply of bonds) increases, pushing the interest rate back up toward its initial level. We refer to this as the 'nominal-income effect'. (Chapter 5 explains this process more fully.) Since we assume an increase in the money growth rate, the nominal interest rate will eventually rise above its initial level. Fisher (1896) explains this increase by noting that lenders, who expect repayment in dollars of shrunken purchasing power, require, and borrowers concede, compensation by an inflation adjustment in nominal rates. We refer to this as the 'inflation allowance' or 'Fisher effect'.

Although Fisher most clearly presented the real/nominal rate relation, Humphrey (1983b) argues that several eighteenth- and nineteenth-century economists had already stated it. Its most elaborate formulation is: $n = r + p + rp$, where n is the nominal interest rate, r is the real interest rate, p is the expected rate of inflation, and rp is a cross product that accounts for the impact of inflation on the real value of interest receipts (Humphrey, 1983b, p. 5). The usual presentation of the Fisher effect ignores this cross-product term because as the multiplicative product of two small terms, it is usually insignificant enough to be disregarded. The resulting equation with the cross-product term dropped is, of course, only an approximation, albeit a very close one.

With different monetary effects and their different lags at work and with nonmonetary influences occurring also, the relation between money growth and interest rates is ambiguous, at least over short periods. Sustained rapid monetary growth though is likely to make the positive inflation allowance or Fisher effect dominate. It is a myth that 'loose money' always brings low rates and 'tight money' causes high rates (Friedman, 1968b).

Miller (2002, p. 12) identifies the following 'puzzle': interest rates rose in the United States in the short run during the 1970s despite increases in the money growth rate. Yet since that time the short-run response has been consistent with the liquidity effect, which Miller refers to as 'traditional thinking'. Why was the response perverse in the 1970s? Melvin (1983) even speaks of the 'vanishing liquidity effect of money on interest...' Our answer to the alleged puzzle focuses on heightened inflationary expectations stemming from the excessive expansion of the US money supply in the 1970s.

Interest Rate Targeting

When the monetary authority pegs or targets the interest rate, it is committed to buy or sell bonds as necessary in order to maintain the target rate. The money supply is 'endogenous' in the sense that it may respond to the public's demand for and supply of bonds (loans). We question though whether the money supply is 'demand-determined', that is, passively responding to the public's *demand for money* (compare Laidler, 1992 [1997a]). The literature provides many examples of confusion between endogenous and demand-determined. For example, Kaldor (1982, pp. 24, 70) and Moore (1988, p. xi) maintain that under interest rate pegging the money supply is always demand-determined; it could never be in excess supply. King (2000, p. 58) states: 'money is demand-determined under an interest rate rule, so that the monetary authority is implicitly saying to the private sector, "any quantity of money which you desire at the specified nominal interest rate...will be supplied"'.[6]

Greenfield and Yeager (1986) provide the following counterexample that shows how interest rate targeting can create an imbalance between money supply and money demand. Suppose that people's preferences shift from bonds toward commodities with no change in their demand for money. Ordinarily the resulting increase in the supply of bonds would raise the interest rate. However, in targeting the rate the authority buys the excess bonds, thereby increasing the money supply despite no increase in money demand having taken place. Now the nominal demand for money must adjust to the increased supply, rather than the other way around (Greenfield and Yeager, 1986, p. 365; Judd and Scadding, 1982, p. 1013).

For a second counterexample, consider the situation posed on page 117 above. People's tastes shift so that money and bonds are in excess demand and commodities are in excess supply. To resist a fall in the interest rate, the authority sells bonds. The money supply decreases despite the excess demand for it (Greenfield and Yeager, 1986) .

For a third counterexample, suppose that the authority arbitrarily decides to lower the target rate by buying bonds. When people sell bonds to the authority, it is not because they demand more cash balances. On the contrary, people are generally willing to sell bonds to whoever offers the most attractive price. When the authority is the buyer, it may create an excess supply of money with inflationary consequences.

Under interest rate targeting, the money supply is endogenous in the sense that changes in it may occur as a *by-product* of the authority's pegging operations in the bond market. However, the money supply is not demand-determined, that is, always responding to the public's demand for money, as the three counterexamples illustrate. The money supply process as described in money and banking textbooks is still relevant, since actions by the authority may create an excess supply of or excess demand for money, with the respective inflationary or contractionary consequences.[7]

In discussing his pure credit economy, Wicksell did not distinguish between 'endogenous' and 'demand-determined' (Humphrey 2002). We say 'pure credit' because Wicksell did not consider demand deposits to be money. In his system the public's demand for loans determined the quantity of loans and as a by-product the quantity of demand deposits. However, Wicksell incorrectly believed that these deposits were determined by the public's *demand for deposits* and hence could not be in excess supply. Humphrey (2002, p. 71) concludes that Wicksell 'conflated a non-demand-determined variable (deposits) with a demand-determined one (loans)'.

Much confusion in the literature likely stems from the failure to distinguish between 'the demand for money' and 'the demand for loans or credit' (Greenfield and Yeager, 1986). For example, when people go to the bank in order to borrow money newly created by the banking system, they are demanding loans or credit and not necessarily money. (Recall that 'money demand' refers to the desire to hold cash balances.) Since borrowers most likely want to spend the new money they receive, an excess demand for commodities results matched by an excess supply of money. Only after prices and incomes have risen sufficiently (to increase money demand) would monetary equilibrium again prevail. The increase in the money supply would be fully demanded at first in the unlikely event that borrowers desired to add the entire increase to their cash balance holdings.

Some Ambiguous Relations Involving Interest Rates

It is not always meaningful to simply inquire about the effect of a change in the interest rate on some economic variable, since the relevant market experiment requires specification of just what has disturbed the existing market situation. Failure to fully specify the initial disturbance invites invalid generalizations about associations between the interest rate and other magnitudes, as we now illustrate.

One often hears that high interest rates 'choke off' expansions and cause recessions. This implies a direct relation between high rates and slumping business. But what makes the rates rise? Often during economic expansions, it is a strong demand for loans. Sometimes price inflation is the cause. Low rates, conversely, do not necessarily promote expansions. Rather, they may reflect depressed economic activity and a slack demand for loans, as happened in Japan beginning in the 1990s (see pages 138–9 below).

Similar comments apply to the relation between the interest rate and saving. The supply schedule of saving as a function of the rate may indeed slope upward, but that individual experiment result does not imply a positive market experiment relation. An increased rate, for example, may result from a reduced willingness to save.

The relation between the interest rate and money's velocity also depends on the nature and source of disturbance. It is sometimes said that an increased rate and increased velocity go together, since the higher rate reduces the demand for money and so stimulates spending on output. (In Keynesian theory, higher velocity means higher income, increased money demand and so higher interest rates.) However, if an increase in the interest rate was caused by a shift of demand toward money and away from bonds (as on pages 154–6 below), a decrease in velocity and output would be associated with an increased rate.

A similar argument applies to the relation between the interest rate and a currency's foreign exchange value. A rise in the rate may be accompanied by either appreciation or depreciation of a floating currency. A rise in the home interest rate associated with economic expansion might well attract capital inflows and strengthen the home currency on the exchanges. Inflationary money supply growth, on the other hand, would both raise the home interest rate and depreciate the currency. Government budget deficits might both raise the rate and either weaken or strengthen the currency, depending on whether or not they were taken as signs of inflation to come. As so often in economics, we must be clear about the exact nature of the initial disturbance.

Uncertainties about the Definition of Money

Do uncertainties about the definition of money for statistical purposes invalidate an analysis focusing on its supply and demand? The answer is no. Regardless of just where we draw the boundary between money and other things, once we have money defined, the concepts of its quantity demanded and its actual quantity and of equilibrium or disequilibrium between these quantities remain meaningful. Disequilibrium between supply of and demand for money broadly defined almost certainly entails disequilibrium in the same direction for narrow money. Regardless of money's exact statistical definition, the distinctive roundabout process whereby its desired and actual quantities tend to be brought into equilibrium, perhaps painfully, retains its significance. So does the stickiness of prices quoted in money. While uncertainties about a definition may pose problems for policy, they do not discredit a theory focusing on the supply of and demand for narrow money.

Yet a live question remains: what should be included in the statistical measure of the money supply for use in policy or prognostication? Focusing on money's function as medium of exchange does rule out definitions that are too narrow (for example, the monetary base or high-powered money) and ones that are too broad (for example, ones including all noncheckable deposits). Laidler (1991b, p. 296) acknowledges a related difficulty:

> ... modern quantity theorists, myself included ... have argued that money is best defined as that aggregate for which the most stable demand function exists, and have hence made themselves vulnerable to a charge of circular reasoning; they have, in

effect, chosen as the appropriate definition of money only that which will confirm the theory they are purporting to test.

Interest on Demand Deposits

What would happen if money bore interest, as checking accounts held by individuals have already come to do? (It is convenient and legitimate here to blur the distinction between demand deposits and currency or to suppose that currency also bears interest.) Would money's interest yield serve as a flexible price equilibrating supply and demand without a painful roundabout process? Would money lose its distinctiveness? Pesek and Saving (1967, especially pp. 105–11) did suggest that money loses its monetary quality to the extent that it bears interest.

Explicit interest on money would become a new dimension of competition among individual banks, but its rate would not become a price that equilibrated money's overall demand and supply. Even bearing interest, money would remain the means of pricing and paying for everything else. Its supply and demand still would not directly confront each other 'at the banks', or on any other particular market. (With noncheckable deposits, in contrast, supply and demand do confront each other at the institutions offering them; and the interest rate paid on them can function as a kind of deputy for a price.) Money would still lack a single, definite, flexible price whereby its value in goods and services might readily adjust to equilibrate its supply and demand. Narrow money remains a distinctive focus of attention, largely because of the distinctive way in which it is supplied and demanded.

For example, suppose the central bank increased the banking system's excess reserves through open-market purchases. The banking system would not have to increase the explicit interest paid on newly created demand deposits in order to persuade people to accept them. Rather, because money is the medium of exchange, the banking system could simply make loans or buy bonds from people and pay with newly created deposits; no one would refuse to accept the new money. After all, in the past individuals have willingly accepted deposits paying zero explicit interest. Why should payment of, say, 3 percent interest make any difference? The postulated excess supply of money would then become fully demanded through the Wicksell Process. Even without any change in money's hypothesized pecuniary yield, its MER would still adjust to equal the MERs on other assets through changes in its nonpecuniary component (compare Brunner, 1989, p. 78).

Tobin's 'New View'

One objection denies the uniqueness of money and of the institutions that issue demand deposits. (At the time the following view first became popular, only commercial banks issued demand deposits.) Tobin's (1963) 'new view' of money and banking emphasizes that expansion of bank credit, as of credit from other sources, is limited by cost and revenue factors in an environment of rivalry for customers and that even in the absence of reserve requirements, a 'natural economic limit' to the size of the banking system would exist, similar to the limits restraining financial intermediaries that do not issue actual media of exchange. Given their wealth and their asset preferences, says Tobin, people will voluntarily hold additional demand deposits only if yields fall on alternative assets. But then loans and investments afford lower yields to the banks, making further lending and investing unprofitable for them beyond some point. 'In this respect the commercial banking industry is not qualitatively different from any other financial intermediary system.' Even without reserve requirements, the banking system's expansion 'would be limited by the availability of assets at yields sufficient to compensate banks for the costs of attracting and holding the corresponding deposits' (Tobin, 1963, pp. 414, 416). Restating these ideas, Crockett (1976) says that banks and nonbank intermediaries, both as individual institutions and as systems, face similar cost and demand constraints on expansion of their deposits and their portfolios.

Proponents of this view are evidently not attributing the natural economic limit to limitation of base money and to a finite money multiplier, for that would be old stuff and not a 'new' view. Those familiar limitations operate on the supply-of-money side, while the new viewers emphasize limitations on the demand side.

Tobin and his followers slight some familiar contrasts. No obstacle on the demand-for-money side blocks lending and spending new bank demand deposits into existence. No one need be persuaded to invest in the routine medium of exchange before more of it can be created, since people will always accept payment in money. If they do not desire to continue holding it, then instead of causing it to go out of existence, they will pass it along to someone else. Through the repercussions of the Wicksell Process, the supply of money creates its own demand in a momentous roundabout way. In contrast, undesired savings or nontransactions deposits will quickly disappear – or will not be accepted in the first place.

It is hard to imagine why a bank might find it more profitable to hold reserves in excess of what the law and prudence call for than to buy riskless short-term securities with them. Contrary to Tobin's tacit assumption, the individual bank is trying to maximize its own profits, not those of the banking system as a whole.

Suppose, then, that a cut in reserve requirements, expansion of the monetary base, or shift of the public's preferences from currency to deposits initially gives the banks more excess reserves. The individual bank finds it profitable to invest any it may have. The seller of whatever security the bank buys deposits the check he receives somewhere, providing his bank with more excess reserves to invest. And so on.

Even applied to the banking system as a whole, something is incorrect with the idea that a decline in yields obtainable will restrain expansion of loans and investments and deposits. As money expansion raises nominal incomes and prices, the dollar volume of loans demanded rises also, even at given interest rates. An unconstrained 'cumulative process' can even lead to embodiment of inflationary expectations in interest rates as described by Fisher (1930 [1955], Chapter 2 and *passim*). The great inflations of history discredit any notion of expansion being limited as marginal revenues fall in relation to marginal costs.

The quantity of nominal money cannot be explained by a cost-and-revenue approach that treats its issuers like manufacturers of refrigerators. In contrast, cost-and-revenue and supply-and-demand analysis *do* apply to the nominal volume of noncheckable deposits held at financial intermediaries. In the aggregate as well as individually, institutions must induce depositors to acquire and hold such claims against them.

In summary, an individual bank can expand its operations indefinitely as long as depositors furnish it with the necessary funds at costs it does not find excessive. Even if it had trouble finding qualified borrowers, it could buy securities. While an individual bank is of course limited in size by the public's willingness to hold its liabilities, the same is not true of the money and banking system as a whole.

THE QUANTITY THEORY AND MONETARISM

According to the quantity theory, 'broadly interpreted', the quantity of money in existence and the desires of the public to hold cash balances determine the economy's total nominal spending stream (recall Figure 1.3). This stream interacts with the level of prices and has some bearing on whether or not full employment prevails. A 'stricter' or more 'rigid version' (examined by Patinkin, 1956, 1965, and reviewed in our Chapter 5) goes further by asserting a strict proportionality between the quantity of money and the price level. This result holds strictly only for fiat money, which has no nonmonetary use and no cost of production closely resembling the cost of ordinary commodities.

The quantity theory should not be confused with Fisher's equation of exchange, $MV = PT$, or the $MV = PQ$ that we have used. The theory, unlike the equation, is no mere tautology (which is not to say that tautologies are useless). The theory rests on empirical facts, such as that people are concerned with cash balances for the purchasing power they represent rather than for their sheer nominal sizes or for their physical properties. A second fact is that people do not want to add all of any increase in the money supply directly and permanently to their cash balances. Equilibrium between the supply of and demand for money will not be restored until spending, prices and income have increased sufficiently to make people desire cash balances totaling the entire expanded money supply.

Empirical evidence of money's influence on spending, income and prices appears not only in the everyday decisions of people and business firms but also in historical events, in 'experience covering centuries in time and spanning the globe in space' (Friedman, 1959a [1969], p. 136). The role of money in classic hyperinflations and severe deflations is unmistakable. Even in prisoner-of-war camps during World War II, increases and decreases in the quantity of cigarettes, which served as money, resulted in effects described by the quantity theory (Radford, 1945; recall Chapter 2, pages 25–6).

Brunner coined the term 'monetarism' and expressed the core of the doctrine in three propositions (1968, p. 9):

> First, monetary impulses are a major factor accounting for variations in output, employment and prices. Second, movements in the money stock are the most reliable measure of the thrust of monetary impulses. Third, the behavior of the monetary authorities dominates movements in the money stock over business cycles.

Brunner cites empirical support for these hypotheses in the research of Brunner and Meltzer, Cagan (1965), and Friedman and Schwartz (1963). Clark Warburton really belongs on the list (many of his articles, dating from 1945, are collected in his book of 1966), and much work done since Brunner wrote in 1968 has further supported monetarist propositions.

Monetarism has often been identified with several other beliefs. However, we prefer to focus on Brunner's original propositions, which accord with the 'monetary-disequilibrium hypothesis' set forth and documented by Clark Warburton.

THE MONETARY TRANSMISSION MECHANISM: ELABORATION OF THE WICKSELL PROCESS

We are concerned here with the question of how changes in the money supply affect nominal income, postponing until Chapters 6, 7 and 8 the question of how changes in nominal income are split between changes in prices and changes in output. A change in the money supply can affect spending and income both directly and indirectly through the Wicksell Process. In what follows we assume three types of goods: (1) money; (2) newly produced commodities, interpreted to include services *and labor* and (3) nonmoney assets, physical as well as financial. We also suppose the money supply decreases. In the direct channel of the Wicksell Process, people and firms try to restore what they consider deficient money holdings by straightaway decreasing their demand for commodities. The indirect channel operates when people and firms try to restore their deficient money holdings by selling assets, thereby raising interest rates and lowering asset prices, and when people and firms decrease their demand for commodities in response to the increased rates (rather than directly in response to the perceived deficiency of cash balances). Mishkin (1995, pp. 3–10) surveys the main types of monetary transmission mechanisms found in the literature. None portray changes in the money supply as affecting aggregate demand and income through the direct channel of the Wicksell Process. The Federal Reserve Bank of St Louis *Review* of May/June 1995, devoted entirely to the channels of monetary policy, also ignores the direct channel. Similarly, the Federal Reserve Bank of New York *Economic Policy Review* (May 2002) presents the proceedings of its conference on financial innovation and monetary transmission. The overview or survey article (Kuttner and Mosser, 2002, pp. 15–26) does not mention the direct channel even while supposedly presenting 'all' the major channels of monetary transmission found in the literature. It does, however, speak of a 'monetarist channel', which focuses on changes in *relative asset prices*. The authors also recognize an 'exchange rate channel' and the empirical difficulties of pinning it down.

We acknowledge that several 'subchannels' exist through which monetary policy can affect nominal income, as these publications illustrate. We choose, however, to focus on the two channels of the Wicksell Process. Besides these channels, a complete presentation of the Wicksell Process recognizes two other effects of each channel besides the one Patinkin (1965) emphasizes in discussing his 'real-balance effect', also known as the wealth effect or Pigou effect. Real money balances form part of their holders' wealth, and a decrease in them, other things being equal, makes their holders less eager to buy commodities and nonmoney assets. This is true, anyway, of so-called 'outside money', money not matched by private debt. Prime examples are commodity money and government fiat money. 'Inside money' has less claim to being counted as part of private sector net wealth, since it is matched by private debt. The prime example is banknotes and deposits created in connection with loans to private borrowers.[8] Although the Pigou effect was originally thought of as working through price deflation (Pigou, 1943, 1947; Haberler 1952), later writers including Patinkin broadened the concept to cover as well a change in the real money supply brought about through a change in the nominal money supply or increase in prices.

Patinkin does not describe two other effects of the Wicksell Process – not explicitly, anyway. A second might be called the Cambridge effect, referring to 'Cambridge k', the inverse of desired velocity (see pages 9–11 above). The idea, though not the name, comes from Sir Dennis Robertson (1963, pp. 443–4).[9] People hold money largely for transactions purposes and are concerned with the size of their cash balances relative to income and expenditure. A decrease in the relative size of these balances, whether through a decrease in the nominal quantity of money or a rise in the prices at which income and expenditure flows are evaluated (or through a rise in real economic activity) would make people feel that they were holding too little money and so make them less willing to buy commodities and nonmoney assets and more willing to sell.

A third effect, the portfolio-balance effect, hinges on people's concern for the composition of their asset holdings (both money and nonmoney). The internal rate of discount (IRD) or marginal rate of time preference also enters into the analysis, which Chapter 2 discusses at length. Here we briefly review it. Suppose people start with portfolios they consider satisfactory and then experience a decrease in money's share in them, whether through a decrease in the nominal quantity of money or a general rise of prices. People find that their portfolios contain relatively too little money. In accordance with the principle of diminishing marginal yield, their MERs on money are now above the MERs on nonmoney assets and above their IRDs. People set about trying to replenish their cash balance holdings by buying fewer commodities and nonmoney assets and by selling more. The operation of this portfolio-balance effect (like the Cambridge effect, if not the wealth effect) does not seem to hinge on whether money is of the outside or inside type.

Chapter 2 differentiates the portfolio-balance effect, whereby changes in the money supply can affect spending and income through both the direct and indirect channels, from the portfolio-adjustment models found in the literature. In almost all of these models monetary policy affects spending and income only indirectly, by changing interest rates and asset prices, including the prices of existing real (physical) assets relative to the costs of producing them new (see pages 45–6 above).

A total of six 'aspects' of the Wicksell Process exist: the direct and indirect channels, each operating through the wealth, portfolio-balance and Cambridge effects. In the operations of the direct channel, people try to remedy what they consider excessive or deficient cash balance holdings by straightaway (directly) altering their behavior in the markets for commodities. In the operations of the indirect channel, people try to remedy excessive or deficient cash balances by altering their behavior in the markets for securities and debt. The resulting changes in interest rates and credit terms and availability then (indirectly) induce people to alter their behavior in the market for commodities.

The three effects of the Wicksell Process – each operating through the direct and indirect channels – are not distinct, separate components of that process. They are, as we said, 'aspects', meaning views or slants on how real cash

balances affect the demand for commodities. The borderline between direct
and indirect operation of each of the three effects is blurred in reality, yet the
distinction is illuminating. Analogously, we view a statue from several different
angles, obtaining a better appreciation of it than from one angle only. But the
views overlap; they are views of a single reality, the whole statue.[10]

Both the real-balance effect and its broader version, the Wicksell Process,
pertain to interaction of the demand for money with the actual quantity.[11] Just
as individuals try to adjust their cash balances in light of their stocks of other
assets and the prices, incomes and interest rates confronting them, so their
efforts to make these adjustments in the face of a given nominal money supply
affect the intensities of demands and supplies in various markets and so the
prices, incomes and interest rates that result. A focus on influences running
from confrontation between desired and actual cash balances to the economy's
macroeconomic variables yields a description of the Wicksell Process or the
real-balance effect, broadly conceived.

The real-balance effect is sometimes said to be a disequilibrium phenomenon
that vanishes in equilibrium. If this remark merely means that economic
variables are in the process of change in consequence of disequilibrium between
desired and actual money holdings only when such a disequilibrium prevails,
well, that is obviously true. The effect makes things happen only outside of
equilibrium. In a less trivial sense the real-balance effect and Wicksell Process
characterize a monetary economy even in equilibrium. People are concerned
about the real sizes of their money holdings and act to maintain them at or
restore them to levels they consider appropriate. Even in the imagined case of
a full general equilibrium, the determinacy and stability of prices depend on
this concern for real holdings confronting the nominal money supply.

The Wicksell Process also affects investment by firms through the direct
channel as firms respond to their money holdings (Miller and Orr, 1966),
although the usual presentation of the real-balance effect focuses narrowly on
consumption. After a monetary contraction, for example, the increased MERs
on money held by firms make the MERs on new factories, machinery and other
capital goods (as well as goods in inventory) look relatively less attractive and
therefore depress investment.

Bernanke (1983) provides a useful insight. During the Great Depression,
financial intermediation was greatly impaired, with severe real effects on the
economy. Well, monetarists recognize that monetary disorder operates through
other channels besides the two of the Wicksell Process, including interference
with the channels of financial intermediation. However, the Wicksell Process
played a major role in the depression's financial crises. Indeed, Brunner and
Meltzer (1988, pp. 448–9) argue that the financial crises were endogenous
events, 'conditional on the monetary propagation mechanism'.

Both the direct and indirect channels of the Wicksell Process operate regardless of whether the counterpart of money supply contraction on the banks' balance sheets is a smaller volume of business and consumer loans or reduced holdings of government securities. We do not deny that the details and the intensity of the effect are influenced by the balance sheet counterparts of the monetary contraction. Under our current system, the initial impacts of a tightening of monetary policy may fall largely on bank-credit-dependent activities. This follows from our particular institutional structure. But it is illegitimate to downplay the importance of the quantity of money by a narrow focus on initial impact effects (see, for example, the many writings of Milton Friedman and David Laidler).

We must clarify an important but potentially confusing point. An excess demand for money following a decrease in the money supply does not imply that the direct channel of the Wicksell Process is operating. In both channels a fall in the money supply is met by an excess demand for money and an excess supply of commodities. However, in the indirect channel the excess demand for money first shows up as decreased spending on bonds, raising the interest rate, and thereby depressing the demand for commodities so that an excess supply of commodities occurs.

THE MONETARISTS' BLACK BOX

A charge often levied against monetarists is that they have not adequately described the process whereby changes in the money supply affect real income and prices. Monetarists, critics claim, work with a 'black box', leaving money to exert its effects in some mysterious way not specified in sectoral and sequential detail.

Yet the critics have not shown that a detailed or quantitative account of the transmission mechanism is an appropriate objective. What reason is there to suppose that the sequence and other details of how a monetary disturbance affects prices and activity in various sectors of an economy are the same at different times and places and under different technological and institutional conditions? The characteristics that different episodes of monetary disequilibrium do have in common, including the nature of obstacles to easy adjustment of money's value so as to restore equality between its demand and supply, may well not amount to anything reasonably described as a 'detailed' transmission process.

Monetary disequilibrium has widespread and diverse effects. The forces tending to restore a disturbed monetary equilibrium are diffused over the entire economic system for reasons already mentioned. If money's value is out of line with its quantity, if its desired and actual real quantities diverge, then 'things

will happen'. Precisely what things will happen depends on contingent circumstances, including those affecting the stickiness of prices and wages (see
Chapters 6, 7 and 8). As Milton Friedman has long insisted, the response to a
change in the money supply consists of *long and variable lags*. Moreover, while
monetarists do not place great importance on the first-round effects of a change
in the money supply, they do recognize that those initial impact effects vary
by episode. At the centerpiece of the monetarist transmission mechanism is the
Wicksell Process, operating through the two channels and three effects of each
channel. We would not expect these six overlapping aspects to produce the
same pattern of results in each and every episode.

It is the task of theory in any field, of course, to discern uniformities amidst
apparent diversity, but hardly to imagine uniformities in greater detail than the
subject matter admits of. We believe, though, that we have shone some light into
the monetarists' black box through our elaboration of the Wicksell Process.

THE MONETARY TRANSMISSION MECHANISM: THE CREDIT VIEW

Some articles have called into question what they call the 'money view' of the
monetary transmission mechanism and have offered an alternative 'credit view'.
Bernanke (1983, 1988, 1993, and Bernanke and Blinder, 1988) is one of the
leading proponents of the credit view. He presents (1993, p. 55) the 'conventional' interpretation of the money view:

1. The monetary authority sells bonds, reducing banks' reserves.
2. Banks decrease the money supply.
3. The deficiency of money raises interest rates.
4. Higher interest rates decrease aggregate demand.

Bernanke finds the money view, as he understands it, too weak to account
for the large effects of monetary policy on spending sometimes observed (1993,
p. 55). Bernanke and Gertler (1995), Cecchetti (1995) and Hubbard (1995)
emphasize that the alternative credit view actually consists of two channels:
'bank lending' and 'balance sheet'.

In the bank lending channel:

1. The monetary authority sells bonds, reducing banks' reserves.
2. Banks decrease the supply of loans to firms.
3. Bank-dependent firms curtail planned spending.

In the balance sheet channel, borrowers have better information than lenders, who charge a premium to compensate. This 'external finance premium' varies inversely with the firm's net worth. In this channel:

1. The monetary authority sells bonds, resulting in monetary contraction and higher interest rates.
2. Higher rates reduce firms' net worth since higher rates are usually associated with declining asset prices.
3. Lower net worth means firms have less collateral for loans, which raises their external finance premium.
4. Firms cut back on spending.

A burgeoning literature has attempted to determine empirically the importance of the credit view. Reviewing the literature on the bank lending channel, Thornton (1994, p. 48) finds the revived interest in that particular channel unusual, since financial innovation and deregulation should have eroded its strength.

The conventional money view presented by Bernanke is very narrow. The broad view that we embrace focuses instead on the two channels of the Wicksell Process, each operating through its three effects. Moreover, this view is compatible with other subchannels of the monetary transmission mechanism, including those mentioned in Bernanke's writings.

A MONETARIST VIEW OF A 'CREDIT CRUNCH'

The Gurley and Shaw literature (1960 and articles preceding that book) illuminates how extensions and improvements in financial intermediation favor real economic development. Conversely, reverse changes in financial intermediation, perhaps reflecting heightened caution on the part of banks, can impair economic activity. This disruption would be in the nature of a non-monetary or real disturbance as it operates on the supply side of the market for commodities by limiting the economy's productive capacity.

But how would a credit crunch operate on the side of spending or aggregate demand? In answering this question, we shall make use of the money-supply-and-demand framework. If the money supply remains unchanged, as we do suppose to distinguish between a credit shock and a money shock, then any decline in nominal spending presupposes a decline in desired velocity, that is, a rise in Cambridge k. The quantity of money demanded relative to income and expenditure must rise, perhaps because the worsened business conditions have made people more cautious and liquidity-minded. Again we observe that a deficiency of demand for commodities must realistically be associated with an excess demand for money. Our analysis provides another illustration of the usefulness of the translation test.

MONEY FINANCING vs. BOND FINANCING OF A BUDGET DEFICIT

We consider the difference between financing a government budget deficit by the issue of money and financing it by the issue of bonds. Since this difference is what concerns us, we may ignore the spending side of the deficit and simply compare adding new money and adding new bonds to total private holdings.

Alternatively, we are comparing the familiar thought experiment of a helicopter drop of new money with a similar drop of new government bonds. (Compare Tobin's quote on page 115 about a 'rain' of money or bonds.) This section further illuminates the differences between money and bonds.

In the case of money financing people desire to increase their spending on commodities and bonds. Because money is the medium of exchange, people can spend it without having to first convert it to something else. As the Wicksell Process runs its course, nominal income rises until money demand fully absorbs the increased supply. Far from being a constraint on income, bonds play a temporary expansionary role as people's increased demand for them lowers the interest rate and hence increases spending on commodities, though indirectly. It is implausible that money financing of a deficit would have a contractionary effect on nominal income.

Suppose instead that the financing occurs through the issue of bonds. Because bonds are a part of gross financial wealth in the sense of Gurley and Shaw (1960), bond recipients desire to spend part of their increased wealth on commodities. Unlike money, bonds are not a medium of exchange. Their recipients must first convert them to money on the bond market, thereby depressing bond prices and increasing the interest rate. The rise in the rate induces people to hold smaller cash balances than otherwise in relation to income and spending (Cambridge k decreases). The rise in desired velocity allows the increase in spending and nominal income to take place. In this manner, bond financing can stimulate economic activity.

On the other hand, if people desire money holdings positively related to the total sizes of their portfolios – if a wealth argument appears in the demand-for-money function – and if government bonds count as part of the gross wealth of the private sector (as following Gurley and Shaw we assume they do), then the additional bonds tend to increase desired holdings of money. Conceivably, if not very plausibly, this wealth effect tending to reduce the velocity of the (unchanged) money supply could outweigh the above-mentioned interest rate effect tending to increase it, resulting in a shrinkage of total spending and nominal income. In this case the fall in income chokes off an excess demand for money. The greater the role wealth plays in the demand function for money, the less far-fetched is the possibility that bond financing may be contractionary on balance.

We thus observe an asymmetry in the methods of financing the deficit. With money financing no decline in nominal income is plausible, since bonds are not a constraint on expansion. With bond financing the constant money supply is such a constraint. In the conceivable contractionary case, which we call 'the perverse result', the wealth-induced increase in money demand dominates any interest-induced decrease so nominal income actually falls. Whether this situation occurs or whether the bonds wind up being net wealth – that is, they increase spending and nominal income – is an economic question whose answer is reflected in the sizes and signs of the relevant partial derivatives given in the following algebraic model.

This model of bond financing focuses on the conditions that are necessary for the perverse result of a fall in nominal income.[12] We assume that the bonds are short-term obligations in order to abstract from the fringe complication in which the increased interest rate resulting from the bond sale reduces gross financial wealth by lowering the price of previously outstanding bonds. (Havrilesky and Boorman, 1978, p. 314n, assume all bonds are fixed-price variable coupon bonds in order to avoid this complication.) We also assume the economy starts at full-employment equilibrium. We use the following notation:

Y = nominal income.
B = nominal value of outstanding bonds.
M = nominal money supply.
$W = B + M$ = total nominal financial wealth.
r = the interest rate.

The small letters y, b and m signify amounts of commodities, bonds and money demanded and also serve as the functional symbols of the demand functions. When these letters contain subscripts, they become partial derivatives, whose economic meanings are *propensities*. For example, y_r is the partial derivative of the amount of commodities demanded with respect to the interest rate. The greater its absolute value, the greater is the fall in this amount for a given increase in the rate.

The following are the equilibrium conditions:

$$m(Y,r,W) = M \tag{1}$$
$$y(Y,r,W) = Y \tag{2}$$
$$b(Y,r,W) = B \tag{3}$$

Using differentials, we rewrite equation (1):

$$m_y dY + m_r dr + m_w dW = dM \qquad (4a)$$

where dB is positive; $dM = 0$; $dW = dB + dM = dB$. Rewriting yields:

$$m_y dY + m_r dr + m_w dB = 0 \qquad (4b)$$

Similarly, we rewrite equations (2) and (3):

$$y_y dY + y_r dr + y_w dB = dY \qquad (5)$$
$$b_y dY + b_r dr + b_w dB = dB \qquad (6)$$

Rewriting equation (4b) yields:

$$dY = (-1/m_y)\,(m_r dr + m_w dB) \qquad (7)$$

From (7) the very direction of change in Y, *nominal income*, depends on whether $m_r dr$ or $m_w dB$ is larger in absolute value – on whether the interest-induced decrease in money demand is greater or less than the wealth-induced increase in it. The very possibility of the perverse result depends on the existence of this wealth effect. If $m_w dB$ is greater in absolute value income decreases. The larger is m_y (the effect of nominal income on money demand), the more it dampens the change in income whether upward or downward. For example, the greater m_y is, the less is the decrease in nominal income needed to eliminate a given excess demand for money.

We gain further insight by solving for dY in terms of the exogenous dB and the partial derivatives that express propensities. That is, we solve for dy/dB in terms of those propensities alone.

Rewriting (4b), (5) and (6) gives:

$$m_y dY + m_r dr = -m_w dB \qquad \text{(money equation)} \qquad (8)$$
$$(y_y - 1)dY + y_r dr = -y_w dB \qquad \text{(commodities equation)} \qquad (9)$$
$$b_y dY + b_r dr = (1 - b_w)dB \qquad \text{(bond equation)} \qquad (10)$$

Because transactions are two-sided and the budget constraint applies, only two of the equations are independent. We therefore can solve for dY/dB using any two.[13] We choose to solve the commodities and money equations because the solution does not include bond propensities. Our reasons for avoiding them are given below. The likely signs for the propensities appear above them:[14]

$$dY/dB = \frac{\overset{+}{y_w}\overset{\pm}{m_r} - \overset{+}{m_w}\overset{\pm}{y_r}}{\underset{-}{m_r}(1 - \overset{+}{y_y}) + \overset{+}{m_y}\overset{\pm}{y_r}} = \frac{?}{-} \tag{11}$$

Since $dY/dB = ?/-$, the solution is negative, that is, the perverse result occurs, if the numerator is positive. The absolute value of $(y_w m_r)$ must be less than the absolute value of $(m_w y_r)$ for this result. Rewriting, we obtain our necessary condition: the absolute value of (m_r/m_w) must be less than the absolute value of (y_r/y_w). Nominal income *falls* if the interest sensitivity of money demand is slight, the wealth sensitivity of money demand is great, the interest sensitivity of spending is strong, and the wealth sensitivity of spending is weak. The following elaborates:

1. A weaker interest sensitivity of money demand implies a smaller decrease in money demand for a given increase in the interest rate, tending to diminish the rise in desired velocity. (We realistically assume the rate increases in the case of bond financing.)
2. A stronger propensity to devote increased wealth to money holding means a greater increase in money demand for a given rise in wealth, thereby tending to hold down the increase in desired velocity and even to promote its fall.
3. A stronger interest sensitivity of spending implies less spending on commodities for a given rise in the interest rate, tending to restrain the increase in nominal income and even to promote its fall.
4. A weaker propensity to devote increased wealth to spending means less spending on commodities for a given increase in wealth, tending to restrain the increase in income.

If we solve for dY/dB using either of the other two pairs of equations, we obtain ambiguous results because the solutions contain bond propensities. Interest sensitivities regarding money, bonds and commodities are interrelated as illustrated in note 14. The interest sensitivity of bond demand thus tends to be associated with a fall in income if it is accompanied by a relatively weak interest sensitivity of money demand and a strong interest sensitivity of spending. It tends to be associated with a rise in income under opposite conditions. Similarly, wealth sensitivities are interrelated as illustrated in note 14. The wealth sensitivity of bond demand tends to be associated with a fall in income if it is accompanied by a relatively strong wealth sensitivity of money demand and a relatively weak wealth sensitivity of spending. Under opposite conditions, it tends to be associated with a rise in income.

We thus observe another difference between bonds and money. The influences of interest and wealth sensitivities are ambiguous for bonds but not for money.

The foregoing analysis has further implications. On page 115 above we suppose a good fairy gives a country's inhabitants $1 billion worth of blankets. By increasing people's wealth and hence demand for money, this gift could conceivably lead to a decline in spending and income. The literature examines the effect of a rise in stock market prices and hence wealth on consumer spending (for example, see Poterba, 2000; Mehra, 2001 and Starr-McCluer, 2002). Yet the increase in wealth, through its influence on the demand for money, could conceivably lower spending and nominal income (compare Greenfield, 1994, pp. 14–16). Indeed, using quarterly data from 1961 to 1986, Friedman (1988) finds a positive relation between stock market wealth and the demand for money (defined as M2). He finds, however, that annual data for a longer period seem to contradict this result (Friedman, 1988, p. 239).

THE RICARDIAN EQUIVALENCE PROPOSITION

Controversy exists in the literature concerning the financing of a tax cut through the government's issue of bonds, a situation analogous to the helicopter bond drop. The 'Ricardian equivalence proposition' maintains that the additional bonds are not net wealth, which means they do not increase consumption, aggregate demand and hence income. People supposedly realize that bond-financed tax cuts will result in greater future tax liabilities in order to pay off the new debt as well as the interest payments on it. In essence, the expansionary effect of a tax decrease today is completely offset by saving in anticipation of the corresponding tax rise in the future. In terms of the public's balance sheet, the added bonds on the asset side are matched by expected future taxes on the liability side, leaving net wealth unchanged. People supposedly buy the new government bonds with their increased saving. Interest rates therefore do not change and no 'crowding out' of private spending occurs (see Seater, 1993, p. 145; Tobin, 1980b, p. 51).

Barro (1974) argues that people would still save the full amount of the tax cut even if the anticipated tax levies were shifted to future generations. Since people care about the well-being of their offspring, they would save the entire amount of the tax cut in order to leave bequests to them. The children would then be able to pay the future tax increase without cutting their consumption. The equivalence proposition derives its name because financing a new deficit with bonds or an alternative lump sum tax would have equivalent effects on income. That is, replacing bonds with an equal amount of taxes would have no impact on income.

Seater (1993, p. 184) reviews the literature and concludes that while the proposition is not literally true, it does appear to be a good approximation to reality. On the other hand, Stanley (1998) rejects the proposition by using a meta-analysis (quantitative review) of 28 empirical studies.

Our analysis, which focuses on the effect of increased wealth on the demand for money, offers an alternative explanation for the lack of stimulus that may follow a bond-financed tax cut. It is also more consistent with crowding out, since the interest rate rises in our model but remains constant according to the Ricardian equivalence proposition.

THE CONSENSUS MODEL OF MONETARY POLICY

The 'consensus model of monetary policy' that emerged in the literature contains three equations (Meyer, 2001; McCallum, 1999). The first is a version of the familiar IS curve in which the real interest rate affects spending and output. The second is a price-adjustment specification that is often referred to as the 'new Keynesian Phillips curve' (see page 137 below). The third equation stipulates a policy rule that is adhered to by the monetary authority. The policy instrument is a nominal interest rate set by the authority according to the rule. Taylor (1993) is the inspiration for this model, and economists refer to the 'Taylor rule' that supposedly describes the Federal Reserve's policy behavior over time. This model combines the rigorous techniques of real business cycle theory with the price stickiness proposition of new Keynesian economics. (Pages 169–70, 208–209 below describe both schools of thought.)

Conspicuously missing from the model is any mention of money. McCallum (2001) even speaks of 'monetary policy analysis in models without money'. According to Leeper and Zha (2001, p. 84), in this model money has no role at all to play in the setting or transmission of monetary policy; it is 'a sideshow'. A key assumption of the model is that the money supply is demand-determined by the public because the authority targets the interest rate. The authority simply accommodates the public's demand for money at this rate. One could add a fourth equation, an LM relation, that would include money supply and money demand. However, it would be redundant since it would just indicate how much money the authority supplies to meet the public's demand for it.

Meyer (2001, p. 3) and McCallum (1999, p. 7) note that the model used by the staff of the Federal Reserve Board of Governors is a large-scale version of the consensus model. Meyer further observes that monetary policy becomes totally ineffective in the model once the policy instrument, a nominal interest rate, hits the zero lower bound, as happened in Japan in the late 1990s.

Monetary-disequilbrium theory helps illuminate the many problems with the consensus model; here we concentrate on five major ones. First, monetary policy supposedly affects spending and nominal income only by first affecting the interest rate. The model completely overlooks the operation of the direct channel of the Wicksell Process. Second, at the zero lower bound interest rate, monetary policy becomes impotent because the economy is in the alleged 'liquidity trap'. Chapter 2 explains why the notion of the trap is untenable. People will not add unlimited amounts to their cash balances. Third, the model assumes that the money supply is 'demand-determined' because the authority targets the interest rate. Pages 118–20 above explain why this assumption is invalid. Fourth, the 'new Keynesian Phillips curve', the model's second equation, contradicts reality as Mankiw explains on page 231 below. Fifth, the policy rule diverts attention away from the fact that the monetary authority creates the inflation to which it is supposed to respond.

Japan's long bout with stagnation beginning in the early 1990s illustrates the model's problems. Japan's low (and sometimes zero) interest rate stemmed from a tight (contractionary) monetary policy and was a sign of a sick economy rather than of loose policy. (Pages 117–18 above argue that the interest rate can be a misleading indicator of monetary policy.) Contrary to the literature, no liquidity trap existed in Japan. The zero lower bound interest rate pertains to the bond or loan market and not to the nonexistent 'money market'; the narrow interest rate is the price of loans and not money. Japan may well have been in the quasi-equilibrium described in Chapter 3, in which the money supply is equal to the effective or actual stock demand for money, which has been reduced through poverty. But we question whether people's demand for money was 'satiated', as some economists claimed. Rather, Japan's sick economy reflected monetary disequilibrium, that is, an effective transactions-flow excess demand for money and a full-employment stock excess demand for money, as explained in Chapter 3. Both could have been removed through adequate expansion of the money supply. In short, Japan's deflation was a monetary phenomenon (compare Hetzel, 2003) .

Because of Japan's experience, fear of deflation spread to the United States. For example, Federal Reserve Board Governor Ben Bernanke addressed the issue of deflation in remarks before the National Economists Club in Washington D.C. on November 21, 2002. However, monetarists recognize the similarity between Japan's experience and that of the United States during the Great Depression (see Friedman, 1997). In both cases overemphasis on interest rates led to misguided policy and economic tragedy. Both economies would have recovered as the direct channel of the Wicksell Process operated following adequate monetary expansion.

The monetary authority could always increase the money supply, if necessary by spending it into existence. Because money is the medium of exchange, no one would refuse to accept it. As a last resort, the monetary authority could combine its efforts with the fiscal authority by having a tax cut financed through money creation, a situation analogous to the helicopter drop of new money (see pages 132–3 above).

NOTES

1. Keynes (1936, Chapter 17, especially pp. 230–32). Keynes puts his own emphasis on how an asset with the properties in question might hold the interest rate above the level at which investment would be adequate for full employment. He does not specifically draw the Walras's Law implications of an excess demand for money. For an example of concern with possible excess demand for nonmonetary assets, see Loeb (1946, pp. 93–4).
2. Morgan (1969) describes the first and second ways as well as the alternative described below that is peculiar to money.
3. The narrowly conceived wealth effect concerns how money affects spending only by being part of people's net wealth, as explained below.
4. Compare J.B. Say (1836, pp. 133–4), quoted in Chapter 1, page 19.
5. Miller and Struthers (1979, pp. 1–9, preceded by an approving introduction by Mark H. Willes, President of the Federal Reserve Bank of Minneapolis), and Miller (1980, pp. 2–4). The quotations come from page 2 in each of these publications. In a footnote to the latter, Miller cites other authors who also, he says, perceive the essential similarity of bonds and money. Also see N.J. Simler's letter to the *Wall Street Journal*, 10 August 1981, p. 19.
6. A similar line of argument concerns an open economy under fixed exchange rates, in which the domestic money supply is supposedly 'demand-determined'. The balance of payments acts as an equilibrating mechanism to assure this result. Chapters 3 and 9 provide counterexamples to this argument (compare Rabin and Yeager, 1982).
7. Laidler (1992 [1997a], p. 366) speaks of 'monetarism's unfinished business' of getting the money supply process back onto the monetary research agenda.
8. The distinction between outside and inside money was introduced by Gurley and Shaw (1960 and articles preceding that book).
9. Humphrey (1994, p. 71) argues that John Wheatley (1807, 1819), an overlooked classical monetary theorist, also had the idea of the Cambridge effect, although neither uses that name. Wheatley believed that monetary shocks affect only monetary variables (Humphrey, 1994, p. 70).
10. Zincone (1967, 1968) recognizes the two channels and three effects presented here. However, our exposition differs in numerous ways from his 1967 dissertation.
11. Patinkin's first edition (1956) contains a broad conception of the real-balance effect, while his second edition (1965) shifts emphasis to the narrow wealth-effect-only conception (Trescott, 1989; Zincone, 1967, Appendix ii). In passages departing from his usual narrow conception, Patinkin (1965, pp. 18, 83) calls the real-balance effect the inverse of the familiar demand for money. Moreover, on pages 294 and 298 he appears to recognize a portfolio-balance effect that operates only indirectly. An imbalance in the money market is matched by one in the bond market.
12. Meltzer and Brunner (1963) hint about how a bond-financed deficit could conceivably have a deflationary impact. Timberlake (1964) alludes to a similar possibility, though without necessarily claiming realism for it. Silber (1970) and Havrilesky and Boorman (1978) also recognize the possibility of the perverse result.
13. The model avoids the question of supply: how changes in nominal income are split between changes in output and prices. (That question is addressed in Chapters 6, 7 and 8.) One may therefore ask whether Walras's Law 'applies' in this model. Our response is twofold. Any model or theory that contradicts the Law must be wrong. In that sense the Law always applies. However, by neglecting the question of supply we cannot accurately describe the new 'equilibrium' situation. At one extreme, if the decrease in nominal income solely reflects a decrease in prices, the economy remains at full-employment equilibrium. At the other extreme, if the

decrease in nominal income solely reflects a decrease in output, then the quasi-equilibrium of Chapter 3 results.

14. Although different propensities (partial derivatives) appear in the different solutions to the three paired equations, no contradiction exists. The reason is that the economic meaning of the propensities requires them to be interrelated in such ways that the apparently different solutions are consistent with each other. The following illustrates the interrelations of the different propensities. Remember, each is a partial derivative of quantity demanded:

$$y_r + b_r + m_r = 0$$
$$y_w + b_w + m_w = 1$$
$$y_y + b_y + m_y = 1$$

5. Patinkin's monetary theory and extensions

PATINKIN'S CONTRIBUTION

We have been considering how money affects spending and how an excess demand for or excess supply of money weakens or strengthens demand relative to supply on the markets for individual goods and services and securities. All this reconciles with Patinkin's (1956, 1965) superficially rather different exposition of the 'strict' or 'rigid' quantity theory. (Pages 124–5 above distinguish between broad and strict versions of the theory; for the latter, it is necessary that only fiat money exists.) Going beyond mere mechanics and algebraic tautologies, his work explains the role of the real-balance effect in the logic of the theory. It builds bridges between macroeconomics and microeconomics, tracing macro phenomena of prices and incomes back to the decisions of individual economic units. Along with presenting his positive analysis, Patinkin clears up some inconsistencies in earlier monetary theory.

Patinkin shows that several assumptions apparently necessary for the strict quantity theory are not in fact necessary. For example, omission of the interest rate from Fisher's equation of exchange seems to presuppose that that rate does not affect the demand for or velocity of money. Actually, the theory requires no such assumption. The conditions that *are* necessary are not fully met in the real world, which helps explain why the quantity theory does not hold *rigidly* true. Yet the forces Patinkin describes, notably the real-balance effect, do indeed operate in reality.

COMPARATIVE STATICS

At one stage of his exposition, Patinkin (1954, pp. 132–4) presents a comparative-static analysis of the equilibriums corresponding to two different nominal quantities of fiat money. Following that exposition, and postponing review of the necessary assumptions, we write equations for equilibrium in the markets for the four groups into which all exchangeable items are aggregated – commodities (including services), labor, bonds and money. Besides symbols for the demand and supply functions, the following symbols appear:

Y_0 = full-employment output of commodities (that is, full-employment real income).
p = price level.
w = money wage rate.
r = interest rate.
M_0 = exogenously given initial nominal quantity of money.

The following are the equations:

$$F(Y_0, M/p, r) = Y_0 \qquad \text{Commodity equilibrium} \qquad (1)$$
$$N^d(w/p) = N^s(w/p) \qquad \text{Labor equilibrium} \qquad (2)$$
$$B^d(Y_0, M/p, r) = B^s(Y_0, M/p, r) \quad \text{Bond equilibrium} \qquad (3)$$
$$pL(Y_0, M/p, r) = M_0 \qquad \text{Money equilibrium} \qquad (4)$$

Equation (1) shows full-employment output equal to full-employment demand for commodities, which depends on full-employment real income, real money balances and the interest rate. Equation (2) shows labor equilibrium, demand and supply both depending on the real wage rate. More elaborate labor supply and demand functions would not affect the analysis. Equation (3) expresses equilibrium between demand for and supply of bonds, each expressed in real terms and depending on full-employment real income, real money balances, and the interest rate. Equation (4) shows that real money balances demanded depend, according to the L( ) function, on real income, real balances themselves and the interest rate. Nominal balances demanded are real balances demanded multiplied by the price level. They are equal in equilibrium to the nominal money supply.

By Walras's Law, if supply and demand are in equilibrium for any three of the four markets, then they must be in equilibrium for the fourth market also. If any three of the equilibrium conditions are written in explicit functional form, complete with numerical coefficients, then they together already imply the fourth one in complete detail; and writing it explicitly would add no new information. Writing all four equations does no harm provided we remember that only three of them are mathematically independent.

If the four equations are satisfied for quantity of money M_0, price level p_0, wage rate w_0, and interest rate r_0, then, when the quantity of money is multiplied by k and becomes kM_0, the equations are satisfied at price level, wage rate and interest rate of kp_0, kw_0 and r_0. This result is obvious from inspecting the equations after making the indicated substitutions. In the new equilibrium, prices and wages have changed in the same proportion as the quantity of money and the interest rate is unchanged.

Patinkin (1965) assumes perfect competition throughout his analysis. The economy starts in 'general equilibrium', which implies that all markets are clearing. After a change in the money supply, it again winds up in general equilibrium. Only prices change during the adjustment process, with output held constant at its full-employment level. Since Patinkin is mainly concerned with the forces at work that restore the economy to its general-equilibrium level, he is able to avoid the complications that arise in discussing the disequilibrium of depression (and that are highlighted in chapters 3 and 4). For example, he need not worry about the distinction between stocks and flows, which is so crucial in understanding the depths of depression. Similarly, he need not distinguish between output and supply, since the economy remains at full-employment output.[1]

REAL BALANCES

The M_0/p_0 term appearing in the commodity, bond and money equations (and, after the money supply change, kM_0/kp_0, which has the same value) is the real value of money balances held. Patinkin's 'real-balance effect' is the dependence of demands and supplies in the markets for commodities, bonds and money itself on this term, the purchasing power size of the money supply. If some exogenous disturbance were to shrink real balances, then people being poorer than before on that account would be inclined to economize on purchases of commodities and even on real money holdings themselves and would probably desire smaller creditor and larger debtor positions in real size. (Fuller discussion of this effect, interpreted more broadly as the Wicksell Process, came earlier. That real balances form part of people's wealth is not the whole story.)

The real-balance term could have been left out of the commodity or bond or money equation without upsetting the comparative-static proposition about proportionality of prices and wages to the money supply. We did leave that term out of the labor equation, although we could have included it. Empirically, it is highly plausible that a real-balance effect operates in the commodity market. Its operation there is not strictly necessary, however, for the quantity theory result. An increase in the nominal quantity of money not yet matched by price increases could conceivably stimulate the demand for bonds relative to the supply, *temporarily* depressing the interest rate and so stimulating spending on commodities until prices had risen in proportion to the quantity of money after all and real balances were no longer larger than originally.

The real-balance effect must operate in some market if the quantity theory is to hold. If it operated nowhere – neither directly in the commodity or labor market nor indirectly there through the bond market and the interest rate – then an increase in the nominal quantity of money would leave the initial equilibrium undisturbed in each market. No pressures would be working to change the price and wage levels or the interest rate. To reflect this absence, the money equation would be written to show a plastic and passive demand for real balances, that is, a demand for nominal balances accommodating itself to the actual nominal quantity regardless of the price and wage level. Under those conditions, furthermore, even apart from any change in the quantity of money, the price level would be indeterminate, in neutral equilibrium. Any arbitrary or accidental fall or rise, spelling a rise or fall in real balances, would leave behavior unaffected on all markets and so would exert no pressure for its own reversal. Such a total absence of the real-balance effect is empirically unbelievable.

If the real-balance effect operates anywhere, as empirically it must, then it must operate in the markets for at least two things. Equilibrium cannot be disrupted at the old price in one market alone. Walras's Law provides the reason. Market transactions are two-sided: one thing exchanges for another.

This point about at least two markets may seem to require one qualification. Patinkin (1965, p. 514) imagines a far-fetched case in which 'the real-balance effect is dissipated entirely in increasing the demand for money balances'. The real-balance effect 'operates exclusively in the market for money', assuring continuous monetary equilibrium. (Compare our description above of a passive money demand function resulting in neutral equilibrium and price level indeterminacy.) Patinkin's exceptional case is the Keynesian liquidity trap. All additions to wealth through increments to real balances are devoted to nothing else than acquiring those additional real balances. But is it correct to say that the real-balance effect is 'operating' even when it is 'dissipated' as Patinkin says by being confined to 'the market for money'? The issue is purely semantic. Although the case in question is empirically unbelievable, it is worth mentioning because it illuminates reality by the contrast it presents.

NECESSARY AND UNNECESSARY ASSUMPTIONS

The key assumption necessary for Patinkin's comparative-static result – strict proportionality of the price level to the money supply – is absence of money illusion. Before explaining what that means, let us review the more familiar assumptions. Some are routinely made in theorizing of this general type, such as that an initial equilibrium exists, that stable functional relations hold among the variables and that extraneous disturbances do not occur. Strict price/money proportionality presupposes, further, that no distributional effects occur, or that if any do occur, they cancel each other out. In actuality, increases in the money supply and the price level (unexpected increases, anyway) do redistribute real wealth away from creditors toward debtors, making creditors economically weaker and debtors economically stronger in expressing their tastes in market transactions. Unless the tastes of the two groups happen, by fantastic coincidence, to be similar in just the right way, not merely the price level but also the pattern of relative prices undergoes at least some change. Perfect indexing of all debts to prices in the first place would avoid these particular distribution effects. Other distribution effects occur because increases in the quantity of money cannot occur uniformly in practice. Some people receive the new money relatively early or benefit from a lag in price increases of things they buy behind those of things they sell; others suffer in opposite positions. In other discussions, such effects are important; but Patinkin justifiably abstracts from what are mere fringe complications for his exposition of the bare logic of the quantity theory. The complications of reality can be better understood through comparison with the extreme case of their absence.

In his comparative statics, Patinkin does not *assume* that the real or nominal flow of spending on commodities is proportional to the total of real or nominal money balances held. Those propositions are true, but they follow as conclusions instead of being needed as assumptions. The distinction between individual and market experiments helps clarify this remark. In the individual experiment, people do not necessarily exercise demand for commodities in proportion to their holdings of real or nominal cash balances. A doubling of the money supply, ceteris paribus, would probably not exactly double desired nominal spending. In the market experiment, however, we increase the money supply and inquire into the nature of the new equilibrium position. The resulting change of prices in proportion to money, with relative prices and real quantities remaining unchanged, means that all nominal money magnitudes, including total purchases of commodities evaluated at their money prices, change in the same proportion (see Patinkin, 1954, pp. 147–8). This proposition is a result, not an assumption, of the analysis.

Patinkin also needs no assumptions about the strength of the real-balance effect. How strong the upward pressures are that an increased nominal (and temporarily increased real) money supply exerts upon commodity prices is unimportant to the comparative statics. Those pressures might be feeble and work slowly. They might even work only indirectly, through the interest rate, as in the unrealistic case of a commodity demand function lacking any real-balance term. Even so, prices would not come to rest before reaching the level that made actual and demanded real quantities of money equal again at their original level. The question of how quickly and easily a new monetary equilibrium is reached is different from the questions of comparative statics.

Just as Patinkin need not assume any specific strength of the real-balance effect in the commodity market or any specific form of the commodity demand function, so he need not assume any specific form of the demand-for-money

function. For example, he can recognize the influence of the interest rate on
the demand for money. It is no paradox to say that the quantity of money
demanded depends on the interest rate but that the interest rate does not depend
on the quantity of money. The first proposition relates to an individual
experiment, the second to a market experiment (see pages 113–14 above). When
a change in the quantity of money has completed its effects, the interest rate will
have returned to its original level and so will not lead people to demand real
balances different from those initially held. (Compare pages above in which
we allude to 'temporary' changes in the rate during the adjustment process.)

Patinkin can also recognize motives beyond the transactions-precautionary
motive for holding money even in equilibrium. Contrary to what Keynes seemed
to suggest (1936, pp. 208–9), it is not necessary to rule out the 'speculative'
motive in equilibrium. People may indeed hold 'idle' cash balances. What is
important is that they be concerned with their real sizes.

Finally, it is unnecessary for Patinkin to assume away rigidities *as such*. The
assumed absence of money illusion already rules out, for example, workers'
stipulating for wages in nominal terms instead of being solely concerned with
real wages. It rules out anyone's insisting on a particular nominal price for a
commodity regardless of other prices.

Now we must explain 'money illusion' and its absence. People suffer from
it if their behavior depends in some respects on the mere numbers – the nominal
money magnitudes – attached to the real situation confronting them, quite apart
from what those numbers mean for the realities. If, for example, all prices,
incomes, holdings of money and other financial assets, and all debts should
double in nominal money terms, leaving relative prices, real incomes, real
money holdings and all other realities quite unchanged, and if people nevertheless altered the real quantities of things that they attempted to exchange on
the markets, they would be suffering from money illusion. People are illusion-
free if a change affecting neither relative prices, the rate of interest, real income,
nor the real values of money holdings and other assets and debts leaves all real
aspects of economic behavior unchanged, the only difference being the height
of the nominal money magnitudes attached to those unchanged realities. People
free of illusion *will* react to real changes, including changes in real cash
balances, whether brought about by a change in the nominal money supply or
by a change in the absolute price level.

Of course, people are not totally free of money illusion in the sense defined;
and it helps in understanding the concept to review the bits of illusion that do
exist in reality – such as the requirement for reporting automobile accidents
causing damage above a stated dollar amount and the income tax brackets
formerly (before indexing) defined by dollar amounts. The relevance of Patinkin's
analysis depends only on people's being *essentially* free of money illusion, with
its real-world examples making the analysis fuzzy only at the fringes.

If people are substantially free of money illusion, a change in the quantity of money not directly matched by a change in the demand for it must lead, somehow, to a corresponding change in the price level. Similarly, a change in the real purchasing power quantity of money demanded (perhaps because of real economic growth), if not satisfied by a change in the nominal quantity of money, must cause a change in the price level. Otherwise, people would be holding larger or smaller money balances than they desired and would be trying to adjust them in the way described by Wicksell. Pressures would be at work on the price level until it had risen or fallen enough to make people content, after all, with their nominal money holdings.

THE PROCESS UNDERLYING THE QUANTITY THEORY

By now we have gone beyond comparative statics. Patinkin examines the process of response to a changed quantity of money. He assumes that output remains at the full-employment level, leaving prices as the variable that responds. Figure 5.1 represents the real aggregate demand for commodities as depending on real balances and other variables. Line 0, as well as the similar lines in shifted positions, slopes upward from left to right to represent the real

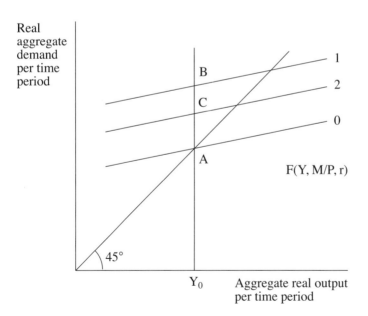

Figure 5.1   Aggregate real output and alternative demands for commodities

demand for output as depending partly on real income itself. Line 0 represents the aggregate demand function for the initial nominal and real money balances. A vertical line at Y_0 reflects the assumption of full-employment output. Point A portrays initial equilibrium between aggregate demand and output.

Now the government engages in deficit spending financed by issuing new money. The shift of the F( ) function line to position 1 represents the strengthening of real aggregate demand. Distance AB represents excess demand in the commodity market. Next the government discontinues its deficit spending, and aggregate demand falls to position 2. It does not yet fall all the way back to position 0, since the already issued new money remains in circulation; and since prices have not yet risen fully in proportion, real balances are larger and are making the demand for commodities stronger than in the initial situation. Excess demand of AC remains and exerts continuing upward pressure on prices. Eventually, though, prices rise enough to reduce real money balances to their initial level, and commodity demand is back in position 0. So precise an outcome is an oversimplification, of course; but the points being made about the nature of the process remain qualitatively valid. In actuality, the government deficit spending would itself be a change in the realities of the situation, and it would cause distribution effects.

If the rise of prices were at one stage to overshoot the mark, then real balances would be lower than initially, and negative excess demand for commodities would bring the overshot prices down to their new equilibrium level.

In principle, the interest rate enters into the adjustment process. Before prices have caught up with the expanded money supply, people want to unload their excessive real balances not only in buying commodities but also in buying bonds. Their actions depress the interest rate, which further stimulates the demand for commodities in accordance with the F( ) function. But as the rise in prices continues to erode real balances, it also reverses the strengthening of demand for bonds that had temporarily depressed the interest rate, which now recovers.

A stage in the adjustment process is barely conceivable at which prices have not yet fully responded to the increased nominal money supply but at which the increased real balances are being fully demanded, quite in accordance with the demand-for-money function, because the interest rate is depressed (temporarily). With the demand for and supply of money again in equilibrium, why doesn't the process simply come to a halt? The answer is that the monetary equilibrium is merely a partial equilibrium. The bond and commodity markets remain out of equilibrium. In particular, the depressed interest rate continues causing excess demand in the commodity market. Prices and the rate undergo further change, disrupting the temporary and partial monetary equilibrium. Monetary equilibrium in this model cannot be fully restored except as part of a general equilibrium of all markets.

As noted on pages 102–107, an excess demand for commodities matched solely by an excess supply of bonds but not of money, as in the above partial monetary equilibrium, is paradoxical. If such a situation did occur, the flexibility of bond prices and interest rates would tend to come into play, eliminating any excess supply of bonds unaccompanied by an excess supply of money. Moreover, the situation is implausible for another reason: how can a low interest rate stimulate the demand for commodities if people are frustrated in getting all the loans they want at that rate? (Recall that an excess supply of bonds is equivalent to an excess demand for loans.) Ordinarily we think that a low rate is stimulatory because it indicates cheap availability of credit, but things are different if the low rate is a disequilibrium rate and credit is in short supply. Realistically, any excess demand for goods would be accompanied by at least some excess supply of money, even if along with an excess supply of bonds as well.

PATINKIN'S DIAGRAMMATICS

Figure 5.2, presented earlier as Figure 4.1, includes lines (not necessarily straight ones) representing pairs of price level and interest rate that equate supply and demand for each of the three composite goods into which we now aggregate all

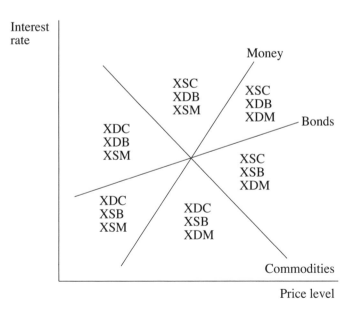

Figure 5.2   Conditions of equilibrium

the goods of the economy. These composites are commodities-and-labor
(hereafter called simply 'commodities'), bonds and money.[2] A point on one
line alone represents partial equilibrium in its market. The intersection of all
three lines represents general equilibrium. Regions of excess demand are labeled
XDC, XDB and XDM for commodities, bonds and money, respectively; XSC,
XSB and XSM indicate excess supplies. The diagram presupposes a fixed
nominal quantity of money (as well as given real conditions affecting the supply
of commodities); changes in the quantity of money must be represented by
shifts in the lines, as will be explained.

   Why the disequilibrium regions are as they are and why the lines slope as they
do may be explained together. Starting from a position of equilibrium on the
commodity line, consider a horizontal move, representing an arbitrary increase
in the price level with no change (yet) in the interest rate. The attendant fall in
the real value of the given nominal money supply dampens the demand for
commodities, leaving them in excess supply. Since the demand for commodities responds to the interest rate also – inversely – a sufficient fall in that rate
would restore commodity equilibrium, a partial equilibrium, at a new point on
the line southeast of the original point.

   Next consider a rightward move from a point on the bond line. The decline
in real balances thus represented is supposed to dampen the demand for bonds
in real terms, and the squeeze on real liquidity might also increase desired
borrowings. Bonds would thus be in excess supply unless a rise in the interest
rate achieved a new (partial) equilibrium at a point on the bond line northeast
of the initial point.

   While excess supplies appear to the right and excess demands to the left of
both the commodity and bond lines, the reverse is true of the money line. To
the right of it, the shrinkage of real balances has caused an excess demand for
money. It could be removed by a sufficient rise in the opportunity cost of
holding money, the interest rate; thus the line slopes northeastward.

   We may see in two ways why the money line slopes upward more steeply
than the bond line. First, it is reasonable that equilibrium or disequilibrium in
a given market should depend more sensitively on the price prevailing there
than on the price in another market. The diagram represents this condition by
the bond line's being more nearly perpendicular to the interest rate axis and the
money line's being more nearly perpendicular to the price level axis. (The
narrow interest rate is the price established in the bond or loan market as argued
in Chapter 4. While money has no single price or market, we view money's
price as its purchasing power, represented here by its reciprocal – the commodity
price level.) Starting from the general-equilibrium intersection, consider a
rightward move, representing a rise in the price level that causes disequilibrium for both bonds and money (as well as for commodities). Now, the rise in
the interest rate required to re-equilibrate the bond market is smaller than the

rise required to re-equilibrate money. Relative to the influence of the price level, the interest rate evokes a more sensitive response in the bond market than in the money market, which is eminently reasonable.

The second explanation notes that if the relation were the reverse of the one shown, it would violate Walras's Law. If the bond line sloped upward more steeply than the money line, then the diagram would contain a sector of commodities, bonds and money all being in excess demand and a sector of all three being in excess supply. The reader should check this assertion.

A CHANGED QUANTITY OF MONEY

The solid and the dashed lines in Figure 5.3 represent equilibrium conditions for an original and a doubled nominal quantity of money. At each level of the interest rate, the horizontal distance out to each new line is twice the distance to the corresponding old line. This construction reflects the absence of money illusion and of distribution effects. If a particular market was initially in equilibrium at a rate r_0, nominal money supply M_0, and price level p_0, then that market is again in equilibrium at r_0, $2M_0$ and $2p_0$, for the rate and real balances are both the

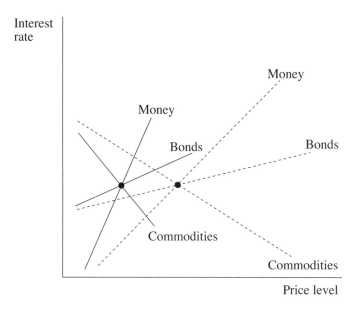

Figure 5.3   Equilibrium conditions for an original and a doubled nominal quantity of money

same as before. The new general-equilibrium point occurs at the initial interest rate and a doubled price level. The diagram illustrates the comparative statics of the strict quantity theory under the assumptions necessary for it.

THE TRANSITION PROCESS

The diagram can also show something about the path of adjustment. To avoid clutter, Figure 5.4 omits the initial equilibrium lines and shows only their point of intersection. The new lines, being the only ones shown, may now be drawn solid, leaving dashes for the transition path. Since any two equilibrium lines suffice to locate the general-equilibrium intersection, we omit the money line. The labeling of the four sectors indicates whether commodities and bonds are in excess demand or excess supply. The east and west sectors do not violate Walras's Law, since the money disequilibrium in each is the opposite of the commodity and bond disequilibrium. The horizontal and vertical arrows indicate market pressures on the price level and interest rate. In the north sector, for example, the excess supply of commodities is pushing the price level down, while the excess demand for bonds is pushing the interest rate down.

The old general-equilibrium point lies in the sector of excess demand for both commodities and bonds with respect to the lines drawn for the doubled quantity of money. The upward pressure on commodity prices and downward pressure on the interest rate combine, diagrammatically, into a southeastward

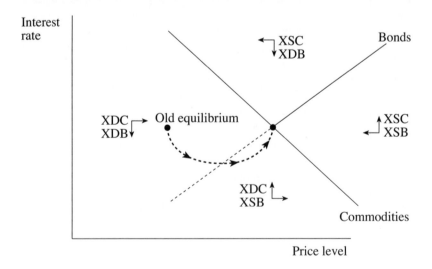

Figure 5.4   The transition after a doubling of the nominal quantity of money

movement along the dashed path. The path is horizontal where it crosses the sectoral boundary, reflecting the absence of direct pressure on the interest rate at that point. Once in the south sector, the point tracing the transition path moves northeastward. It might move directly to the new general-equilibrium point, as drawn in the diagram, or it might spiral towards that point through the east and north sectors. If the path did cross the commodity line, it would do so in a vertical direction, reflecting absence of direct pressure on the price level *on* that sectoral boundary. Either directly or with spirals, the path reaches the equilibrium point of a doubled price level and unchanged interest rate.

As the dashed path shows, the rate first falls under the pressure of the expanded money supply on the bond or loan market and then recovers as the rise of the price level erodes real money balances back towards their original level. This interest rate movement is quite intelligible in terms of people's behavior, is amply illustrated in history, and was described in detail by John Stuart Mill over a century ago.[3]

CHANGES IN UNDERLYING CONDITIONS

Patinkin's apparatus helps analyze the consequences of changes in tastes. The shift from the solid to the dashed position of the line in each of the three parts of Figure 5.5 represents a strengthening of the taste for (or of demand for relative to supply of) commodities, bonds and money. The horizontal component of the shift is rightward for commodities and bonds but leftward for money. Any point on the old commodity line, representing a combination of price level and interest rate that formerly equilibrated the commodity market, now lies in a region of excess demand. To eliminate the excess demand, a rise in the price level (which shrinks real balances) or a rise in the interest rate, or some combination of each, is necessary; hence the northeastward shift of the line. In the bond market, eliminating the excess demand now prevailing at any point on the old line requires a fall in the interest rate or a rise in the price level (which shrinks real balances, reducing the demand for bonds relative to supply). Removing the excess demand for money requires either a fall in the price level, increasing real balances, or a rise in the interest rate – the opportunity cost of holding money.

In a complete diagram, a shift of any one line must be accompanied by a shift of one or both of the others to make a new common intersection possible. This relation has economic meaning. Tastes or other circumstances cannot change, initially disequilibrating one market, without initially disequilibrating one or both other markets as well. For example, people's tastes cannot shift away from commodities – from current consumption, which means increased thriftiness – without by that very token shifting in favor of some vehicle of thrift, namely, bonds or money.

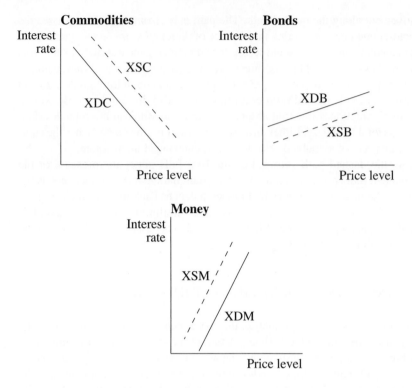

Figure 5.5   Intensification of demands for commodities, bonds and money

FURTHER EXAMPLES OF THE APPARATUS AT WORK

Figure 5.6 represents an increase in thrift in favor of both bonds and money. Comparison of the general-equilibrium intersections shows declines in both the price level and the interest rate. The rate declines because of increased thrift and strengthened demand for bonds; money gains purchasing power because of strengthened demand for it.

Figure 5.7 shows no change in tastes for commodities – in thrift – but a simple shift in tastes away from bonds and toward money. Nevertheless, the rate changes: it rises. This result in no way vindicates the liquidity preference theory of interest. Instead of being purely monetary, the change has occurred in the underlying realities of the situation, specifically, in tastes. With bonds now considered less attractive than before to hold in comparison with money, the reward for holding bonds and opportunity cost of holding money must rise to maintain equilibrium. The fall in the price level – rise in real balances – is

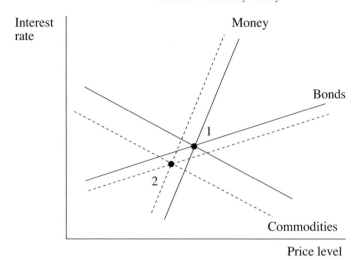

Figure 5.6   Shift of demand from commodities toward bonds and money

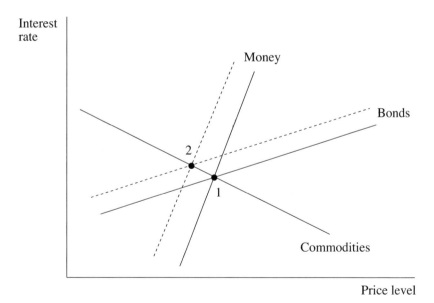

Figure 5.7   Shift of demand from bonds toward money

appropriate to the shift in tastes toward money. In the commodity market, the rise in real balances offsets the tendency toward excess supply created by the rise in the interest rate.

Patinkin (1965, p. 249) uses the term 'Keynesian case' to describe the situation portrayed above in which the increase in liquidity preference is solely at the expense of bonds. However, not every increase in the demand for money results in a rise in the interest rate. If liquidity preference strengthens solely (or mainly) at the expense of commodities, as in Figure 5.8, the price level and interest rate both fall. An increase in liquidity preference that raises the rate 'must be one which in some sense is at the expense of bond holdings more than at the expense of commodities' (Patinkin, 1965, p. 248). In what Patinkin calls the 'classical' case, an increase in liquidity preference is neutral, affecting the desirability of both bonds and commodities relative to money but not that of bonds and commodities relative to each other. In this case, portrayed in Figure 5.9, the price level falls and the equilibrium rate remains unchanged.

For a final example of the apparatus at work, Figure 5.10 portrays a case already used (page 47) to illustrate the translation test. Inventions or improved 'animal spirits' have raised business firms' assessments of the rate of return obtainable on investments in capital goods. Their intensified demands for capital goods and for the resources with which to construct them account for a strength-

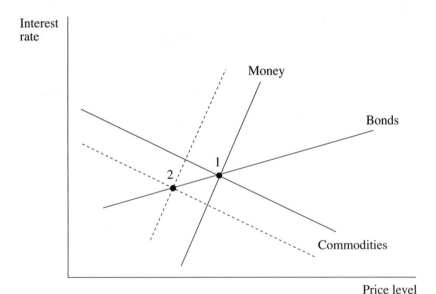

Figure 5.8   Shift of demand from commodities toward money

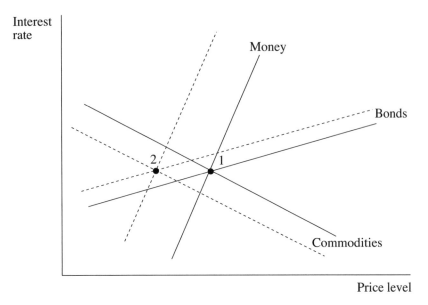

Figure 5.9   Shift of demand from commodities and bonds toward money

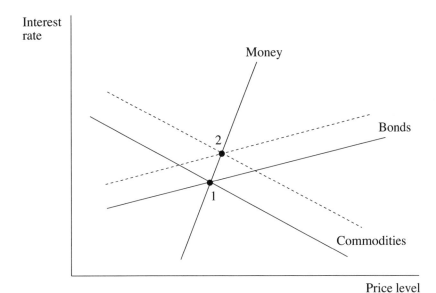

Figure 5.10   Intensification of (investment) demand for commodities and of supply of bonds

ening of total demand for commodities and labor. They desire to issue more bonds to finance the capital investment. Hence the commodity and bond lines shift as shown. Tastes for money have not directly changed, and the new general-equilibrium intersection lies on the unshifted money line. Comparison shows a rise in the price level and interest rate both. An increase in the reward for thrift is appropriate to the situation supposed. This rise in the opportunity cost of holding money has reduced Cambridge k quite in accordance with an unchanged money demand function; increased velocity of the unchanged nominal money supply accounts for the higher price level. The supposed underlying changes also result in a changed mix of production – more investment goods and less consumption goods – but Patinkin's apparatus is not designed to display that sort of change.

In later chapters we shall reinterpret Patinkin's diagrammatics for use beyond the narrow context in which pressures in the commodity market are supposed to impinge only on the price level and not on quantities traded and produced. Changes in the price level may be regarded as symptomatic of changes in nominal income, leaving for further investigation how these nominal changes are split between price and quantity changes.

PATINKIN'S CRITIQUE OF NEOCLASSICAL MONETARY THEORY

Patinkin clears up some inconsistencies in neoclassical monetary theory after showing that its expositors embraced two related fallacies, the 'invalid dichotomy' and the 'homogeneity postulate'. (Patinkin, 1965, pp. 174–5, indicts Walras, Fisher, Pigou, Cassel, Divisia, Lange, Modigliani, Schneider and others.)

Following Patinkin (1965, p. 174) and in line with earlier literature, we assume an economy with commodities and money but not bonds. The dichotomy separates the economy into two sectors, real and monetary. It supposes that relative prices are determined in the real sector, while the price level is determined in the monetary sector. We may restate this dichotomy in terms of excess-demand functions. The excess-demand function for a good represents the aggregate amount of positive and negative desired changes in initial holdings as depending on various prices; in equilibrium this amount is zero. This is true in a simple model of a productionless exchange economy, anyway. In a production economy, the excess-demand quantity is the difference between total desired purchases and total desired sales of the good. According to the invalid dichotomy, the real sector is described by the excess-demand functions for commodities, in which only relative prices appear as arguments.

The monetary sector is described by the excess-demand function for money, in which not only relative prices but also the absolute price level appear.

The dichotomy embraces the homogeneity postulate, which states that the excess-demand functions of all commodities are homogeneous of degree zero in prices, meaning that quantities demanded and supplied depend on relative prices only and not on the absolute price level.[4] An equivalent statement is that excess demands for commodities are unaffected by real cash balances. For if, with a given nominal money supply, an equiproportionate change in all prices does not affect the commodity markets – since it does not affect relative prices – then the change entailed in real cash balances does not affect those markets either.

The neoclassical writers evidently did not recognize that the homogeneity postulate and the invalid dichotomy contradict the quantity theory. To see how, suppose that the postulate and dichotomy were valid. Starting from general equilibrium, an arbitrary doubling of all prices would not affect any of the excess-demand functions in the real sector and so would not disturb the equilibrium in the commodity markets. By Walras's Law, the money market would also remain in equilibrium, since we have assumed an economy without bonds. The absolute price level would be indeterminate, since if any set of prices were an equilibrium set, any multiple of that set would also provide equilibrium as relative prices remained unchanged. Each of the infinitely many possible equilibria would be a 'neutral' equilibrium, with no forces working to reverse deviations from it. This situation contradicts the quantity theory, which envisages a unique equilibrium level of prices *for a given nominal quantity of money*.

To probe this contradiction further, we introduce the 'mirror image' excess-demand function for money. By Walras's Law, the excess demand for money must be equal in size but opposite in sign to the aggregate value of excess demands for all nonmoneys. In particular, if the aggregate excess demand value for all things but money depends on all prices in a specific way, then the excess demand for money, with opposite sign, must depend on all those prices in exactly the same way. Detailed and correctly written excess-demand functions for all things but money also implicitly specify the excess-demand function for money itself; making the implication explicit is simply a matter of mathematics. The resulting mirror image excess-demand function for money and the excess-demand functions for all other things reflect each other. If the markets for each individual thing except money were in equilibrium at a definite set of prices, the excess demand for money would necessarily be zero also.

If the 'homogeneity postulate' held true – if the markets for nonmoneys were unresponsive to the absolute price level – then any set of relative prices that equilibrated all these other markets would necessarily make the demand for and supply of money equal also. The absolute price level would be indeterminate.

Valavanis (1955), echoed by Ackley (1961) and Tsiang (1966), interpret this result as leaving room for a separate Cambridge or Fisher equation representing determination of the absolute price level. According to Valavanis (1955, pp. 356–61, 366–7), the mirror image excess-demand function for money, instead of describing decisions and behavior regarding money, just passively reflects commodity-market behavior; hence it is not contradicted by a quantity theory equation grafted onto the system. Valavanis contends (in Tsiang's paraphrase, 1966, p. 334n) that the mirror image function is 'totally different from the kind of demand for money shown in the quantity equation'. Valavanis and Tsiang apparently mean that the commodity functions describe what are fundamentally supplies and demands occurring *as if* in a barter economy, with money a mere lubricant of exchanges, and that it is pointless if not downright illegitimate to infer a mirror image function for money from the commodity-market functions.

Accepting for the sake of argument Patinkin's interpretation of the mirror image condition implied by the homogeneous commodity functions as saying that no particular price level is necessary for monetary equilibrium and that any absolute price level will do if relative prices are correct, the Valavanis camp replies that the additional Cambridge or Fisher equation 'selects' from the innumerable price levels compatible with the mirror image the one particular price level that provides equilibrium *for a given quantity of money* (see, in particular, Ackley, 1961, p. 123). At that price level the quantity of money is just adequate, especially in view of institutionally determined transactions 'needs'.

All this is a misconception. The contemplated mirror image equation, which sets the excess-demand function equal to zero to specify monetary equilibrium, leaves no room for selecting out a specific price level. It does not say that any price level will do as far as it itself is concerned and that further information is necessary to specify the equilibrium price level. Instead, it flatly denies that any particular price level characterizes equilibrium. Selection of a particular equilibrium price level contradicts and does not merely supplement the mirror image. It is no answer to dismiss the mirror image equation as a mere armchair implication of the commodity equations. If these equations refer to human decisions and desired market behavior, then anything they mathematically imply must do so just as fully. How can people's behavior regarding money be affected by the absolute price level unless their behavior regarding supplies and demands for other things is also affected by it? After all, each transaction involves not only money but also some other thing.

Rather than accept homogeneous commodity excess-demand functions whose mirror image implies indeterminacy of the absolute price level, we must realize that the excess demands for commodities do indeed depend to some extent on the absolute price level, given the quantity of money, and not merely on relative prices. An equivalent statement is that those excess demands also depend on the real money supply. Then the corresponding mirror image excess-demand equation for money does not imply indeterminacy, and any supposed distinction between it and an additional monetary equation simply vanishes. Properly formulated, the two equations amount to the same thing and cannot contradict each other. The most that could be made of the distinction would be to conceive of the Cambridge or Fisher equation as a sort of simplification or condensation of the correct mirror image equation, useful when one does not wish to apply the full general-equilibrium analysis to price level determination. Though containing less detail, that equation would neither contradict nor supplement the mirror image equation.

As Patinkin argues (1965, pp. 180–81), if the model of the invalid dichotomy were expanded to include bonds and if the bond excess-demand function were also homogeneous of degree zero in prices, then the absolute price level would still be indeterminate – for the reasons given above. On the other hand, if the absolute price level appeared as an argument in the bond excess-demand function, then prices would be determinate. For now, starting from general equilibrium, an arbitrary doubling of all prices would disturb equilibrium in the bond market. The resulting excess supply of bonds would raise the interest rate, which in turn would lower the demand for commodities, forcing prices back down to their original level. This situation is comparable to the case presented earlier in which the real-balance effect appears in the bond market but not in the commodity markets. But as Patinkin argues (1965, p. 180), this variation of the dichotomy is also unacceptable, for exclusion of the real-balance effect from the commodity markets is unrealistic empirically.

A VALID DICHOTOMY

Patinkin recognizes one valid dichotomy: the equilibrium values of relative prices, the interest rate, and the real quantity of money are independent of the nominal quantity of money and can be determined – 'determined' in a special sense explained below – even without knowledge of it. The analysis divides into two stages. In the first, tastes and resources are the independent real variables, and technology also in a model of an economy with production. These real 'givens' determine the dependent real variables: relative prices, the interest rate and the real money supply. In the second stage the nominal money supply determines – again in the special sense explained below – the absolute price level. An increase in the quantity of money does not disturb any of the equilibrium real values determined in the first stage, while it raises the price level equiproportionately in the second stage (given the assumptions of the quantity theory).

Suppose that, starting from equilibrium, the money supply doubles, and so – until prices change – does the real money supply. We assume that people's taste for real balances has not changed, so prices must double to restore real balances to their initial equilibrium level. Doubling the money supply leaves the equilibrium values of relative prices, the interest rate and the real quantity of money unaffected. These variables are 'determined' apart from the nominal quantity of money: they can be calculated from sufficiently detailed equilibrium equations without knowledge of this quantity. ('Determined' in this special context means 'calculated' or 'made calculable'.)

Similarly, the nominal money supply 'determines' the absolute price level in the second stage. That level is simply the ratio of the given nominal money supply to the real money supply determined in the first stage of analysis. Again we use 'determined' in the special sense of 'calculated' or 'made calculable'.

The invalid dichotomy states that given *all* the commodity and bond equations *and* the money supply, one more equation, a distinct monetary equation, is needed to determine the absolute price level. The valid dichotomy recognizes that given *all* this information, the absolute price level *is already determined*. It is a simple ratio and therefore no monetary equation distinct from the mirror image is necessary or even permissible.

The valid dichotomy is purely conceptual, notes Patinkin (1965, p. 173), since the real and monetary independent variables are 'specified' simultaneously in an actual economy.

UNIFORM UNITARY ELASTICITY OF DEMAND FOR MONEY

Many neoclassical writers, Patinkin notes, believed that the demand for nominal money as a function of the inverse of the price level had uniform unitary elasticity, an elasticity of (minus) 1; the curve was a rectangular hyperbola, as in Figure 5.11. Evidently they envisaged alternative vertical money supply curves intersecting it for equilibrium price levels. This issue of elasticity is not important in its own right, but it serves as a vehicle for exposing and resolving some confusions that also spawned the homogeneity postulate and the invalid dichotomy.

Actually, the demand curve for nominal money is steeper than a rectangular hyperbola; its elasticity is less than 1 in absolute value. Doubling the price level makes the individual holder want a nominal cash balance less than twice as large as before, and halving the price level makes him want a nominal cash balance more than half as large as before. Doubling or halving the price level reduces or increases the desired *real* balance. The reason for this result in the individual experiment is that doubling the price level reduces the purchasing

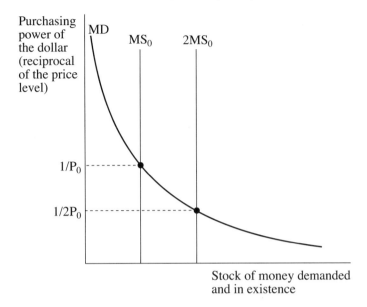

Figure 5.11   Uniform unitary elasticity of the demand for money

power of a nominal cash balance; and being thus slightly impoverished in real terms, its holder must economize on various uses of his income or wealth, including even the holding of real cash balances. Halving the price level makes a money-holder *wealthier* and able to afford somewhat larger allocations of wealth in various directions, including a larger allocation to his real cash balance. (We assume, realistically, that real money holdings are a normal as opposed to inferior good. We also restrict our analysis to Patinkin's narrow view of the real-balance effect as a wealth effect.)

So far we have been considering an individual holder's demand for money. The market demand function is conceptually generated by totaling the quantities of money that all holders would desire at each of the different conceivable price levels. In addition, this function generally depends upon not only relative prices and total real income and wealth (including real cash balances), but also the distribution of income and wealth among members of the community. Anyway, for reasons already explained, the market demand curve for nominal cash balances, like the individual demand curve, presumably has an elasticity less than 1 in absolute value with respect to the purchasing power of the money unit.

This point about elasticity helps clarify and emphasize the distinction already introduced between individual experiments and market experiments. The less-than-unit-elastic money demand curve describes an individual experiment.

Quite distinct from it is a market-equilibrium curve, which portrays the strict quantity theory and does have unit elasticity. In Figure 5.12 the market-equilibrium curve EE joins the points of equilibrium of alternative supplies of money and their corresponding demands. Awkwardly enough, the position of each money demand curve depends in part on the actual money supply: the larger the supply, the further to the right the demand curve appears. Although desirable in principle, it is not always possible to keep supply factors and demand factors in separate categories. In the present case, the stock of actual cash balances does enter into the real wealth of economic units at each price level and does affect their demands for various things, even including cash balances.

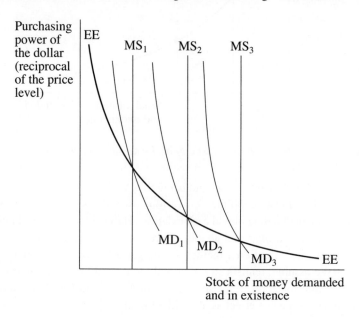

Figure 5.12   The market-equilibrium curve for money

Curve EE is a rectangular hyperbola. Whatever the nominal quantity of money, its total real purchasing power is the same. This characteristic of EE simply illustrates the rigid quantity theory but does not prove it. Yet it is useful. Clarifying the distinction between a demand curve for cash balances and a market-equilibrium curve helps us see that the former curve does not have unit elasticity, even though the latter does.

In summary, the market-equilibrium curve portrays the result of a series of conceptual market experiments. It shows that the equilibrium purchasing power of the money unit is inversely related to the quantity of money; that is, it has unit elasticity. On the other hand, the demand curve for nominal money represents individual experiments: it shows how desired cash balances depend on the inverse of the price level, the total of actual nominal cash balances being one of the magnitudes *held constant*.

PATINKIN ON CLASSICAL INTEREST RATE THEORY

Patinkin argues that classical and neoclassical writers held that the interest rate is invariant with respect to changes in the money supply under the conditions necessary for the quantity theory to hold. They recognized, for example, that the increase in the money supply would have to be distributed among people in proportion to their initial holdings (Patinkin, 1965; pp. 45, 164, 371). They understood the interdependence among markets. An increase in the money supply would cause an increase in the demand for commodities and bonds, temporarily depressing the interest rate. As the price level increased so would the demand for loans (supply of bonds), causing the interest rate to return to its initial equilibrium level. (Pages above discuss this process in detail.)

Patinkin (1965, p. 371) mentions that these writers recognized one exception, 'forced savings', that involves distribution effects. In this case, a rise in the money supply accrues mainly to entrepreneurs, who increase investment in capital goods. The resulting rise in the price level causes the necessary decrease in consumption, that is, 'forced savings'. Furthermore, the increased capital stock lowers its marginal productivity and hence depresses the equilibrium rate of interest.

Patinkin (1965, pp. 371–2) argues that since classical and neoclassical writers recognized the foregoing exception, they probably would have acknowledged that a change in liquidity preference or open-market operations could also alter the equilibrium rate. However, he (1965, p. 380) suggests that the following hypothesis would represent their views:

> Variations in the average long-term rate of interest...have originated primarily in technological changes which have affected the marginal productivity of capital, and in time-preference changes which have affected the desire to save; they have not originated primarily – or even significantly – in changes in the quantity of money or shifts in liquidity preference.

Figure 5.6 shows how an increase in thrift can lower the equilibrium rate, while Figure 5.10 illustrates how an increase in the productivity of capital can raise it. Figures 5.7, 5.8, and 5.9 illuminate the different ways a change in liquidity preference can affect the equilibrium rate of interest. An open-market purchase by the monetary authority would increase the relative scarcity of bonds, raising their price and lowering the interest rate.

Chapter 10 views the interest rate, broadly interpreted, as primarily a real phenomenon. Building on the discussions in Chapter 2, it focuses on the inter-dependence of markets and the mutual determination of the rate.

MONEY, BARTER AND NEUTRALITY

Patinkin (1965, p. 75) argues that mere conversion of a barter economy to one with money would not affect the real general equilibrium; introduction of money would be 'neutral' – neutral in the sense of leaving all realities, all quantities and relative prices, the same as they would otherwise be. Patinkin conceives of a barter economy 'as the limiting position of a money economy whose nominal quantity of money is made smaller and smaller'. The equilibrium values of relative prices and the interest rate remain unchanged as the quantity of money approaches zero as a limit. Patinkin argues that we can get as close as we want to a barter economy while preserving the neutrality of money. Yet he senses a flaw in his own argument: as the nominal quantity of money approaches zero, so does the price level, leaving the real quantity of money unchanged. 'Thus the limiting position that we have defined as a barter economy is one in which there exists the same real quantity of money as in a money economy!'

Actually, the difference between the two economies is no mere quantitative one concerning levels of prices and sizes of money supplies; the difference is the momentous qualitative one of whether money exists and functions at all. Patinkin's contention is a curious slip in an otherwise impressive work of sustained analysis.[5] If we take seriously the tremendous services of money reviewed in Chapter 2, we cannot suppose neutrality with respect to money's very existence.

We *can* conceive of money's being neutral, leaving the real equilibrium unaffected, with regard to its nominal quantity; that is what the strict quantity theory maintains. In this case, a one-time increase in the nominal money supply could come by way of donations to holders in proportion to their existing holdings. This proportionality would avoid the distribution effects whose absence strict neutrality presupposes. Even in the absence of such propor-tionality, the distribution effects associated with a one-shot change in money would tend, relative to other influences, to become vanishingly small over time, as argued by Archibald and Lipsey (1958). In the long run, neutrality would still hold.

Less plausible is neutrality with respect to money's nominal *growth rate*. Different growth rates entail different rates of rise (or fall) of prices, different costs (or rewards) of holding real money balances, and different total real quantities of money in existence. By the principle of general interdependence, different real money supplies entail different real sizes of other magnitudes also. Yet a far-fetched case is conceivable after all in which neutrality – so-called 'superneutrality' – would hold even with regard to money's growth rate. In that case, continuing increases in the money supply would have to come by way of donations to holders in proportion to their existing holdings, thereby just canceling the price-inflation disincentive to the holding of real balances and also avoiding distribution effects.

We have now considered three imaginable types of neutrality. The third, superneutrality, presupposes continuing changes in the money supply in an utterly implausible and pointless manner. The second, the quantity theory concept, is the most nearly plausible of the three. Yet, as we know, reality does not strictly satisfy the conditions necessary for the exact quantity theory result. The first concept, denying any real difference between barter and monetary economies, is downright wrong.

A barter economy might get stuck away from full employment at disequilibrium relative prices. While the aggregate of excess demands for all goods and services must be zero, with excess demands in some sectors matching excess supplies in others, these sectoral imbalances still could entail overall unemployment. Adjustment of barter prices to market-clearing levels is more difficult than adjustment of money prices. Money existing in a 'correct' or adequate quantity could lessen the effects of nonmonetary disorders by providing a kind of cushion as described on pages 109–11 above. On the other hand, monetary disorder can pose disturbances unknown to a barter economy.

CONCLUSION

According to a broad or loose version of the quantity theory, the money supply, together with the demand for cash balances, determines the stream of spending and nominal income. The rigid or strict theory goes on to assert an exact proportionality between the nominal money supply and the price level. Patinkin explains the conditions necessary for the latter version, conditions not fully met in reality. Changes in the money supply affect output quantities and relative prices as well as the price level. The real world exhibits disequilibrium, as explained in our next chapter, not the general equilibrium of Patinkin's book. Nevertheless, his analysis, especially of the real-balance effect, contributes greatly to understanding the real world. His diagrammatic apparatus can be applied and extended in illuminating ways (see pages 212–15 below).

NOTES

1. Patinkin departs from his focus on general equilibrium when he discusses involuntary unemployment in Chapters 13 and 14. He distinguishes between 'output' and 'supply' in Chapter 13

(see pages above). In his 'Introduction to second edition, abridged', Patinkin (1989) further elaborates on his disequilibrium approach to macroeconomics.

2. Patinkin avoids explicitly considering labor by assuming enough flexibility of nominal and real wage rates to keep its market always in equilibrium. We prefer getting rid of a separate labor market by aggregating labor with commodities, which also include services as mentioned above.

3. Looking up Mill (1848 [1965], pp. 653–8) is well worth the trouble.

4. In mathematics a function is said to be homogeneous of degree n if multiplying each of its independent variables by a positive constant k makes its value k^n times its original value. If $f(kx, ky) = k^n f(x,y)$, then the function is homogeneous of nth degree.

   Homogeneous functions of degree 1, also called linear homogeneous functions, are familiar in economics. The standard example is a production function exhibiting constant returns to scale: an equiproportionate change in the quantities of all inputs changes output in the same proportion.

   A homogeneous function of degree zero has its value unaffected by an equiproportionate change in its independent variables. A simple example is the identity saying that real income equals nominal income divided by the price index: doubling both nominal income and prices leaves real income unchanged. When Patinkin refutes the 'homogeneity postulate', he refers to particular zero-degree functions, namely, commodity demand and supply functions having the supposed property that quantities demanded and supplied are unaffected by an equiproportionate change in money prices – *given* the money supply.

5. Wonnacott (1958) makes this criticism of Patinkin.

6. Disequilibrium economics (1)

THE MONETARY-DISEQUILIBRIUM HYPOTHESIS

Among theories of macroeconomic fluctuations that accord a major role to money, at least three rivals have confronted each other. One is orthodox monetarism – 'the monetary disequilibrium hypothesis', as Warburton has called it (1966, selection 1, and elsewhere). A second is the so-called 'Austrian theory of the business cycle'. A third is part of the 'new classical macroeconomics', which features two main hypotheses: 'rational expectations' and 'equilibrium always' (also known as continuous market-clearing or the Walrasian general-equilibrium model). This latter hypothesis consists of two strands: the theory of misperceptions in which money does have a role to play, and real business cycle theory. What monetarism offers toward understanding and perhaps improving the world becomes clearer when one compares it with its rivals.

When monetary disequilibrium occurs, 'things begin to happen' that tend eventually to restore equilibrium. Instead of adjusting rapidly, however, prices and wages are 'sticky', so adjustment in the short run involves quantities rather than prices alone. Theories emphasizing an infectious failure of markets to clear have been criticized by adherents of the new classical macroeconomics. Yet a microeconomic rationale of disequilibrium behavior is available and will be presented here. It recognizes that most markets are not and cannot be perfectly competitive. It shares some strands with new Keynesian economics, which we review in the next section.

NEW KEYNESIAN ECONOMICS

New Keynesian economics contributes to our understanding of why prices and wages are sticky. It is a response to criticisms lodged by new classical economists that Keynesian economics lacks rigorous microeconomic foundations because it simply assumes prices and wages are rigid. New Keynesians address this issue by realistically assuming imperfect competition in their models. Agents are wage-and-price setters, not takers as in the perfectly competitive model.

No single new Keynesian theory exists. Rather, many compete for attention. Some new Keynesians even complain about too many theories, as in Blinder

(1986), Blanchard (1992) and Mankiw (1995 [1997a]). We integrate new Keynesian explanations of price and wage stickiness throughout our chapters on disequilibrium economics.

In his exposition of new Keynesian economics, Gordon (1990b, pp. 1137–8) notes the lack of attention paid to the pioneering works of Patinkin, Clower, Leijonhufvud and Barro and Grossman (see page 67 above for his full statement). He argues that new-Keynesian theories are 'riddled with inconsistencies' because they neglect constraints and spillover effects.

A growing new-Keynesian literature focuses on the problem of coordination failures (van Ees and Garretsen, 1996 provide an annotated bibliography; Cooper and John, 1988 is the seminal article). 'Coordination failures' in this literature refers to multiple, welfare-ranked equilibria. Game theory is often used to illustrate how economies can get stuck at low-output equilibria, leaving a role for government intervention to move economies to Pareto-superior equilibria (Mankiw and Romer, 1991, pp. 8–9).

Many new Keynesians embrace rational expectations as well as the rigorous techniques and methods of 'dynamic general equilibrium theory', which was formerly known as 'real business cycle theory'. Like their new classical counterparts, new Keynesians are frequently occupied with the *microfoundations of macroeconomics*. They refrain from using the term 'disequilibrium', since that would supposedly imply failure of agents to realize 'perceived gains from trade' (Gordon, 1990b, pp. 1136–7). New Keynesians believe that recessions and depressions represent market failure on a grand scale (Mankiw, 1993, p. 3). Rather than interpreting disequilibrium as a defect, flaw, or failure of the market, we recognize that 'market imperfections' are simply a fact of life (compare Gordon, 1990b, p. 1163; Brunner and Meltzer, 1993, p. 141; and the literature of the Austrian school).

We argue on pages 201–202 below that new Keynesian economics is neither 'new' nor 'Keynesian'. Mankiw (1992 [1997a], pp. 449–50) realizes that 'old classical economists' like David Hume allowed for changes in the money supply to have real effects in the short run. He suggests: 'with new Keynesians looking so much like old classicals, perhaps we should conclude that the term "Keynesian" has out-lived its usefulness'.

A major difference between monetary-disequilibrium theory and new Keynesian economics is that the former focuses on the centerpiece of orthodox monetarism: a disequilibrium relation between the nominal quantity of money and the general level of prices and wages. Moreover, the former takes a broad view of coordination and the role that money and prices play in achieving or obstructing coordination. It recognizes that the 'coordination problem', explained on pages below, is the central problem bridging microeconomics and macroeconomics. Further, it focuses on processes and people's behavior rather than on sheer mechanics.

THE WALRASIAN WORLD AND THE WORLD OF POSSIBLE DISEQUILIBRIUM

Robert Clower and others initiated – or resurrected – a line of research that takes certain familiar but fateful facts seriously.[1] In a developed economy, goods and services exchange for each other not directly but through the intermediary of money. No process works swiftly and smoothly enough to keep markets continuously in equilibrium or to restore disturbed equilibrium instantaneously. Disequilibrium in some markets can spread to others.

The world envisioned by writers in this tradition becomes clearer by contrast with the influential Walrasian vision (not to be confused with Walras's Law). In Walras's general-equilibrium system as commonly interpreted (and here is not the place to question an admittedly questionable interpretation), markets are cleared as if by an 'auctioneer' or 'secretary of the market'. In effect, this imaginary personage finds market-clearing prices by trial and error. He announces a trial set of prices and learns how much of each good or service each market participant would like to buy or sell at those prices. Some items turn out to be in excess demand, others in excess supply. The auctioneer raises or lowers their prices accordingly, announces the new set, observes the new and presumably smaller pattern of market imbalances, adjusts prices again and continues adjusting until he has found the prices that equate supply and demand quantities for each item. Alternatively, the auctioneer somehow has all individual demand and supply functions programmed into his computer and simply calculates the market-clearing prices. Not until then does he give the signal for actual trading to take place. Each participant delivers and receives the quantities that he had expressed willingness to sell and buy at the prices that now take effect, receiving and making payments for them. (Until then, indicated transactions were contingent on whether the trial prices turned out to be equilibrium prices.)

In such a world, no redistribution of wealth occurs through transactions at disequilibrium prices. In the real world, by contrast, people gain in relation to what the general-equilibrium outcome would have been whenever they buy at lower and sell at higher than equilibrium prices. People in opposite positions lose.

Furthermore, precisely because the auctioneer ensures market-clearing prices, no excess demand or excess supply frustrates transactors in making all the purchases or sales they desire. In a superidealized vision, the auctioneer even cuts through information problems by putting trading partners costlessly in contact with one another. Every commodity is perfectly salable at its equilibrium price and so is perfectly usable in paying for whatever its owner might be buying. Each transactor's budget constraint becomes, in effect, nothing more than the condition that his sales equal his purchases in total value. Money, along with securities and commodities, is just one of the many things that might be sold or bought. Everything is just as marketable as money, so money plays no distinctive role. Its appearance in the Walrasian general-equilibrium model seems rather artificial. Patinkin (1965), too, has to graft money onto his general-equilibrium system in an artificial way, through his random payments process, and Clower criticizes him for not taking seriously money's distinctiveness as the medium of exchange.

The Walrasian world affords no scope for distinguishing between desired purchases (or sales) of some item when the parties do and when they do not meet frustration in carrying out other desired transactions. Market-clearing prices preclude any such frustration. They also obviate any distinction between desired and actual transactions. At those prices people successfully accomplish the transactions they desire. In the real world, though, the distinctions mentioned do apply.

Here, regrettably, we must make a terminological digression. Trading without the Walrasian auctioneer is often called the *nontâtonnement process*. The words 'tâtonnement' and 'nontâtonnement' have come to be used, it seems, in senses rather different from their original ones. Instead of judging 'what Walras really meant', we consider what the words mean today. 'Tâtonnement', literally 'groping', was Walras's word for the way that the economic system actually approaches the equilibrium values of prices and quantities, as distinguished from an economist's merely calculating them by solving the simultaneous equations describing the system. Prices fall for commodities in excess supply and rise for ones in excess demand, bringing prices and quantities closer and closer to their equilibrium values. The doctrinal issue is whether Walras conceived of a process centrally conducted by an auctioneer who withheld the signal for actual transactions until he had found the equilibrium prices. Or was Walras referring instead to the decentralized process of the real world, where transactions do take place at disequilibrium prices, but with the pressures of competitive bids and offers by frustrated transactors driving prices toward market-clearing levels? Current usage implies the former interpretation. The auctioneer conducts the tâtonnement on paper and forestalls any disequilibrium trading.

Nontâtonnement processes, then, are the subject matter of disequilibrium economics. Trading can occur even before the equilibrating processes have done their work. Markets can fail to clear. Frustration of desired transactions can cumulatively impair production.

NOTIONAL AND EFFECTIVE DEMANDS AND SUPPLIES

In such a world, the real world, we must make the distinctions just introduced. We must distinguish, furthermore, among the notionally, effectively and successfully demanded (or supplied) quantities of each item, elaborating on concepts already introduced in Chapter 3.[2]

The 'notional' demand for something is the quantity that buyers would demand at a specified set of prices if no market disequilibrium were frustrating any of their attempted purchases and sales of other items. An 'effective' demand is the quantity that demanders want to buy and are prepared to pay for in view of whatever frustrations they may actually be experiencing in markets other than the one in question. Neither notional nor effective demand is necessarily 'successful', for the buyers may not find enough willing sellers.

Similar distinctions apply to supply. The quantity of something notionally supplied is the volume of desired sales, absent any frustration in other markets. Effective supply, when it diverges from notional supply, is desired sales as affected by such frustration. Neither notional nor effective supply is necessarily 'successful', for the sellers may not find enough willing buyers.

Clower illustrates the distinction, which is briefly presented in Chapter 3. Suppose he meets no frustration. In particular, he can sell as much of his economic consulting services as he wants at the going price. His demand for champagne at its going price is then his notional demand for it. His effective demand is the same in this absence of frustration. Now suppose, in contrast, that he does encounter frustration in selling his services. His income is smaller than in the first case, and his effective demand for champagne accordingly falls short of his notional demand.

In the notional demand (and supply) functions of the Walrasian system, incomes do *not* appear along with prices as independent variables. The reason is that incomes are already implied by the various factor supply functions and by the assurance of prices that clear markets and prevent frustrations. Each person's income is the sum of the values at equilibrium prices of the factor quantities he would supply at those prices. The total of everyone's incomes is thus implicitly specified also, and no room remains for specifying it again as a separate independent variable.

When we recognize that disequilibrium prices may frustrate some transactions, however, incomes do enter as independent variables into effective demand (and supply) functions. Clower's income, reflecting his possibly only partial success in selling his services, is an argument in his effective champagne demand function.

DUAL DECISION THEORY AND THE DICHOTOMIZED BUDGET CONSTRAINT

The contrast between Clower's alternative behaviors in the champagne market according to his success or frustration in the consultation market epitomizes what he calls 'dual decision theory'. A person's decision on transactions in a particular market will differ according as he does or does not succeed in carrying out his desired transactions in other markets. If he meets success in the other markets, then his effectively desired and notionally desired transactions in the particular market coincide. If he meets frustration, his effective and notional decisions regarding the particular market diverge.

Recognizing that not all goods in the real world are as readily marketable as money, dual decision theory points to the further notion of the 'split budget constraint'. The conventional Walrasian budget constraint is not split. It says, in effect, that the aggregate value of the commodities and money that an individual desires to wind up with after his market transactions equals the aggregate value of the commodities and money that he begins with. In symbols: $\sum_{i=1}^{n} p_i(d_i - s_i)$ + desired money holding − initial money holding = 0, where the p_i is price and the d_i and s_i are desired and initial quantities, respectively, of commodities (here interpreted to include factor and other services, as well as securities). According to Clower (1967 [1984], p. 86), this 'familiar budget constraint effectively admits as feasible trades all pairwise combinations of commodities that are traded in the economy'. Initial commodity quantities enter the constraint in the same way as initial money holdings. Commodities are indistinguishable from money as sources of effective demand.

Such a constraint, Clower continues, does not appropriately describe the choice alternatives in a money economy. He supposes that all money prices except labor's wage rate are free to vary. Now part of the money stock is destroyed. Prices of all commodities other than labor fall as far as necessary to clear their markets, so their excess demands remain zero. The wage rate, nominally fixed, has risen in real terms so the quantity of labor demanded falls. By Walras's Law, the money value of unsold labor equals the excess demand for money. Now someone autonomously increases the quantity of labor that he offers. This, according to the conventional *un*split budget constraint, constitutes an increase in the demand for nonlabor commodities, whose prices rise in response. In that way, the hypothesized autonomous increase in the labor supply − and in unemployment − reduces the real wage rate and so increases employment and output after all. More generally, in the Walrasian general-equilibrium world, with its unified budget constraint, an increase in the unsold stocks of any commodity with a fixed nominal price will raise the general level of other prices and so indirectly stimulate purchases of that commodity by reducing its relative price. With the Walrasian auctioneer at work, an increase in the supply of any particular thing, whether money or something else, supports an increased demand for other things (except its substitutes). In such a centralized market, money has no particular function.

In this world, the magical appearance of a great quantity of blankets from heaven, far from being contractionary, would support an increased demand for other things and tend to raise their prices. (It would do so, anyway, unless an inelastic demand for blankets and flexibility of their price caused the total exchange value of the increased stock to be less than the stock's value before its increase.) The auctioneer makes blankets just as usable as money in paying for things bought and in serving as a reserve of ready purchasing power. Whether a good fairy added $1 billion worth to a country's stock of blankets or gave its inhabitants $1 billion of new money, demands for (other) commodities would respond in the same way. Yet the form of the gift *is* relevant to behavior in the real world. A nonmonetary gift could quite conceivably have a contractionary effect because people's additional wealth would increase their desired holdings of money. Chapter 4 deals explicitly with this possibility.

A properly formulated budget constraint for the real world recognizes 'the requirement that money be offered or demanded as one of the commodities entering into every trade' (Clower, 1967 [1984], p. 86). It recognizes a clear separation between (1) offering to sell commodities and take money in exchange and (2) offering to buy commodities and pay money for them. (Compare the two stages of exchange mentioned on page 99 above.) The first branch of the budget constraint, called the 'income constraint', specifies that the sum of prices times quantities of commodities offered equals the amount of money desired in exchange. It recognizes that all (net) offers to sell commodities involve, in the first instance, a desire to acquire just one other thing, money. The second branch, the 'expenditure constraint', specifies that the sum of prices times quantities of commodities demanded equals the amount of money offered in exchange. It recognizes that demands for commodities count on the markets of a monetary economy only if desires are backed up by readiness to pay money – money obtained by selling commodities in our broadened sense of the term, which includes bonds.

An individual's plans might satisfy his unified budget constraint yet fail to satisfy his more realistic split constraint. For example, his intended sales might cover his intended purchases, leaving his cash balance unchanged. If some of his intended sales fell through, however, he could not use the unreceived money to cover his intended purchases.

IMPAIRED SIGNALS AND CONTAGIOUS DISEQUILIBRIUM

In a model that realistically recognizes the use of money in substantially all transactions, increased initial endowments of some commodities do not directly increase the demands for other commodities. As the splitting of the budget constraint recognizes, supply of some commodities constitutes demand for others only if the commodities supplied are sold successfully for money with which to demand the others. No deficiency of aggregate demand exists provided that no monetary disequilibrium is obstructing the intermediated exchanges of commodities for commodities. Clower's analysis directs attention to this crucial proviso (compare the discussion in Chapter 1 of the 'goods-against-goods approach').

A hitch involving money impairs the communication mechanism of the market. Clower might want to supply his services indirectly or directly for champagne, yet run into difficulty informing producers of his 'willingness to solve their market research problems in exchange for copious quantities of their excellent beverage' (Clower, 1965 [1984], p. 48). More generally, workers might want to buy more consumer goods if only they could get jobs, and firms might want to hire more workers if only they could sell more consumer goods, yet both sides might run into difficulty in signaling and accomplishing these desired exchanges.

Here is the place for a broad, intuitive summary. Traditional Walrasian general-equilibrium theory tacitly supposed, in each supply or demand function, that markets cleared for all items except the one in question. (The clearing of its own market was neither assumed nor denied, since the necessary conditions were under investigation.) The theory assumed that the individual transactor could succeed in buying or selling things at market-clearing prices in whatever amounts he desired, as described by his demand and supply functions. His demand functions (and factor-supply functions) did not have to include his income specifically as an independent variable, since its equilibrium level was already implicitly specified by the market prices of factors and his own factor-supply functions (as well as whatever accounted for his share of business profits).

This theory committed a serious oversight. Some of the prices confronting the individual (for example, the price of his labor) may be disequilibrium prices at which he cannot deal in the quantities he desires. If so, his effective demand and supply functions diverge from the notional ones traditionally written. In a situation of generally deficient effective demand (interpreted here as one in which prices and wages are generally too high in relation to the nominal quantity of money), real incomes are lower than what the Walrasian general-equilibrium equations (implicitly) indicate. Because disequilibrium constrains real incomes, effective demands for most commodities are weaker than they would be in general equilibrium.

This formulation alludes to what Clower calls the 'income-constrained process', the process of *cumulative disequilibrium*. When disequilibrium prices constrain sales and therefore production of particular commodities, their producers by that very token suffer cuts in real income. These producers' effective demands for the outputs of other sectors of the economy are accordingly weaker than their notional demands. With demands weakened, what might have been market-clearing prices for the products of these other sectors are now too high, and prices already too high are now still further above equilibrium levels.[3] The drop in sales, output and real incomes in these other sectors reduces demands for and production of the outputs of still other sectors, and so on cumulatively. In short, the drop in production in the sectors first thrown out of equilibrium spells a drop in real buying power and in the real demand for the outputs of other sectors, which suffer in turn. And so on.

In the reverse direction, revival in some sectors constitutes increased buying power over the outputs of other sectors. Even if left unchanged, prices of those other outputs are now less excessive in relation to their market-clearing levels than they were before. Recovery spreads still more widely.

The cumulative character of recession and recovery is an element of truth that the mechanistic Keynesian multiplier distorts. Multiplier formulas convey a spurious impression of precision. They draw attention away from the role of prices. Degrees of disequilibrium, of its pervasiveness, and of the wrongness of prices are inherently fuzzy. Little warrant exists for simply assuming dependable quantitative relations in these matters.

MONETARY CONTRACTION: THE MODEL OF BARRO AND GROSSMAN

Gordon (1990b, p. 1138) contrasts the inconsistencies in new Keynesian economics with the work of Barro and Grossman (1971, 1976) in particular. Their work illuminates what determines quantities of output and employment when prices and wages are sticky. Emphasizing constraints and spillovers among markets that fail to clear, they merge the complementary theories of Clower (1965 [1984]), and Patinkin (1965, Chapter 13). Clower argues that workers' demand for commodities is constrained by their success in selling labor, while Patinkin argues that firms' demand for labor is constrained by their success in selling commodities.

Patinkin's Chapter 13, which focuses on the causes of involuntary unemployment, foreshadows much of the disequilibrium theory developed by Clower, Leijonhufvud and Barro and Grossman. Patinkin recognizes that involuntary unemployment does not presuppose an excessive and rigid real wage rate and that cutting real wages may be neither necessary nor sufficient for restoring full-employment equilibrium. What follows helps explain the logic behind these observations.

At the analytical core of Barro and Grossman's book of 1976 is their assumption that nominal wages and prices respond sluggishly if at all to shifts in demand. Markets can fail to clear. If disequilibrium prices and wages are restricting possibilities of exchange, then output and employment do depend on aggregate demand. A deficiency of demand for commodities depresses employment through a multiplier process. Clower's distinction between effective and notional demand and supply functions becomes relevant.

Employment can be depressed even if the real wage rate remains fixed at its full-employment equilibrium level. A decline in the effective demand for commodities reduces the effective demand for labor, and these shifts do not presuppose a rise in the ratio of wages to prices. Money prices and wages might both be too high, even in the same degree, in relation to the nominal quantity of money.

If exchange is voluntary, actual transactions in a good are whichever is smaller, the demand quantity or the supply quantity. Failure of a market to clear spells frustration for parties on one side or the other and constrains their ability to deal in other markets. Most obviously, a person frustrated in finding a job is constrained in buying consumer goods.

In reality, opportunities to build up and run down inventories dampen the contagion of disequilibrium. To focus attention on that contagion, however, Barro and Grossman assume that firms do not hold inventories.

In the case of general excess supply (deficient demand), firms are producing less output than they would want to produce and sell at going levels of prices and wages. They are employing less labor than they would want to employ if they were meeting no frustration in sales. Firms' actual output is smaller than their notional supply quantity, so their effective demand for labor is smaller than their notional labor-demand function indicates. Households, selling less labor than their notional supply, are effectively demanding fewer commodities than their notional functions would indicate.

The constraints on firms' sales of commodities and so on their demands for labor (compare Patinkin) and the constraints on households' sales of labor and so on their demands for commodities (compare Clower) interact and reinforce each other. This process of interaction and reinforcement, akin in a way to a Keynesian multiplier process, does not go so far as to reduce economic activity to zero. Instead, production, consumption and employment settle at a 'quasi-equilibrium' below full employment, as explained in Chapter 3.

To help make the point that households will adjust to their current constraint on earning incomes not entirely by curtailing current consumption but partly by other adjustments also, Barro and Grossman introduce distinctions between different spans of time. We omit these details here.

We now consider the process determining actual income and employment. We suppose that wages and prices are initially consistent with full-employment equilibrium, but that some exogenous disturbance such as a decrease in the nominal quantity of money renders their unchanged levels too high now. As the Wicksell Process unfolds, households meet frustration in selling labor, firms in selling commodities. The fall in labor earnings (and in households' share in business profits) causes households to reduce further their effective demands for commodities. At the same time, the reduction in effective demand for and sales of commodities further reduces the profits of firms and their effective demand for labor. The cumulative decline persists until the actual levels of output and employment 'settle' below their full-employment levels.

To look at the process in a somewhat different way, real output and income deteriorate until the quantity of money actually (effectively) demanded as cash balances, as distinguished from the quantity that would be demanded at full employment, no longer exceeds the actual money supply. If, as we are supposing, no cuts in nominal wages and prices reduce the nominal demand for money, then real activity must deteriorate to reduce the quantity of money that people feel they can 'afford' to hold. As argued in Chapter 3, however, an effective transactions-flow excess demand for money still persists in the quasi-equilibrium as workers are frustrated in supplying labor and firms are frustrated in supplying commodities. Disequilibrium actually prevails.

The stickiness of prices and wages poses obstacles to prompt adjustment that are understated by the slight degree of disaggregation – into commodities-in-general and labor-in-general – that Barro and Grossman consider. In the very finely disaggregated real world, problems of information and of piecemeal decisionmaking go far toward explaining the sluggishness of price and wage adjustments, as explained in Chapter 7.

Figure 6.1 portrays the case of generally deficient demand. Employment is measured along the horizontal axis, real output along the vertical. Dashed lines perpendicular to the axes indicate employment and output at full employment and meet at point A. The curve labeled 'Firms' represents a physical relation, the production function. Its diminishing slope reflects the diminishing marginal productivity of labor. In the present case of deficient demand, the curve shows the volume of commodities demanded required to motivate employing the corresponding amount of labor. Because of the diminishing marginal productivity of labor, the contemplated demand for commodities required to motivate each contemplated increment in employment rises less and less. In the present case, then, the curve for firms shows volumes of output associated with both effectively demanded and actually employed amounts of labor. (We ignore here the question of whether real balances belong in the production function and whether the decrease in cash balances would shift it.)

A curve for households, drawn dashed, shows the association between amounts of labor supplied and commodities demanded, given a full-employment real quantity of money. The solid curve for households also shows the demand for commodities arising from indicated amounts of actual employment. Its being drawn lower than the dashed curve shows the actual demand schedule for commodities depressed because real money balances are now inadequate for full

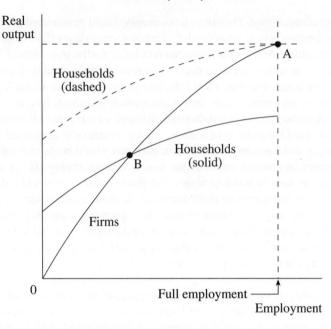

Figure 6.1   The case of deficient demand

employment. Its positive intercept on the output axis shows that people would demand some commodities even at zero employment, paying out of savings.

In the region between the two curves nearer the origin from their intersection at point B, the firms' curve shows more labor being effectively demanded at a given level of output than the amount of employment that, according to the households' curve, would generate enough demand to absorb that much output. At a given level of employment – to shift the point of view – the output produced according to the firms' curve is less than the output demanded according to the households' curve. Either point of view indicates interacting *upward* pressures on employment and output.

In the region outward from point B, at a given output less labor is demanded according to the firms' curve than the volume of employment necessary, according to the households' curve, to sustain a demand for that much output. At a given level of employment, the output produced according to the firms' curve is greater than the output demanded according to the households' curve. Interacting *downward* pressures are at work.

Point B corresponds to the quasi-equilibrium. On this interpretation, the diagram is loosely similar to the standard Keynesian 45-degree-line diagram of the textbooks. One difference here is that employment rather than income is measured along the horizontal axis. (Keynes himself, in his *General Theory*

(1936), described but did not actually draw a diagram with employment measured along the horizontal axis and demand for and supply of output along the vertical axis.) Barro and Grossman's curve for firms is loosely analogous to Keynes's aggregate supply function, which shows the volume of expected purchases of output that would just make it worth while for firms to offer the corresponding volume of employment. The curve for households is loosely analogous to Keynes's aggregate demand function, which shows the volume of households' purchases of output that businesspeople do expect at the corresponding volume of employment. (Barro and Grossman did not point out these analogies and bear no responsibility for our interpretation.)

Barro and Grossman (1976, p. 62) emphasize that a real wage rate above the equilibrium level 'is a sufficient condition, but not a necessary condition, for underemployment'. In the case presented here, underemployment traces to a deficient demand for commodities. The real wage could be *at* or even *below* its full-employment equilibrium level. Barro and Grossman mention that cuts in the real wage might superficially *seem* to be a remedy. Wage cuts might reduce and eventually eliminate the excess supply of labor by decreasing the amount of labor *effectively supplied*. They would not, however, achieve full-employment equilibrium.

MONETARY EXPANSION IN A RECESSION

Suppose that something, perhaps a fall in the money supply, has already caused a recession. Now the nominal money supply expands sufficiently. A depressed level of activity is no longer needed to choke off the effective excess demand for money that caused the recession. People no longer feel pressed to curtail their buying to restore or conserve cash. They feel freer to spend. Restoring full activity does not necessarily require a fall in the real wage rate. The demand for labor increases as producers find that they can sell more output. Barro and Grossman even suggest that the recovery of output and employment may be accompanied by a rising real wage. This procyclical change 'differs from the conventional view that employment and real wages must be inversely related' (1971, p. 87). The conventional view at the time, as expressed in Friedman's seminal 1967 address to the American Economic Association, was that a lower *actual* real wage was necessary to convince producers to increase output. Workers would agree to supply more labor because they *misperceived* the real wage (see pages 206–208 below).

The case of recovery from recession is again portrayed in Figure 6.1. Now, though, the increase in the money supply shifts the curve for households upward, so the relevant curve is the dashed line. Point A represents the new equilibrium at full employment.

LIMITS TO CONTAGION

Our expository apparatus must not mislead us into supposing that the process of cumulative disequilibrium and recovery works with precision. In the real world, the behaviors of inventories and money limit its self-feeding character. One function of a firm's inventories – of purchased materials and parts, of work in process, and of finished products awaiting sale – is to serve as buffers absorbing the impact of short-run fluctuations in deliveries of inputs and in demands for output. A firm may want its inventories to average out, over a period of months or longer, to a stable level or into a stable relation with its flows of inputs and output. Yet its inventories may vary over shorter periods. A drop off in demand for its product may be a fluke, soon to be reversed. While seeking further information on the market situation, the firm may well continue producing output and even buying materials as before, letting its inventory of unsold output grow. So doing, it avoids cutting the incomes of its suppliers and employees and avoids the spread of recession on this account.

Of course, if production persists despite fallen demand long enough for inventories to rise clearly above a level felt tolerable, the firm will adjust production. In the opposite direction, similarly, a firm may initially respond to a spurt in sales by drawing down inventories. But if the spurt persists, it cannot maintain that passive response.

The idea that firms may passively allow inventories to fluctuate within certain ranges and will actively adjust production only when inventories move outside them has given rise to a so-called *corridor theory* of economic fluctuations. Within a supposed corridor on a time-series diagram of economic activity, the buffer function of inventories tends to absorb shocks, especially as long as fluctuations remain sectorally localized. This buffer role of inventories puts a further element of play and indefiniteness into the contagion of recession and recovery. The income-constrained process does not operate with mechanical precision. But the theory of that process does not become otiose.

Only when shocks are severe enough to push activity outside the corridor do deviations become self-aggravating. (Anyway, this is the theory of Leijon-hufvud, 1973 as interpreted by Blinder, 1981.) This is an intriguing but unproved idea. It seems to ignore an opposite kind of corridor effect whereby cash balances can resist the further worsening of substantial and pervasive fluctuations. A steady or moderately growing nominal money supply can have this dampening effect. We have less reason to expect a monetary dampening of merely minor or localized fluctuations because people will not act to maintain a *precise* ratio between their incomes and their cash balances. The buffer role of cash balances – absorbing short-run or random spurts and slumps and mismatchings of receipts and payments – accounts for a certain passiveness of response to such fluctuations. A sustained and pervasive disturbance to income, however, would disrupt income/money ratios enough to elicit the response described in Chapters 3 and 4.

MONETARY EXPANSION AND A CONCEIVABLE FALL IN OUTPUT

An increase in the money supply at full employment could bring either of two results. In the case we take up second, output rises temporarily.

First, though, we consider the model of Barro and Grossman, which assumes that firms do not hold inventories and that wages and prices are rigid or sticky both upwards and downwards. In their model, a general *excess* of aggregate demand (and not only a general deficiency) could impair real activity.

From full-employment equilibrium, the money supply expands, causing general excess demand. The individual household now meets frustration trying to buy the commodities that it notionally demands. Accordingly, it reduces its effective supply of labor below its notional supply. (Why keep on working full time to earn income and acquire money when one already meets frustration spending it?) The reduced effective supply of labor constrains actual employment and makes output fall further short of demand. In this model, monetary disorder – excess as well as deficiency – disrupts exchanges and so restricts employment and production.

When the average household is unable to buy all the commodities that it notionally demands, does it fully substitute leisure for the unavailable consumption? Most likely it compromises between two responses, effectively supplying less labor and effectively accepting more real money balances. The latter implies a greater than notional effective demand for future consumption. Cash balances are the only vehicle of saving in the model.

The average firm perceives a supply-imposed constraint on its employment of labor, which not only reduces its profits but also causes it to reduce its actual output. This induced reduction in output further constrains consumption, which induces a further reduction in effective labor supply. (On the other hand, the induced reduction in profits distributed to households creates a partially offsetting stimulus to effective labor supply.) A cumulative decline persists until the actual levels of output and employment 'settle' below their full-employment levels.

Figure 6.2 portrays this case of general excess demand. The 0A curve is the same as in Figure 6.1, reflecting the production function of firms. The interpretations, however, require different emphases. In the excess supply (of commodities) case of Figure 6.1, the 0A curve indicates the commodity demand necessary to motivate firms to offer the indicated amount of employment. Here,

in the case of excess demand, the curve indicates the amount of labor required
if the firm is to supply the indicated amount of commodities.

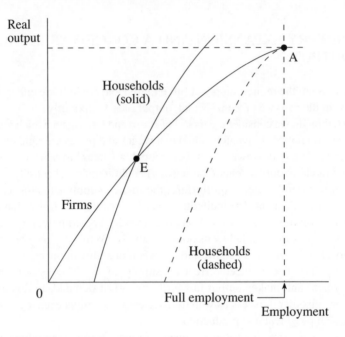

Figure 6.2   The case of excess demand

In the excess supply case, the curve for households shows the demand for
commodities arising from specified amounts of actual employment. Here the
solid households' curve shows how much labor would be offered if the indicated
amounts of commodities were available. Here the curve has a positive horizontal
intercept, suggesting that households would offer some labor, presumably to
accumulate buying power over commodities in the future, even if none were
currently available. (The diagram ignores the question of how workers could
supply any work without any current consumption. Perhaps the households'
curve should be left undrawn in the vicinity of the horizontal axis.) The dashed
households' curve is drawn for a real quantity of money sufficient for full
employment. It passes through point A, since households would provide
sufficient labor at full-employment output.

The contrasting positions of the solid curve for households in the two cases
reflect opposite monetary disorders – real balances too small for full-
employment equilibrium in the earlier case, too large in this one. The curves
answer different questions: earlier, how much commodities would households
demand if they could obtain indicated volumes of employment?; here, how

much labor would households supply if they could obtain indicated amounts of commodities?

In Figure 6.2, the curves for firms and households intersect at point E. In the region between the curves inward from this point, at a given volume of output, labor offered by households exceeds the labor necessary to produce that output. At a given level of employment, conversely, the output producible with that much labor exceeds the output whose availability is necessary to motivate the supply of that much labor. On either view of the situation, interacting pressures operate to increase output and employment.

In the region outward from point E, at a given level of output, the labor supplied by households falls short of the amount necessary to produce that output. At a given level of employment, conversely, the output producible falls short of the amount necessary to motivate the supply of that much labor. From either point of view, interacting pressures are at work to shrink output and employment. Shrinkage of the amount of commodities available leads households to withhold their labor all the more, while reduced labor input entails further shrinkage of commodity output.

Point E represents the quasi-equilibrium of Chapter 3. Excessive real cash balances have reduced output and employment from their full-employment equilibrium levels at point A. Yet output and employment do not fall all the way to zero. Furthermore, point E is a disequilibrium, since people and firms are frustrated. The transactions-flow excess demands for commodities and labor are matched by an effective transactions-flow excess supply of money. Upward pressure on wages and prices still exists.

A certain symmetry holds between the cases of generally deficient and generally excessive aggregate demand. Both cases illustrate how monetary disorder can obstruct the process of exchange. The disorder is not, of course, purely monetary. Rigidity or stickiness of wages and prices is also involved. For if they always moved swiftly to their market-clearing levels, *any* nominal quantity of money would be an equilibrium *real* quantity. Still, any impairment of exchange by that very token impairs production of goods destined to be exchanged. Again the simple point stands out that goods exchange for goods – but through the intermediary of money.

Impairment of activity by overall excess demand is presumably of slight practical importance. First, if workers ever do experience frustration in spending their money, they may well expect the situation to be temporary only. Instead of responding entirely by withholding their labor, they may go on working and accumulate savings to spend when commodities become available again. Such behavior was evident during World War II. Second, sales from inventory by real-world firms lessen the frustration of worker-consumers and limit the perverse interaction described above. Third, wages and prices are not rigid.

Some commodities may be in short supply, but realistically, workers will still find some things to spend their earnings on.

Nevertheless, the excess demand case has more than theoretical interest. Historical examples can be found, as in Germany before the monetary reform of June 1948. Despite an inflated money supply, the price and wage controls of the Hitler era remained in force under the Allied occupation, entailing excessive cash balances, consumer frustration, and worker absenteeism. Instead of remaining at work earning more of the money that was so hard to spend anyway, workers found it sensible to take time off for expeditions to the countryside to engage in barter with the farmers. This was especially true because trips on the government railroads were among the few things that people could successfully spend money on and were bargains at the fares charged. Contemporary accounts describe jam-packed trains, with passengers sitting on the roofs and clinging to the sides.

Then the reform lifted price controls and drastically shrank the quantity of money. Again it was sensible to stay at work producing things, for money earned became the key to obtaining commodities, now available. Economic activity zoomed almost overnight. The great contrast provided further insight into the earlier disequilibrium.

MONETARY EXPANSION AND A RISE IN OUTPUT

In the more intuitively plausible second case of an increase in the money supply at full-employment equilibrium, this increase can temporarily raise output and employment beyond their initial levels, and without necessarily reducing the real wage rate. Here a stimulus comes from monetary expansion *not* fully absorbed by price increases.

When the money supply and spending increase, business firms encounter strengthened demands for their products. Quite generally, each firm or the average one is willing to meet increased demand with increased sales, and at a substantially unchanged price, as long as it can get the necessary capital goods, materials, labor and other inputs at unchanged cost. Whether it can get them depends largely on other people's willingness to run down their inventories, work their factories more nearly at maximum capacity, work overtime, take less leisure between jobs, enter the labor force, postpone retirement and so forth.

To some extent, other people are willing to do so. A chief reason for holding inventories in the first place is to be able to accommodate possibly temporary spurts of demand over output. Moreover, sellers of finished goods, goods in process and materials are willing to draw down inventories without price increases if they think they can readily replenish them. So now the average firm is willing to order more inputs and offer more jobs. Even though wages may not have risen, workers more easily find jobs as good as they already considered satisfactory; less 'job search' is necessary. Workers are willing to put in more overtime or to postpone taking time off between jobs because they think they might as well seize overtime or job opportunities while available. Their response is, in a sense, an increase in the current supply of labor. Consequently, sales and output expand.

In this story, nothing on the wage side has changed to make expansion more attractive to firms. Rather, the individual firm sees a chance to do more business. In effect, its curve of marginal physical product of labor has shifted to the right. This curve for any factor is conventionally drawn against the background of supposedly fixed amounts of other factors. But here the firm is not thinking of a worsened mix of labor in relation to other factors. Rather, it expects to be able to put increased quantities of other factors into use along with labor. (And capital equipment is not always fully employed. Some flexibility exists in the system.) Furthermore, the easier sale of output means that the curves of *marginal revenue product* and of marginal revenue product deflated by price have shifted to the right. The concept of marginal revenue product recognizes that a firm's demand for labor depends not merely on how much the labor can physically contribute to production but also on what this additional physical output can add to the revenue of the firm. Extra physical output that cannot be sold adds nothing to the firm's revenue.

Since it takes time for prices to rise as explained in Chapter 7, output may expand in the meantime, and activity may temporarily exceed its full-employment level. Perceptions have been at work that eventually result in what superficially looks like a fallacy of composition.

Actually, there is none. There would be one if business firms and workers were making the above-mentioned decisions as a single aggregate entity. But they are deciding *individually*. And each one, from his own point of view, is not committing a fallacy or being fooled. ('Fooling' is essential in the branch of new classical macroeconomics that relies on 'misperceptions', as explained in Chapter 7.) The individual firm's opportunity to do a bigger volume of business at substantially unchanged costs and prices is a genuine one, even though it will prove temporary. Why not seize it while it lasts? As for the worker, why should he pass up the opportunity for overtime work that he would be glad to do some time or other or pass up the opportunity to find a job easily, even though (or especially though) the opportunity may prove fleeting? Why not postpone leisure? Firms and workers rationally respond to increased spending by producing and working more because they have to make their decisions individually, even though such behavior would be irrational if decided on *collectively*. No misperception or irrationality is necessarily involved. The key to the scenario is that people make the relevant decisions in a decentralized, piecemeal, nonsynchronous manner. (We examine the important concepts of individually and collectively rational behaviors on pages 195–6.)

How does this scenario ever end? It looks as if everybody has become happier than before at no cost. By its very nature, however, the situation can last only a while. Inventories available to be run down are not unlimited in size, nor are workers willing without limit to postpone leisure. Inflated demands get transmitted back to primary materials and factors of production, bidding up their prices and creating what superficially looks like a 'cost-push' process (see pages below). The inflated flow of spending impinges on limited real supplies (and supply schedules), and the economy turns out only temporarily escaping the impact on prices that standard theory describes. As resource and inventory limitations manifest themselves, as costs and prices and living expenses rise, and as the initially attractive sales and job opportunities accordingly come to look less attractive after all, the initial quantity impact of the inflated aggregate spending gives way to a price impact. P rises and Q drops back, even if MV remains at its new inflated level. Output and employment drop back again after temporarily rising beyond their sustainable rates.

Three points deserve emphasis. First, although price increases may accompany the monetary stimulus to output and employment, they are far from being an essential part of the process and are actually in rivalry with the stimulus. Second, although a cut in the real wage rate might indeed have an expansionary effect on output, it is not necessary for that effect (see the next section). Third, it is unnecessary to decide here whether the gain in output and employment should ultimately prove to have been only a borrowing against the future as, later, workers recoup postponed leisure and suppliers rebuild rundown inventories. Even if monetary factors should prove to have affected real output only by shifting it in time, and if this could happen only in a special case, the point would remain that monetary factors could indeed have a real bite even on an initial situation of full employment.

Let us examine the nature of the disequilibrium process in this case. The initial increase in the money stock raises the demand for commodities. Transactions, production and employment respond. These real accommodations to increased spending are unsustainable, however. Output eventually falls back for the supply-side reasons given above. This relapse manifests itself in an excess demand for commodities and productive factors, matched by an excess supply of money. The bidding up of costs and prices helps to clear the relevant markets. On the demand side, the increased prices mean decreased real balances and real expenditure. Both demand and supply factors, then, reverse the initial temporary stimulus to output and employment.

The analysis of this section might seem to contradict that of the previous section, which explains how general excess demand could shrink real activity. Actually, no contradiction exists. The rise in output in the second case is avowedly temporary. It hinges on rational decentralized decisionmaking, on workers' postponements of leisure, and on suppliers' rundowns of inventories, which serve the buffer purpose for which they were held in the first place. In the counterintuitive case of Barro and Grossman, workers not only do not postpone leisure but withdraw some of their labor because they cannot succeed in spending all of their earnings. Those authors assume, in their book, that firms hold no inventories (and their article of 1971, p. 85, 'abstracts from inventory accumulation or decumulation'). While the second case seems more plausible, the excess demand case of Barro and Grossman could develop, with no significant (further) leisure postponements and inventory rundowns taking place and with employment and production reduced below their full-employment equilibrium levels.

REAL WAGES AND THE BUSINESS CYCLE

Keynes (1936, p. 17) attributed to classical economists the belief that real wages are countercyclical: 'In general, an increase in employment can only occur to the accompaniment of a decline in the rate of real wages. Thus I am not disputing this vital fact which the classical economists have (rightly) asserted as indefeasible'. We question though whether most classical economists ever squarely faced this issue of the real wage.[4] Nevertheless, the belief that real wages are countercyclical was adopted by Keynesians and later became an important feature of Milton Friedman's 1967 AEA address. Yet according to monetary-disequilibrium theory, in the second case of monetary expansion, we cannot predict whether the real wage will increase, decrease, or remain the same. If the demand for labor increases more than the supply, then the theory is consistent with a rise in the real wage. This may be more in accord with Phillips's (1958) original formulation of the Phillips curve (discussed on pages 209–12 below), since a higher nominal and real wage may now accompany tightness in the labor market. A rise in the real wage would be consistent with the rise in the marginal productivity of labor.

Numerous empirical studies of the movement of real wages over the business cycle have provided no firm conclusions (a fact itself suggesting that the association, whether procyclical or countercyclical, is not strong and dependable). For example, Basu and Taylor (1999) study business cycles from 1870 to 1999 for 15 countries in what they call the largest such panel of data ever studied over this time frame in terms of country coverage (p. 46). They divide the 130 years covered into four periods according to the distinct international monetary regime that prevailed at the time. They find that real wages have been more procyclical recently, which they conjecture may account for the popularity in the current literature of models that predict procyclical real wages (p. 63). However, they argue that no distinct wage pattern emerges over time and place.

Although we attach no great theoretical importance to how real wages move over the cycle, we find nothing paradoxical about procyclical movement. High real wages are more feasible when effective coordination is contributing to the efficiency of the economic system and its component units than when monetary disequilibrium is impairing coordination. One aspect of this greater efficiency or productivity is that economic units can find trading partners more readily. Fewer resources are used up in market search. A related aspect is that fixed costs can be divided over more units of output, thereby increasing profit margins. Greater profits or profit margins in economic expansions need not be attributed to erosion of real wages. On the contrary, the circumstances conducing to greater profits may also permit somewhat increased wages.

THE SPLIT BETWEEN PRICES AND OUTPUT

One of the unanswered questions in money/macro theory that has puzzled economists for decades is the division of a change in nominal income between a change in output and a change in price. According to the equation of exchange, any increase in nominal spending and nominal income (MV) must be matched by an increase in the *value* of output, split between increases in price (P) and real output (Q). Given a definite, constant or fixed price/output split, the greater the price rise, the greater the underlying spending expansion so indicated and therefore the greater the accompanying output expansion. A given price/output split presupposes idle productive capacity available to be activated. Given the expansion of spending and nominal income, however, with the split a *variable*, the more the expansion goes toward raising price, the less it can go toward expanding output. In this case price increases are in *rivalry* with output expansion; they are inversely related. The following paragraphs explore this issue.

We write the equation of exchange in terms of percentage changes:

% change in M + % change in V = % change in P + % change in Q.[5]   (1)

Rewriting, we obtain:

% change in Q = % change in M + % change in V − % change in P.   (2)

Equation (2) illustrates that changes in output (Q) and price (P) are *inversely* related for a given change in nominal income.

For example, assume the economy starts at full-employment equilibrium with no inflation. Suppose that the money supply, spending, and hence nominal income, rise by 5 percent. At one extreme, prices increase by the full 5 percent leaving no room for an increase in output. At the other extreme, prices are rigid so that the entire increase in nominal income shows up as a 5 percent rise in output. We can infer that given an increase in nominal income (MV), the greater the increase in price, the smaller will be the expansion of output. While this example may seem simplistic, the next two chapters illustrate violations of the equation of exchange found in the literature.

It is the expansion of money and spending *itself* that increases output (if perhaps only temporarily). Price and wage inflation is one of the incidental and counterproductive consequences. Sluggishness of price response helps preserve the monetary stimulus to output.

When a monetary change impinges relatively heavily on real activity and only lightly on prices, we call such a split 'favorable' for an expansionary monetary change but 'unfavorable' for a contractionary or disinflationary one. Conversely, when a monetary change mainly impacts upon prices and has little effect on output, we call such a split 'unfavorable' for an expansionary monetary change but 'favorable' for a contractionary or disinflationary one.

How favorable the actual split is depends partly on what people expect. If following an increase in the money supply, people expect inflation and thus readily adjust prices, little stimulus remains for output. On the other hand, expectations serving to retard price adjustments leave greater scope for output to rise.

With the most favorable split conceivable, a contraction or slowdown of money growth, spending and nominal income would work entirely to reduce the price level or restrain the price uptrend, damaging real activity not at all. With the most unfavorable split, a contraction or slowdown would impinge entirely on real activity, with no reduction in the level or uptrend of prices. In general the impact falls partly on real activity and partly on prices. The factors tending to make the split favorable or unfavorable are relevant to the ease or difficulty of stopping an inflation. With a monetary policy geared toward disinflation, the split depends on the circumstances governing how persistent an inflationary momentum is, as explained in Chapter 8.

The following circumstances affect how the split generally occurs: (1) the process of adjusting away an excess demand for or excess supply of money takes time; (2) most markets are not perfectly competitive, so individuals are price-setters and wage-negotiators; (3) wages and prices are therefore not perfectly flexible; (4) the quantity of something actually exchanged on the market is the smaller of the quantity demanded and the quantity supplied; (5) frustration in undertaking some desired transactions affects the volume of other transactions attempted; (6) price trends and trends in the real volume of economic activity respond with differential lags to changes in money supply trends; and (7) people's expectations play a role in determining these lags. We elaborate on these items throughout the book.

NOTES

1. See Clower (1965 [1984], 1967 [1984]); Leijonhufvud (1968); Tucker (1971) and Barro and Grossman (1971, 1976). On why the text says 'or resurrected', see Yeager (1973, 1985, 1986, 1988, 1991 [1997]).
2. Clower does not explicitly introduce the concept of successful demand (or supply), but it appears in Fitoussi (1974) as 'realized' demand (or supply).
3. Hutt (1963, 1974, 1979) stresses this aspect of the contagion. What he calls 'withheld capacity' – pricing too high for market-clearing – in one line of production impairs activity and income earned in that line and so weakens demand for the outputs of other lines of production, rendering unchanged prices there too high also. In that way withheld capacity tends to spread. Hutt's theory of cumulative deterioration in a depression is remarkably similar (except in terminology and associated moralizing) to the theory of Clower and Leijonhufvud. Yet far from believing, as Clower and Leijonhufvud at least initially did, that he is giving an interpretation of Keynes, Hutt regards his own doctrine as quite different from that of Keynes. While not actually tackling the question of who more correctly understood what Keynes really meant, Glazier (1970) shows that Clower, Leijonhufvud and Hutt 'agree more on some of the fundamental issues of disequilibrium than they do on the history of doctrines' (Glazier, 1970, p. 3).
4. Humphrey (1991, pp. 6–7) shows that some classical economists (for example, Henry Thornton and Robert Torrens) argued that wages are more sticky than prices. An increase in the money supply would therefore lower real wages, raise profits and stimulate output and employment.
5. To be mathematically precise, a third term should be included on each side of the equation. It is the product of the two percentage changes on each side. Following the literature, we assume it is a small number and therefore can be omitted.

7. Disequilibrium economics (2)

THE LOGIC OF PRICE AND WAGE STICKINESS

Prices and so the purchasing power of the money unit do not dependably adjust fast enough to maintain continuous equilibrium between desired and actual quantities of money. A theory spelling out the reasons and implications may be eclectic, but so what if it corresponds to reality?

Brown (1931, pp. 88–9, 104) explained why price cuts would not immediately absorb a contraction of money, credit and spending. Producers, dealers and workers would not easily see why they should accept reduced prices and wages. Rather, they would hesitate making changes until they were sure that their costs or expenses had also been reduced. Brown was alluding to the 'who-goes-first problem' explained below. It is illegitimate to suppose that people somehow just know about monetary disequilibrium, know what pressures it is exerting for corrective adjustments in prices and wages, and promptly use this knowledge in their own pricing decisions. One cannot consistently suppose that the price system is a communication mechanism – a device for mobilizing and coordinating knowledge dispersed in millions of separate minds – and *also* suppose that people *already* have the knowledge that the system is working to convey (compare Garrison, 2001, p. 27). Business firms do not have a quick and easy shortcut to the results of the market process. They do not have it even when the market's performance is badly impaired.

Even if an especially perceptive entrepreneur did correctly diagnose a monetary disequilibrium and recognize what adjustments were required, what reason would he have to move first? By promptly cutting the price of his own product or service, he would be cutting its relative price, unless other people cut their prices and wages in at least the same proportion. How could he count on deep enough cuts in the prices of his inputs to spare him losses or increased losses at a reduced price of his own product? The same questions still apply even if monetary conditions and the required adjustments are widely understood. Each decisionmaker's price or wage actions still depend largely on the actual or expected actions of others. A businessperson's difficulties in finding profitable customers or a worker's in finding a job are not likely, as explained below, to trace wholly, and perhaps not even mainly, to his *own* pricing policy or wage demands.

To expect the market system to solve the 'coordination problem' automatically – or, rather, to keep it from arising – is to fail to understand that problem. What ensures that people act together in a sensible pattern? What makes people's economic activities mesh? What makes individual price adjustments add up to sensible outcomes? No one takes on this responsibility. The economy does not stay at full-employment equilibrium once reached. How close or how far away it is depends on how severe and how recent shocks have been in 'wants, resources and technology' – and monetary conditions.

The impossibility of perpetual full coordination is no defect of the market system. It is an inevitable consequence of circumstances confronting any economic system. One of the market system's virtues is that it does not require or impose collective decisions. The dispersion of knowledge and the fact that certain kinds of knowledge can be used effectively only through decentralized decisions *coordinated through markets and prices* – rather than coordinated in some magically direct way – is one of the hard facts of reality. It forms part of the reason why monetary disturbances can be so pervasively disruptive: they overtax the knowledge-mobilizing and signaling processes of the market.

Forces of unbalanced supply and demand tend, to be sure, to press disequilibrium prices toward their market-clearing levels. Since economic plans and activities stretch out over *time*, the coordinating forces do not operate rapidly enough to maintain full-employment equilibrium. Impediments to transactions can reinforce each other to a degee that shows up as recession or depression. Such considerations help argue for putting the *micro* semester of a principles of economics course before the *macro* semester. Students can hardly understand disruptions to economywide coordination, the subject matter of macroeconomics, until they know that a coordination problem exists in the first place and understand how the market process solves it when it is working ideally.

Coordination requires more than correct prices and wages. In Walrasian general-equilibrium theory, the 'auctioneer' not only achieves the whole array of market-clearing prices, but also puts trading partners in contact with one another, obviating the mutual searches that would otherwise be necessary. In the real world, however, a worker may be unemployed not necessarily because he insists on too high a wage rate but because he and a suitable employer have not yet made contact. Moreover, transactors encounter difficulties in finding trading partners in 'thin' as opposed to 'thick' markets (compare Diamond, 1982; Howitt, 1990 and Hall, 1991). Various startup costs of a new employer–employee relation also enter into the story.

Individual wages and prices are interdependent. This interdependence is central to the who-goes-first problem (compare Cagan, 1980, p. 829 and Schultze, 1985). It appears in input–output tables[1] and in the attention given to production costs, the cost of living and notions of fairness in price and wage setting. Concerned about maintaining their market shares over the long run, sellers try to keep their customers loyal by treating them reasonably in good times and bad, charging prices based on costs and fairly stable percentage markups. Although price and wage strategies help maintain good relations over the long run among customers and suppliers and workers and employers, they do undercut the sensitivity of prices and wages to short-run supply and demand. (Okun, 1975, 1979, 1981; Okun distinguishes between 'auction' and 'customer' markets and speaks of an 'invisible handshake' between labor and management in the latter.)

The holding of inventories (of materials and semi-finished and finished products) testifies to the rationality of price stickiness and to the role that incomplete knowledge plays in this stickiness.[2] Build-ups and rundowns of inventories absorb random fluctuations and mismatchings of supply and demand. Not every little inventory fluctuation calls for a price change. When, by exception, a fundamental or nonrandom supply or demand change does occur, the inventory-holder does not immediately recognize its nature. Nor is it rational for him that he should, for his being able to do so would have entailed the costs of obtaining and processing detailed knowledge about market conditions and the underlying fundamentals. Even – or especially – when the demand for particular materials or products changes as one aspect of a monetary disequilibrium, the necessity for a price change is likely to go unrecognized for a while.

Chapter 6 (pages 186–9) explains how firms and workers, following an increase in the money supply at full employment, may individually 'seize the opportunity' to increase quantities even though such behavior would not be collectively rational. Similarly, in a depression, when it would be collectively rational to cut the general level of prices and wages and other costs enough to make the money stock adequate for a full-employment volume of transactions, the individual may not find it rational to move first by cutting the particular price or wage for which he is responsible. He may rationally wait to see whether cuts by others, intensifying the competition he faces or reducing his production costs or his cost of living, will make it advantageous for him to follow with a cut of his own. The individually rational and the collectively rational may well diverge, as in the well-known example of the prisoners' dilemma (compare Olson, 1965 and Schelling, 1978). Taking the lead in downward price and wage adjustments is in the nature of a public good, and private incentives to supply public goods are notoriously inadequate.[3]

The divergences between individual and collective rationality and incentives, together with the interdependence and piecemeal determination of prices and wages and other costs, go far toward explaining the stickiness of price and wage levels and the persistence of monetary disequilibrium. This distinction between individually and collectively rational behaviors gets much play in several strands of microeconomics. We wonder why it took so long to receive due attention in macro.

Some noneconomic examples will help make it clearer. Most members of a lecture audience might want to avoid sitting in the first few rows, so those arriving early take seats toward the middle or rear. Those arriving later take seats behind the people already seated, leaving the front of the auditorium nearly empty. Most people wind up sitting further back than they really desire. Individually they do not want to move forward, but they wish that the audience as a whole would somehow move forward, leaving its members' relative positions unchanged (Schelling, 1978, Chapter 1). Most of the drivers waiting in a gasoline line, for another example, might wish that the line would form later in the morning (or wish that there were no panicky tank-topping in the first place), but since each one is powerless to change the behavior of the others, he adjusts to it by joining the line early.

Many more or less analogous circumstances make price and wage stickiness reasonable from the standpoint of individual decisionmakers. As a result, quantities adjust and markets do not clear following a disturbance. For example, the workers foreclosed from a particular employment by too high a wage rate may well be only a minority of the candidates, victims of a seniority system or of bad breaks. The more senior or the luckier workers who remain employed are not acting against their own interest in refusing to accept wage adjustments toward a market-clearing level.

According to the 'insider–outsider theory', insiders are currently employed workers whose jobs are protected by high turnover costs. Outsiders are the unemployed workers whose interests are neglected by the insiders. The market power of insiders accounts for sticky (and higher) real wages (Lindbeck and Snower, 1985, 1986, 1988a, 1988b).

For the employer as well, the costs of obtaining and processing information may recommend judging what wage rates are appropriate by what other people are paying and receiving and by traditional differentials. If changed conditions make old rules of thumb no longer appropriate, it takes time for new rules to evolve. An employer may offer a wage higher than necessary to attract the desired number of workers so that he can screen ones of superior quality from an ample applicant pool (compare Weiss, 1980, 1990). Considerations of 'morale' are relevant to many jobs that involve providing informal training to one's less experienced fellow workers (compare Solow, 1979, 1980; Akerlof, 1982 and Akerlof and Yellen, 1988, 1990).[4] Performance in this and other respects is hard to monitor, and workers may withhold it if they come to feel that they are being treated unfairly. Employers may offer higher real wages to discourage workers from 'quitting' or 'shirking' (compare Stiglitz, 1974; Schlicht, 1978; Salop, 1979; Shapiro and Stiglitz, 1984).

The 'efficiency wage theory', which Gordon (1990b, p. 1157) calls the 'rage of the 80s', assumes that the productivity of workers depends directly on the real wage received and that firms are therefore willing to pay higher wages, as in the foregoing examples.[5] Some new Keynesians argue that such theories provide a rationale for the existence of *underemployment equilibrium*, which supposedly exists when the real wage is kept at a high level (compare Snowdon and Vane, 1997a, p. 18; Snowdon, Vane and Wynarczyk, 1994, Chapter 7). We argue, however, that this unemployment would be 'structural' rather than 'cyclical'.

For some goods and services as well as labor, actual or supposed correlations between price and quality may provide reasons for not relying on market-clearing by price alone. Transactors on one side of a market or the other may not be able to know exactly what they are buying or selling. They may value the privilege of dealing with a trustworthy seller or buyer enough to pay a higher price or accept a lower price than they otherwise would. Some price–quality relations are likely to be genuine. Physicians charging higher fees may be able to 'afford' more time per patient, or the more conscientious physicians, treating fewer patients, may 'require' higher fees. A higher average level of prices for used cars may induce owners of well-functioning cars who might otherwise have kept them to trade them in or put them on the market after all.

Suppose now, in a more general context, that some seller is willing to offer his output at below the prevailing price, even at a price that is low in relation to quality. He would cut his price *if* doing so would attract enough customers. But if he feared that customers might take his price cut as a sign of a reduction, even a disproportionate reduction, in the quality of his product, he might well forgo that cut at least until after his competitors had shown the way.[6]

More broadly, money's general purchasing power is sticky because of a banal but momentous fact discussed in Chapters 3 and 4: money, unlike all other goods, lacks a price and a market *of its own*. When the purchasing power of money is wrong in relation to the money supply, no *single* adjustment will restore equilibrium. Rather, the pressures of monetary disequilibrium are obscurely diffused over myriads of individual markets and prices. This very diffusion renders the correction of monetary disequilibrium sluggish.

Alternatively, while individuals may set the prices of their own particular goods or services, with regard to the *overall* purchasing power of money they are *price-takers*. Each seller sees his own behavior as having little or no effect on it. He must take it as given in deciding how to adjust his own price. This very fact helps explain the sluggishness of the pressures working to correct a disequilibrium value of the money unit.

Price and wage stickiness as we explain it does not hinge on long-term contracts, although they do contribute to it and receive emphasis in new

Keynesian economics (Gordon, 1987, p. 229; 1990a). For example, Fischer (1977) and Phelps and Taylor (1977) show that with long-term wage contracts, nominal shocks to aggregate demand can have real effects even if expectations are formed rationally. Taylor (1980) extends the analysis to include *staggered* overlapping *wage* contracts, while Blanchard (1983) focuses on staggered overlapping *price* contracts.

In seminal new Keynesian articles, Mankiw (1985) and Akerlof and Yellen (1985) argue that small barriers or frictions to price adjustment on the level of the individual firm can produce large price rigidities in the aggregate. Mankiw focuses on *menu costs*, while Akerlof and Yellen speak of *near rationality* in which firms simply forgo small amounts of profits by not adjusting prices frequently. Their arguments are further developed by Blanchard and Kiyotaki (1987) and Ball and Romer (1990).

The reader may wonder whether the foregoing arguments do not prove too much. How does too high a price level ever adjust? Well, some sellers will have to cut their prices and even sell at a loss to avoid still greater losses. An extreme example would be a seller faced with a credit squeeze, growing inventories and a scarcity of storage space, yet obliged under long-term contracts to accept continuing deliveries of materials. For sellers in such a position, further delays in price adjustments become less reasonable as time goes on. When they finally do reduce their prices, the attendant changes in costs and competitive conditions make it both easier and more necessary for others to follow.

The argument about reasons for delaying adjustments refers, furthermore, to *administered* prices and wages. Some prices, however, are determined impersonally in *atomistic* markets and their sensitive responses do facilitate the subsequent responses of administered ones. The commodities whose prices respond first are by and large primary commodities embodying relatively small amounts of inputs produced by other economic sectors. For them the *interweaving* of prices and wages and other costs is a relatively slight impediment to price adjustments. The prompter and wider price swings of primary products than of highly fabricated products is consistent with this interpretation. The sensitive responses of some prices to disequilibrium keeps the overall price level from being actually *rigid*.

An instructive analogy holds between a wrong *level* of prices and wages and an established *trend* of prices and wages. By first considering the simpler question of how a mere level is established and adjusted, we have prepared for exploiting the analogy in Chapter 8 between the inertias of a level and a trend.

In conclusion, rational behavior does not preclude disequilibrium. Attaining a new level and pattern of prices and wages that would correct a monetary disequilibrium can be a long, drawn-out and painful process. Hence the importance of a policy, which need not be a particularly activist one, of not causing monetary disturbances.

POSSIBLE DIFFICULTIES RESOLVED

Critics of disequilibrium theory[7] might claim that it assumes nonmaximizing behavior. To let disequilibria persist – to leave nonmarket-clearing prices unadjusted – is to throw away gains from trade, irrationally. Critics might further argue that emphasizing price and wage stickiness is a cop out, a fig leaf to cover the theorist's own perplexity. Prices, broadly interpreted, have many dimensions: unofficial discounts, speed of delivery, associated services, credit terms and so on and on. Similarly, many conditions besides dollars per hour can be manipulated to modify effective wage rates. Considering all these possibilities, we must recognize prices and wages as effectively flexible. 'Stickiness' is not the cause of business fluctuations.

Disequilibrium theorists would reply that stickiness must not be taken overliterally as saying that prices and wages are immovably rigid. Rather, it is a traditional shorthand expression referring to various circumstances that keep prices and wages from promptly moving to a new full-employment equilibrium after a major disturbance. The point that a typical price has several dimensions besides the cut-and-dried dollars-per-unit dimension underlines the complexity, not the ease, of achieving a new equilibrium.

In making his observations about discoordination and the complexities of recoordination, Leijonhufvud (1981) quite explicitly does *not* appeal to rigidity or stickiness of prices and wages in any overliteral sense. Mere changeability of prices and wages does not ensure that they all change promptly and in the proper degrees into a new equilibrium relation with each other. They are flexible in the long run, but the question is how quickly they can achieve a new full-employment equilibrium.

Critics of disequilibrium theory could hardly mean that people have always already maximized utility or profit or wealth and have already reaped all potential gains from trade. Such a view would deny all miscoordinations, including depressions. Disequilibrium theorists, like others, recognize that people act rationally and purposefully. But people have no way of achieving desired results instantly and costlessly. Through their time-consuming behavior on markets, hampered by 'transactions costs' and 'imperfect information', they must grope for better coordination of their own plans and activities with those of millions of other people. They must cope as best they can with constant changes in wants, resources, technology, institutions, legislation – and monetary conditions. They are rarely in a position of already having achieved complete success.

The issue is how fast or slow and with how much smoothness or difficulty the processes of groping operate. The decisions required as people seek to coordinate their activities are interdependent, yet are made piecemeal. Whether a particular prospective transaction can go forward to the advantage of both prospective parties may depend not just on their own pricing decisions but also on decisions of *third parties,* decisions they cannot directly control.

Suppose that a house owner and his teenage neighbor want to make a deal for the teenager to mow his lawn. Lawnmowers and lawnmower rentals happen, however, to be priced prohibitively high. At no wage rate, then, could the two people strike an advantageous bargain. The obstacle is not one that either or both of them can remove, and their failing to remove it is no sign of irrationality. Similarly, whether a manufacturer can afford wage rates attractive to workers may well depend on land rents, interest rates, prices of materials and equipment and fuel and transport, prices charged by competitors and prices entering into workers' cost of living.

The point of these examples is that attaining a full-employment pattern of prices and wages is not simply a matter of bilateral negotiations between the two parties to each potential transaction. Comprehensive multilateral negotiations are infeasible or prohibitively costly, so groping must take place instead through decentralized, piecemeal, sequential, trial-and-error setting and revision of individual prices and wages. Price-setters and wage-negotiators cannot obtain the information necessary for setting the 'correct' prices and wages, whatever they might be, in some magical, nonmarket way. The market process has work to do, including work in transmitting information. That process works better than any alternative set of institutions we can imagine. Still, it cannot work miracles.

Does stickiness 'cause' business fluctuations? No, the cause is whatever disturbances inflict widespread discoordination. The subsequent price changes are indicators and symptoms of those disturbances and curative (though only partially curative) responses to them.

In part these responses aggravate the discoordination. A 'catch-22' is at work. The economy is damned if it does and damned if it does not exhibit a high degree of price flexibility in response to the disturbance. Fisher (1933) emphasized the 'debt-deflation' aspect of downward price and wage flexibility. Through increasing the real burden of debts and in other ways, downward flexibility contributes to bankruptcies, impairs the value of collateral against loans, undermines credit and financial intermediation and causes other but related kinds of damage, such as rendering much information obsolete (compare Bernanke, 1983). Another problem with downward flexibility concerns 'expectations'. If people see the purchasing power of money increasing, they may very well delay their spending in hopes of even lower prices.[8] On the other hand, somehow keeping prices and wages inflexible in the face of a major disturbance would itself obstruct recoordination.

The term 'stickiness' alludes to many reasons why lapses from coordination and waste of potential gains from trade do not show that people are irrational.

Economic history illustrates that discoordination can persist for months and even years after a severe disturbance.

A second line of criticism of disequilibrium theory might question its concern with knowledge having to be conveyed through markets. Some information – as about monetary aggregates, interest rates and so forth – is publicly available outside of markets. For many reasons, including elements of money illusion built into the economy quite rationally from individual points of view, monetary changes just cannot be neutral in their effects on real quantities. Even if people rightly understand the ultimate consequences of a monetary situation and act accordingly, they still run the risk of being right too soon because of 'long and variable lags' (to use Milton Friedman's expression). The public availability of monetary numbers and other information does not discredit what we have said about the time-consuming and glitch-beset process of maintaining or regaining coordination in the face of disturbances.

Critics might suggest, thirdly, that 'the assumptions about economic behavior used to account for the relation between money and real activity should be consistent with the assumptions used to explain resource allocation and income distribution' (Grossman, 1986, p. 402). But consistency surely does not mean using identical assumptions in all strands of analysis, however different. In theorizing about some physical questions, it is appropriate to neglect – to 'assume away' – air friction. In theorizing about others, air friction is central and must not be neglected. Similarly, in comparative-static theorizing about the long-run consequences of specified changes in technology or taxes or whatever, the frictions of transition processes are legitimately neglected. In macroeconomic theorizing, however, which deals with disturbances to coordination among decentralized activities, the frictions besetting coordinating processes and the absence of perfect competition are central to the story.[9]

THE HISTORICAL ROOTS OF DISEQUILIBRIUM THEORY

Theories of monetary disequilibrium involving price stickiness far antedate Keynes. It was not a hallmark of classical and neoclassical economics to believe that markets always clear or that automatic market-clearing forces are always more potent than disturbances to equilibrium. When concerned, as they usually were, with the long-run equilibrium toward which fundamental market forces were driving patterns of prices and resource allocation, classical and neoclassical writers (including Ricardo, Mill and Marshall) did abstract from the shorter-run phenomenon of monetary disequilibrium. But they recognized that such disequilibrium does occur and sometimes paid explicit attention to it (Warburton, 1981 and an unpublished book-length manuscript; see also Humphrey, 1991).

For example, Hume (1752b [1970], pp. 38–40) explained that monetary expansion exerts a real stimulus only during a transition period, before prices have risen fully. And though less clearly, he saw the corresponding point about a contractionary monetary change. Thornton (1802 [1978], pp. 119–20) was more explicit and even noted that wages tend to adjust downward more stickily than prices. Scrope (1833, pp. 214–15) implicitly recognized the stickiness of at least those prices that enter into the 'producing cost' of commodities. To jump to early twentieth-century America, Davenport (1913, pp. 298–320) and Brown (1931, pp. 85–104; 1933) provide examples of pre-Keynesian emphasis on wage and price stickiness. (Yeager, 1991 [1997] provides further examples, including quotations from Brown's (1933) hard-to-find article written just a few days before Franklin D. Roosevelt took office as president.)

THE AUSTRIAN THEORY OF THE BUSINESS CYCLE

One quite specific theory of the business cycle was cultivated by Ludwig von Mises and F.A. Hayek in the early 1930s and is popular nowadays with members of the resurrected Austrian school.[10] Briefly, this theory attributes recession or depression to a preceding excessive expansion of money and credit. It does not flatly deny any possible role of their contraction during the depression, but it insists that misguided expansion has already, before the depression begins, caused the damage fated to follow. A hard-core version of the theory even suggests that resistance to contraction is then useless or even harmful. Depression must be dealt with early by forestalling the unhealthy boom in which it originates.

Let us review the supposed process. Perhaps in response to political pressures for lower interest rates, the monetary authority begins expanding bank reserves through its discount or open-market operations. Business firms find credit cheaper and more abundant. These signals suggest, incorrectly, that people have become more willing to save and so free resources for investment projects that will make greater consumption possible in the future. Accordingly, firms invest more ambitiously than before. In particular, they construct *higher-order* capital goods, goods relatively remote from the final consumer: machine tool factories, for example, as opposed to retail stores and inventories of consumer goods. Relatively long times must elapse before resources invested in such goods ripen into goods and services for ultimate consumers. This large time element makes demands for higher-order goods relatively sensitive to interest rates. That is why credit expansion particularly stimulates their construction.

Actually – so the theory continues – the underlying realities have not changed. Resources available for long-term-oriented investment have not become more abundant. Shortages and price increases reveal a keen struggle for resources among industries producing higher-order capital goods, *lower-order* (closer-to-the-consumer) capital goods, and *consumer* goods. This struggle intensifies as workers in the artificially stimulated industries, whose contributions to ultimate consumption are far from maturity, try to spend their increased incomes on current consumption.

Price signals, especially the interest rate, have been falsified. Sooner or later appearances must bow to reality. Shortages or increased prices of resources necessary for completing some capital-construction projects will force their abandonment, spelling at least partial waste of resources already embodied in them. A tightening of credit, with loans no longer so readily available and interest rates no longer so artificially low as they had become, may play a part in this return to reality. For policies of expanding money and credit could not doggedly persist without threatening unlimited inflation.

Cutting back long-term-oriented investment and even abandoning some partially completed projects for the reasons just mentioned means laying off workers, cancelling orders for machines and materials and cancelling some rentals of land and buildings. The downturn is under way. In the ensuing depression, unwise projects are liquidated or restructured and the wasteful mis-allocation of resources begins to be undone – but painfully.

This scenario of boom and downturn is conceivable, but so are others. It does not explain the ensuing depression phase. Depression is a pervasive phenomenon, with customers scarce, output reduced, and jobs lost in almost all sectors of the economy. Whatever might be said of the boom and downturn, the depression phase can hardly be portrayed as an intersectoral struggle for productive resources exacerbated by distorted signals in interest rates and other prices. Austrian economists can hardly explain the continuing depression – unless they invoke a 'secondary deflation', meaning monetary factors going beyond their own distinctive theory.

Furthermore, the Austrian theory is an unnecessarily specific scenario. It envisages specific consequences of specific price distortions created by the injection of new money, but it demonstrates neither the necessity nor the importance of those specific distortions to the downturn into the depression, let alone to the depression itself. Monetary-disequilibrium theory, in contrast, can handle the phenomena of economic expansion and depression with less specific suppositions. Unlike the Austrian theory, it does not disregard 'Occam's Razor'.

Both Austrian and monetarist theories recognize that expansion and contraction of money affect credit conditions. The specific Austrian scenario is not necessary to understand why demands for capital goods, particularly of higher orders, fluctuate more widely over the cycle than demands for investment goods closer to final consumption and for consumer goods. Firms invest in view of prospects for profitable sale of the consumer goods and services that will ultimately result, and investment is more susceptible to postponement or hastening than is consumption. In the short and intermediate term, then, investment can exhibit a *magnification* of observed or anticipated fluctuations in consumption demands. In a world of uncertainty, furthermore – uncertainty exacerbated by monetary instability – hindsight will reveal some investment projects to have been unwise, some even being abandoned before their completion. The Austrian theory is not needed to account for these facts. Monetary-disequilibrium theorists put less stress than the Austrians on shifts in the interest rate and relative prices. The reason is *not* that they deny such shifts.[11] The reason rather is that such shifts, though crucial to the distinctively Austrian scenario, are mere details in the monetary-disequilibrium account of business fluctuations. Understandably the monetarists emphasize the 'centerpiece' of their story – a disequilibrium relation between the nominal quantity of money and the general level of prices and wages.

RATIONAL EXPECTATIONS

The next three sections review another alternative to monetary-disequilibrium theory, the new classical macroeconomics. It features two main hypotheses: *rational expectations* ('RE' for short) and *equilibrium always* (the continuous market clearing of the Walrasian general-equilibrium model). Although initially RE was thought to be the distinguishing characteristic of this school, the assumption of equilibrium always has now taken its place. In fact, many new Keynesian economists accept the RE hypothesis.

How people act depends on what they expect about future circumstances and the behavior of other people. Two approaches to modeling expectations are labeled 'adaptive' and 'rational'. The adaptive expectations approach implies that economic units base their expectations of future magnitudes on a weighted average of actual values during previous periods or on observed discrepancies between current outcomes and past expectations. But, claims the RE camp, it is irrational to ignore new information about the present and future. The RE view supposes that people, in forming their expectations, will use all information available (at costs worth incurring). The information used is not confined to past values of economic variables. Rather, it may include all kinds including political news.

According to the RE doctrine, people will process their information by employing at least tacitly sensible economic theories and models. One implication is that in devising a realistic model involving expectations, the economist should suppose that people form expectations in a way that is compatible with his model. Otherwise he would be making contradictory assumptions. But is that necessarily true? Might not the economist, without contradicting himself, believe that his own theory is correct but that people generally accept and act on some different and wrong theory? Critics of the 'real-bills doctrine' recognize that policymakers have often believed in and even acted on that fallacious doctrine.[12]

What reason is there to suppose that people will acquire information sensibly and use it with sensible theories and models? In part, the argument appeals to a kind of natural selection. People who act on expectations formed with inadequate information and poor theories will tend to lose money and positions of influence in economic life, leaving the field to those who do behave sensibly.

Arbitrage and speculation also enter into the story. If economic variables did happen to be determined under the predominant influence of people who used poor information and poor judgment, then others with better information and judgment could make profits. In so doing they would move the variables into correspondence with their fundamental determinants. This argument has some plausibility when applied to prices of things traded on organized markets, such as securities, standard commodities and perhaps foreign currencies. It applies less well to variables such as GDP and the unemployment rate. How does one speculate on those magnitudes in such a way as to move them toward levels that are in some sense correct?

RE doctrine does not require everyone to behave rationally in the sense described. It simply requires enough people to behave that way. People have a profit-and-loss incentive to behave rationally, a weeding out process operates, and the behavior of the rational people tends to dominate aggregate economic behavior.

RE doctrine does not say that expectations are correct. Not even rational people can foresee the future in detail. But expectations will not be systematically and dependably wrong – wrong in a particular direction and degree. If they were, people who perceived the systematic errors could earn profits by 'realizing perceived gains from trade', and their transactions would tend to wipe the errors out. Economists should therefore model behavior on the supposition that expectations are right *on average* in the light of the best available information and theory, although perhaps varying widely around the average.

Lucas (1976 [1981] [1987]) draws a related implication of RE in a proposition known as the 'Lucas critique'. Parameters econometrically measured under one policy regime will not necessarily stay the same under another. (Some examples of alternative regimes are: gold standard versus fiat money, fixed versus floating exchange rates, and macro policy under a political administration committed to avoiding inflation versus policy under one known to favor fighting unemployment even at the risk of inflation.) Parameters are unlikely to stay the same because people take account of the policy regime in forming and acting on their expectations.

RE econometricians try to form models that will remain valid across regimes by taking account of how the perceived regime affects expectations and behavior. They look for parameters of structural equations describing aspects of people's behavior that remain constant across a range of environments or regimes, such as parameters characterizing technologies and preferences (Sargent, 1986, Chapter 1).

EQUILIBRIUM ALWAYS AND MISPERCEPTIONS

The doctrine of equilibrium always comes close to assuming that prices and wages are so flexible that markets always clear (or should be modeled as if they do). This doctrine is not logically bound up with rational expectations, and not all RE writers combine the two doctrines. Yet the two often do occur together.

How do equilibrium always theorists handle the palpable fact that business fluctuations do occur and that what appears to be severe involuntary unemployment sometimes develops and persists for months or even years? The first version or strand of equilibrium always invokes the theory of misperceptions, connected with the 'Lucas supply function'. Focusing on the fact that workers and firms have incomplete or imperfect information, Lucas presents 'an equilibrium model of the business cycle' (1979 [1981] [1987], pp. 179–214).[13] The second version or strand adopts the real business cycle theory, with its emphasis on shocks to technology and supply conditions.

In the strand based on *misperceptions*, money has a role to play in business fluctuations. Markets are still clearing at the going wages and prices, although people may be supplying and demanding quantities of labor and commodities based on misinterpretations of what nominal wages and prices mean in *real* terms. In an apparent depression, for example, workers are not supplying as much labor as usual because they mistakenly perceive real wages as too low to motivate a normal supply.

One scenario of misperceptions goes as follows. Suppose monetary expansion unexpectedly raises prices in general. Firms recognize that relative to the increased prices of their own particular products, constant or even somewhat increased nominal wage rates represent real wage cuts. Accordingly, they demand more labor. Workers are willing to supply more labor, for they do not know enough about the prices of the whole range of consumer goods and services to recognize that the somewhat increased nominal wage rates actually represent cuts *relative* to their own cost of living. Because workers are fooled, actual employment and output rise. Yet all transactors are operating on their demand or supply curves, even though the labor supply curve has been distorted by misperceptions of the real wage.

Suppose, conversely, that monetary shrinkage causes an unexpected decline in the price level. Firms are more aware of the prices of the particular things they sell than worker-consumers are of the prices of all the things they buy. Constant or even somewhat reduced nominal wage rates appear as real increases to firms but as real reductions to workers, so firms demand and households supply less labor. Output falls even though everyone is operating on his labor demand or supply curve (labor supply curves being distorted by misperceptions). In this view the unemployment that results is voluntary.

The foregoing scenario is based on Friedman (1968a) and focuses on the fooling of *workers*. Lucas (1973, p. 333) extends Friedman's model to include fooling of firms, which 'misinterpret general price movements for relative price changes'. Lucas also introduces rational expectations into his model instead of the adaptive expectations used by Friedman. Birch, Rabin and Yeager (1982) observe that the misperceptions theory has implications at odds with reality and squares poorly with the equation of exchange. Our pages below elaborate on these points.

Sargent and Wallace (1975, 1976) show that the misperceptions strand of equilibrium always, together with the RE doctrine, yields the 'policy-invariance proposition'. The former attributes output fluctuations to errors in expectations or perceptions. The latter suggests that people will not make such errors in response to systematic, predictable, or perceivable monetary or fiscal policy. Hence, such policies are ineffective in changing output and unemployment. The emphasis is on 'systematic' policy because that is the kind that people can catch onto and make allowance for in their setting of wages and prices. For example, if people come to perceive that every time a recession begins, the monetary authority increases the money supply, they will anticipate this response. Instead of marking down their wages and prices in the face of slumping demand, they will anticipate the monetary expansion and will maintain their wages and prices or even raise them in line with the expected money supply increase. The systematic policy will have no real bite.

Unsystematic, random, haphazard policy cannot come to be expected and allowed for and so will have a real bite. But precisely because such a policy is pointless and haphazard, its real effects can hardly be systematically beneficial. The best to be expected of macroeconomic policy is that it be simple, steady, easy to catch onto, and therefore nondisturbing. This branch of new classical macroeconomics arrives at almost the same policy recommendations as earlier monetarists, but by a different route.

Yet it is hard to believe that anticipated monetary expansion would do no good even in the depths of depression, simply exhausting itself in price and wage increases. After all, prices and wages are already too high for the nominal quantity of money. Monetary expansion would increase real cash balances up to the full-employment level in a simpler and quicker way than through the slow and painful process of price and wage deflation, with its adverse side effects on existing debts and through postponement of spending. New classical economists are disinclined, however, to dwell on this case. They are uncomfortable with the very concept of disequilibrium, especially of the severe and prolonged kind that a deep depression would represent.

The notion of equilibrium always is hard to accept. It seems more straight-forward to recognize that monetary disturbances may disrupt the clearing of the markets for labor and commodities. Whether or not people suffer from mis-perceptions, various circumstances including the complex interdependence of very many separately determined prices and wages keep them from *all* adjusting swiftly to market-clearing levels.

What assumptions we should make about flexibility of prices, nearness to pure competition and the strength of market-clearing forces depend on what questions we are tackling (compare page 201 above). In tackling microeco-nomic questions, assumptions about market perfection may be legitimate simplifications. But in macroeconomic theorizing, departures from market perfection are close to the center of the story. One reason for some theorists' belief in equilibrium always seems to be that they (for example, Barro 1979, especially p. 55) are sliding from a warranted skepticism about activist government policies into an unwarranted attribution of near-perfection to markets. Yet no human institution is perfect. The imperfection of one, the state, does not imply the perfection of another, the market. It does not imply the capacity of the market to cope quickly even with severe shocks. We should not go too far in personifying markets and attributing powers of coping to them. *Individuals* and not markets are the actors in the economic drama.

EQUILIBRIUM ALWAYS AND REAL BUSINESS CYCLE THEORY

While money does play a role in the theory reviewed in the last section, it has no role in real business cycle theory, the second strand of equilibrium always. This theory attributes business cycles to real or supply shocks, such as changes in technology. Kydland and Prescott (1982) and Long and Plosser (1983) are two of the seminal articles in this literature. In explaining observed correlations between changes in money and output, the theory stresses 'reverse causation'. Instead of changes in the money growth rate causing changes in income, changes in income cause changes in that rate (King and Plosser, 1984). As in misper-ceptions theory, unemployment in a recession is voluntary. Government stabilization policy is unnecessary and even undesirable (see below).

This theory does not fully explain the technology shocks that supposedly occur. It simply assumes they do exist. In historical fact it is implausible to blame real disturbances for the major recessions and depressions actually expe-rienced. Instead of being readily attributable to changes in capacities to produce output, recessions and depressions exhibit what look like pervasive deficiencies of demand, pervasive difficulties in finding customers and finding jobs. The theory ignores the questions of coordination, information and transactions costs. It usually assumes a 'representative agent', that is, all individuals are identical. In effect it considers how Robinson Crusoe might rationally react to techno-logical shocks (Plosser, 1989 [1997a], pp. 399–400).

In Figure 1.1, real business cycle theory eliminates the trend line represent-ing potentional output. It assumes instead that real shocks have permanent effects so that potential output constantly shifts. Since it assumes that actual and potential output are the same, the equilibria that result are Pareto optimal; government stabilization policy is not needed and not desirable. Proponents of the theory often refer to it as 'dynamic general equilibrium theory'. The consensus model of monetary policy, described on pages 137–9 above, merges the quantitative techniques and methods of this theory with the price stickiness of new Keynesian economics.

Market clearing is at the core of real business cycle theory, and as we argue above, equilibrium always is hard to reconcile with the facts. On the other hand, monetary-disequilibrium theory explains how erratic money has especially great scope for causing discoordination. It can point to ample historical and statistical evidence from a wide range of times and places suggesting that erratic money has in fact been the dominant (which is not to say the exclusive) source of business fluctuations. Such episodes defy being talked away with the 'reverse causation' argument. Laidler (1988 [1990a], p. 22n) suggests that the plausibility of that argument is greatly reduced by the long and variable time lags inherent in the real-world phenomena discussed in the monetarist literature. We add that many episodes of money supplies being changed by causes independent of incomes and price levels also discredit that argument.

Monetary-disequilibrium theory recognizes that monetary disturbances can have real effects not only in the short run, but also in the long run (see pages above) . One does not have to resort to real business cycle theory in order to explain how the Great Depression badly impaired capital formation, leaving the U.S. economy to recover from a lower productive base than it otherwise would have.

THE PHILLIPS CURVE TRADEOFF BETWEEN INFLATION AND UNEMPLOYMENT

In the first chapter of his 2001 textbook, *Principles of Economics*, Mankiw looks at the 'ten principles of economics'. The last of these is: 'society faces a short-run tradeoff between inflation and unemployment' (Mankiw, 2001a, p.

14). He writes in a journal article (2001b, p. c46) that the tradeoff is both 'inexorable' and 'mysterious' and that 'the economics profession has yet to produce a satisfactory theory to explain it'. He continues: 'Indeed, the standard models of inflation-unemployment dynamics are inconsistent with conventional views about the effects of monetary policy. Resolving this inconsistency is a prominent outstanding puzzle for business cycle theorists'.

We recognize that an increase in the money supply may not immediately cause people to revise their expectations about the price level. A lag in the response of expectations and prices leaves room for expanded spending to stimulate real output. Not price inflation but rather the lack of it is what permits a real stimulus. No causality exists between changes in prices and changes in output. Rather, both are the result of the underlying monetary expansion that brings them about.

One early version of the Phillips curve held that monetary policy can exploit a 'long-run tradeoff' between unemployment and inflation. After the seminal articles of Friedman (1968a) and Phelps (1967), the notion of a 'short-run tradeoff' between unemployment and unanticipated inflation took its place. The sequence of events runs from an unanticipated increase in the money supply to an unanticipated increase in prices to an increase in output. Unanticipated inflation supposedly causes output to rise as explained on pages 206–207 above. Birch, Rabin and Yeager (1982) argue that this scenario is at odds with reality. In general, the sequence is the other way around, so that output rises before prices. (Compare Cagan, 1974, p. 39; and the many empirical studies of Milton Friedman.) Laidler (1990b) also recognizes this inconsistency in the literature.

While inflation itself is supposed to stimulate output and reduce unemployment, what actually stimulates output is the monetary change not fully absorbed by inflation. David Hume (1752b [1970], p. 38) put this central point correctly by saying that in the process of inflation, 'it is only in this interval or intermediate situation, between the acquisition of money and rise of prices, that the encreasing quantity of gold and silver is favourable to industry'. If the price increase was somehow kept down, a given degree of monetary expansion would go further in expanding output. Eventually though, costs and prices would respond and output recede to the full-employment level as described on pages 186–9 above.

We present our argument more formally by writing the equation of exchange as taken from page 190 above: (1) % change in Q = % change in M + % change in V – % change in P. This equation implies that given a change in nominal income (MV), the output change (Q) is inversely related to the change in price (P). Since the equation of exchange is a tautology, it must hold at every point in time. Anything that conflicts with it or contradicts it is therefore bound to be wrong.

The following equation is one formulation of the so-called 'expectations-augmented Phillips curve':

(2) output gap = f (p − p^e), where the output gap is actual output minus potential output, p is the actual rate of inflation, p^e is the anticipated (expected) rate of inflation, and f' is greater than zero. Given the level of potential output and the anticipated rate of inflation, any change in actual output is directly related to the change in the actual rate of inflation (p). We assume the economy starts with no inflation (actual and anticipated) and then increases occur in the money supply, spending, and hence nominal income. According to equation (2), it is the increase in prices that causes the increase in output. More specifically, the greater is the (surprise) inflation, the greater will be the increase in actual output.

On the other hand, equation (1) implies that for a given increase in nominal income (MV), the greater is the rise in prices, the smaller will be the increase in actual output. A contradiction clearly exists between equation (1), the equation of exchange, and equation (2), the expectations-augmented Phillips curve, and the latter equation is just plain wrong. Note that we are not taking equation (2) as an aggregate supply curve which must then be combined with an aggregate demand curve. Rather, following the literature we take it as a causal proposition about reality. It incorrectly implies that (surprise) inflation causes output to increase. One might try to argue that when inflation occurs, velocity also increases as the demand for real balances shrinks. The rise in velocity then supports the greater output. However, this increase in velocity would result from anticipated inflation and not the unanticipated inflation of equation (2).

We interpret the 'tradeoff', if we must, as temporarily securing greater output today at the expense of an increase in prices in the future. Any price increase today detracts from this real stimulus. More importantly, it is the rise in the money supply and hence spending that cause both increases. And as we have argued, it takes time before prices fully respond.

An alternative specification of the expectations-augmented Phillips curve is:

(3) p = p^e + f (output gap), where the terms are the same as before and f' is greater than zero. Chapter 8 examines this version and concludes that it too contradicts the equation of exchange and therefore must also be wrong. Moreover, Chapter 8 illustrates that a sticky price level has its analogue in a sticky price uptrend. Monetary-disequilibrium theory can explain both phenomena and is a viable alternative to the 'new Keynesian Phillips curve', which Mankiw (2001b, p. c52) calls the 'workhorse for much recent research on monetary policy'. While it may have some virtues, Mankiw acknowledges that this relation has one glaring defect: it is contradicted by the facts (see page 231 below) .

Our interpretations and formulations of the expectations-augmented Phillips curve are based on Humphrey (1978, 1982, 1985a, 1985b). Humphrey (1985b) argues that the 'Phillips curve tradeoff' did not originate with Phillips (1958). Rather, he shows that at least ten predecessors over a period of 250 years are associated with it. Humphrey (1984, p. 16) points out that Irving Fisher's seminal 1926 article was reprinted in 1973 under the title 'I discovered the Phillips curve'. Fisher (1926 [1973], p. 502) incorrectly argues:

> But as the economic analysis already cited certainly indicates a causal relationship between inflation and employment or deflation and unemployment, it seems reasonable to conclude...that the ups and downs of employment are the effects, in large measure, of the rises and falls of prices, due in turn to the inflation and deflation of money and credit.

UNANTICIPATED VERSUS ANTICIPATED CHANGES IN THE MONEY SUPPLY

Lucas (1996, p. 678) believes that the distinction between unanticipated and anticipated changes in the money supply is the major theoretical lesson of the 1970s. Supposedly only unanticipated changes in the money supply have real effects. Anticipated changes just lead to inflation. However, one of the lessons of this book is that an increase in the money supply could restore the economy to full employment *regardless of whether or not the change in the money supply was anticipated (predictable)*. For in a depression a full-employment excess demand for money exists that can be satisfied through an actual increase in the money supply. The latter is an alternative to price deflation as a way of increasing the real money supply. Deflation has to work through a sequence of millions of piecemeal price and wage decisions. The alternative of nominal money expansion puts no such demands on the economy's coordinating mechanisms. It is incorrect to assume that predictable changes in the money supply will always result in higher prices (although such changes would presumably have whatever effects they do have sooner if expected than if not).[14]

DIAGRAMMATICS: THE STRADDLE MODEL

The literature portrays two polar graphical models. Hicks's IS-LM graph holds prices constant while Patinkin's model assumes output is constant at full employment. The straddle diagram lies somewhere in between. It measures the interest rate on the vertical axis and nominal income on the horizontal. Unlike the other two models, it avoids the question of how changes in nominal income are split between changes in output and prices. The diagram can be useful as a heuristic and expository device in illustrating, for example, the stimulatory effects of an increase in the money supply on nominal income.

Figure 7.1 illustrates the straddle diagram. Line YY represents equality between the nominal demand for commodities and nominal income. It slopes downward for reasons similar to why Hicks's IS curve and Patinkin's commodity curve slope downward. Line MM represents equality between the demand for and supply of money. It slopes upward for reasons similar to why Hicks's LM curve and Patinkin's money curve slope upward. Line BB portrays equality between the demand for and supply of bonds. Its slope is drawn horizontally. However, there is no clear presumption that this line slopes either upward or downward, although because transactions are two-sided and because of the budget constraint, it must slope less steeply upward than the MM line and less steeply downward than the YY line. We do not lose much of importance by assuming that the BB line is horizontal, as in Patinkin (1965, pp. 331–2). The three lines intersect at a common point, which is not necessarily at full-employment equilibrium, since the diagram avoids the issue of supply (see note 13 on pages 139–40 above).

Figure 7.2 illustrates the case of an increase in the money supply. Line MM shifts to the right and line BB shifts downward, in keeping with the traditional literature. However, line YY also shifts to the right as people respond to their increased money holdings in part by directly increasing their purchases of commodities. That is, the direct channel of the Wicksell Process operates, contrary

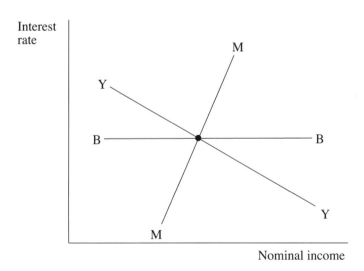

Figure 7.1   The straddle diagram

to the usual presentation in the IS-LM model, which only shifts the LM curve
to the right. The interest rate decreases because bonds are now relatively scarce
in people's portfolios.

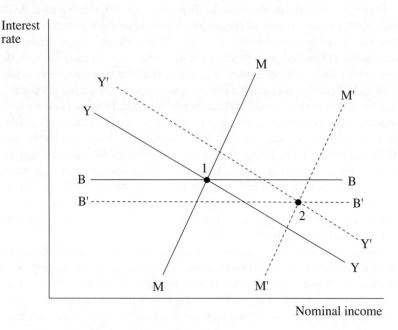

Figure 7.2   An increase in the money supply

Figure 7.3 illustrates the 'perverse result' of bond financing of a tax cut in
which nominal income falls, a possibility that is introduced on pages 132–6
above. Line BB shifts upward, line MM shifts to the left and line YY shifts to
the right. The following conditions promote this fall in nominal income:

1. a relatively steep MM line;
2. a large leftward shift of MM;
3. a relatively flat YY line;
4. a slight rightward shift of YY.

These conditions correspond to the conditions presented in our algebraic model
on page 135 above:

1. a weak interest sensitivity of money demand;
2. a strong propensity to devote increased wealth to money-holding;
3. a strong interest sensitivity of the demand for commodities;
4. a weak propensity to devote increased wealth to spending.

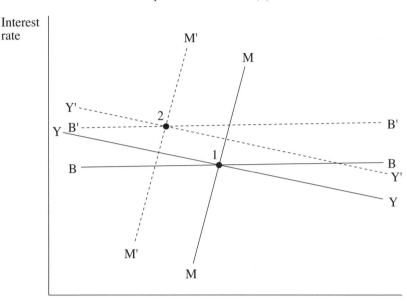

Figure 7.3   Bond financing (perverse result)

CONCLUSION

The new classical macroeconomics challenges disequilibrium theory by asking why people throw away the gains from trade. We can reverse this question: how can it be rational for individuals to behave in ways that result in depression? Why do they let exchange be snarled up? This chapter illustrates that people may indeed be acting rationally. What is individually rational, however, may not be collectively rational.

We present three theories that accord a major role to money in explaining macroeconomic fluctuations. Monetary-disequilibrium theory accords better with reality in our view than the Austrian theory or the new classical theory centered on misperceptions. Changes in the money supply can have an impact on real income and output in the short run. Getting the theory straight does not necessarily entail recommending discretionary and activist stabilization policy.

When the money supply increases, what stimulates output is the expansion of money and spending itself, while price inflation detracts from it. No dependable causal tradeoff exists between unanticipated inflation and output.

Disequilibrium theory can be extended to deal with inflation and stagflation and with the adverse side effects of disinflationary monetary policy by working out a close analogy between the stickiness of a price and wage *level* and the momentum of an entrenched *uptrend*. Chapter 8 examines these issues.

NOTES

1. Gordon (1990b) emphasizes the input–output table approach in which multiple buyer–supplier relations exist.
2.. Some of the points that follow are mentioned in Howitt (1979), especially p. 61.
3. Blanchard and Kiyotaki (1987) argue that an 'aggregate demand externality' exists in which one firm's decision *not* to adjust prices can affect other firms' decisions and therefore can have a large *social* cost.
4.. Bewley (1999) examines surveys consisting of interviews with employers and concludes that the 'morale theory' best explains wage rigidities.
5. Gordon (1990b, p. 1157) notes that the terms 'efficiency wages' and 'efficiency earnings' appear in Marshall (1920, pp. 456–69).
6. Some of the ideas in the preceding paragraphs appear in Stiglitz (1979, 1987); Wilson (1979); Buiter (1980, p. 41); Pettengill (1979); Thurow (1980, around p. 56) and Okun (1980).
7. One of them is Grossman (1986, 1987).
8. Haberler (1958); De Long and Summers (1986); Driskill and Sheffrin (1986); Caskey and Fazzari (1987); Greenwald and Stiglitz (1993) and Tobin (1993) recognize that a high degree of wage and price flexibility may worsen the discoordination.
9. Musgrave's (1981) article, and especially what Musgrave has to say about 'negligibility assumptions', is relevant here.
10. We recognize the many contributions of the Austrian school toward understanding the real world. Here we are only concerned with its business cycle theory. See Garrison (2001) for his exposition of 'capital-based macroeconomics'.
11. For documented refutation of Austrian charges that monetarists deny or unduly neglect relative price effects, see Humphrey (1984).
12. Laidler (1986 [1990a], p. 71) argues that Barro's (1977, 1978) empirical work on output and prices in the United States in the 1945–76 period is inconsistent, for he assumes people behaved *then* as though they believed in the new classical model. Laidler observes that *if* people really held those beliefs at that time, 'there would have been no need for a new-classical revolution'.
13. Hoover (1988, as cited in Snowdon, Vane and Wynarczyk, 1994, p. 196) notes: 'To explain the related movements of macroeconomic aggregates and prices without recourse to the notion of disequilibrium is the *desideratum* of new classical research on the theory of business cycles'.
14. Mishkin (1982) and Gordon (1982) find empirical evidence that not only unanticipated, but also anticipated changes in the money supply affect output and employment.

8. Inflation

THE COSTS OF INFLATION

Chapter 2 emphasizes how the use of money helps make production efficient and responsive to people's wants. If we take these services seriously, we should recognize how erosion and instability of money's purchasing power impair them.

Most obviously, unanticipated price inflation redistributes income and wealth between debtors and creditors, payers and receivers of fixed incomes, and buyers and sellers of goods and services under long-term contracts. Even if inflation is anticipated, its rate and duration can hardly be allowed for accurately. (Okun, 1971 observes that steady and easily allowed for inflation is a myth; compare Dowd, 1996, p. 435; and Laidler, 1993b [1997a], p. 331.) Debtors lose if the inflation premium they pay in nominal interest rates turns out to be an overestimate, making the actual real interest rate excessive. The uncertainty inflation brings impairs accounting and economic calculation, as well as the meeting of minds between potential parties to long-term contracts. Indexing can alleviate such problems but brings difficulties of its own (see Yeager, 1983, pp. 305–26).

Inflation at an extreme rate increases the costs of transactions as people try to get rid of money soon after receiving it. An observer of the Austrian scene in the early 1920s noted the constant shopping and queuing and the loss of family time to frenetic shopping expeditions. Such costs fell mainly on the humbler elements of society, since servants could do the shopping for upper-class households (Maier, 1978, p. 71n, citing Arlt, 1925).

Several other costs of inflation, although almost impossible to quantify, are nevertheless real and should be counted in an overall assessment of the costs of inflation. Business and personal habits (like the allocation of a family's housekeeping money) have been based on the assumption of stable prices and are not easily broken; yet leaving them unbroken in the face of severe inflation creates obvious distortions. Accounting and tax systems, and even the legal system, have also been based on the assumption of stable money. Rapid change in money's value twists them out of shape.[1] Legislation to put these things right again (for a time) requires reopening closed issues and spending time and energy on political discussions. Notions of fairness are also involved.[2] Prices and wages are 'made' in most markets, not just impersonally 'determined' by supply and demand. Prices and wages stand a better chance of seeming fair to the parties concerned if they are set in accord with precedent on the presumption that what was acceptable before will be acceptable again. A rapidly changing price level invalidates this approach. Moreover, people become wary of long-term contracts, sacrificing the several advantages of such contracts as well as costing resources in more frequent negotiations (Ackley, 1978, p. 153).

Inflation degrades the information transmitted by prices. Ideally, each price tells the prospective buyer of a good how much sacrifice of other goods buying it would entail, as well as how attractive an offer each prospective seller is making in comparison with his rivals' offers. Inflation renders such information obsolete or unreliable more quickly. Because of the amount of new information needed to find the best deal, Ackley (1978, p. 153) likens the difficult shopping situation to that of one's suddenly beginning to use a foreign currency, with all of its laborious calculations and comparisons.

Another cost is that firms must devote real resources to marking up prices, changing pay phones, vending machines and cash registers, and revising catalogs more often – the so-called 'menu costs'. Book jackets show list prices less commonly than they formerly did. Publishers thus save on these costs, but by depriving reviewers and readers of useful information.

Prices and interest rates are distorted by the particular ways or channels in which inflationary amounts of new money are injected into the economy. Some prices are less promptly flexible than others, so that inflation distorts relative prices. It simply cannot occur uniformly and predictably. Incorrect price signals and incentives affect patterns of resource allocation. The price system becomes less efficient in responding to consumers' tastes and to objective circumstances and in coordinating economic activity. Even if inflation does not shrink the overall real volume of economic activity, somehow measured, it may well reduce the ultimate human satisfactions derived from that total because of changes in its composition.

To mention one obvious example, resources are diverted into books and periodicals on financial survival in inflation and into investment consultations and seminars. Patinkin (1989, p. xlix) notes that with a higher rate of inflation, more people are employed in the financial services sector and less in the 'real' sectors of the economy. Regarding financial services as an intermediate good, he concludes that real output suffers.

Not only does inflation alter the mix of real economic activity, it also reduces the relative rewards of sober activity devoted to improving products or cutting the costs of producing or distributing them. It increases the relative rewards of being a crafty operator – of predicting prices and policies, of cleverly wheeling and dealing, of sizing up the intellects and moral characters of potential trading partners and associates. It also puts a relative premium on trying to protect oneself through political activities, broadly conceived, in contrast with more market-oriented activities. Leijonhufvud (1981, Chapter 9) develops some of these points. As Milton Friedman (1977, p. 466) says, prudent behavior becomes reckless and reckless behavior prudent.

The German inflation of the 1920s, according to a keen observer (Bresciani-Turroni, 1937, pp. 391–2), suspended the process of selection of the fittest firms. When people are so anxious to part with their melting money that they do not shop around as carefully as they otherwise would, even sellers of shoddy and overpriced goods will find some customers. Although this erosion of the competitive process of rewarding efficiency and punishing inefficiency is most clearly evident in hyperinflations, it presumably occurs in more moderate degree in more moderate inflations.

The time and effort devoted to coping with inflation, as well as the uncertainty and sheer anxiety it causes, count negatively in a comprehensive assessment. So do the lost opportunities and personal anguish that may result. Seeking to protect their savings, savers must look beyond the familiar financial intermediaries and beyond the stock market. Wise stock market investment, never easy, becomes all the harder when inflation interacts with conventional accounting and with the tax laws to erode profitability or at least to make it more difficult to assess. Alternatives, including real estate, art objects and all sorts of collectibles, are touted as inflation hedges. Placement of savings becomes a less impersonal matter than it is when money is stable. Wise investment in nonstandard assets requires detailed knowledge. Savers themselves must grope amateurishly for the expertise that they could leave to financial intermediaries in calmer times. The relevant information, being more specific and heterogeneous than information about the conventional outlets for savings, is more subject to obsolescence.

The demand for collectibles as an inflation hedge represents some diversion of people's propensity to save and accumulate wealth away from construction of capital goods or from the purchase of securities issued to finance capital construction. Bidding for collectibles raises their prices. Their increased value – not merely nominal value but value relative to other goods and services – represents an increase in wealth for individual holders and helps satisfy their propensities to save and hold wealth. Yet the increased values of collectibles do not represent any increase in real wealth from the social point of view. The same point holds for increases in the value of land.[3] The more people satisfy their desires to hold savings by holding wealth of a privately genuine but socially spurious kind, such as the bid-up value of collectibles and land, the less they satisfy their desires for savings by holding capital goods (or securities that are a counterpart of capital goods).[4]

On the other hand, the erosion by inflation of real wealth held as cash balances promotes greater saving insofar as people try to recoup this lost wealth

(Mundell, 1963). Furthermore, what amounts to a tax on real cash balances motivates people to allocate a given volume of saving less toward them and more toward real capital formation. Allais (1947) and Tobin (1965 [1979]) recognize this possibility (see pages 50–51 above). However, even if inflation did prod individuals to accumulate more real capital and hold less real balances, they would be getting less of real-balance services, which would itself tend to impair real production (compare Marty and Thornton, 1995, p. 31).

Insofar as the propensity to save is diverted into and satisfied by bidding up the prices of land and collectibles, our worry about capital formation is justified. If inflation and disrupted asset markets make providing for the future difficult and risky – as illustrated by the resort to exotic inflation hedges – why not live for today? Total *saving* is thereby reduced. Furthermore, by impairing the functioning of money, inflation makes financial intermediation less efficient, thereby tending to obstruct real capital formation and economic growth.

If the tax system continues treating interest income fully as income, not distinguishing between real interest and the inflation allowance in nominal rates, the consequent reduction in the real after-tax rate of return, which may even become negative, hinders capital formation. This effect could be counteracted to the extent that borrowers receive a tax deduction for interest paid.

We question any attempts to measure accurately the costs of inflation. Many of them are almost impossible to quantify but are nevertheless real. The traditional method of measuring these costs assumes a fully anticipated inflation. The welfare cost is measured in terms of the appropriate area under an aggregate demand-for-money function (Laidler, 1990c [1990a] and Dowd, 1996, pp. 381–437). The area represents the value of the real cash balances forgone as people adjust to the anticipated inflation. (Recall that inflation reduces the demand for real balances as explained in Chapter 2.) But as a result of general interdependence, the reduction in real balances affects in principle *all* real magnitudes thus increasing the costs of inflation. Again we argue that 'superneutrality' of money does not hold (see pages above).

THE MONETARY NATURE OF INFLATION

In Milton Friedman's famous dictum (1963 [1968c], p. 39), 'inflation is always and everywhere a monetary phenomenon'. This does not mean that an increase in the money supply is the cause of every one-shot increase in the price level. It means that every sustained inflation has a monetary basis.

Admittedly, a purely nonmonetary account of inflation is barely conceivable. Even such an account would have to square with the equation of exchange. With neither M nor V continuously rising, continuing price inflation would presuppose a continuing fall in real economic activity, Q. This case is implausible.

Alternatively, if the total flow of nominal spending were to keep on rising despite a steady M, then V would have to keep on rising, and rising faster and faster in such a way as to produce an accelerating inflation. A steady inflation would not be sufficient, since it would be inconsistent with standard assumptions about how real balances demanded depend on the rate of change of the price level. With inflation recognized as steady, real balances demanded would be constant, though constant at a lower level than with no inflation. Yet the arithmetic of inflation would be steadily shrinking their actual amount. It is implausible that the price level would keep rising despite a growing excess *demand* for money. Merely steady inflation would not motivate the continuing rise of velocity that 'bootstrap inflation' would require.

An accelerating inflation could do so. While actual real balances were shrinking as a matter of arithmetic, the quantity demanded would shrink exactly in step as people responded to the continuing rise in the cost of holding money. Each shrinkage would cause the other: the accelerating erosion of real balances would keep cutting the demand for them, while the falling demand would keep shrinking the actual real stock.

Such phenomena, which might seem to shake the foundations of monetary theory, rest on the assumption that people instantly readjust their real-balance holdings to the changing current rate of inflation. However, significant *lags* might characterize either people's perceptions of the current inflation or their adjustments of their real-balance holdings in accord with their revised perceptions. Such sluggish behavior would thwart a bootstrap process.[5] Realistically, continuing price inflation must involve continuing monetary expansion.

Let us consider the nature of the monetary disequilibrium in the inflationary process. We suppose that an economy starts at full-employment equilibrium without inflation. The monetary authority then increases the money supply. The Wicksell Process helps explain why spending increases. If prices and wages do not immediately adjust, an excess demand for goods and services is matched by an excess supply of money. Chapters 6 and 7 illustrate that output may rise under certain circumstances, if only temporarily, with a rise in prices eventually following.

Suppose that the money supply and prices come to grow at a steady rate. Do money supply and demand remain out of equilibrium during this process? Hardly: ever-higher prices keep raising the nominal demand for money approximately in step with supply. A kind of moving equilibrium holds for both money and goods. An actual excess supply of money keeps being staved off by the rise in prices.

Stagflation is understandable if the monetary authority now reduces money growth. Prices and wages continue rising for a while, thereby raising the nominal demand for money into an excess demand, with goods in excess supply. Inflation, though usually attributed to an excess supply of money and an excess demand for goods, can thus coexist with recession, usually attributed to an excess demand for money and an excess supply of goods. Stagflation exhibits the consequences of both excessive and deficient growth in the quantity of money, the excess occurring earlier and the deficiency currently. The earlier excessive growth establishes an inflationary momentum that now keeps eroding the real value of the money supply, which is no longer growing so fast. (Pages 231–4 below elaborate on inflationary momentum.) Against a background of too much spending earlier, spending becomes deficient in real terms now and output falls. This diagnosis does not necessarily recommend, however, revving up money again. It also illustrates that one need not resort to supply shocks in order to explain stagflation. On page 237 below we argue that this analysis can account for stagflation in the United States during the mid-1970s.

What causes the monetary expansion that fuels inflation? No one answer always applies: different causes have operated in different historical episodes. Saying this is no mere lame eclecticism. It corresponds to the way things are. As an expository device – the distinction is far from sharp – we may classify the causes or sources of monetary expansion under two headings. First are factors 'exogenous' to the process of setting wages and prices. Money growth is cause rather than consequence. Second are ways in which money growth 'accommodates' nonmonetary upward pressures on prices and wages instead of occurring independently. Several different circumstances belong under each heading.

EXOGENOUS MONETARY EXPANSION

Gold discoveries and improvements in mining and refining provide examples of exogenous monetary expansion under a gold standard. Another obvious example involves government deficit spending, perhaps in wartime, with the deficit covered by printing money or the equivalent. A government deficit may result from the pressures of democratic politics, which lead to governmental hyperactivity and a bias toward overspending. As has often been illustrated in Latin America, money issue may cover the deficits of government-owned enterprises.

Monetary expansion may result from pursuit of a low-interest-rate policy, perhaps again in response to political pressures. In early twentieth-century Chile, a conservative government dominated by a landowner class with heavy mortgage debts apparently pursued almost deliberately inflationary policies (Fetter, 1931).

The early 1970s provide many examples, although hardly history's earliest examples, of 'imported inflation'. Trying to keep the exchange rate of a country's currency fixed in the face of balance-of-payments surpluses expands the home money supply. Monetary expansion of that sort hardly occurs in response to domestic wage and price setting, so it belongs on our list of exogenous types. A dubious contention that even such a monetary expansion comes by way of accommodation to already accomplished price and wage increases – a contention made by the 'strong version' of the monetary approach to the balance of payments – is examined on pages 264–5.

The causes of monetary inflation have sometimes included fallacious ideas underlying policy. One has been the idea (compare Chapters 6 and 7) that expansionary policy can reduce unemployment and stimulate production beyond the full-employment level, and better than just temporarily.

Another influential fallacy involves failure to understand the relation between nominal and real quantities of money. In Germany in 1923, eminent financiers and politicians and even economists (notably Karl Helfferich) argued that no monetary or credit inflation was occurring. Although the nominal value of the paper money supply was enormous and skyrocketing, its real value or gold value was much lower than that of the money supply before the war. This doctrine overlooked the obvious reason why the real money stock had become so small: inflation itself was deterring people from holding wealth in that form.

Rudolf Havenstein, president of the Reichsbank, expounded a related fallacy – the doctrine that exchange rate depreciation was due to an unfavorable balance of payments (involving, in this instance, Germany's heavy reparations obligations). This fallacy dates at least as far back as discussions of 'the high price of bullion' in Great Britian during the Napoleonic wars, when the Bank of England had temporarily been relieved of the gold-redemption restraint on banknote issue but when anti-quantity-theorists could blame depreciation on outward payments to support allies on the Continent.[6] The fallacy consists in emphasizing a minor nonmonetary factor, whether merely imagined or even actual, at a time when the dominant cause of price increases and exchange rate depreciation is monetary expansion.

In August 1923, Havenstein denied that money and credit expansion had been feeding inflation in Germany, observing that the loan and investment portfolio of the Reichsbank was worth well under half of its pre-war value in gold (Bresciani-Turroni, 1937, pp. 155–6). As the Reichsbank kept pouring out new money on loan to the deficit-spending government and to businesspeople, who borrowed eagerly in the warranted expectation of repaying later in sharply depreciated marks, its president adhered to the 'real-bills' or 'needs-of-trade' fallacy. He considered it his duty to supply the growing amounts of money needed to conduct transactions at the ever higher price level. At one point Havenstein seriously expressed hope that installation of new high-speed currency printing presses would overcome the supposed shortage of money.[7]

The just-mentioned 'real-bills doctrine', although demolished as long ago as 1802 by Thornton (1802 [1978]), keeps being rediscovered as if it were a profound and original truth.[8] In essence – but variations do occur – the doctrine holds that new money is not inflationary if used to finance productive activities, since additional goods to spend it on will soon match it (compare Humphrey, 1982a). In part, the fallacy consists in believing that what happens to the price level depends not so much on the quantity of money as on the particular way in which new money initially comes into circulation. The doctrine fails to realize that creating new money to finance particular activities ordinarily does less to increase total production than to bid productive resources from other activities into the favored ones, while at the same time the intensified bidding for productive resources raises costs and prices.

Related to the fallacy that the quantity of money is less important than its quality or the nature of its issue is the notion that money is not inflationary if it is solidly backed. Proponents of issuing the assignats during the French Revolution argued that the issues would be harmless, indeed beneficial, because they were backed by nationalized lands. Preoccupation with backing has sometimes made the authorities passive in the face of the danger of imported inflation. Creation of money to buy up gold and foreign exchange was supposedly acceptable because, after all, the new money was being backed by the additional reserves acquired in the process.

Another fallacy is that the introduction of floating exchange rates promotes inflation. For example, the acceleration of worldwide inflation in 1973/1974 occurred at about the same time that floating rates replaced the Bretton Woods system of pegged but adjustable exchange rates. While some economists blame the speed up of inflation on the new regime of floating rates, Chapter 9 argues instead that it was a result of the last-ditch attempts to defend the Bretton Woods system.

An idea often encountered is that the monetary authority is not responsible for what happens to the quantity of money because it is passively responding in part to changes in income and prices. Indeed it may be, as when the authority is subordinating control of the money supply to some other objective, such as low interest rates or a fixed exchange rate. Having institutions that made the money supply behave passively in some such way would count as an action of the monetary authority, interpreted broadly to include legislators or constitution-makers.

ACCOMMODATING MONETARY EXPANSION

The real-bills doctrine recommends monetary expansion to accommodate supposedly increased 'needs of trade'. Meeting an increasing demand for real cash balances associated with real economic growth need not be inflationary, true enough, since it may simply avoid price deflation. What bears on theories of inflation is meeting the 'need' for additional nominal money at increased wages and prices that trace in turn to nonmonetary upward pressures.

Theories of this type envisage either 'automatic' accommodation to these pressures, or more plausibly accommodating policy actions. On this view the authorities are practically forced to expand the quantity of money in the face of nonmonetary upward pushes on wages and prices. If they did not do so, the old nominal quantity would become inadequate in real purchasing power, inadequate for a full-employment volume of productive activity. Recession and unemployment would result. In the equation of exchange, with M (and MV) approximately steady, a pushed-up P would entail a fall in Q.

This line of theorizing might be caricatured as blaming inflation on 'one damn thing after another'. All sorts of developments may be tending to raise particular prices or wages – a crop failure here, a flood there, predation by OPEC or other energy shocks, and increased unionization or union militancy. In its most naive form, this is the man-in-the-street theory of inflation. The general level of prices and wages rises because newsworthy events are pushing up particular prices and wages. We shall first discuss conceivable *nonmonetary* causes of upward pushes and then consider whether accommodating these pushes would be beneficial.

Sometimes business firms are blamed for inflation as well as unions. References appear to 'sellers inflation', to 'administered prices' of goods and labor alike, to 'profit pushes' as well as 'wage pushes'. Developments are conceivable, of course, that enhance the monopoly power of particular business firms and enable them to raise prices and profit margins. In general, though, a contrast holds between labor unions and business firms as sources of sustained inflationary pressure. (Only this contrast is what concerns us here. We are not contending that labor unions are generally a major cause of inflation.)

A firm has a goal of maximum (or satisfactory) profit, and under given demand and cost conditions, pushing the price of its product still higher would not even be in its own interest. Strengthened demand or increased costs may make a higher price than before the most profitable one, but a satisfactory explanation then must focus on whatever has changed these conditions. Besides, continually raising prices is not the business executive's mission in life. He takes no pride in doing so and feels some need to make excuses when he does raise prices.

A union leader's mission, however, is to raise the price of his members' labor; a union's goal is 'more'. Unions are partly political institutions, often exhibiting rivalry among actual and potential leaders in the same and different unions. Each leader wants to seem effective in comparison with his rivals and counterparts. A union has no goal as nearly definite as a business firm's profit goal, no such goal whose attainment would clearly suffer from excessively grasping behavior. Even if a union leader does recognize why a general wage–price–money spiral is self-defeating, he has little incentive to practice restraint. If others keep pushing for 'more', his own members will lose relatively or in real terms, and he personally will look ineffective unless he joins in the push. Pattern bargaining and concern for maintaining or improving traditional wage differentials enter into this story.

Given a concern for wage patterns or differentials, even a sectoral (nonuniform) gain in productivity can exert an inflationary tendency. Suppose that a particular labor group enjoys a gain in productivity and insists on a corresponding wage increase, which the employers might well be able to grant. This increase upsets the accepted pattern of wage differentials, triggering wage demands even in sectors where productivity lags. Similar consequences could follow from a strengthening of demand for the output of a particular group of workers. 'The unifying characteristics of this diverse class of theories is the notion that the labour market is not a competitive market at all'.[9]

Some theorists have traced the inflations typical of developed countries since World War II to efforts by economic interest groups to enlist the political process in improving their income shares, even if this amounts to trying to divide total income into shares totalling more than 100 percent. Such a struggle is self-defeating, of course, while the very struggle may impair the size of the whole. Even so, no group with political clout has reason to withdraw from the struggle, for doing so would impair its income share even worse. The self-interest of the individual politician likewise requires him to respond to political realities that he might regret but is individually powerless to remedy. Here we have another example of tension between individual rationality and collective rationality. A decent restraint in clamoring for government action to redistribute income from others to oneself is a public good, not a private good.[10]

The 'ratchet' theory of Charles Schultze (1959 [1969]) centers on shifts of demands among economic sectors and on the greater upward than downward flexibility of prices and wages. Even if demand is not excessive overall, excess demand in some sectors causes price and wage increases there that decreases in sectors of deficient demand do not fully balance out. Downward rigidities, efforts to maintain wage patterns, and pricing on the basis of costs act like a ratchet on the price level, producing an inflationary bias. We note, however, that intersectoral shifts of demand – shifts between investment and consumption goods and between durable goods and nondurables and services – stem largely from general business fluctuations and so would be less severe in an environment of monetary stability.

Questions arise: does the monetary authority have good reason for allowing the quantity of money to behave in an accommodating manner? Does it do any lasting good – does it enduringly cope with troublesome realities – to cause or allow accommodation? Suppose, for example, that upward pressures and downward rigidities affecting wages and prices do trace to a struggle to divide up total national output into shares totaling more than 100 percent. Attempts to do the impossible are bound to fail. Why should they be allowed to fail in the context of inflation rather than of stable money? How can persistent monetary accommodation improve the underlying realities?

In the context of ongoing inflationary monetary accommodation, price- and wage-setters will realize what is happening and will frame their demands accordingly. Rigidities and pushes in relation to a steady wage and price level will spawn their counterparts in relation to an entrenched upward trend and will damage production and employment as before.

Monetary accommodation cannot really alleviate the harmful consequences of rigidities and pushes, or not more than temporarily. This discussion, remember, concerns accommodation of *nonmonetary* upward pushes on wages and prices. Once an inflation becomes well entrenched, wages and prices can acquire such an upward momentum of their own that the monetary authority may feel obliged to continue accommodating it to avoid recession or stagflation. In arguing the undesirability of accommodation, we are not considering this difficulty of stopping an entrenched money-fueled inflation. Instead, we are considering conceivable cases of inflation initiated by nonmonetary upward pressures.

Might not accommodation help alleviate the effects of an adverse supply shock? Suppose that the shock mechanically, arithmetically, raises the general price level. Real cash balances shrink, and with them the volumes of transactions, production and employment they can support. In this case the monetary authority might expand the money supply to restore real balances, resist unemployment and so cushion the shock.

We do not dismiss this argument out of hand. We can imagine a severe shock to which accommodation would be a less undesirable response, on balance, than any alternative policy. Yet the argument is not decisive. For accommodation clinches the price-raising effects of the shock. Without it, some prices would fall sooner or later. A policy of accommodation once embarked upon and accepted poses a temptation to accommodate even more minor shocks. What Buchanan (1975) has called the 'Samaritan's dilemma' may develop. Giving in to a problem or threat (for example, an airplane hijacking) just invites more of the same. Accommodating even minor supply shocks could result in chronic inflation.

Once a momentum of interacting wage and price increases has become established, regardless of just how, the authorities face the question whether to ratify those increases by money supply expansion. Having to make this choice is near the heart of the problem of stopping inflation and will occupy us at length later.

THE DECEPTIVE APPEARANCE OF COST PUSH

An inflation fueled by monetary growth can appear to result from cost push instead. In some stages of the process, costs may seem to rise first, with prices following. Yet this sequence may be spurious as evidence of causation. A firm's standard response to strengthened demand is to try to have larger quantities of its products to sell. A retailer will order more goods. A manufacturer will order more materials, seek more labor and perhaps try to expand his plant and equipment. Each individual business firm might think that, given time, it could meet the increased demand without raising prices. Yet as firms transmit the increased demand for final products back to the factors of production, competing for materials, labor and plant and equipment, they bid up these elements of cost.

To the individual firm, then, the chief circumstance justifying and requiring a rise in its selling prices is the rise in its costs. It may see the inflation as a cost-push process, even though costs are in fact rising as inflationary demands for final products are transmitted back to factors of production (compare Cagan, 1974 and Humphrey, 1979a and 1979b). The foregoing process helps explain the *long and variable lags* mentioned in the monetarist literature and throughout this book.

THE ANALOGY BETWEEN LEVELS AND TRENDS OF PRICES

An analogy holds between the inertia of an established price and wage level and the inertia of an established trend. Something like Newton's first law of motion is at work. Just as a body resists being set in motion or having the speed or direction of its motion changed, so prices on the average resist changes in their level or their trend, particularly cuts in their level or moderation of their uptrend (Pazos, 1972, p. 70). When a change in the volume or growth of money and spending has changed what would be the equilibrium level or trend of prices, this new equilibrium is not reached immediately. Prices are 'sticky' in the complex sense explained in Chapters 6 and 7. Adjustment of the level or trend of money's value stretches out over time, so inflation can 'persist' even after its monetary basis may have been stopped. Production and employment suffer as long as price trends do not fully absorb the deceleration of money and spending.

This unfavorable split between price and output responses could be avoided or mitigated if people saw convincing reasons to believe that the inflation was in fact being stopped. Unfortunately, no policymaker and no individual seller can confidently guess when prices might decelerate in response to monetary restraint. The individual seller knows only that this result does not depend on his own sales and price decisions (Fellner, 1974 [1979], p. 91). Just as individual price-setters and wage-negotiators have reason for reluctance to go first in reducing a level of prices and wages that is too high for the nominal quantity of money, so they are reluctant to go first in breaking an established uptrend. Again, individual rationality and collective rationality may well diverge.

Suppose an individual business executive recognizes that a new policy of monetary restraint ought to stop inflation. (The effect that a policy 'ought' to have is the one that it is designed to have in the light of correct economic theory, or that it would have if people understood it and modified their behavior accordingly.) Even so, how can the individual count on others' having the same perceptions and modifying their behavior accordingly? How can he be confident that his workers will restrain their wage demands and his suppliers and competitors their prices? He has good reason to postpone changes in his own pricing policy until he gets a better reading on what the situation is, including, in particular, on how other people may be modifying their price and wage policies. His policy, like theirs, had been to keep marking up his selling prices in line with the entrenched general trend unless faced with definite conditions of costs and competition that recommend doing otherwise. Of course, if he and all other price-setters and wage-negotiators were to make their decisions collectively and simultaneously, then it would be in their collective interest to avoid the side effects of the new policy of monetary restraint by practicing appropriate price and wage restraint. In fact, though, they make their price and wage decisions piecemeal, opening the way for divergence between collective and individual rationality.

The implication is not to give up and let an entrenched inflation roll on. Doing so, as we shall argue, would make the attempted cure all the more painful when belatedly undertaken (see pages 236–7 below).

THE SIDE EFFECTS OF TRYING TO STOP INFLATION

The explanation of sluggish reduction of a disequilibrium price level carries over to sluggish deceleration of an entrenched price uptrend. Even if a solution to underlying difficulties (such as government deficit spending) does permit checking monetary expansion, prices and wages can continue rising for months with a 'momentum' of their own. With nominal money growth slowed, the stock of real money balances shrinks, contributing to monetary disequilibrium and thus to a slowdown in production and employment. Stagflation results. Just as a shrinkage that makes the *quantity* of money inadequate to sustain the prevailing *level* of prices impairs real economic activity, so a cutback that makes the money *growth rate* inadequate to sustain an entrenched *uptrend* in prices curtails real economic activity or at least cuts its growth. On many such occasions of reduced monetary growth, the unwanted real side effects have apparently made the monetary authority lose its nerve and switch back to a policy of 'growth', as in the United States during the late 1960s and the 1970s. (The very prospect of side effects may block a determined disinflationary policy in the first place.) Yet from a longer-term perspective than the authority may feel politically able to adopt, no conclusion follows in favor of increasing monetary growth again, since doing so would make the 'stagflation dilemma' worse later on as distortions worsened (see pages 236–7 below).

Reference to the withdrawal pangs of trying to end inflation raises the question of how the impact of restraint on money and spending is split between prices and real activity. The greater and quicker the impact on the price uptrend, the less real activity suffers. It is a familiar but 'inexact remark' that slow real economic growth or actual recession restrains inflation (and, conversely, that rapid real growth causes inflation). The reverse accords better with the equation of exchange, as illustrated below. Underlying the remark, presumably, is the idea that slowed real growth is one consequence and indicator of a slowdown in the growth of nominal income and the money supply. If this is what it means, however, the standard formulation is misleading. Imagine – trying to gauge the disinflationary intensity of monetary policy by an unwanted side effect of that policy, namely, a real slowdown, especially since the equation of exchange indicates that the side effect competes with the desired price deceleration.

One version of the 'expectations-augmented Phillips curve' implies the causality mentioned in the 'inexact remarks' above. The following price-adjustment equation depicts that version and is taken from page 211 above:

(1) $p = p^e + f$ (output gap), where p is the actual rate of inflation, p^e is the anticipated (expected) rate of inflation, the output gap is actual output minus potential output, and f' is greater than zero. According to this equation, for a given anticipated rate of inflation and a given level of potentional output, the change in the actual rate of inflation is directly related to the change in actual output. Specifically, greater actual output (higher real economic growth) causes a greater actual rate of inflation. Conversely, lower actual output (or recession) causes a lower actual rate of inflation. These invalid propositions repeat the inexact remarks mentioned above.

To see why equation (1) is invalid, we again appeal to the equation of exchange, now written as:

(2) % change in M + % change in V = % change in P + % change in Q. The change in the sum of the components on the left side of the equation must equal the change in the sum of the components on the right side. That is, a change in the growth rate of nominal income (MV) is *split* between a change in the actual rate of inflation and a change in the growth rate of output. More specifically, the latter two changes are inversely related for a given change in the growth rate of nominal income . For example, given an expansionary monetary policy that raises the growth rate of nominal income, the larger is the increase in the growth rate of output, the smaller will be the acceleration in the actual rate of inflation. Conversely, given that a disinflationary monetary policy has reduced the growth rate of nominal income, the larger is the decrease in the growth rate of output, the smaller will be the deceleration in the actual rate of inflation. As

a proposition about reality, equation (1) contradicts these results and therefore must be wrong. Moreover, our analysis is consistent with the high output growth and low inflation in the United States during the 1990s.

THE NEW KEYNESIAN PHILLIPS CURVE

On pages 137–9 above we present the 'consensus model of monetary policy', which consists of three equations. The second, a price-adjustment equation, is often referred to as 'the new Keynesian Phillips curve' . We write it as:

(3) $p = p^e + f$ (output gap), where p^e is inflation expected to prevail in the future. The rest of the equation is already familiar. The different price-adjustment equations that have appeared in this model derive from Calvo (1983), Rotemberg (1982), and Taylor (1980).

Mankiw (2001b) interprets the new Keynesian Phillips curve as a causal relation that contradicts the facts for three reasons. First, contrary to reality, a credible disinflation in this model causes booms as shown by Ball (1994). Second, Fuhrer and Moore (1995) illustrate that the model cannot account for the persistence of inflation. Given a change in the money growth rate, the effect on inflation is immediate. Third, Mankiw (2001b) examines impulse response functions, which are the dynamic paths of inflation and unemployment in response to monetary policy shocks. He concludes that model simulations cannot produce the delayed and gradual effect that in reality a monetary shock has on inflation.

Most versions of the consensus model ignore the important analogy between the inertia of an established price level and the inertia of a price uptrend. This analogy helps illuminate the adjustment process. McCallum (2002, p. 90) notes 'the profession's poor level of understanding of the precise nature of...price adjustment relations'. However, insistence on quantitative precision overlooks the fact that changes in the money growth rate are followed by 'long and variable lags' in changes in the rates of inflation and output growth, and for very good reasons illuminated by monetary-disequilibrium theory. (Compare pages 129–30 above which address the alleged lack of detail in the monetarist explanation of the monetary transmission process.) The following section elaborates on the reasons for the persistence of inflation.

INFLATIONARY MOMENTUM

Price and wage momentum has two main aspects, 'catching up' and 'expectations' (compare Humphrey, 1979b). Both involve complex interrelations and time lags. Prices and wages and other costs are determined in piecemeal and decentralized ways. Some firms' selling prices are other firms' costs. Only during hyperinflations do various prices and wage rates rise nearly in step with each other, month by month and week by week. Only the prices of securities and standardized commodities traded on organized exchanges respond to supply and demand from hour to hour and minute to minute. Most individual prices and wages are adjusted only from time to time. As a result, the structure of relative prices is constantly undergoing distortions and corrections. At any time, many prices and wages are temporarily lagging behind others in the inflationary procession. They still have catching up to do after monetary expansion is checked. Somehow keeping them from catching up would leave them stuck away from market-clearing levels, and the distorted structure of relative prices and costs would interfere with some transactions and so with production and employment. In abstract theory, these distortions could be corrected by declines in some prices and wages that averaged out further increases in others. Actually, the difficulties that impede a mere leveling off of upward trends impede all the more any cuts of particular prices and wages. Catching up does obstruct any instant end to inflation.

For these and other reasons, a change in monetary policy and in the flow of spending on final goods and services has its impact spread over many months. If monetary policy were to be tightened and an inflationary expansion of demand checked, much of the adjustment of prices to the earlier demand inflation would remain to be completed.

Extreme inflation has a possible silver lining. As inflation persists and becomes faster and more fully expected, people shorten the intervals between price and wage adjustments. Transmission of higher wages and other costs into higher prices and of higher prices into higher wages occurs more rapidly (Okun, 1979, p. 2). This shortening of lags means that disinflation policy has less of a problem of prolonged catching up to contend with. In this respect it may be easier to stop an extreme inflation than a merely moderate one. (Yeager and associates, 1981 provide some examples.)

Expectations are the second aspect of inflationary momentum, overlapping with the catch-up aspect, while the interaction of various costs and prices enters into both. When prices and wages have been rising conspicuously for several years, people recognize what is happening, expect it to continue, and make their own pricing decisions and wage demands accordingly. They do so, anyway, unless some clear-cut change in circumstances provides a reason for doing otherwise. With particular adjustments being made not every day but only from time to time, people take account of the erosion of the purchasing power of the prices or wages that they receive. In adjusting their own prices or wage demands, they not only allow for any erosion already experienced since their last adjustment, but also allow for further erosion expected to come in the months ahead. Strong anticipations of inflation can reduce the direct influence of demand on prices (and also of prices on quantities demanded). Cost increases are more readily and fully passed along despite weakness in demand if that weakness is viewed as temporary and prices are expected to continue in an uptrend. Costs and prices push each other up with less friction (Cagan, 1972, p. 143). As buyers become accustomed to repeatedly paying increased prices and find it increasingly difficult to keep abreast of and compare the prices asked by rival sellers, they become less sensitive to price competition. Sellers become accustomed to passing actual and even expected cost increases on to their customers without meeting too much buyer resistance.

Even a seller of some product or type of labor for which demand is currently deficient – a businessperson dissatisfied with his sales or a union leader dissatisfied with his members' employment – may well forgo cutting or may even increase his money price anyway. He can reduce his real or relative price in order to attract buyers simply by keeping its nominal increase smaller than the general inflation rate. When prices and wages are generally rising, to join in the procession is not necessarily to push for an increased price in real terms but simply to avoid an unnecessarily large markdown. Why take less than the market will bear? Why sacrifice to the advantage of others? Even if a seller should experience some drop or lag in sales attributable to an excessive nominal price increase, he could expect the continuing general inflation of costs and prices to make his price soon competitive and acceptable after all. Why reverse a slightly premature price increase that customers will soon be willing to pay?

Momentum has its policy aspects. Irresoluteness is one of them. Authorities have often feared the side effects of discontinuing their accommodation of an entrenched uptrend. (The old analogy between inflation and an addictive drug is instructive.) Another policy aspect hinges on the fact that some people do succeed in adjusting to inflation and would suffer if their adjustments were rendered no longer appropriate. A vivid example concerns young couples who buy more expensive houses than would otherwise be prudent, incurring almost crushing burdens of mortgage payments in relation to income. They do so because they expect their incomes to rise with inflation, shrinking the payments relatively. An end to inflation would penalize such people in a double-barreled way. First, mortgage payments would remain a crushing burden unless they sold their houses. Second, prices would probably drop because the exceptional demand for real estate as inflation hedges would have vanished. More generally, taking inflation and the inflation premium out of interest rates would alter property values, benefiting some persons and firms and victimizing others (Warburton, 1974, p. 15). Still more generally, certain activities flourish more in an inflationary than in a stable environment. Their shriveling would hurt people who had devoted their money and careers to them. Inflation continuing and becoming deeply ingrained puts more and more people into such a position.

Political pressures from them, even if only unorganized pressures, work to keep inflation going.

CREDIBILITY

The expectational aspect of inflationary momentum makes the credibility of a disinflation policy crucial to how severe the withdrawal pangs will be.[11] If a program of monetary restraint is not credible – if price-setters and wage-nego-tiators think that the authority will lose their nerve and switch gears at the first sign of recessionary side effects – then people will expect the inflation to continue and will make their price and wage decisions accordingly. The unintended consequence will be an 'unfavorable' split between the price and quantity responses to monetary restraint. If, on the contrary, people are convinced that the authority will stick to its disinflationary course no matter how bad the side effects, so that the price and wage inflation is bound to abate, then everyone should realize that if they nevertheless persist in price or wage increases at the same old pace, they will find themselves ahead of the stalled inflationary procession and will lose customers or jobs. People will moderate their price and wage demands, making the split more 'favorable' to continued production and employment. It is only superficially paradoxical, then, that in two alternative situations with objectively the same degree of monetary restraint, the recessionary side effects will be milder when the authority is believed ready to tolerate them than when the authority is suspected of irresoluteness.

While a resolute and credible disinflation program could thus conceivably turn expectations around almost at once, the catch-up aspect of inflationary momentum appears less tractable. Still, if the turnaround in inflationary expec-tations were quick and complete enough, relative prices could conceivably be restored to an approximate equilibrium pattern through declines in previously leading prices that averaged out catch-up increases in previously lagging prices. As mentioned above, this is just an extreme benchmark case and not a practical possibility.

The game-theoretic literature on 'time inconsistency of policy' and 'reputation' attempts to explain the importance of a credible monetary policy. Kydland and Prescott (1977) and Barro and Gordon (1983) are the seminal articles in this literature. When the monetary authority is free to conduct dis-cretionary policy, an incentive supposedly exists for it to announce a conservative (noninflationary) policy and then renege in order to exploit the Phillips curve tradeoff and thus lower unemployment. If people believe the authority's announcement, then the ensuing inflation will be a surprise and will increase output. However, people with rational expectations will understand the authority's incentive to cheat and will therefore expect it to do so. Consequently, the game-theoretic result is no output gain with higher inflation. Rogoff (1985) proposes a solution to the above policy dilemma: appoint a conservative (and reputable) central banker in order to ensure credibility of the monetary authority.

While we are also concerned about the inflationary bias that often plagues an economy in which the monetary authority has discretionary powers, we do question the key assumption in this entire literature: some version of the Phillips curve. Surprise inflation is *not* what gives rise to an increase in output. Rather, emphasis belongs on the expansion of money and spending that cause *both* phenomena.

In 1990, New Zealand and Chile introduced the notion of 'inflation targeting'. Neumann and von Hagen (2002, p. 127) list 17 countries in all that have tried it. Since many countries have now attained low inflation, a key question is: 'what is the "optimal" rate of inflation?' (Fuhrer and Sniderman, 2000). The Federal Reserve Bank of Boston sponsored a 1999 conference devoted to 'the conduct of monetary policy in a low-inflation environment'. The chief concern among participants was that the inflation rate and interest rate might become *too low*. Japan's alleged experience in the liquidity trap was the motivating factor for this concern.

CONTROLS

Imposing wage and price controls might be a disinflationary device, though one of limited scope and importance. Perhaps the most nearly respectable argument is that controls can dramatize a policy shift and so help break the expectations that had been contributing to the momentum of inflation (Lerner and Colander, 1979, p. 212). Some such hope underlay the controls instituted by President Nixon in August 1971 (Fellner, 1972, p. 256). A related argument is that controls could be a synchronizing mechanism and in effect impose a coordinated decision to stop raising prices and wages. The usual piecemeal method of setting prices and wages, under which everyone has reason to wait for everyone else to go first in practicing restraint, would be temporarily set aside (Keller, 1980). The split between price and quantity responses to monetary restraint would become more favorable.

Using temporary controls during a period of economic slack to break an inherited inflationary spiral must be distinguished from trying permanently to suppress the pressure of excess demand. While the case for temporary controls to hasten a transition warranted by monetary and fiscal restraint is more nearly respectable than the case for permanent controls, it is far from conclusive. The US control policy of 1971 could devise only arbitrary criteria for regulating *relative* wages and prices while the general rate of inflation was being reduced (Fellner, 1972, p. 256). Because controls lock relative prices into what is or soon becomes a disequilibrium pattern, success with their use probably must come quickly if it is to come at all. Even when adopted as part of a comprehensive program for stopping monetary expansion, controls are less likely to work successfully if recent experience with their inappropriate use has discredited them with the public. For example, the failure of controls under Nixon probably precluded their use later on.

Moreover, controls might divert attention away from the true monetary nature of inflation. They might be used in place of monetary restraint, causing an excess supply of money to build up. During the period of Nixon's controls the rate of money growth accelerated sharply. In 1972 alone, the first full year of the controls, it was over 9 percent, the highest rate since World War II. It is therefore not surprising that inflation shot up when the controls were removed in 1974, and that for the duration of the 1970s it remained higher than in the pre-control period.

OTHER ASPECTS OF STAGFLATION

The diagnosis of stagflation that focuses on how the momentum of price and wage increases erodes real money balances and the flow of real spending is incomplete. Inflation impairs the information-transmitting and coordinating properties of the price mechanism and distorts relative prices, frustrating some exchanges. Just how inflationary quantities of money enter the economy can be relevant, and interest rates may figure among the prices that are distorted. Inflation distorts the pattern of production and resource allocation – in favor, for example, of supposed 'inflation hedges' as well as the financial services sector. If a policy of trying to reduce inflation seems to be working, then people will tend to shift production and resource allocation back toward more normal patterns, giving rise to frictional losses of production and employment.

Part of the purpose of ending inflation is to reverse inflationary distortions of resource allocation. If stabilization reinstates the competitive process of selecting the fittest firms, then some firms that were being kept afloat by the peculiarities of the inflationary situation will fail. Their plants and equipment and employees will have to shift into the hands of better management or into more desired lines of production. The shifting will involve frictions, and real activity will suffer for a while.

These considerations help explain why it is practically impossible to stop inflation without any adverse side effects. They also argue that delay makes stopping inflation all the more painful by letting distortions worsen in the meantime.

The distinction between credit-intensive and noncredit-intensive businesses and products is relevant to the side effects of monetary restraint. In our type of money and banking system, a slowdown in money supply growth will transitionally tighten credit. During the transition, however, the particular burdening of credit-intensive firms can be a further source of resource reallocation and frictions. (Compare Colander, 1979, p. 105n; and the literature on the 'credit view' of the monetary transmission mechanism.)

STAGFLATION IN THE UNITED STATES

Monetary-disequilibrium theory helps explain the episode of stagflation in the United States during the mid-1970s. One does not have to resort to the oil price shock of 1973/1974 in order to understand it.

Barsky and Kilian (2001, p. 138) argue that in the popular press, in textbooks and in the literature, 'oil price shocks are an essential part of the explanation of stagflation'. Their alternative interpretation of the US experience is similar to the monetarist explanation. They argue that as a result of expansionary monetary policy, inflation in the early 1970s had already begun to accelerate before OPEC's increase in oil prices. *Tightening* by the monetary authority then led to stagflation. Indeed, some economic indicators pointed to recession nine months *before* the oil crisis even began but immediately after the monetary tightening occurred (Barsky and Kilian, 2001, p. 149). These authors also argue that OPEC's increase in the price of oil during 1973/1974 was in large part a response to global monetary expansion and excess demand rather than solely a response to the political events in the Middle East, a point often made by Leland Yeager.

MONEY, INFLATION AND VELOCITY

Friedman (1974) confronts a supposed puzzle over the relation between money and velocity. Following a distinct increase in the rate of monetary growth, velocity tends to decline. Friedman (pp. 47–8) implies that it declines for a period of up to nine months, rising only later. Why this lag?

Suppose that, starting from a stable price level and full employment, money growth occurs or speeds up. Arithmetically velocity declines since money serves as a buffer. The increase is willingly accepted, even willingly held at first. As people finally decide they do not desire the increased cash balances, they increase their spending on goods and services and securities as the Wicksell Process operates. The goods bought are likely to come first out of firms' inventories, which also serve as buffers. Several months may elapse before output fully responds to the increased money supply (assuming that resources and capacity permit its rise). Meanwhile, velocity has fallen.

As output and then prices finally rise, velocity not only recovers but is also likely to rise above its initial level if monetary expansion continues. Once people come to expect the resulting inflation, they choose to hold smaller real cash balances. Prices must therefore rise more than in proportion to the nominal money supply, leaving velocity greater than originally. Prices overshoot for a second reason. When temporarily stimulated output shrinks back to its full-employment level, prices must temporarily rise at a faster rate as the equation of exchange indicates.

On the other hand, the ending of inflation produces an increase in real money demand and decrease in velocity. Yeager and associates (1981) describe several episodes in which monetary authorities were able to increase their issues to accommodate the increased demand for real balances once inflation had subsided.

Starting from full-employment equilibrium monetary contraction results in an increase in real money demand and decline in velocity, following the transitory 'arithmetical' rise because of money's buffer role. Theories of difficulty in making contact with potential trading partners (see Chapters 6 and 7) help illuminate this familiar decline in velocity. In recession or depression, with many desired sales thwarted, people find themselves holding more cash balances than usual relative to their incomes and expenditures. The grim business scene together with uncertainty encourage increased holdings that would otherwise seem excessive. Velocity falls in the process. Moreover, when prices decrease, people hold larger real cash balances once the deflation becomes anticipated.

APPENDIX: THE REAL-BILLS DOCTRINE

The real-bills doctrine relates the value of money more to its origin or quality or backing than to its quantity. The name comes from a 'real bill of exchange'. This is a draft drawn by a seller of merchandise ordering the buyer to make payment after a specified short period of time. During that time (say three months), the buyer enjoys credit. Ordinarily the drawee – the buyer in this example – signs the bill to confirm his obligation to make payment at maturity, thereby converting the bill into an 'acceptance', effectively a promissory note. If the seller chooses not to wait for payment, he may discount the accepted bill at a bank, which takes over the drawer's role as lender. A 'real bill' arises in connection with an underlying real commercial or industrial transaction.

The real-bills doctrine stretches the concept of real bill to any method of granting bank credit to finance short-term commercial or industrial transactions. Most straightforwardly, the bank makes an ordinary short-term loan to a merchant or manufacturer. It lends money for three months to a shoe store owner laying in inventory or to a tablecloth manufacturer buying raw materials. If all goes as expected, the store owner will sell his shoes or the manufacturer will sell his tablecloths for enough money to repay the loan with interest and with profit remaining on the operation. The loan is relatively safe for the bank because it is self-liquidating, that is, it finances operations expected to bring the borrower more than enough funds to make repayment. While recommending such loans, the real-bills doctrine discourages bank loans to consumers for cars, medical bills, or vacations; loans to executives undertaking leveraged buyouts of their companies; and even long-term loans to industrial enterprises.

Conformity to the doctrine is supposed to regulate the money supply properly. The deposits (and banknotes, if any) on the liability side of banks' balance sheets are matched or backed by sound assets, namely, by loans to merchants and industrialists who will shortly be bringing new goods onto the market. In effect, money is backed by goods, and changes in its quantity are matched by changes in the quantity of goods. Its quantity conforms to the 'needs of trade', hence the doctrine is sometimes also called the 'needs-of-trade theory'. Abiding by the doctrine supposedly maintains money's purchasing power. In practice the doctrine works perversely. It approves increasing bank credit and money in a business expansion and contracting them in a slump, thereby intensifying business fluctuations.

The doctrine commits the fallacy of composition. The individual shoe store owner or tablecloth manufacturer may indeed be able to bring more goods to market with than without a bank loan, but it does not follow that expanding total bank credit and money will bring more goods in total to market. Monetary expansion may indeed promote recovery of output from a recession, but this special case does not justify forgetting the problem of allocating scarce

productive resources. It neglects the rationing function of interest rates along
with other prices. To extend bank credit all across the board means giving
various lines of production more money with which to bid against each other
more intensely for limited resources. The result is higher resource prices, costs
and product prices. Money, made less scarce, loses purchasing power.

At increased prices, the real-bills doctrine allows a firm that will bring a
given physical quantity of goods to market to obtain a proportionately increased
loan in dollar terms. Rising prices call for an increase in the quantity of money,
falling prices for shrinkage of money. The real-bills doctrine ties the nominal
quantity of money to the nominal values of goods, not their physical quantities.
No physical quantity, whether of gold or anything else, defines the dollar. Its
purchasing power depends on the quantity of money interacting with the
demand for money, and the quantity of money under the real-bills doctrine
depends on the price level. Thus the quantity of money is anchored to a consequence of itself, which means not being anchored at all. The purchasing power
of the dollar is not anchored either. The real-bills doctrine, by itself, leaves the
money supply and price level indeterminate. In terms of Chapter 2, it lacks a
critical figure.[12]

Thornton (1802 [1978]) exposed the fallacy of the doctrine, yet it is
remarkably durable. In the United States it was one of the leading ideas
underlying the Federal Reserve Act of 1913, particularly in provisions for redis-
counting of short-term commercial and industrial loans (as well as agricultural
loans). The doctrine was one of the ideas contributing to the German hyperinflation that climaxed in 1923 (see pages 223–4 above).

NOTES

1. Dowd (1996, p. 430) presents some examples of how inflation can actually undermine the
   original intent of a law.
2. Hicks (1977, pp. 114–16) and Okun (1979, pp. 1–5) discuss these matters, including the role
   of notions of equity in setting prices and especially wages.
3. Allais (1947) explicitly mentions land as well as money in his argument about unproductive
   diversion of the willingness to save (see pages 50–51 above). Fry (1988, p. 17) also recognizes
   the point.
4. For eloquent remarks about the sidetracking of savings from capital formation into gold,
   jewels, foreign money and foreign securities, luxury cars, furniture, real estate, and so forth;
   about the appearance of easy gains; about the separation created between activities that are
   privately and those that are socially most profitable; and about social tensions bred by inflation
   – conditions observed in Latin America – see Costanzo (1961, pp. 130–35).
5. Yeager (1976a) provides a fuller, partly mathematical, discussion of bootstrap inflation.
6. Several of the essays in Humphrey (1993) deal with the bullionist controversy.
7. He regarded money supply growth as accommodating rather than exogenous. For insight into
   his thinking, see League of Nations (1946, pp. 16–17, 31) and his address to the executive
   committee of the Reichsbank on 25 August 1923, reprinted in Ringer (1969, pp. 93–6).

8. The doctrine was so called because it held that money issues were sound if connected with the banks' discounting of 'real bills', that is, lending on bills of exchange associated with the production or marketing of actual goods. For further discussion, see, besides Thornton's book, Mints (1945), Humphrey (1982a) and this chapter's Appendix.

9. Trevithick (1977, pp. 94–5), attributing the ideas summarized to J.R. Hicks and R.F. Kahn, among others.

10. A growing literature has developed concerning the political business cycle. Snowdon and Vane (1997b) provide a summary.

11. Fellner long insisted on points like these. See, for example, 1976, especially pp. 2–3, 12–15, 116–18 and 1978, pp. 1–12.

12. Humphrey (1982a) notes the similarity between the real-bills doctrine and the attempt by the monetary authority to peg permanently the interest rate at too low a level. He argues (1983a) that classical and neoclassical economists recognized that the authority could not permanently peg the real rate of interest.

9. Money in an open economy

This chapter shows how monetary theory expounded without attention to the outside world can be adapted to an open economy. It stresses the role of money in balance-of-payments equilibrium, disequilibrium and adjustment. It contrasts the processes determining a country's money supply under fixed and floating exchange rates. It illustrates the problems of compromise systems and reviews experience accumulated and theoretical contributions made since floating became widespread in 1971–73. Again the Wicksell Process plays a major role in the analysis.

THE INTERNATIONAL GOLD STANDARD

Under a gold standard, a country's monetary authority keeps the national monetary unit and a definite quantity of gold equal in value on free markets. It stands ready to buy (or coin) unlimited amounts of gold at a definite price and also to sell unlimited amounts at the same or nearly the same price, as by redeeming its paper money. An international gold standard exists among all countries that tie their moneys to gold and allow its unrestricted import and export.

The international gold standard, which ended in 1914, limited exchange rate fluctuations. Each government or monetary authority made its currency and gold freely interconvertible at a fixed price. The United States would coin gold into money and redeem money in gold at the rate of $20.671835 per fine troy ounce. The British pound sterling 'contained' 4.86656 times as much gold as the dollar. When the dollar price of sterling *on the foreign exchange market* rose above this 'mint par' of $4.86656 by more than roughly two cents, arbitrageurs could make a profit. They would redeem dollars in gold, ship the gold to England, have the gold recoined there into pounds sterling (or sell it to the Bank of England at a corresponding price), thereby obtain sterling for dollars more cheaply than at the exchange rate, and sell the sterling on the foreign exchange market for more dollars than they started with. In so doing, the gold arbitrageurs would check any further rise in the dollar rate on sterling. At the opposite extreme, when the dollar price of sterling fell more than roughly two cents below mint par, arbitrageurs could profitably redeem sterling in gold, ship the gold to the United States and convert it into dollars, thereby obtain more dollars for their sterling than corresponded to the exchange rate, and have a profit in dollars after buying back their original amount of sterling on the foreign exchange market. So doing, they would check any further fall in the dollar rate on sterling.

The spread between the mint par and each of the two so-called 'gold points' on either side of it corresponded to the costs of crating and shipping and insuring the gold, the interest lost on wealth tied up in gold in transit, and other costs of carrying out the arbitrage. Since the interest loss and other costs of gold arbitrage changed from time to time and since some of the costs were matters of rough estimate anyway, the spread was not constant and precise. Still, the limits to exchange rate fluctuation under the gold standard ordinarily stayed close to mint par as in our example.

Each government (except in a few countries on a gold exchange standard) ordinarily left exchange rate stabilizing operations to private gold arbitrageurs. With minor exceptions, it restrained itself to maintaining two-way convertibility between its monetary unit and a fixed amount of gold.

When a gold standard currency had weakened almost to its so-called 'gold export point', people would realize that it could not weaken much further and that it would probably rise. Speculative or quasi-speculative capital movements then came to the support of the currency and tended to keep gold exports from actually becoming profitable. At the other extreme, outflows of speculative capital from a country whose currency had almost reached its 'gold import point' would tend to keep inward gold arbitrage from becoming profitable. The danger of distrust and destabilizing speculation was slighter under the gold standard than under the compromise systems that followed because preserving two-way convertibility between each national money unit and a fixed quantity of gold was then seen as almost an overriding goal of financial policy.

The permanence of this policy depended in turn on a connection between a country's monetary gold stock and its stock of all kinds of money, including banknotes and bank deposits. In a country losing gold because of excess imports of goods, services and securities, the total money supply decreased. A country gaining gold experienced monetary expansion. Governments had little scope to manage money supplies to suit themselves, even if full employment and price level stability had been their objectives. Money supplies, prices, employment, production and incomes had to respond to the requirements of keeping foreign transactions balanced at fixed exchange rates. Each country had to let deflation and inflation at home keep generally in step with world-wide monetary conditions (see pages 252–4 below). Because countries gave up their monetary independence in order to keep their exchange rates fixed, we say that they adhered to the 'rules of the game'.

MONEY AND THE BALANCE OF PAYMENTS

When exchange rates are fixed but a country's currency is weakening under the pressure of excess imports of goods, services and securities, the monetary authority supports it by buying it with foreign exchange (broadly interpreted to include gold) held in reserve for that purpose. In doing so the authority fills the gap between the total value of imports of goods, services and securities and the smaller value of total exports. This gap is the balance-of-payments deficit.[1]

Actually, the authority maintains as well as fills the gap, for if it were not filled it could not exist. Unless it is financed, overimporting cannot occur. Instead, the value of the country's imports would necessarily shrink to the value of its exports in some way or other, perhaps by depreciation of the home currency or by controls designed to choke off demands for foreign exchange. In keeping the exchange rate fixed, the authority can go on filling the gap only as long as it has reserves left or is able to borrow more abroad.

An opposite imbalance, a surplus, requires the authority to absorb foreign exchange and pay with home money to prevent its currency from strengthening. In doing so and thus financing and maintaining the country's excess of sales over purchases in foreign transactions, it faces no limit as definite as the one in the opposite situation. It can create home currency to keep it from strengthening, but it cannot of course create foreign exchange in the deficit case.

The authority's sale or purchase of foreign exchange is similar in its monetary consequences to its open-market sale or purchase of domestic securities, but with one important difference. Although open-market operations are usually undertaken at the authority's discretion, foreign exchange sales and purchases are practically automatic if the authority is committed to a fixed exchange rate. Therefore, a payments deficit will shrink its base of high-powered money and its money supply in turn. Conversely, a surplus will cause multiple expansion of its money supply. The authority may try, however, to 'sterilize' these results by undertaking deliberate open-market operations with opposite monetary consequences. For example, it may try to match purchases of foreign exchange with sales of domestic securities. Sterilization though would violate the 'rules of the game' for fixed rates.

DEMAND-DETERMINATION OF THE MONEY SUPPLY UNDER FIXED RATES

According to the fundamental proposition of monetary theory, incomes and prices adjust to make desired nominal cash balances equal in the aggregate to the actual money supply. This proposition holds in a closed economy or an open economy with floating rates. It does not necessarily hold in an open economy with fixed rates. Suppose, for example, an excess supply of money exists. The Wicksell Process operates as people try to dispose of cash balances by purchasing more goods and services and securities. This increased demand shows up partly at the water's edge as residents develop an excess of purchases over sales in transactions with foreigners. The excess money figuratively 'leaks abroad' through the payments deficit as the authority absorbs it and supplies foreign exchange. Conversely, an excess demand for money may create a payments surplus and a rise in the money supply.

In a closed economy or in an open economy with floating rates, the demand for nominal cash balances adjusts to the money supply, but in an open economy with fixed rates the nominal supply may adjust to the demand for it. Under both sets of arrangements, we recall, the actual real quantity of money adjusts to the real quantity demanded. But under fixed rates the same actual-to-demanded adjustment may occur even for nominal quantities.

CASES IN WHICH THE MONEY SUPPLY IS NOT DEMAND-DETERMINED

Not all payments surpluses or deficits occur as mere responses to excess demands for or supplies of money. In an open as in a closed economy, it is an error to assume that money being actually accepted is necessarily being demanded. Because the medium of exchange is routinely used and accepted on all markets, an increase in its actual quantity, whether occurring through a payments surplus or as a result of domestic policy, does not necessarily correspond to an increased demand for it. Conversely, a shrinkage does not necessarily represent a deliberate and desired rundown of individual holdings.

One must distinguish sharply between the demand for home currency on the foreign exchange market and the demand for cash balance holdings, for which no market actually exists. When residents demand home currency on the foreign exchange market, they prefer it to foreign exchange on that market, but they do not necessarily want to hold this money. Because this acquisition merely reflects the home currency's role as medium of exchange, the transaction can create an excess supply of cash balances.

Let us reconsider a case first met in Chapter 3. The supposed action would be absurd or sadistic as an actual policy, but it introduces an instructive analysis. Anyway, the monetary authority revalues the home currency upward, cutting in half the pegged home-currency price of foreign exchange. The consequent price changes make purchases of goods and services and securities from abroad more attractive than sales abroad, and the country runs a payments deficit. By making foreign exchange a bargain and selling it lavishly out of its reserves, the authority takes out of circulation the home money received in payment. Yet this monetary contraction in no way represents an intentional rundown of private money holdings. On the contrary, it leaves an excess demand for money with its painful contractionary consequences.

Suppose instead that the authority devalues the home currency, leaving the price of foreign exchange too high. The resulting payments surplus expands the money supply with inflationary consequences. Rather than the result of an excess demand for money, the surplus is part of the process that creates an excess supply.

An unintended change in the money supply can occur through an 'imposed' surplus or deficit. If foreign demand falls for some of the home country's export goods, an imposed deficit results that creates an excess demand for money. Conversely, an imposed surplus creates an excess supply of cash balances. We say that these payments imbalances are 'imposed' because they stem from actions *external* to the home country.

BALANCE-OF-PAYMENTS ADJUSTMENT UNDER FIXED RATES

A balance-of-payments disequilibrium can be cured 'automatically' in three ways, that is, without direct orders from some authority but rather through appropriate incentives to private economic units concerned with their own incomes and cash balances and expenditures. To correct a deficit (and conversely for a surplus), the first and second ways involve a fall in the ratio of total home nominal income to total foreign nominal income. This ratio is not an indicator by which people and firms govern their decisions and actions. We use it simply as a device for organizing a comparison of the mechanisms. (1) The ratio could conceivably fall as home nominal income fell entirely through cuts in the prices and wages at which goods and services were valued and without any decline in the overall physical volume of domestic production and employment. (2) Home nominal income and its ratio to foreign nominal income could fall through a shrinkage in the physical volume of goods and services produced, with prices and wages unchanged. (3) The Wicksell Process plays a role in both these mechanisms but deserves separate mention.

All three mechanisms operate automatically providing countries abide by the 'rules of the game', as in the gold standard example discussed at the beginning of this chapter. That is, they must give up their monetary independence in order to keep the exchange rate fixed. The relative importance of the automatic mechanisms depends in part on how frictionlessly price and wage levels adjust up and down. One reason for focusing on this adjustment process is to better understand the weaknesses of the compromise system of 'pegged-but-adjustable exchange rates'.

We mention two temporary palliatives of disequilibrium. First, on page 243 above we illustrate how speculative inflows or outflows of capital can be equilibrating under the gold standard when the exchange rate reaches one of its 'gold points'. Second, changes in interest rates can motivate short-term capital flows that are equilibrating. However, neither of these palliatives 'cure' the payments disequilibrium. Accordingly, we abstract from them in the analysis that follows.

THE PRICE LEVEL MECHANISM UNDER FIXED RATES

In the convenient German terminology, the home country is called 'Inland', while another country or all other countries together are 'Outland'. Also for convenience, we take up our three mechanisms or aspects of the adjustment process one by one. We first suppose that monetary contractions and expansions impinge only on prices and not on real activity.

We also suppose that a real disturbance, such as a shift of Outland's tastes away from some of Inland's export goods, imposes a deficit on Inland. The adjustment mechanism may operate from the start, conceivably even forestalling the deficit, but for expository convenience we suppose that it actually develops before corrective processes prevail. The deficit drains money out of Inland, whose price level falls accordingly. Opposite developments take place in Outland, where a payments surplus expands the money supply and thus raises prices. The relative cheapening of Inland goods shifts some purchases by Inlanders from imports to domestic goods. Outlanders also have reason to buy the relatively cheapened Inland goods. Inland's payments deficit shrinks or vanishes.

If the initial disturbance is an increase in Inland's money supply, then price increases there turn Inlanders and Outlanders from buying Inland to buying Outland goods. The resulting payments deficit reverses Inland's rise in money and prices, thus removing its own source.

The foregoing description invokes the price-specie-flow mechanism of David Hume (1752a [1969], p. 27). Hume hypothesized that if four-fifths of the money supply in Great Britain was annihilated overnight, prices would sink in proportion, leading to a balance-of-trade surplus. As money flowed into Britain, prices would rise again and the surplus would disappear.

One might criticize Hume's (and our) supposedly disregarding the 'law of one price'. It is unrealistic, critics say, to suppose that the price of a good could differ between countries by more than the trading costs (broadly interpreted).

Inland's and Outland's price levels could not diverge as Hume envisaged. His mechanism, however, can be defended by distinguishing between traded and nontraded goods. Changes in their relative prices contribute to adjustment. Our preliminary suggestion that export prices fall and rise along with general price levels in the two countries was an oversimplification. The prices of each country's import and export goods do not keep exact pace with its general price level because they are determined by supplies and demands on the world market rather than just by local conditions. In the flexible price context of mechanism one, monetary contraction in a reserve-losing deficit country chiefly affects the prices of goods like houses and haircuts and labor, which do not typically move in international trade. Of course, the dividing line is fuzzy and shiftable. Even local services can be 'exported' by sale to visiting foreigners, and large enough spreads between foreign and domestic prices could motivate trade in goods ordinarily too costly to ship in relation to value. Still, the distinction is meaningful, along with emphasis on world determination of traded goods prices and local determination of nontraded goods prices.

After the supposed real disturbance (the shift of tastes), Inland's payments deficit depresses its money supply and so reduces the prices of its nontraded goods. Because these become relatively cheaper, Inlanders shift their buying onto them and away from imports and exportable goods, while concentrating their production and sales efforts on the sectors of the foreign market that have now become more favorably priced. Corresponding but opposite price shifts and incentives in Outland reinforce this balance-of-payments adjustment.

Two objections may arise. First, if the supposed drop in foreign demand for some exports has cut aggregate demand in Inland, how can we speak of a shift of purchases toward nontraded goods? Our answer recognizes that the combined nominal demand for traded and nontraded goods has indeed fallen. The deficit-induced money supply shrinkage depresses the prices of nontradables in particular. Since tradables, specifically those not hit by the supposed initial drop in export demand, do not fall in price in the same proportion, some demand shifts away from them onto nontraded goods, moderating the price declines in that sector. Still, overall nominal demand for Inland's goods has diminished including the total nominal demand for nontraded goods. Second, one might ask why Inland firms switch into production of traded goods, since the initial disturbance was a drop in demand for Inland's exports. The answer is, in part, that only some and not all export goods were hit by the initial disturbance, so that the adjustment process including declines in factor prices does encourage production of other exports (including, perhaps, goods just now made profitably exportable). The reduced relative price of nontradables helps push productive factors into the export sector. Our conclusions do not contradict the assumption of an initial decline in total demand for Inland's goods and productive factors.

We now focus specifically on prices of factors of production, which are among a country's goods and services least directly involved in international trade. Wage rates, land rents and other factor prices fall as reserve losses deflate Inland's money supply, while prices of traded goods experience relatively less deflation. These changes imply a fall in the real purchasing power of productive factors and in the real incomes of their owners. Neither this fall nor the response of individuals in reducing their consumption and investment necessarily entail an overall decline in production and employment, since we have been assuming flexible wages and prices. Nor is the fall identical to a worsening of the terms of trade in the ordinary sense of the ratio of export to import prices, although those terms are indeed likely to worsen in our supposed case of a drop in demand for Inland's exports.

In the face of the initial adverse disturbance, continued exchange rate pegging by sale of reserves of foreign exchange at a price too low to equate supply and demand had in effect been *subsidizing* the incomes of and expenditures by Inland's individuals and business firms. The fall in factor prices *relative* to traded goods prices, when it finally occurs as the Inland money supply shrinks, offsets or discontinues this subsidy. The country's worsened real economic position comes to bear on the decisions of individual economic units. The fixed exchange rate again becomes an equilibrium price, and the deficit comes to an end. Note that the fall in the price of nontraded goods helps remove the excess demand for money caused by the deficit.

Our alternative disturbance under a fixed rate, an increase in the money supply in Inland, raises the prices of goods and services supplied and demanded in world markets less than the prices of Inland's nontraded goods and services and factors of production. The real incomes of workers and other factor owners rise. The real economic position of the country as a whole has not improved, yet the positions of individual economic units have improved because their incomes and expenditures are being subsidized by official sale of foreign exchange at what is now a bargain price. Importable and exportable goods become relatively attractive to Inland buyers, contributing to the payments deficit.

Any correction of the deficit involves bringing to decisionmakers' attention the fact that the country's real economic position has not in fact improved. The disinflation caused by the deficit-induced shrinkage of the money supply makes the fixed rate an equilibrium one again and reverses the subsidization of incomes and expenditures. In particular, reversal of the temporary increases in domestic factor prices *relative* to traded goods prices brings the real incomes of factor owners back into correspondence with the country's real economic position. As the prices of nontraded goods and services and factors of production return roughly to their pre-inflation levels, the relative attractiveness of traded goods and its contribution to the deficit is removed.

THE INCOME MECHANISM

With prices and wages unchanged, variations in real income and employment constitute a second aspect of automatic adjustment. The initial drop in Outland's spending on Inland's exports reduces Inland's real income. The deficit-induced fall in the money supply exacerbates this decrease. As they become poorer, Inlanders cut back on their purchases of nontraded goods, imports and exportable goods and domestic goods made with factors capable of shifting into export production. The initial fall in Inland's exports is partly allayed as Outlanders take advantage of Inland's more eager sales efforts, which may include faster deliveries of exports. The income mechanism also works in Outland, where spending and real income rise as permitted by the slack in productive capacity that we tacitly assume. With the rise in income promoted by the increase in cash balances, Outland's decrease in purchases from Inland is restrained for this second reason. This dual restraint along with the money-and-income-induced fall in Inland imports help restore payments equilibrium.

We do not consider the alternative case of a rise in Inland's money supply since numerous scenarios exist. For example, we could assume implausibly that only real income rises. Or we could assume that prices only rise, but they do not fall. At any rate, changes in real income are part of the adjustment process.

The variation of real income as one corrective of external imbalance represents a departure from a theoretically ideal system frictionlessly maintaining equilibrium on all goods and factor markets through prompt price and wage adjustments. Regrettable though the fact may be, changes in real income represent one mechanism in the automatic adjustment process under fixed rates.

THE OPERATION OF THE WICKSELL PROCESS

More directly influencing the balance of payments than price and income changes are the monetary developments to which those changes are themselves a response. After the real disturbance, the drop in Outland's demand for Inland's exports, cash balances shrink in Inland as the deficit drains reserves. Cash balances become and remain smaller than before not only in nominal amount but also in real purchasing power, at least until prices and wages have fully responded to the monetry shrinkage. (They probably remain smaller even afterwards, since discontinuance of the subsidy constituted by pegging the exchange rate at what had temporarily become a disequilibrium rate now represents a fall in real incomes from private points of view, in conformity with the country's worsened economic position. With their real incomes reduced, Inlanders tend to hold smaller real balances.) Meanwhile, concerned not to let their cash balances shrink too far, Inlanders cut their purchases of both nontraded and traded goods and probably become more eager to make sales. The Wicksell Process comes into play and helps terminate the deficit.

Moreover, the Wicksell Process provides part of the answer to the skeptical question sometimes asked: how can a mere change in its price level correct a country's tendency, as evidenced by its deficit, to consume and invest in excess of its current production? The answer focuses on what accompanies, and indeed helps to cause, the price change. The monetary contraction resulting from Inland's deficit leaves money temporarily in excess demand. The operation of the Wicksell Process helps remove this excess demand for money by shrinking spending and hence the prices of nontraded goods and services and factors of production. By reducing the relative price of nontraded to traded goods and by making traded goods less attractive for Inlanders to buy, the Wicksell Process helps eliminate the payments deficit.

When domestic monetary expansion constitutes the disturbance, Inlanders increase their spending abroad as well as at home as the Wicksell Process unfolds. The deficit removes this excess supply of money, thereby restoring external balance. If money were 'to leak abroad' rapidly enough, unrealistically rapidly, changes in prices and production in Inland would not even be necessary. No excess supply of money would occur in the sense of Walras's Law. Inlanders' purchases of goods and services in excess of current national production, or 'overabsorption', would be the real counterpart of the money creation and leakage. This unusual case illustrates how a payments deficit could prevent monetary disequilibrium and frustration from arising after a monetary expansion. In the limiting case, the authority's purchase of domestic assets would not cause any monetary expansion in the first place, for its loss of foreign exchange reserves would keep pace with its acquisition of domestic assets from the start, leaving high-powered money and thus the money supply unchanged.

TRANSMISSION OF BUSINESS FLUCTUATIONS UNDER FIXED RATES

Examples already considered suggest a double relation between domestic business conditions and foreign trade. Inflation, depression, external surplus and external deficit do not go together in any simple way. Causation depends on the nature of the initial disturbance.

On the one hand, the 'adjustment process' operates. Suppose a deficit in Inland results from decreased Outland demand for its exports, as in the case of the real disturbance analyzed above. The adjustment process that helps terminate Inland's deficit may cause depression there. Conversely, the adjustment process that helps eliminate an imposed surplus in Inland may create inflation there. In short, Inland's deficit results in depression and its surplus results in inflation.

On the other hand, a 'transmission process' operates. Monetary expansion in Outland can cause inflation and a corresponding payments deficit. The inflation is then transmitted to Inland through an imposed surplus. Conversely, monetary contraction in Outland can cause a depression and a corresponding payments surplus. The depression is then communicated to Inland through an imposed deficit. In this process, Outland's inflation goes together with its payments deficit, and its depression goes together with its payments surplus. When Inland is on the receiving end of the transmission process, we speak of 'imported inflation' or 'imported deflation' in Inland. We conclude that the same factors that operate in the adjustment process also operate in the international transmission of business fluctuations.

IMPORTED INFLATION

Imported inflation occurs through two main channels involving (1) monetary and (2) direct price transmission (compare Yeager, 1976b; Rabin, 1977 and Rabin and Yeager, 1982).

The Monetary Channel of Imported Inflation

Inflation can be transmitted among countries in a manner similar to Hume's price-specie-flow mechanism. As we have just seen, inflation in Outland (taken to be the rest of the world) and its accompanying payments deficit impose a surplus on Inland. Monetary expansion in Inland then results in imported inflation there. Because the prices of Inland's nontraded goods are not determined directly on world markets, Inland's overall inflation rate may temporarily lag behind Outland's. The monetary channel of imported inflation then operates to align Inland's rate with the worldwide average by increasing the prices of Inland's nontraded goods.

Inflation can be imported even though the current account remains in balance. The monetary effects of an overall payments surplus are the same whether the surplus occurs mostly on capital or mostly on current account. In either case it expands high-powered money and the money supply.

Two related aspects of the monetary channel are *shortage-of-goods* and *spending* effects. First, Inland's current account surplus spells withdrawal of real goods and services. Less than the full value of its current production is available for satisfying demands in Inland, resulting in 'underabsorption'. Second, the increase in Outland's spending on Inland's traded goods and services also operates in the expansionary direction. While these two aspects by themselves may help explain a once-and-for-all rise in Inland's price level, they cannot account for a continuous rise in prices (unless, perhaps, the trade surplus itself keeps growing implausibly for some autonomous reason). In the process of imported inflation, these two aspects must be subordinate to the monetary consequences of an overall payments surplus.

The Direct-Price-Transmission Channel of Imported Inflation

Under fixed rates, an increase in the price of traded goods in Outland spreads to Inland according to the 'law of one price'. Commodity arbitrage keeps each good selling in Inland and Outland at the same price translated at the exchange rate, apart from transportation costs and the like. The increase in the price of traded goods may then raise the price of Inland's nontraded goods through linkages involving factor prices and substitutabilities in production and consumption. Especially if Inland is a small open economy with a large traded goods sector, it may not be unrealistic to assume that its overall inflation rate is directly tied to the inflation rate for traded goods in the outside world. Its price level comes close to being an externally imposed exogenous variable.

For the direct-price-transmission channel to operate, a payments surplus need not actually develop in Inland. An externally imposed increase in its price level raises the nominal demand for money, which can then be satisfied through a payments surplus. But if the authority expands the money supply sufficiently by buying domestic assets instead, it keeps the surplus from developing. It may well make this choice, reasoning that if its commitment to a fixed rate makes inflation inevitable in any case, it may better buy domestic securities instead of foreign exchange. When the direct-price-transmission channel dominates, the role of money is to accommodate externally imposed price increases.

An Eclectic Theory of Imported Inflation

When the outside world is inflating, an economy with a fixed exchange rate catches the inflation through either of the two channels. The direct-price-transmission channel may dominate at some times, the monetary channel at others. The two channels are complementary; they are 'two sides of the same coin' (Fellner, 1975, p. 129).

A payments surplus coupled with inflation at home may trace to a combination of both channels. However, a price rise of traded goods followed by a price increase of nontraded goods does not necessarily indicate that the direct-price-transmission channel has dominated. At issue here is the sequence of price rises. Quite conceivably, monetary expansion through a payments surplus may have inflated the prices of nontraded goods, although with the typical lag

mentioned in the monetarist literature. In this case the monetary channel may
have dominated (compare pages 259–60 below).

Imported Inflation Versus Domestic Inflation

A country adhering to fixed rates may face a choice between accepting imported
inflation and inflating at home. If the authority wants to acquire additional
foreign exchange reserves, it may choose the former course. If it refuses to give
foreigners the loans that the acquisition of reserves represents, it chooses the
latter. Under fixed rates the country cannot resist worldwide inflation. It must
either import it or keep in step with it through domestic policy.

THE EXCHANGE RATE MECHANISM: FLOATING RATES

We explore how a system of freely floating rates operates to maintain the
exchange rate regime. We assume that the dollar is the medium of exchange
in Inland and the peso in Outland. For a real disturbance we again suppose
that Outland's tastes shift partially away from Inland's exports. The old
exchange rate leaves Inland's dollar in excess supply and Outland's peso in
excess demand on the foreign exchange market. Depreciation of the dollar
under market pressures raises the dollar prices of Inland's imports and also of
its exports (other, presumably, than the particular goods for which foreign
demand may have dropped off). On the other hand, appreciation of the peso
cuts the peso prices of Inland's exports. Outland's increased purchases of them,
other than of the particular exports affected by the initial shift of tastes,
represent a movement along its existing demand schedule as a function of peso
prices. From Inland's point of view, the demand schedule as a function of
dollar prices has strengthened for some of its exports, producing the increase
in their dollar prices mentioned above. The important fact is that Inland's
imports and exports both rise in price relative to prices of its nontraded goods
and factors of production. This relative price rise causes Inlanders to cut down
on importing and on domestic consumption of exportable goods and to concentrate more than before on production for export. The fuzzy dividing line
between traded and nontraded goods may shift so as to make more goods than
before profitably exportable.

Opposite effects occur in Outland, where appreciation of its peso causes an
apparent decline in Inland demand for its exports, lowering their peso prices as
well (although their dollar prices rise). Since the peso prices of Outland's
imports from Inland also fall, nontraded goods and factors of production rise
in price relative to traded goods. Outlanders shift toward buying traded goods
from Inland and away from producing them. Loosely speaking, the smaller

Inland is in relation to Outland, the more the price incentives to adjustment occur in Inland.

If monetary inflation in Inland provides the initial disturbance, a depreciation of its dollar prevents some price distortions by allowing the dollar prices of traded goods to keep pace with domestic cash balances and the prices of nontraded goods. It avoids overabsorption promoted by false price signals and financed by drawing down on the authority's foreign exchange reserves.

The exchange rate mechanism is similar in key respects to the price level mechanism under fixed rates described earlier. Consider the real disturbance. First, under fixed rates the deficit shrinks nominal and real cash balances in Inland, while under floating rates depreciation of Inland's currency lowers the purchasing power of the unchanged nominal money supply (by raising the prices of Inland's imports and exports). Second, under either system nontraded goods and services in Inland fall in price relative to traded goods, so the real purchasing power of productive factors and in the incomes of their owners fall. However, under the price level mechanism the general levels of Inland's prices and factor incomes fall while the prices of traded goods remain more nearly unchanged. Under the exchange rate mechanism the dollar prices of Inland's traded goods rise while nontraded prices and factor incomes remain nearly unchanged. But relative movements are ideally the same.

Smooth adjustment under fixed rates requires an unrealistically high degree of downward as well as upward flexibility in domestic wages and prices. Since the price level mechanism will not promptly bear the whole burden of adjustment, the unpleasant income mechanism involving employment and production levels must operate. Market adjustments in floating rates, by contrast, help bring the prices of import and export-type goods into an appropriate relation between them and the prices of nontraded goods and factors of production. When wages and prices are sticky, floating rates can in effect make them flexible as translated into the currencies of other countries, giving them 'quasi-flexibility' (Yeager, 1976b, pp. 104–6).

Under freely floating rates, with the monetary authority staying out of the foreign exchange market, the balance of payments does not directly affect the home money supply. The fundamental proposition of monetary theory again applies. Undesired holdings of domestic money do not 'leak abroad' as they do under fixed rates. Instead, prices or real incomes or both rise to make undesired money fully demanded after all. Conversely, an initially deficient money supply brings deflation or depression. The exchange rate is one of the many prices that change during the adjustment process. Each monetary authority can, if it wishes, insulate its money supply from external domination and try to stabilize its size or growth rate as suits conditions at home. This is not to say, however, that floating or any other exchange rate regime can insulate a country from foreign economic disturbances. Rate fluctuations associated with capital movements can be disruptive, as noted on pages 262–3 below.

PEGGED-BUT-ADJUSTABLE EXCHANGE RATES

The two exchange rate systems reviewed above are polar arrangements. Each has advantages and disadvantages that have been widely discussed in the literature. In the sections that follow we shall investigate the 'compromise system' of pegged-but-adjustable exchange rates, which attempts to reap the advantages of both purely fixed and freely floating rates.

An international monetary system cannot achieve simultaneously all three of the following goals: (1) freedom for each country to pursue an independent monetary policy; (2) freedom from controls on international trade and capital flows and (3) fixed exchange rates. Any two of these are possible together, but not all three. With controls ruled out, the so-called 'doctrine of alternative stability' holds that a country must choose between domestic stability and exchange rate stability, since each of the two kinds of stability rules out the other. For example, to maintain a fixed rate system each country must sacrifice its monetary independence and allow domestic incomes and prices to keep in step with worldwide developments. Each must adhere to the 'rules of the game'. Under a compromise system, countries have often sought to sacrifice two or three of the above objectives in part rather than one of them completely.[2]

Under the international gold standard, which ended in 1914, independent monetary policies were usually sacrificed in order to keep exchange rates fixed. Speculative capital flows were often stabilizing because exchange rates were trusted to be maintained. On the other hand, vulnerability to one-way-option speculation is a major feature of the compromise system of pegged-but-adjustable exchange rates. When a pegged rate is suspected of being overvalued or undervalued, speculators have practically a sure thing. They may have some doubt as to whether the monetary authority will actually make a rate change, but they have no doubt as to its direction. They win big if the change occurs, but lose little if it does not. Moreover, bear speculation against a weak currency may actually force its devaluation as the monetary authority's reserves are depleted. Even worse, rumors of a currency's impending devaluation, even if untrue, might force devaluation through destabilizing speculation and thus make themselves true after all. Even if fundamentals do not justify a devaluation, speculation on it can be self-fulfilling. History contains many examples of minor events and rumors triggering major repercussions (see Yeager, 1976b). What usually sets the stage for currency crises is some compromise system between fixed and freely floating rates. Below we examine one example in detail: the collapse of the Bretton Woods system of pegged-but-adjustable exchange rates.

STERILIZATION

Under pegged-but-adjustable exchange rates countries have often tried to sterilize or neutralize the monetary effects of a payments deficit or surplus. With a fractional-reserve banking system, official sales of foreign exchange shrink the volume of high-powered money and set the stage for multiple contraction of the money supply. To avoid causing a business recession, the authority may act to sterilize (offset) the deficit's contractionary impact by buying domestic securities, which restores high-powered money to banks. By returning the home currency collected for foreign exchange sold, sterilization impairs any automatic adjustment process. Speculation on exhaustion of external reserves may even force a devaluation of the deficit country's currency.

Much the same holds true in reverse for a country with a payments surplus. To resist inflation, the authority may sterilize its monetary repercussions by selling domestic securities. Awkwardly, this policy may well create an interest rate differential that attracts capital inflows and deters outflows. This shift toward a surplus on capital account increases the amount of foreign exchange that the authority must buy to keep the rate fixed, compounding the problem. Speculation on an upward revaluation can turn the problem into a crisis on the foreign exchange market.

Under the Bretton Woods system Germany tried for years to resist imported inflation.[3] Even if it could have completely sterilized the monetary increases produced by the surpluses, it would still have been vulnerable to the direct-price-transmission channel of imported inflation. Indeed, Fels (1969) emphasizes this channel in discussing Germany's bout with imported inflation. Only under the subsequent protection of floating rates was Germany successful in pursuing domestic monetary policy without interference (Bundesbank, 1973, p. 27). Otmar Emminger, Deputy Governor of the Bundesbank, offers this illuminating assessment of Germany's struggles (quoted in Brunner and Meltzer, 1976, pp. 5, 6):

> In the Bundesbank we consider March 1973, when we went over to floating, to have been a sort of watershed not only in international but also in domestic monetary affairs...from the beginning of 1970 to March 1973, we were obliged under the Bretton Woods system...to take in $23 billion worth of foreign exchange, and to convert these foreign exchange inflows into D marks, which led to a runaway increase in our money supply. As central bankers, we were no longer independent agents but were at the mercy of these destabilizing international money movements...whatever we did in order to sterilize these funds inevitably attracted additional money from abroad...After

the suspension of this inflation-prone system the Bundesbank quickly regained control over domestic money supply...

THE BRETTON WOODS SYSTEM OF PEGGED-BUT-ADJUSTABLE EXCHANGE RATES

The post-war Bretton Woods system was a compromise system that lacked any automatic adjustment process and that finally broke down as it experienced severe bouts of one-way-option speculation. The world paid dearly for the valuable lessons the system provided – lessons that in many cases have only begun to be understood in light of the currency crises of the 1990s.[4]

Instead of letting national money supplies rise, and especially instead of letting them fall as necessary to restore payments equilibrium, monetary authorities often sterilized any undesirable changes as they pursued domestic full-employment policies. They certainly avoided the 'rules of the game'. They were allowed to alter their declared parities in cases of 'fundamental disequilibrium', but exactly what that consisted of was never fully explained.[5]

The newly created International Monetary Fund loaned financial resources for 'waiting out' balance-of-payments deficits hopefully expected to go away of their own accord. It stood 'ready to subsidize this breath-holding policy'. Unless by exercising moral suasion over its members' domestic financial policies or by authorizing infrequent deliberate adjustments in levels of exchange rate pegging, it did nothing positive to promote equilibrium. It simply helped improvise ad hoc solutions for crises (Allen, 1961, pp. 159–64). Exchange controls on trade and capital movements, though contrary to the spirit of the IMF charter, remained available as a partial substitute for a continuously operating adjustment process. Other 'patchwork' expedients also characterized the system. Quite appropriately, Mundell (1968, p. 217) spoke of the 'international disequilibrium system' (although he later became nostalgic about it).

Disequilibrium showed up in crises of one-way-option speculation that periodically swept the system. Even when the defenders of existing parities did succeed in riding through a crisis, it caused much disruption. While exchange rate changes did not occur often, when they did occur they tended to be devaluations rather than revaluations, which helped contribute to the eventual overvaluation of the dollar. When all else failed, deficit countries would devalue as a last resort rather than face deflation. On the other hand, surplus countries were more prone to inflate, since revaluation was usually not viewed as a viable alternative. The system thus had a devaluation and inflationary bias. (Yeager, 1976b elaborates on these points.)

In the 1960s, it was common to speak of the system's three major problems: 'liquidity', 'confidence' and 'adjustment'. The liquidity problem stemmed from the need for more international liquidity so countries could 'ride out' their deficits. Yet that implied the United States, the main supplier of international liquidity (see the next section), would have to run large deficits. Confidence in the dollar would be adversely affected, hence the confidence problem.[6] While the liquidity problem held most economists' attention, such emphasis was probably misplaced, for the liquidity and confidence problems both derived from the adjustment problem. With an adequate adjustment process operating, the other problems would not have arisen. Because no such process did exist, the system eventually collapsed.

In 1971, the US payments deficit reached nearly $30 billion as foreign monetary authorities added more dollars to their official reserves than in all of human history up to that time. During the period 1970–72 and the first quarter of 1973, they increased their dollar reserves by 346 percent. These last-ditch attempts to defend the system – to keep rates pegged by buying dollars – not only transmitted inflation but actually generated it. The huge surpluses led to internal disequilibrium by creating excess supplies of cash balances. This monetary 'explosion' fueled the subsequent acceleration of worldwide inflation.[7] (Besides *International Financial Statistics*, see also Ingram, 1974; Rabin, 1977 and Rabin and Yeager, 1982.)

Since monetary expansion affects prices with the usual lag of roughly two years, superficial observers had an opportunity to blame the acceleration of worldwide inflation in 1973–74 not on the defense of the system, but rather on the floating exchange rates left after its demise. Yet this acceleration actually began *before* fixed rates finally collapsed in 1973 and, we might add, *before* the oil supply shocks of 1973–74 (see page 237 above).

Some economists have argued that the acceleration of inflation could not have been caused by imported inflation, since the United States had a lower rate of inflation and monetary growth than the outside world during this period. The argument does not recognize that the acceleration was primarily generated by the monetary channel of imported inflation. Countries could import inflation even though it was not exported elsewhere (that is, through the direct-price-transmission channel).[8] An already accelerated price inflation in the United States was *not* a necessary condition for the acceleration of worldwide inflation to occur.

While prodigious efforts to defend the Bretton Woods system stretched over several years, the demise finally came in 1973. Some economists have blamed it on the United States' termination in 1971 of its commitment to convert dollars to gold. Our response comes in three parts. First, in practice, convertibility ended in 1968 with the collapse of the gold pool and its replacement by a two-tier price system (see Yeager, 1976b, pp. 574–5). Second, despite this lack of convertibility the system of pegged rates was restored in 1971 (after its initial collapse) under the Smithsonian agreement. Third, countries were 'forced' to give up their defense of pegged rates as speculators enjoyed one-way options on a mammoth scale. For example, on 1 March 1973 the Bundesbank was compelled to purchase $2.7 billion, at that time 'the largest amount of foreign exchange a central bank has ever had to acquire within a single day' (Bundesbank, 1973, p. 66). The following day it gave up support of the dollar and floated its exchange rate.

THE UNIQUE POSITION OF THE UNITED STATES

Because of the dollar's special international role as the dominant transactions, intervention and reserve currency, the United States came close to retaining even under the Bretton Woods system the domestic monetary independence made possible by floating. Other countries pegged their currencies to the dollar, while the dollar was nominally pegged to gold. In the United States high-powered money and the domestically-held part of the money supply were not usually affected by payments disequilibrium. For example, when the US ran a payments deficit foreign monetary authorities acquired dollars. Typically they chose to hold their dollar reserves not in currency and demand deposits but in short-term US government securities. The actual money remained under US ownership. Hence, the fundamental proposition of monetary theory held for the United States even under pegged-but-adjustable exchange rates.

PURCHASING POWER PARITY

Supply and demand determine a freely floating exchange rate. The purchasing power parity doctrine concerns the approximate level at which supply and demand will balance. The doctrine notes that people value currencies for what they will buy. If one Inland dollar buys as much goods and services as three Outland pesos, a free exchange rate would hover in the range of three pesos per dollar, 33 cents per peso. An actual rate that unmistakably undervalued the peso, say 20 cents, would make Outland goods seem great bargains to Inlanders and make Inland goods seem overpriced to Outlanders. Inland eagerness to buy Outland goods and Outland reluctance to buy Inland goods would flood the foreign exchange market with dollars seeking to buy scarce pesos. The imbalance would eventually bid the rate back toward its purchasing power parity. Corrective pressures would operate through changes in both the quantities and the mix of goods traded.

Comparing two countries' price levels to calculate a purchasing power parity presupposes some one assortment of goods and services that can be priced in both countries and that accurately represents the types and relative quantities of various goods and services produced and consumed in each. In fact, no one assortment can typify the patterns of production and consumption in both of two countries, so a direct comparison of purchasing powers is impractical or dubious. If a calculation is nevertheless required, it is typically a makeshift. The current parity exchange rate is estimated from changes in the purchasing powers of the two currencies since some past base period when the actual rate was supposedly in equilibrium. If the Inland price level has tripled over a certain period of time while the Outland level has been multiplied by six – if Outlanders have suffered twice as much price inflation as Inlanders – then the dollar should be worth about twice as many pesos as before.

The convenience of using each country's own price index, constructed in its own way and representative of the local economy, is also a source of weakness. The purchasing power parity doctrine is mainly concerned with the forces at work determining an exchange rate at a given point in time, yet the calculations deal with price level changes over a span of time, during which many sorts of changes may have robbed a price index of accuracy and even of clear meaning. For many reasons, moreover, the base period actual exchange rate used in the calculation may not have been an equilibrium rate. Tariffs and other trade barriers may have become more or less severe since the base period.

All these difficulties concern makeshift calculations and do not impugn the logic of the purchasing power parity doctrine itself. Fundamentally the doctrine is a theory of monetary influences on exchange rates – monetary influences reflected in price levels. It is closely associated with the quantity theory of price level determination. Meinich (1968) generalizes Patinkin's quantity theory (1956, 1965) to an open economy. Making simplifying assumptions similar to Patinkin's and working on a similar level of abstraction, Meinich shows, for example, that doubling the supply of domestic money, given unchanged money supplies abroad, would result in a doubled price level and a doubled home-currency price of foreign exchange. Similarly, Patinkin (1989, pp. xxxix–xlii) generalizes his 1965 model of the neutrality of money to the small open economy. He also shows how a doubling of the money supply results in a doubling of the price level and price of foreign exchange with an unchanged rate of interest.

Correctly understood, neither the quantity theory nor the purchasing power parity doctrine denies that all sorts of influences besides money affect price levels and exchange rates. 'Real' factors affecting terms of trade and capital movements, and even speculative capital movements, can of course affect exchange rates. When these factors are strong, they can swamp and obscure the influence of relatively small monetary changes reflected in price levels.

A major theme of this book is that one must go beyond the simple mechanics of the quantity theory (or in this case purchasing power parity) in order to

understand the processes of adjustment at work. When monetary expansion
thrusts initially excessive cash balances onto people, no reason exists to suppose
that they try to unload them onto nontraded goods first and that only later, in
response to changed price relations, they try to unload them onto traded goods
and foreign exchange. On the contrary, traded goods may be among the first
things onto which people try to unload excessive cash balances. When a
currency is losing value in consequence of monetary expansion, it does not lose
value at one stroke or at a uniform pace against all goods and services. Some
prices are stickier than others and an uncontrolled exchange rate is among the
least sticky of prices. It is sensitive and mobile in reflecting actual and anticipated changes in price levels and in their underlying monetary causes. The
phenomenon of exchange rates outrunning (or 'overshooting') their purchasing
power parities is illustrated particularly clearly in the classical hyperinflations.
Market participants do look ahead, taking account of whatever clues they have
to future relative purchasing powers. Demands for cash balances of a country's
currency, for assets denominated in that currency, and for that currency on the
foreign exchange market respond to expectations of future monetary expansion
and to other speculative factors. (On anticipatory movements in exchange rates,
compare Mises, 1912 [1934] [1981], pp. 243–6.)

VOLATILITY OF EXCHANGE RATES

Since 1971–73 floating rates have moved erratically. Over periods of hours,
months and perhaps even years, capital transactions have far overshadowed
trade in goods and services in determining exchange rates. 'As someone who
has always strongly favored floating exchange rates', Milton Friedman (1985)
admits that he 'did not anticipate the volatility in the foreign exchange markets
that we've had'.[9] Bilateral rates have fluctuated 10 and 20 percent over periods
of months and sometimes several percent from day to day or even within days.
Contrary to hopes pinned earlier on the development of market institutions and
the accumulation of experience, rate fluctuations appear not to have been getting
milder over time. How serious its consequences are is not clear. Volatility seems
not to have impaired the volume of international trade, or not enough for the
effect to be detectable beyond dispute (Aschheim, Bailey and Tavlas, 1987,
especially pp. 433–41). Capital movements have flourished, perhaps excessively in some sense.

Exchange rates in part have the character of asset prices, jumping around like
stock prices (if not that widely) as asset-holders seek to rearrange their
portfolios. Movements ('overshooting') of exchange rates ahead of or in exaggeration of or otherwise out of correspondence with the relative purchasing

powers of the currencies involved is readily understandable (compare Dornbusch, 1976). In contrast with the instant flexibility of free exchange rates, the stickiness of many wages and prices comes into play. As Irving Fisher said in a broader context (1922, p. 185): 'Just as an obstruction put across one half of a stream causes an increase in the current in the other half, so any deficiency in the movement of some prices must cause an excess in the movement of others'.

Another apparent cause of volatility is 'noise' (compare Black, 1986). High-technology communications and data-processing bring facts and figures and rumors to the attention of traders more frequently and in more discrete bits than in the past, causing frequent shifts in noise-oriented trading decisions. In the old days, or so one may plausibly conjecture, news spread and its general interpretation changed more gradually as otherwise discrete bits had time partially to neutralize each other.

The current system is by no means one of free and general floating. It contains elements of outright pegging and even floating rates are managed. Yeager (1976b, Chapter 14) explains how official intervention can increase the volatility of floating rates and provides some historical examples. While speculation itself can be stabilizing, private speculation based on trying to guess or anticipate what an authority's activities and intentions are can be destabilizing. It can lead to so-called 'bandwagon effects' or 'herding behavior'. The authority's attempts to smooth rate fluctuations may actually lead to outright pegging, with all of the potentially disruptive consequences mentioned above.

Koppl and Yeager (1996) test the theory of 'big players' and 'herding' in asset markets. A big player is someone who uses discretionary power to influence the market while being immune from its discipline of profit and loss. The authors analyze the behavior of the Russian ruble under two different regimes in the late nineteenth century. One Russian finance minister was an interventionist and big player. The other was a strict rule-follower and hence not a big player (p. 371). Using rescaled-range analysis, which serves to detect herd behavior, they find support that big players do encourage herding. Their results 'may help account for the difficulty of explaining exchange rates in the short to medium run' (p. 379).[10]

Moreover, the special role of the dollar as worldwide reserve and intervention currency, a role that all-around free floating would preclude, exposes the dollar rate to changeable pressures beyond those directly associated with US trade and capital flows. A system of managed floating is a compromise one and may very well combine the worst rather than the best features of truly fixed and fully free rates. It certainly lacks the automaticity of the adjustment processes described above.

MONETARY APPROACHES TO THE BALANCE OF PAYMENTS AND EXCHANGE RATES

Throughout this book we have been using the money-supply-and-demand approach or framework to explain our monetary theory. (Pages 2–8 above explain the distinction between approach and theory.) Rabin and Yeager (1982) speak of the 'weak version' of the monetary approach to the balance of payments (MABP) and the 'weak version' of the monetary approach to exchange rates (MAXR). Each weak version is an approach that uses the money-supply-and-demand framework to develop propositions and theories about the open economy. Each is a way of organizing discussion rather than a causal theory.

The weak version of the MABP presupposes fixed exchange rates. Yeager (1976b) and Mundell (1968) argue that the three approaches to balance-of-payments analysis that used to dominate the literature – monetary, elasticities, and absorption – reconcile with one another. Each of these approaches raises questions and focuses attention on certain aspects of reality. Mundell (1968, pp. 150–51) summarizes:

> It is not meaningful to question the validity of the three approaches. The terms can be defined so that they are correct and assert identical propositions, even if capital movements are included...The identity of the three approaches, when they are properly interpreted, does not mean that each approach is not in itself useful. [Each approach] provides additional checks on the logic of balance-of-payments policies.

On the other hand, the 'strong version' of the MABP, associated with Harry G. Johnson and his followers, is a theory that happens not to be generally valid. It identifies a country's balance-of-payments surplus with an excess demand for money and a balance-of-payments deficit with an excess supply of money. It denies the possibility that imposed surpluses and deficits can create monetary disequilibrium. Rather, it views the balance of payments solely as an 'equilibrating mechanism' that helps remove an excess demand for or supply of money. For example, this theory views the surplus that follows a devaluation from equilibrium as a process that eliminates an excess demand for money. Johnson (1972, p. 91; 1976, pp. 273–4) states:

> The effect of devaluation is transitory, working through the restoration of the public's actual to its desired real balances via the impact of an excess demand for money in producing a surplus...The balance-of-payments surplus will continue only until its cumulative effect in increasing domestic money holdings satisfies the domestic demand for money.

The devaluation automatically raises the domestic price level, which creates an excess demand for money and hence the payments surplus. On the other hand, we have argued on pages 245–6 above that the payments surplus resulting from the devaluation may be part of the process that creates an excess supply of money, with its inflationary consequences.

A similar story applies to the case of imported inflation. The strong version of the MABP completely neglects the monetary channel of imported inflation. Instead, it focuses solely on the direct-price-transmission channel. As in the case of devaluation, it is higher prices (imported from abroad) that cause an excess demand for money and hence a payments surplus. We conjecture that it is the failure to recognize that massive surpluses were imposed on countries in 1971 and again in 1973 that led to widespread misdiagnoses of the breakdown of the Bretton Woods system and of the acceleration of worldwide inflation that followed (see Rabin, 1977; Rabin and Yeager, 1982 and pages 258–60 above).

Advocates of the strong version of the MABP believe that the domestic money supply is always 'demand-determined'. They thus commit the same errors as those economists who argue that when the monetary authority pursues interest rate targeting, the money supply is always demand-determined (see pages 118–20 above).

The strong version of the MAXR is analogous to the strong version of the MABP. It too is a theory that happens not to be generally valid. It unequivocally associates a currency's depreciation on the foreign exchange market with an excess supply of money and an appreciation with an excess demand for money. While these associations may be typical, they are not necessary. Rabin and Yeager (1982) provide counterexamples to the strong version of the MAXR as well as to the strong version of the MABP. (In several of his articles and in his book of 2002, Norman C. Miller also recognizes the errors of the strong versions.)

NOTES

1. This definition accords with the 'official-reserve-transactions' (ORT) concept.
2. See Yeager (1976b, pp. 651–2) for a full discussion of these points. Dorn (1999, p. 314) recognizes the argument presented here. Kenen (2000, p. 113) notes that 'a system of stable but adjustable exchange rates' is an oxymoron, since 'stability is incompatible with adjustability'.
3. Yeager (1976b) documents Germany's struggle against imported inflation from the early 1950s until the system's demise.
4. The international currency crises of the 1990s have spawned an enormous literature. Flood and Marion (1998) present a technical review of this research, some of which dates back to the early 1980s.
5. Under the Bretton Woods system, rate fluctuations of one percent on either side of the peg were allowed, but in reality they were usually held to 0.75 percent. The Smithsonian agreement of 1971 widened the permissible range to 2.25 percent on either side.

6. Triffin (1966) diagnoses the contradictions inherent in the system, especially the conflict between the liquidity and confidence problems.
7. Meiselman (1975, p. 72) correctly identifies the system as an 'engine of worldwide inflation'.
8. Greenfield (1994, p. 69) also recognizes this point
9. Friedman (1999, p. 140) attributes the variability in exchange rates to the wider variability in inflation rates among countries. He views this exchange rate variability as a 'necessary reaction, maybe over-reaction, to what was going on'. He points out that trying to maintain fixed rates under these conditions would have posed major problems.
10. Flood and Marion (1998, p. 41) argue that not only exchange rate models, but 'all asset-price models based on underlying fundamentals work poorly'. Taylor (1995) reviews the literature on exchange rates and notes that most models cannot forecast better than the random walk.

10. Interest rate theory

This chapter views the interest rate, broadly interpreted, as basically a real phenomenon and addresses the following two questions. What factors determine the interest rate? What functions does it perform in a market economy? While it is convenient to speak of 'the interest rate' as well as of 'the wage rate', we recognize that in reality no single rate of either kind prevails. Yeager (1994b) cites the contributions of the following to interest rate theory: Allais (1947), Böhm-Bawerk (1959), Cassell (1903 [1956]), Eucken (1954), Fisher (1930 [1955]), Hirshleifer (1970) and Wicksell (1934).

INTEREST AS A FACTOR PRICE

We can simplify capital and interest theory, tie it in better with general micro theory, and clear up certain puzzles by resurrecting the view that the interest rate is the price of 'waiting', a factor of production. Waiting is the service performed by *holding* financial and physical assets instead of selling them and devoting the proceeds to current consumption or to other current exercise of command over resources. Waiting has the dimensions of value over time. We do not claim that this view of the interest rate is the only valid one. We invoke the distinction made in Chapters 1 and 9 between an approach and theory. The approach we take here is compatible with other approaches to the interest rate (for example, compare Chapter 2).

A.R.J. Turgot noted over two centuries ago that the interest rate is 'the price given for the use of a certain quantity of value during a certain time'. He put this use on a par with other factors of production.[1] Cassel (1903 [1956], p. 67) regarded it as settled, 'once and for all, that interest is the price paid for an *independent and elementary factor of production* which may be called either waiting or use of capital, according to the point of view from which it is looked at'. Dorfman (1959, pp. 367, 370) 'reaffirmed the reality of waiting as one of the primary factors of production, co-ordinate with labor, land, etc...[W]aiting is a genuine scarce factor of production...The unit of waiting [may be taken as] one unit of consumption deferred for one unit of time'.[2]

Waiting so conceived enables the person demanding or acquiring it to devote productive resources to his own purposes sooner or on a larger scale than he otherwise could; he obtains advanced availability. The person who supplies or performs waiting postpones the use for his own purposes of resources over which he could have exercised current command.

Some economists old and recent, even including Irving Fisher, have denied that waiting is a distinct productive factor, apparently not seeing that the supposed issue is spurious. Actually, it is idle to argue over whether the thing whose price is the interest rate is or is not 'really' a productive factor. What to count as inputs into a production function, and just how to conceive of the production function itself, is a matter of convenience in each particular context (see pages 41–2 above). In some contexts it is convenient to regard machines, buildings and other capital goods, or their services, as factors of production and not to probe more deeply or theorize more abstractly. In other contexts, particularly those concerned with what the interest rate is a payment for and what its functions are, it is helpful to regard it as a factor price and probe into the factor's nature.

To interpret capital as waiting gives intelligible meaning to such familiar phrases as 'interest on capital', 'the cost of capital', 'the capital market', 'shortage of capital', and 'international capital movements'. It helps us bypass the supposed need to distinguish between goods that do and goods that do not properly count as physical capital. It enlists familiar concepts of supply, demand and derived demand. It figures in explaining how international trade in goods can tend to equalize interest rates internationally like other factor prices. It permits handling the odd case of a negative interest rate. It helps show what sort of opportunity cost the interest rate measures and, more generally, provides deeper understanding of the logic of a price system by applying that logic to a challenging phenomenon.

In some respects waiting is an unfortunate term. It does not describe the service bought and sold equally well from both the buyer's and seller's points of view. The buyer of the service, such as a borrower, is not acquiring waiting but *avoiding* it; he is paying someone else to do waiting for him. But the term 'labor' runs into similar embarrassments. The buyer is not performing labor but paying someone else to perform it for him. Despite what the term suggests, labor – like waiting – is not always irksome.

Waiting can be supplied or performed and demanded or avoided in many ways besides granting and obtaining loans. Competition, substitution, and arbitrage tend to make waiting performed by lending, by holding an investment in capital goods or in land, and by acting in other ways all bear the same net rate of return – with obvious qualifications about risk, liquidity and the like. (Compare the portfolio-balance condition for equilibrium in Chapter 2.) Consider business firms deciding whether to buy automobiles or rent them. The higher the interest rate on loans in relation to rental charges, the less firms will borrow to buy cars and the more they will rent them. Their doing so will tend to reduce loan rates and increase rates of return in the car rental business.

Conversely, the lower the loan rate in relation to rental charges, the greater the borrowing to buy cars and the less the volume of renting, again tending to bring the interest rate on loans and rental charges in relation to the values of cars into an equilibrium relation.

One methodological point is worth mentioning. How changes in wants, resources, or technology affect such price relations should be explainable in terms of the explicit interest rate determined on the loan market and of substitution and arbitrage between loans and other forms in which people supply and demand waiting. This precept warns against forgetting the literal and 'narrow' definition of the interest rate as the price of loans. (We have argued throughout this book that the interest rate is *not* the price of money.)

No doubt only small portions of total supplies of and demands for waiting confront each other directly on the market for loans. The marginal yields (MERs) on bonds, equities, land and all sorts of capital goods tend to become equal, subject to qualifications already mentioned (again compare Chapter 2). Our emphasis on the mutual determination of marginal yields illustrates the superficiality of theories that consider only the loan market, money and liquidity preference. It also illuminates the pervasiveness and fundamentally 'real' character of the interest rate.

WAITING FURTHER EXAMINED

This section presents a few examples of the demand for and supply of waiting. An occupier of a house might demand waiting in two ways. He might rent the house, paying for its services month by month and letting the landlord wait to receive the value of those services over time. Alternatively, the occupier might buy a house with borrowed money, having the lender perform the waiting. The house occupier's own influence on the general level of interest rates should be about the same in the two cases. But if he has become more thrifty and instead of renting a house buys one after saving to accumulate the purchase price or at least a large downpayment, or else pays for the house out of already accumulated savings that would otherwise have been spent on current consumption, then his thriftiness adds to the supply of waiting and does tend to reduce interest rates. If, conversely, a house owner sells his house and spends the proceeds on a world tour, intending to become a renter when he returns, then his behavior tends to raise interest rates.

Someone who rents a machine, which by its very nature incorporates waiting, is demanding waiting while its owner is supplying it. A firm that itself finances its holdings of capital and intermediate goods while it awaits their ripening into salable products is thereby contributing to the aggregate supply of waiting as well as to the demand. A firm employing capital goods in its operations is playing a role in intermediating the consumers' demands for waiting embodied in the final goods back to the ultimate suppliers of waiting, which could be the firm's owners. Links in a chain of intermediation involve both demanding and supplying waiting. Intermediation and arbitrage in waiting are closely related activities.

BYPASSING UNNECESSARY DISTINCTIONS

The concept of waiting permits bypassing some distracting and often irrelevant questions associated with a physical conception of 'capital'. For example, what types of goods – plant and equipment, inventories of consumer goods and other goods in the hands of producers, durable and nondurable goods in the hands of consumers and improved and unimproved land – should and should not count as capital? Because of such puzzles about classification and for other reasons, the concept of an aggregate of physical capital is inherently fuzzy. Some capital goods are always being worn out and scrapped, and new and different ones are always being constructed. Whether the aggregate is growing or shrinking or staying unchanged may be hard to say, especially since unforeseen changes in technology and tastes are always occurring and raising or lowering the market values and the genuine usefulness of particular capital goods.[3]

Nobody conducts transactions in the aggregate of capital goods, and the prices at which individual capital goods are bought and sold are quite distinct from the interest rate. Waiting for value over time is something more nearly homogeneous than physical capital. It commands a price of the same nature whether it is devoted to fresh accumulation or mere maintenance of physical capital or is used in other ways. In several contexts then, the concept of waiting spares us from trying to distinguish between capital goods and other goods, gross and net production, maintenance and accumulation, and gross and net saving and investment. Those distinctions are vital in dealing with some questions, but they are irrelevant distractions in dealing with some central questions of the nature and functions of the interest rate.

A person can perform waiting and so promote the maintenance or accumulation of physical capital even by just continuing to own a capital good or plot of land or other asset instead of selling it and spending the proceeds on current consumption. The rate of return or interest rate he receives is expressed by the relation between the value of the services of the asset, net of depreciation and the like, and the value of the asset itself.

One might object that the asset will continue to exist whether or not its current owner sells it and spends the proceeds on consumption. How, then, does his continuing to own it promote maintenance or accumulation of physical capital? Most obviously, the owner is not engaging in consumption that he might have engaged in and is not bidding resources away, as he might have done, from maintenance or accumulation of physical capital. His selling the asset would tend to depress the prices of it and competing assets, raising their MERs and tempting people desiring such assets to buy them rather than construct them afresh. One complication involves land. Its owner promotes accumulation of physical capital by holding it. However, the demand for land as a hedge in times of inflation represents some diversion of people's propensity to save and accumulate wealth away from construction of capital goods or from the purchase of bonds issued to finance them (see pages 219–20 above).

The recommended view of the interest rate as the price of waiting in no way entails slipping into the sort of mysticism attributed to J.B. Clark and Frank Knight and criticized by Hayek (1936 [1946], pp. 355–83, especially p. 377; 1941, pp. 5, 93–4, 266–7), among others. We need not conceive of waiting as a sort of abstract homogeneous quantity or fund enduring through time and embodying itself in a changing assortment of physical capital goods. People supply waiting by refraining from currently consuming their entire incomes and wealth and by making loans, owning capital goods and doing other quite unmysterious things. So doing, they contribute by and large to the maintenance or accumulation of physical capital.

The concept of waiting has the further merit of helping us avoid overemphasis on physical capital formation. Waiting can be productively employed in largely nonmaterial ways, as in the training of human beings and in research. Like other factors, too, some waiting is devoted directly to *consumption*: consumer loans are analogous to labor in domestic service and to land maintained for pleasure as gardens or wilderness.

INTERNATIONAL MOVEMENTS OF CAPITAL AND GOODS

International capital movements pose another test of alternative conceptualizations. Capital movements are not shipments of capital goods in particular. People in the lending country are giving up and people in the borrowing country are acquiring something more abstract – current command over goods or resources in general. Through the processes of overall balance-of-payments adjustment, imbalance on capital account tends to be matched by opposite imbalance on current account; the financial side of the capital movement develops its real counterpart. While in general the borrowing country increases its imports and reduces its exports, with opposite changes occuring in the trade of the lending country, this is not necessary. In an extreme case the borrowing country might develop a net inflow of goods and services entirely by reduction of its exports. The 'real transfer' could take place even if no capital goods and no tangible goods were traded internationally; the borrowing country could experience a rise in imports or fall in exports of services. In all such cases, nevertheless, the lenders are waiting to exercise command over real resources, and the borrowers are obtaining advanced command over them.

The conception of capital as waiting also integrates smoothly with the theory of how under certain conditions international trade tends to equalize the prices in different countries of the factors of production 'embodied' in the goods traded. Consider new wine and matured wine produced with relatively little and relatively much waiting. If waiting is relatively scarce and the interest rate relatively high in the home country, matured wine commands a correspondingly large price premium over new wine in the absence of trade. Abroad, where waiting is relatively abundant and cheap, matured wine commands only a relatively small price premium. Now trade opens up. The home country imports high-waiting-content matured wine and exports low-waiting-content new wine (or vodka or other low-waiting-content goods). Trade tends to equalize product prices, reducing the price premium of matured over new wine in the home country and shrinking production of matured wine there. Waiting formerly devoted to the maturing of wine is freed for other uses. Trade lessens the effective scarcity of waiting and so reduces the home interest rate.[4] The opposite occurs abroad.

The interest-equalization tendency does not depend on whether waiting enters directly or only indirectly into production functions of goods. Perhaps waiting enters directly into the production of widgets, which like wine require time to mature. Alternatively, widgets are manufactured with machines that embody much waiting. Still another possibility is that widgets are made by specialists who must undergo years of expensive training. What difference does any of this make for the interest-equalization tendency? Suppose widgets are expensive because their costs include high salaries corresponding to the expensive waiting invested in training technicians. Now international trade brings imports of cheap foreign widgets, shrinking the domestic industry. Waiting formerly devoted to training technicians becomes free for other purposes and as in the wine example the interest rate falls.

NEGATIVE INTEREST

The concept of waiting helps make the unreal but instructive case of a negative interest rate conceivable. That possibility shows by the way that waiting need not imply irksomeness and that time preference – the IRD in terms of Chapter 2 – need not necessarily be positive at the margin.[5] We consider an isolated community where all goods produced are perishable, where no money and no equity securities exist, where land is either superabundant and free or else not subject to private ownership, and where there is no collectively organized or family-centered social security system. We assume a stable population of uniform age distribution and abstract from any differences in people's tastes, including time preferences, at corresponding periods of their lives. People differ only in belonging to different generations. Each person's total production and earnings are the same, furthermore, in both working periods of his life. So strict an assumption is not really necessary, but it is convenient in helping to rule out a positive rate of interest, as serves our purpose in this section.

How can anyone provide for his old age? Retired people cannot live by borrowing because they would be in no position to promise repayment. With accumulation of wealth in other forms ruled out, the only way to store up command over goods to be consumed later is to acquire claims on borrowers. (In the absence of money, loans are expressed in particular commodities or in composite baskets of commodities.) At a zero interest rate the typical person wants a nearly even distribution of consumption over his lifetime. He wants to make loans in each of his two working periods and to receive repayments in retirement. With all people having preferences of this sort, however, desired lending would exceed desired borrowing. Only a negative interest rate can clear the loan market. The rate must be negative in order to persuade people to depart from their otherwise preferred more equal distribution of consumption over their adult lifetimes. Only a reward for borrowing would persuade people to consume especially heavily in their early working years. People in their late working years are willing to pay young people to take loans from them so that they can live on the repayments in retirement.

The typical person must borrow goods in his early working years, both repay this borrowing and lend goods in his later working years, and receive repayment when retired. In his early working years he must consume in excess of his current income, and in his later working years he must consume an amount that falls short of his current income by more than his earlier excess consumption. In retirement he consumes only the repayments of loans he made in his late working years.[6]

All this is easy to say in terms of waiting. Prospects of old age make people want to postpone consumption of part of their current incomes. Yet they are able to wait by making loans only if younger people accommodate them by borrowing. The desired supply of waiting by lenders exceeds the volume demanded by borrowers at a zero interest rate. Clearing the market requires that waiting be penalized and accommodating it rewarded.

Considering the odd conditions necessary for a negative interest rate helps us see, by contrast, why the interest rate is almost always positive in the real world.[7] Among its other features our imaginary economy lacks storable goods, money and scarce privately ownable land. The perishability of all goods implies that waiting has negative marginal productivity.

Just as a negative price of waiting is conceivable, so are a negative marginal productivity and a negative wage rate of labor in a particular occupation. The occupation might be particularly enjoyable or afford particularly valuable training, and workers in it might live on wealth from other sources. Employers would tolerate counterproductive overcrowding if paid to do so, that is if the wage were negative. Our purpose is not to dwell on these odd cases but only to point out that the supply-and-demand theories of the prices of waiting and of labor apply even to them, and in parallel ways.

DERIVED DEMAND AND PRODUCTIVITY

A more general argument for the concept of waiting is that it enlists supply-and-demand analysis as illustrated in the preceding section. In considering what determines the price of waiting, we can explore as we do for other factors of production what accounts for the supply and for the demand. On the demand side we can examine why people will pay to avoid waiting and gain advanced availability of command over resources. On the supply side we can examine why in general and at the margin waiting will not be performed free.

Except for consumption loans, the demand for waiting as for labor and land use derives from the factor's capacity to contribute to output – ultimately, output of consumer goods – and from consumers' demand for that output. The relative strengths of consumer demands for goods embodying relatively large amounts of particular factors affect producer demands for those factors and so affect their prices. A decline in consumer demand for a highly waiting-intensive good tends to lower the rate of interest. This point was illustrated in the example of matured wine, whose importation from abroad reduces the demand for its domestically produced counterpart. A shift of consumers' demand away from low-waiting-content vodka toward high-waiting-content wine tends to raise the interest rate.

Some comments are in order on the productivity of waiting or roundaboutness. 'Roundaboutness' is the opportunity to get greater results from present resources if one can wait a longer rather than a shorter period for those results (see Böhm-Bawerk, 1959). Consider a house of definite specifications to be delivered to the buyer on a definite date. The sooner (within limits) construction can begin and so the more time it can take, the smaller is the quantity of inputs other than waiting required. (Compare Alchian, 1959, especially pp. 31–5, 39 and George 1898 [1941], pp. 369–70.) The house probably could be built in only five days as a stunt, but imagine the attendant inefficiencies and expense. Adelman (1972, pp. 19, 63) notes an example of factor substitutability in the oil industry:

> The productivity of a pool is less than proportional to the number of wells because past a certain point there is well 'interference'. The area over which oil migrates

through permeable sands is very wide, so that one well could ultimately drain a very large reservoir. If time – meaning the value of money – were no object, that would indeed be the best because it would be the cheapest way...If time were no object, with zero rate of return or cost of capital, one well would drain a whole reservoir at lowest cost.

These examples of substitutability at the margin between waiting and other factors show that waiting can indeed 'enter into the production function'.

The opportunity to wait for results is productive because it broadens the range of production processes among which intelligent choices can be made. Business firms will pay for such productive opportunities. Most obviously, they will pay for loans enabling them to adopt more time-consuming production methods or to install plant and equipment already embodying waiting along with other factors. Firms' demands for waiting (-avoidance) derive then from the productivity of waiting and from consumers' demands for goods produced with its aid.

Counting the interest rate among factor prices offers a broadened view of the subjective factors that can affect the interest rate. For example, suppose that tastes shift away from poetry readings towards science fiction movies, presumably a form of entertainment whose production is more roundabout or waiting-intensive; hence the rate rises. The tastes that influence the interest rate are not confined to direct time preferences between present and future consumption. The pattern of tastes for different goods and services all demanded at the same time also plays a role.

THE PERVASIVENESS AND FUNCTION OF THE INTEREST RATE

As the foregoing examples suggest, interest is a pervasive phenomenon. It appears not only in the explicit price of loans but also in price relations among final goods, intermediate goods and factors of production. It even lurks in the price relations between consumer goods embodying relatively large and relatively small amounts of waiting.

This view of the interest rate fits in nicely with the view of the price system as a transmitter of information and incentives. Like other prices, the interest rate is a signaling and rationing device in *allocating resources*. In view of that price, each business firm restrains its use of waiting. It restricts the amount of value that it ties up over time in uncompleted processes of transforming primary productive factors into final consumer goods and services. Prices similarly restrain a firm's employment of labor and land. But why should it restrain itself if it could use additional waiting, labor, or land productively?

The prices of scarce factors indicate that employing units of them in any particular line of production has an opportunity cost. Prices of factors and products force each business firm to consider whether additional factor units would add not merely something to its output but also enough to the value of its output to warrant the necessary sacrifice of valuable output elsewhere. Prices enable the firm in effect to compare consumers' evaluations of the additional output it could offer and the cost as measured by consumers' evaluations of other goods forgone.

For example, constructing apartment buildings that will serve with little maintenance for many years is a more waiting-intensive method of providing housing services than constructing buildings with shorter lives or requiring more current maintenance. Even though the more durable buildings require more labor and other inputs in the first place, their services over their entire lives will be greater in relation to inputs of these other factors. This does not mean that constructing the more durable buildings is unequivocally advantageous, for the longer average interval between inputs of resources and outputs of services, as well as the fact that the economies in maintenance accrue not all at once but only over time, imply an 'opportunity cost'. That cost pertains to other projects and products ruled out because the scarce capacity to wait has been devoted to the durable apartments. The interest rate brings this cost to the attention of business firms.

Prices also bring to the attention of *consumers* the opportunity costs of the waiting (and other factors) embodied in the goods and services from which they have to choose. It leads them to consult their preferences in the light of the terms of choice posed in part by objective reality. It is perhaps an additional recommendation of the concept of waiting that without it Fisher (1930 [1955], pp. 485–7, 534–41) denied that interest measures any genuine cost.[8]

We have one clarification. Waiting can*not* be rationed by the interest rate alone. For example, because of uncertainty about whether borrowers will repay, lenders must practice nonprice rationing to some extent. They cannot grant loans in whatever amount requested to all borrowers promising to pay the going rate of interest.

FISHER'S DIAGRAM AND HIS SEPARATION THEOREM

Figure 10.1 portrays a pure exchange economy, that is, one with no production.[9] The vertical axis measures future consumption and the horizontal current or present consumption. Given an initial endowment at point A, line MN is the individual's budget or wealth constraint. Its slope equals $-(1 + r)$ where r is the given market rate of interest at which he can borrow or lend. We assume perfect and complete capital markets, so that the rate for borrowing is the same as the rate for lending. At point N the individual maximizes present consumption by forgoing all future consumption. The opposite is true at point M. The initial endowment point A lies on indifference curve U_1. Through intertemporal exchange the individual maximizes utility at point B on U_2 by cutting current consumption from C_A to C_B and thus increasing future consumption from F_A to F_B. The individual *lends* at interest rate r. The slope of any straight line tangent to an indifference curve measures the marginal rate of substitution (MRS) between current consumption and future consumption at the point of tangency. This slope equals $-(1 + r_t)$ where r_t is the marginal rate of time preference (or IRD in terms of Chapter 2). At equilibrium point B the slope of U_2 (or MRS) equals the slope of budget constraint MN: $-(1 + r_t) = -(1 + r)$. The given interest rate r therefore equals the individual's marginal rate of time preference r_t in equilibrium.

Figure 10.2 portrays an economy with production but no exchange. Curve PP shows all production possibilities available to the individual given his initial endowment at point A. The slope of any straight line tangent to PP measures the marginal rate of transformation (MRT) of current consumption into future

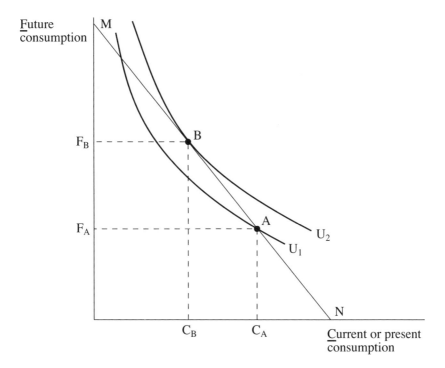

Figure 10.1   Pure exchange economy (no production)

consumption at the point of tangency. This slope equals $-(1 + r_i)$ where r_i is the marginal rate of return on investment in transforming forgone present goods into future goods. Although point A lies on U_1, through investment of $C_A - C_B$ the individual maximizes utility at equilibrium point B on U_2 where MRS = MRT. Since $-(1 + r_t) = -(1 + r_i)$, the individual's rate of time preference r_t equals the marginal rate of return on investment r_i. Note that his consumption in each period (C_B and F_B) equals his actual production in the absence of exchange (Copeland and Weston, 1988, p. 8).

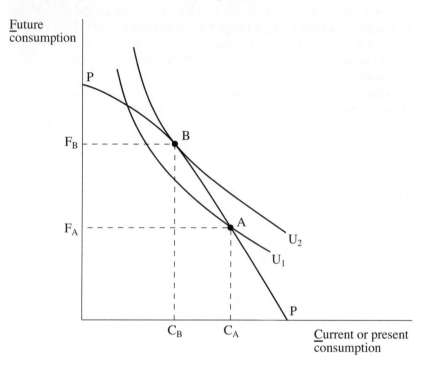

Figure 10.2   Production economy with no exchange

Figure 10.3, which is known as the 'Fisher diagram', portrays an economy with production and exchange.[10] With an initial endowment given by point A, the individual *invests* $C_A - C_B$ in order to maximize wealth at point B, where he reaches the highest attainable budget constraint MN. By *borrowing* at the rate r, he maximizes utility at point D on U_1 where he actually consumes C_D and F_D. At equilibrium point D: MRS = MRT = slope of budget constraint MN. That is: $-(1 + r_t) = -(1 + r_i) = -(1 + r)$. The individual's rate of time preference r_t equals the marginal rate of return on investment r_i, both of which equal the rate of interest r.

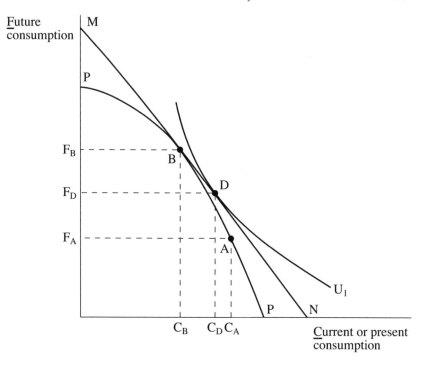

Figure 10.3   Economy with production and exchange

The above analysis implies that the individual's decision process occurs in two separate and distinct stages. First, he invests in order to reach the highest attainable budget constraint MN. Second, through intertemporal exchange he moves from point B on MN to point D, which is the optimal pattern of consumption. Note that point D lies beyond the curve of production possibilities (Humphrey, 1988, p. 5). This separation of the investment and consumption decisions into two stages is what Hirshleifer calls 'Fisher's separation theorem'. The first stage is governed solely by the objective criterion of maximizing wealth (reaching the highest budget constraint), while the second stage is governed by the individual's subjective time preferences concerning consumption. This result implies that investment decisions can be delegated to the firm, whose goal is to maximize wealth, without regard for the subjective time preferences of its owners (Copeland and Weston, 1988, p. 12).

We emphasize that it is a mistake conceptually to identify the interest rate with the marginal rate of time preference or the marginal rate of return on investment. These various rates are mutually adjusting and only tend to become equal. It is a serious error to identify magnitudes whose equality at the margin is an equilibrium condition. While Fisher's diagram helps illuminate the conditions necessary for equilibrium, it is an expository device and therefore a simplification. It should not be confused with the main subject of this chapter, which deals with how the interest rate is determined.

NOTES

1. Turgot (1766) quoted in Cassel (1903 [1956], pp. 20–21). Turgot's formulation, says Cassel, has 'never afterwards [been] surpassed in clearness and definiteness'.
2. Dorfman is mainly concerned to show that the period of investment of waiting and the average period of investment of productive factors are meaningful concepts.
3. Hayek urges points like these in (1941, pp. 296–7, 335–6) and *passim*.
4. Samuelson (1965) reaches a similar conclusion, though without using the concept of waiting and so by a less straightforward route.
5. The IRD (internal rate of discount) must not be confused with the internal rate of return, which is the rate at which a project's net present value equals zero.
6. These paragraphs draw on a discussion among Samuelson (1958, 1959, 1960); Lerner (1959a, 1959b); Meckling (1960a, 1960b) and Cass and Yaari (1966). Earlier, Allais (1947, vol. 1, pp. 48ff) published an essentially similar description of an economy with a negative interest rate. We note that Samuelson's model serves as the basis for the overlapping generations theory of money (see pages 62–3 above).
7. In Japan, nominal interest rates on short-term government bills and on deposits became slightly negative in the late 1990s. Because holding one's wealth in the form of cash can be risky and costly, people were willing to pay a fee for the opportunity to avoid holding cash (Thornton, 1999, p. 1).
8. Recognizing that the value of the amount of waiting required in a physically specified production process depends in part on the price of waiting itself, Yeager (1976c) resolves the 'capital paradoxes' involving reswitching and capital reversal.
9. This section is based mainly on Hirshleifer (1970) and Copeland and Weston (1988).
10. Humphrey (1988, p. 4) argues that Fisher (1907, p. 409) invented this diagram in order to show the gains from *intertemporal* trade. It has become what Baldwin (1982, p. 142) calls 'the sacred diagram of the international trade economist' and has been traditionally used to illustrate the gains from *international* trade. Baldwin's quote appears in Humphrey (1988, p. 3), who traces the early history of 'the sacred diagram'.

Bibliography

Ackley, G. (1961), *Macroeconomic Theory*, New York: Macmillan.

Ackley, G. (1978), 'The costs of inflation', *American Economic Review*, May, 149–54.

Adelman, M. (1972), *The World Petroleum Market*, Baltimore: Johns Hopkins University Press.

Akerlof, G.A. (1975), 'The questions of coinage, trade credit, financial flows and peanuts: a flow-of-funds approach to the demand for money', Federal Reserve Bank of New York, research paper no. 7520, September.

Akerlof, G.A. (1982), 'Labor contracts as partial gift exchange', *Quarterly Journal of Economics*, November, 543–69.

Akerlof, G.A. and J.L. Yellen (1985), 'A near-rational model of the business cycle, with wage and price inertia', *Quarterly Journal of Economics*, supplement, 823–38.

Akerlof, G.A. and J.L. Yellen (1988), 'Fairness and unemployment', *American Economic Review*, May.

Akerlof, G.A. and J.L. Yellen (1990), 'The fair wage-effort hypothesis and unemployment', *Quarterly Journal of Economics*, May, 255–83.

Alchian, A.A. (1959), 'Costs and outputs', in M. Abramovitz et.al., *The Allocation of Economic Resources*, Stanford, CA: Stanford University Press.

Alchian, A.A. (1977), 'Why money?', *Journal of Money, Credit, and Banking*, February, part 2, 133–40.

Allais, M. (1947), *Economie et Intérêt*, Paris: Imprimerie Nationale.

Allen, W.R. (1961), 'The International Monetary Fund and balance of payments adjustment', *Oxford Economic Papers*, June, 159–64.

Archibald, G.C. and R.G. Lipsey (1958), 'Monetary and value theory: a critique of Lange and Patinkin', *Review of Economic Studies*, October, 1–22.

Arlt, I. (1925), 'Der Einzelhaushalt', in J. Bunzel (ed.), *Geldentwertung und Stabilisierung in ihren Einflüssen auf die soziale Entwicklung in Österreich, Schriften des Vereins für Sozialpolitik*, vol. 169.

Aschheim, J., M.J. Bailey and G.S. Tavlas (1987), 'Dollar variability, the new protectionism, trade and financial performance', in D. Salvatore (ed.), *The New Protectionist Threat to World Welfare*, New York: North-Holland, pp. 424–49.

Baldwin, R.E. (1982), 'Gottfried Haberler's contribution to international trade theory and policy', *Quarterly Journal of Economics*, February, 141–8.

Ball, L. (1994), 'Credible disinflation with staggered price setting', *American Economic Review*, March, 282–9.

Ball, L. and D. Romer (1990), 'Real rigidities and the non-neutrality of money', *Review of Economc Studies*, April, 183–202.

Barro, R.J. (1974), 'Are government bonds net wealth?', *Journal of Political Economy*, November/December, 1095–1117.

Barro, R.J. (1977), 'Unanticipated money growth and unemployment in the United States', *American Economic Review*, March, 101–15.

Barro, R.J. (1978), 'Unanticipated money, output, and the price level in the United States', *Journal of Political Economy*, August, 549–81.

Barro, R.J. (1979), 'Second thoughts on Keynesian economies', *American Economic Review*, May, 54–9.

Barro, R.J. and D.B. Gordon (1983), 'A positive theory of monetary policy in a natural rate model', *Journal of Political Economy*, August, 589–610.

Barro, R.J. and H.I. Grossman (1971), 'A general disequilibrium model of income and employment', *American Economic Review*, March, 82–93.

Barro, R.J. and H.I. Grossman (1976), *Money, Employment, and Inflation*, New York: Cambridge University Press.

Barsky, R.B. and L. Kilian (2001), 'Do we really know that oil caused the great stagflation? a monetary alternative', *NBER Macroeconomics Annual*, 137–83.

Basu, S. and A.M. Taylor (1999), 'Business cycles in international perspective', *Journal of Economic Perspectives*, Spring, 45–68.

Baumol, W.J. (1952), 'The transactions demand for cash: an inventory-theoretic approach', *Quarterly Journal of Economics*, November, 545–56.

Baumol, W.J. (1960), 'Monetary and value theory: comment', *Review of Economic Studies*, October, 29–31.

Baumol, W.J. (1962), 'Stocks, flows, and monetary theory', *Quarterly Journal of Economics*, February, 46–56.

Baumol, W.J. (1965), *Economic Theory and Operations Analysis*, second edition, Englewood Cliffs: Prentice-Hall.

Baumol, W.J. and J. Tobin (1989), 'The optimal cash balance proposition: Maurice Allais' priority', *Journal of Economic Literature*, September, 1160–62.

Bernanke, B.S. (1983), 'Nonmonetary effects of the financial crisis in the propagation of the Great Depression', *American Economic Review*, June, 257–76.

Bernanke, B.S. (1988), 'Monetary policy transmission: through money or credit?', Federal Reserve Bank of Philadelphia *Business Review*, November/December, 3–11.

Bernanke, B.S. (1993), 'Credit in the macroeconomy', Federal Reserve Bank of New York *Quarterly Review*, Spring, 50–70.

Bernanke, B.S. and A. Blinder (1988), 'Credit, money and aggregate demand', *American Economic Review*, May, 435–9.

Bernanke, B.S. and M. Gertler (1995), 'Inside the black box: the credit channel of monetary policy transmission', *Journal of Economic Perspectives*, Fall, 27–48.

Bewley, T.F. (1999), *Why Wages Don't Fall During a Recession*, Cambridge, MA: Harvard University Press.

Birch, D.E., A.A. Rabin and L.B. Yeager (1982), 'Inflation, output, and employment: some clarifications', *Economic Inquiry*, April, 209–21.

Black, F. (1986), 'Noise', *Journal of Finance*, July, 529–43.

Blanchard, O.J. (1983), 'Price asynchronization and price level inertia', in R. Dornbusch and M.H. Simonsen (eds), *Inflation, Debt and Indexation*, Cambridge, MA: MIT Press, pp. 3–24.

Blanchard, O.J. (1992), 'For a return to pragmatism', in M. Belongia and M. Garfinkel (eds), *The Business Cycle: Theories and Evidence*, London: Kluwer Academic Publishers.

Blanchard, O.J. and N. Kiyotaki (1987), 'Monopolistic competition and the effects of aggregate demand', *American Economic Review*, September, 647–66.

Blinder, A.S. (1981), 'Inventories and the structure of macro models', *American Economic Review*, May, 11–16.

Blinder, A.S. (1986), 'Keynes after Lucas', *Eastern Economic Journal*, July/September.

Blinder, A.S. and J.E. Stiglitz (1983), 'Money, credit constraints, and economic activity', *American Economic Review*, May, 297–302.

Bohm, D. (1957), *Causality and Chance in Modern Physics*, Princeton, NJ: Van Nostrand.

Böhm-Bawerk, Eugen von (1959), *Capital and Interest*, translated by George D. Huncke and Hans F. Sennholz, 3 vols, South Holland, IL: Libertarian Press.

Bordo, M. and L. Jonung (1981), 'The long-run behavior of the income velocity of money in five advanced countries, 1879–1975 – an institutional approach', *Economic Inquiry*, January, 96–116.

Bordo, M. and L. Jonung (1987), *The Long-Run Behavior of the Velocity of Circulation: The International Evidence*, New York: Cambridge University Press.

Bordo, M. and L. Jonung (1990), 'The long-run behavior of velocity: the institutional approach revisited', *Journal of Policy Modeling*, Summer, 165–97.

Bresciani-Turroni, C. (1937), *The Economics of Inflation*, London: Allen and Unwin.

Brown, H.G. (1931), *Economic Science and the Common Welfare*, 5th edn, Columbia, MO: Lucas Brothers.

Brown, H.G. (1933), 'Nonsense and sense in dealing with the depression', *Beta Gamma Sigma Exchange*, Spring, 97–107.

Brunner, K. (1968), 'The role of money and monetary policy', Federal Reserve Bank of St Louis *Review*, July, 9–24.

Brunner, K. (1989), part of 'General discussion', in M.D. Bordo (ed.), *Money, History, and International Finance: Essays in Honor of Anna J. Schwartz*, Chicago: University of Chicago Press.

Brunner, K. and A. Meltzer (1971), 'The uses of money: money in the theory of an exchange economy', *American Economic Review*, December, 784–805.

Brunner, K. and A. Meltzer (eds) (1976), *Institutional Arrangements and the Inflation Problem*, Amsterdam: North-Holland.

Brunner, K. and A.H. Meltzer (1988), 'Money and credit in the monetary transmission process', *American Economic Review*, May, 446–51.

Brunner, K. and A.H. Meltzer (1993), *Money and the Economy: Issues in Monetary Analysis*, Cambridge: Cambridge University Press.

Bryant, J. and N. Wallace (1979), 'The inefficiency of interest-bearing national debt', *Journal of Political Economy*, April, 365–81.

Buchanan, J. (1975), 'The samaritan's dilemma', in E.S. Phelps (ed.), *Altruism, Morality and Economic Theory*, New York: Russell Sage Foundation, pp. 71–85.

Buiter, W.H. (1980), 'The macroeconomics of Dr. Pangloss: a critical survey of the new classical macroeconomics', *Economic Journal*, March, 34–50.

Bundesbank (1973), *Report for the Year*.

Bushaw, D.W. and Clower, R.W. (1957), *Introduction to Mathematical Economics*, Homewood: Irwin.

Cagan, P. (1965), *Determinants and Effects of Changes in the Stock of Money*, New York: Columbia University Press.

Cagan, P. (1972), in Cagan et al., *Economic Policy and Inflation in the Sixties*, Washington, DC: American Enterprise Institute.

Cagan, P. (1974), *The Hydra Headed Monster: The Problem of Inflation in the United States*, Washington, DC: American Enterprise Institute for Public Policy Research.

Cagan, P. (1980), 'Reflections on rational expectations', *Journal of Money, Credit, and Banking*, November, part 2, 826–32.

Calvo, G.A. (1983), 'Staggered prices in a utility maximizing framework', *Journal of Monetary Economics*, September, 383–98.

Cannan, E. (1921), 'The application of the theoretical apparatus of supply and demand to units of currency', in American Economic Association (eds) (1951), *Readings in Monetary Theory*, Philadelphia: Blakiston, pp. 3–12.

Caskey, J. and S. Fazzari (1987), 'Aggregate demand contractions with nominal debt commitments: is wage flexibility stabilizing?', *Economic Inquiry*, October, 583–97.

Cass, D. and M.E. Yaari (1966), 'A re-examination of the pure consumption loans model', *Journal of Political Economy*, August, 353–67.

Cassel, G. (1903), *The Nature and Necessity of Interest*, New York: Macmillan, reprinted by Augustus M. Kelley (1956).

Cecchetti, S. (1995), 'Distinguishing theories of the monetary transmission mechanism', Federal Reserve Bank of St Louis *Review*, May/June, 83–97.

Clower, R.W. (1965), 'The Keynesian counter-revolution: a theoretical appraisal', reprinted in D.A. Walker (ed.) (1984), *Money and Markets: Essays by Robert W. Clower*, Cambridge: Cambridge University Press, pp. 34–58.

Clower, R.W. (1967), 'A reconsideration of the microfoundations of monetary theory', reprinted in D.A. Walker (ed.) (1984), *Money and Markets: Essays by Robert W. Clower*, Cambridge: Cambridge University Press, pp. 81–9.

Clower, R.W. (1968), 'Stock-flow analysis', in *International Encyclopedia of the Social Sciences*, **15**, New York: Macmillan and Free Press, pp. 273–7.

Clower, R.W. and J. Due (1972), *Microeconomics*, Homewood: Irwin.

Colander, D.C. (ed.) (1979), *Solutions to Inflation*, New York: Harcourt Brace Jovanovich.

Cooper, R. and A. John (1988), 'Coordinating coordination failures in Keynesian models', *Quarterly Journal of Economics*, August, 441–63.

Copeland, T.E. and J.F. Weston (1988), *Financial Theory and Corporate Policy*, 3rd edn, Reading, MA: Addison-Wesley.

Costanzo, G.A. (1961), *Programas de estabilización económica en América Latina*, Mexico City: Centre de Estudios Monetarios Latinamericanos.

Cover, J.P. (1992), 'Asymmetric effects of positive and negative money-supply shocks', *Quarterly Journal of Economics*, November, 1261–82.

Crockett, A.D. (1976), 'The euro-currency market: an attempt to clarify some basic issues', International Monetary Fund staff papers, July, 375–86.

Darby, M.R. (1973), book review of *The Cashless Society* by R.A. Hendrickson, *Journal of Money, Credit, and Banking*, August, 870–71.

Davenport, H.J. (1913), *The Economics of Enterprise*, New York: Macmillan.

De Long, J.B. (2000), 'The triumph of monetarism?', *Journal of Economic Perspectives*, Winter, 83–94.

De Long, J.B. and L.H. Summers (1986), 'Is increased price flexibility stabilizing?', *American Economic Review*, December, 1031–44.

Diamond, P.A. (1982), 'Aggregate demand management in search equilibrium', *Journal of Political Economy*, October, 881–94.

Dorfman, R. (1959), 'Waiting and the period of production', *Quarterly Journal of Economics*, August, 351–72.

Dorn, J.A. (1999), 'Introduction', *Cato Journal*, Winter, 311–20.

Dornbusch, R. (1976), 'Expectations and exchange rate dynamics', *Journal of Political Economy*, December, 1161–76.

Dowd, K. (1996), *Competition and Finance: A Reinterpretation of Financial and Monetary Economics*, New York: St Martin's Press.

Driskill, R.A. and S.M. Sheffrin (1986), 'Is price flexibility destabilizing?', *American Economic Review*, September, 802–7.

Eucken, W. (1954), *Kapitaltheoretische Untersuchungen*, 2nd edn, Tübingen: J.C.B. Mohr (Paul Siebeck).

Feige, E.L. and M. Parkin (1971), 'The optimal quantity of money, bonds, commodity inventories, and capital', *American Economic Review*, June, 335–49.

Fellner, W. (1972), in Cagan et.al., *Economic Policy and Inflation in the Sixties*, Washington, DC: American Enterprise Institute.

Fellner, W. (1974), 'The controversial issue of comprehensive indexation', reprinted in D.C. Colander (ed.) (1979), *Solutions to Inflation*, New York: Harcourt Brace Jovanovich, pp. 88–92.

Fellner, W. (1975), 'Comment' in D. Meiselman and A. Laffer (eds), *The Phenomenon of Worldwide Inflation*, Washington, DC: American Enterprise Institute.

Fellner, W. (1976), *Towards a Reconstruction of Macroeconomics*, Washington, DC: American Enterprise Institute.

Fellner, W. (1978), 'The core of the controversy about reducing inflation: an introductory analysis', in W. Fellner, project director, *Contemporary Economic Problems 1978*, Washington, DC: American Enterprise Institute, pp. 1–12.

Fellner, W. and H.M. Somers (1966), 'Alternative monetary approaches to interest theory', in R.S. Thorn (ed.), *Monetary Theory and Policy*, New York: Random House, pp. 469–81.

Fels, Gerhard (1969), *Der internationale Preiszusammenhang*, Köln: Heymanns.

Ferguson, Adam (1767), *An Essay on the History of Civil Society*, London.

Fetter, F.W. (1931), *Monetary Inflation in Chile*, Princeton, NJ: Princeton University Press.

Fischer, S. (1977), 'Long-term contracts, rational expectations, and the optimal money supply rule', *Journal of Political Economy*, February, 191–205.

Fisher, I. (1896), *Appreciation and Interest*, Evanston, IL: American Economic Association.

Fisher, I. (1907), *The Rate of Interest*, New York: Macmillan.

Fisher, I. (1911, 1922), *The Purchasing Power of Money*, 1st and 2nd edns, New York: Macmillan.

Fisher, I. (1926), 'A statistical relation between unemployment and price changes', *International Labour Review*, June, 785–92, reprinted 1973 as 'I discovered the Phillips curve', *Journal of Political Economy*, March/April, 496–502.

Fisher, I. (1930), *The Theory of Interest*, New York: Macmillan, reprinted by Augustus M. Kelley (1955).

Fisher, I. (1933), 'The debt-deflation theory of great depressions', *Econometrica*, October, 337–57.

Fitoussi, J.P. (1974), *Le fondement micro-économique de la théorie Keynésienne*, Paris: Editions Cujas.

Flew, A. (1971), *An Introduction to Western Philosophy*, Indianapolis, IN and New York: Bobbs-Merrill.

Flood, R. and N. Marion (1998), 'Perspectives on the recent currency crisis literature', *National Bureau of Economic Research working paper No. 6380*, January, 1–57.

Friedman, M. (1959a), 'Statement on monetary theory and policy', in hearings before the Joint Economic Committee, May 25–28, *Employment, Growth and Price Levels*, reprinted in R.J. Ball and P. Doyle (eds) (1969), *Inflation*, Baltimore, MD: Penguin Books, pp. 136–45.

Friedman, M. (1959b), 'The demand for money: some theoretical and empirical results', reprinted in M. Friedman (1969b), *The Optimum Quantity of Money and Other Essays*, Chicago: Aldine, pp. 111–39.

Friedman, M. (1959c), *A Program for Monetary Stability*, New York: Fordham University Press.

Friedman, M. (1961), 'Real and pseudo gold standards', *Journal of Law and Economics*, October, 66–79.

Friedman, M. (1963), 'Inflation: causes and consequences', reprinted in M. Friedman (1968c), *Dollars and Deficits*, Englewood Cliffs, NJ: Prentice-Hall.

Friedman, M. (1964), 'Monetary studies of the National Bureau', reprinted in M. Friedman (1969b), *The Optimum Quantity of Money and Other Essays*, Chicago: Aldine, pp. 261–84.

Friedman, M. (1968a), 'The role of monetary policy', *American Economic Review*, March, 1–17.

Friedman, M. (1968b), 'Factors affecting the levels of interest rates', in *Proceedings of the 1968 Conference on Savings and Residential Financing*, Chicago: United States Savings and Loan League.

Friedman, M. (1969a), 'The optimum quantity of money', in M. Friedman (1969b), *The Optimum Quantity of Money and Other Essays*, Chicago: Aldine, pp. 1–50.

Friedman, M. (1974), 'A theoretical framework for monetary analysis', in R.J. Gordon (ed.), *Milton Friedman's Monetary Framework*, Chicago: University of Chicago Press, pp. 1–62.

Friedman, M. (1977), 'Nobel lecture: inflation and unemployment', *Journal of Political Economy*, June, 451–72.

Friedman, M. (1985), 'Let floating rates continue to float', *New York Times*, 26 December, op-ed page.

Friedman, M. (1988), 'Money and the stock market', *Journal of Political Economy*, **96** (21), 221–45.

Friedman, M. (1993), 'The "plucking model" of business fluctuations revisited', *Economic Inquiry*, April, 171–7.

Friedman, M. (1997), 'Rx for Japan: back to the future', *Wall Street Journal*, 17 December, A22.

Friedman, M. (1999), 'Interview with Milton Friedman', in B. Snowdon and H.R. Vane (eds), *Conversations with Leading Economists*, Cheltenham, UK and Northampton, MA, USA: Edward Elgar, pp. 124–44.

Friedman, M. and A. Schwartz (1963), *A Monetary History of the United States, 1867–1960*, Princeton, NJ: Princeton University Press.

Fry, M.J. (1988), *Money, Interest, and Banking in Economic Development*, Baltimore, MD: Johns Hopkins University Press.

Fuhrer, J.C. and G.R. Moore (1995), 'Inflation persistence', *Quarterly Journal of Economics*, February, 127–59.

Fuhrer, J.C. and M.S. Sniderman (2000), 'Conference summary: the conduct of monetary policy in a low-inflation environment', *Journal of Money, Credit, and Banking*, November.

Garrison, R.W. (1981), 'The Austrian-neoclassical relation: a study in monetary dynamics', Ph.D. dissertation, University of Virginia.

Garrison, R.W. (2001), *Time and Money: The Macroeconomics of Capital Structure*, London: Routledge.

George, H. (1898), *The Science of Political Economy*, reprinted (1941), New York: Robert Schalkenbach Foundation.

Glazier, E.M. (1970), 'Theories of disequilibrium: Clower and Leijonhufvud compared to Hutt', master's thesis, University of Virginia.

Goldfeld, S.M. (1976), 'The case of the missing money', *Brookings Papers on Economic Activity*, vol. 7, 683–730.

Gordon, R.J. (1976), 'Recent developments in the theory of inflation and unemployment', *Journal of Monetary Economics*, April, 185–219.

Gordon, R.J. (1982), 'Price inertia and policy effectiveness in the United States, 1890–1980', *Journal of Political Economy*, **90**, 1087–117.

Gordon, R.J. (1987), *Macroeconomics*, 4th edn, Boston: Little, Brown and Company.

Gordon, R.J. (1990a), *Macroeconomics*, 5th edn, Glenview, IL: Scott, Foresman/Little Brown.

Gordon, R.J. (1990b), 'What is new-Keynesian economics?', *Journal of Economic Literature*, September, 1115–71.

Graham, B. (1933), 'Stabilized reflation', *Economic Forum*, Spring, 186–93.

Graham, B. (1937), *Storage and Stability*, New York: McGraw-Hill.

Graham, B. (1944), *World Commodities and World Currency*, New York: McGraw-Hill.

Graham, F.D. (1942), *Social Goals and Economic Institutions*, Princeton, NJ: Princeton University Press.

Greenfield, R.L. (1994), *Monetary Policy and the Depressed Economy*, Belmont, CA: Wadsworth.

Greenfield, R.L. and L.B. Yeager (1983), 'A laissez-faire approach to monetary stability', *Journal of Money, Credit, and Banking*, August, 302–15.

Greenfield, R.L. and L.B. Yeager (1986), 'Money and credit confused: an appraisal of economic doctrine and Federal Reserve procedure', *Southern Economic Journal*, October, 364–73.

Greenwald, B. and J. Stiglitz (1993), 'New and old Keynesians', *Journal of Economic Perspectives*, Winter, 45–65.

Greidanus, T. (1932, 1950), *The Value of Money*, 1st and 2nd edns, London: Staples.

Grossman, H.I. (1972), 'Was Keynes a "Keynesian"? a review article', *Journal of Economic Literature*, March, 26–30.

Grossman, H.I. (1986), 'Money, real activity, and rationality', *Cato Journal*, Fall, 401–8.

Grossman, H.I. (1987), 'Monetary disequilibrium and market clearing', in *The New Palgrave: A Dictionary of Economics 3*, New York: Stockton Press, pp. 504–6.

Gurley, J.G. and E.S. Shaw (1955), 'Financial aspects of economic development', *American Economic Review*, September, 515–38.

Gurley, J.G. and E.S. Shaw (1960), *Money in a Theory of Finance*, Washington, DC: Brookings Institution.

Haberler, G. (1952), 'The Pigou effect once more', *Journal of Political Economy*, June, 240–46.

Haberler, G. (1958), *Prosperity and Depression*, new edition, London: Allen & Unwin.

Hall, R.E. (1982), 'Explorations in the gold standard and related policies for stabilizing the dollar', in R.E. Hall (ed.), *Inflation: Causes and Effects*, London and Chicago: Chicago University Press, pp. 111–22.

Hall, R.E. (1991), *Booms and Recessions in a Noisy Economy*, New Haven: Yale University Press.

Harrison, G.W. (1987), 'Stocks and flows', in *The New Palgrave: A Dictionary of Economics*, **4**, New York: Stockton Press, pp. 506–9.

Harsanyi, J.C. (1976), *Essays on Ethics, Social Behavior, and Scientific Explanation*, Dordrecht and Boston: Reidel.

Hart, A.G. (1953), *Money, Debt, and Economic Activity*, 2nd edn, New York: Prentice-Hall.

Havrilesky, T.M. and J.T. Boorman (1978), *Monetary Macroeconomics*, Arlington Heights, IL: AHM Publishing Co.

Hayek, F.A. (1936), 'The mythology of capital', *Quarterly Journal of Economics*, February, reprinted in American Economic Association (1946), *Readings in the Theory of Income Distribution*, Philadelphia: Blakiston.

Hayek, F.A. (1941), *The Pure Theory of Capital*, Chicago: University of Chicago Press.

Hayek, F.A. (1945), 'The use of knowledge in society', *American Economic Review*, September, 519–30.

Hayek, F.A. (1967), *Studies in Philosophy, Politics and Economics*, Chicago: University of Chicago Press.

Hetzel, R.L. (2003), 'Japanese monetary policy and deflation', Federal Reserve Bank of Richmond *Economic Quarterly*, Summer, 21–52.

Hicks, J.R. (1935), 'A suggestion for simplifying the theory of money', reprinted in J.R. Hicks (1967), *Critical Essays in Monetary Theory*, Oxford: Clarendon Press.

Hicks, J.R. (1946), *Value and Capital*, 2nd edn, Oxford.

Hicks, J.R. (1965), *Capital and Growth*, Oxford: Clarendon Press.

Hicks, J.R. (1967) , *Critical Essays in Monetary Theory*, Oxford: Clarendon Press.

Hicks, J.R. (1977), 'Expected inflation', in *Economic Perspective: Further Essays on Money and Growth*, Oxford: Clarendon Press.

Hirshleifer, J. (1970), *Investment, Interest, and Capital*, Englewood Cliffs, NJ: Prentice-Hall.

Hoover, K.D. (1988), *The New Classical Macroeconomics*, Oxford: Basil Blackwell.

Howitt, P. (1979), 'Evaluating the non-market-clearing approach', *American Economic Review*, May, 60–63.

Howitt, P. (1990), *The Keynesian Recovery and Other Essays*, Ann Arbor, MI: University of Michigan Press.

Hubbard, R.G. (1995), 'Is there a "credit channel" for monetary policy?', Federal Reserve Bank of St Louis *Review*, May/June, 63–77.

Hume, D. (1752a), 'Of the balance of trade', excerpted in R.N. Cooper (ed.) (1969), *International Finance*, Baltimore, MD: Penguin Books.

Hume, D. (1752b), 'Of money', reprinted in E. Rotwein (ed.) (1970), *Writings on Economics*, Madison, WI: University of Wisconsin Press, pp. 33–46.

Humphrey, T.M. (1978), 'Some recent developments in Phillips curve analysis', Federal Reserve Bank of Richmond *Economic Review*, January/February, 15–23.

Humphrey, T.M. (1979a), 'The interest cost-push controversy', Federal Reserve Bank of Richmond *Economic Review*, January/February.

Humphrey, T.M. (1979b), 'The persistence of inflation', in M.P. Dooley, et al. (eds), *The Political Economy of Policy-Making*, Beverly Hills and London: Sage Publications, pp. 89–113.

Humphrey, T.M. (1982a), 'The real-bills doctrine', Federal Reserve Bank of Richmond *Economic Review*, September/October, 3–13.

Humphrey, T.M. (1982b), 'Of Hume, Thornton, the quantiy theory, and the Phillips curve', Federal Reserve Bank of Richmond *Economic Review*, November/December, 13–18.

Humphrey, T.M. (1983a), 'Can the central bank peg real interest rates? A survey of classical and neoclassical opinion', Federal Reserve Bank of Richmond *Economic Review*, September/October, 12–21.

Humphrey, T.M. (1983b) , 'The early history of the real/nominal interest rate relationship', Federal Reserve Bank of Richmond *Economic Review*, May/June, 2–10.

Humphrey, T.M. (1984), 'On nonneutral relative price effects in monetarist thought: some Austrian misconceptions', Federal Reserve Bank of Richmond *Economic Review*, May/June, 13–19.

Humphrey, T.M. (1985a), 'The evolution and policy implications of Phillips curve analysis', Federal Reserve Bank of Richmond *Economic Review*, March/April, 3–22.

Humphrey, T.M. (1985b), 'The early history of the Phillips curve', in Federal Reserve Bank of Richmond, *From Trade-offs to Policy Ineffectiveness: A History of the Phillips Curve*, pp. 5–12.

Humphrey, T.M. (1988), 'The trade theorist's sacred diagram: its origin and early development', Federal Reserve Bank of Richmond *Economic Review*, January/February, 3–15.

Humphrey, T.M. (1991), 'Nonneutrality of money in classical monetary thought', Federal Reserve Bank of Richmond *Economic Review*, March/April, 3–15.

Humphrey, T.M. (1993), *Money, Banking and Inflation*, Aldershot, UK and Brookfield, USA: Edward Elgar.

Humphrey, T.M. (1994), 'John Wheatley's theory of international monetary adjustment', Federal Reserve Bank of Richmond *Economic Quarterly*, Summer, 69–86.

Humphrey, T.M. (1997), 'Fisher and Wicksell on the quantity theory', Federal Reserve Bank of Richmond *Economic Quarterly*, Fall, 71–90.

Humphrey, T.M. (2002), 'Knut Wicksell and Gustav Cassel on the cumulative process and the price-stabilizing policy rule', Federal Reserve Bank of Richmond *Economic Quarterly*, Summer, 59–83.

Hutt, W.H. (1956), 'The yield on money held', in Mary Sennholz (ed.), *On Freedom and Free Enterprise* (Festschrift for Ludwig von Mises), Princeton: Van Nostrand, pp. 196–223.

Hutt, W.H. (1963), *Keynesianism – Retrospect and Prospect*, Chicago: Regnery.

Hutt, W.H. (1974), *A Rehabilitation of Say's Law*, Athens, OH: Ohio University Press.

Hutt, W.H. (1979), *The Keynesian Episode: A Reassessment*, Indianapolis, IN: Liberty Press.

Ingram, J.C. (1974), 'The dollar and the international monetary system: a retrospective view', *Southern Economic Journal*, April, 531–43.

Johnson, H.G. (1972), *Inflation and the Monetarist Controversy*, Amsterdam: North Holland.

Johnson, H.G. (1976), 'The monetary theory of balance-of-payments policies', in H.G. Johnson and J. Frenkel (eds), *The Monetary Approach to the Balance of Payments*, Toronto: University of Toronto Press, pp. 262–84.

Jones, R.A. (1976), 'The origin and development of media of exchange', *Journal of Political Economy*, August, pt. 1, 757–75.

Judd, J.P. and J.L. Scadding (1982), 'The search for a stable money demand function: a survey of the post-1973 literature', *Journal of Economic Literature*, September, 993–1023.

Kaldor, N. (1982), *The Scourge of Monetarism*, Oxford: Oxford University Press.

Keller, R.R. (1980), 'Inflation, monetarism, and price controls', *Nebraska Journal of Economics and Business*, Winter, 30–40.

Kenen, P.B. (2000), 'Fixed versus floating exchange rates', *Cato Journal*, Spring/Summer, 109–13.

Kessel, R.A. and A.A. Alchian (1962), 'Effects of inflation', *Journal of Political Economy*, December, 521–37.

Keynes, J.M. (1930), *A Treatise on Money*, vol. II, *The Applied Theory of Money*, London: Macmillan.

Keynes, J.M. (1936), *The General Theory of Employment, Interest, and Money*, New York: Harcourt, Brace.

Kim, C.J. and C.R. Nelson (1999), 'Friedman's plucking model of business fluctuations: tests and estimates of permanent and transitory components', *Journal of Money, Credit, and Banking*, August, 317–34.

King, R.G. (2000), 'The new IS-LM model: language, logic and limits', Federal Reserve Bank of Richmond *Economic Quarterly*, Summer, 45–103.

King, R.G. and C. Plosser (1984), 'Money, credit and prices in a real business cycle', *American Economic Review*, June, 363–80.

Kiyotaki, N. and R. Wright (1989), 'On money as a medium of exchange', *Journal of Political Economy*, **97** (4), 927–54.

Kiyotaki, N. and R. Wright (1991), 'A contribution to the pure theory of money', *Journal of Economic Theory*, April, 215–35.

Kiyotaki, N. and R. Wright (1993), 'A search-theoretic approach to monetary economics', *American Economic Review*, March, 63–77.

Kocherlakota, N.R. (1998), 'The technological role of fiat money', Federal Reserve Bank of Minneapolis *Quarterly Review*, Summer, 2–10.

Koppl, R. and L.B. Yeager (1996), 'Big players and herding in asset markets: the case of the Russian ruble', *Explorations in Economic History*, July, 367–83.

Krugman, P.R. (1998), 'It's baaack: Japan's slump and the return of the liquidity trap', *Brookings Papers on Economic Activity*, 2, 137–87.

Kuenne, R.E. (1958), 'On the existence and role of money in a stationary system', *Southern Economic Journal*, July, 1–10.

Kuttner, K.N. and P.C. Mosser (2002), 'The monetary transmission mechanism: some answers and further questions', Federal Reserve Bank of New York *Economic Policy Review*, May, 15–26.

Kydland, F. and E. Prescott (1977), 'Rules rather than discretion: the inconsistency of optimal plans', *Journal of Political Economy*, June, 473–92.

Kydland F. and E. Prescott (1982), 'Time to build and aggregate fluctuations', *Econometrica*, November, 1345–70.

Laidler, D. (1966), 'The rate of interest and the demand for money – some empirical evidence', *Journal of Political Economy*, December, 545–55.

Laidler, D. (1984), 'The buffer stock notion in monetary economics', conference proceedings published in a supplement to the *Economic Journal*, March, 17–34.

Laidler, D. (1986), 'The new-classical contribution to macroeconomics', reprinted in D. Laidler (1990a), *Taking Money Seriously and Other Essays*, Cambridge, MA: MIT Press, pp. 56–78

Laidler, D. (1987), '"Buffer-stock" money and the transmission mechanism', Federal Reserve Bank of Atlanta *Economic Review*, March/April, 11–23.

Laidler, D. (1988), 'Taking money seriously', *Canadian Journal of Economics*, November, reprinted in D. Laidler (1990a), *Taking Money Seriously and Other Essays*, Cambridge, MA: MIT Press, pp. 1–23.

Laidler, D. (1989), 'Comment' in M.D. Bordo (ed.), *Money, History, and International Finance: Essays in Honor of Anna J. Schwartz*, Chicago: University of Chicago Press, pp. 104–10.

Laidler, D. (1990a), *Taking Money Seriously and Other Essays*, Cambridge, MA: MIT Press.

Laidler, D. (1990b), 'The legacy of the monetarist controversy', Federal Reserve Bank of St Louis *Review*, March/April, 49–64.

Laidler, D. (1990c), 'On the costs of anticipated inflation', in D. Laidler (1990a), *Taking Money Seriously and Other Essays*, Cambridge, MA: MIT Press, pp. 41–55.

Laidler, D. (1991a), *The Golden Age of the Quantity Theory*, Princeton, NJ: Princeton University Press.

Laidler, D. (1991b), 'The quantity theory is always and everywhere controversial – why?', *The Economic Record*, December, 289–306.

Laidler, D. (1992), 'Monetarism – the unfinished business', *Cyprus Journal of Economics*, December, reprinted in D. Laidler (1997a), *Money and Macroeconomics: The Selected Essays of David Laidler*, Cheltenham, UK and Lyme, USA: Edward Elgar, pp. 354–68.

Laidler, D. (1993a), *The Demand for Money*, 4th edn, New York: HarperCollins.

Laidler, D. (1993b), 'Price stability and the monetary order', in K. Shigehara (ed.), *Price Stabilization in the 1990s*, reprinted in D. Laidler (1997a), *Money and Macroeconomics: The Selected Essays of David Laidler*, Cheltenham, UK and Lyme, USA: Edward Elgar, pp. 327–52.

Laidler, D. (1997a), *Money and Macroeconomics: The Selected Essays of David Laidler*, Cheltenham, UK and Lyme, USA: Edward Elgar.

Laidler, D. (1997b), 'Notes on the microfoundations of monetary economics', *Economic Journal*, July, 1213–23.

Lange, O. (1942), 'Say's Law: a restatement and criticism', in O. Lange et al. (eds), *Studies in Mathematical Economics and Econometrics* (in memory of Henry Schultz), Chicago: University of Chicago Press, pp. 49–68.

Laudan, L. (1977), *Progress and its Problems*, Berkeley and Los Angeles: University of California Press.

League of Nations (1946), *The Course and Control of Inflation*, Princeton, NJ.

Leeper, E.M. and T. Zha (2001), 'Assessing simple policy rules: a view from a complete macroeconomic model', Federal Reserve Bank of St Louis *Review*, July/August, 83–110.

Leibenstein, H. (1976), *Beyond Economic Man*, Cambridge, MA: Harvard University Press.

Leijonhufvud, A. (1968), *On Keynesian Economics and the Economics of Keynes*, New York: Oxford University Press.

Leijonhufvud, A. (1973), 'Effective demand failures', *Swedish Journal of Economics*, March, 27–48.

Leijonhufvud, A. (1981), *Information and Coordination*, New York: Oxford University Press.

Leijonhufvud, A. (1987), 'Rational expectations and monetary institutions', in M. de Cecco and J.P. Fitoussi (eds), *Monetary Theory and Economic Institutions*, Houndmills: Macmillan.

Lerner, A.P. (1949), 'The inflationary process: some theoretical aspects', *Review of Economic Statistics*, August, 193–200.

Lerner, A.P. (1952), 'The essential properties of interest and money', *Quarterly Journal of Economics*, May, 172–93.

Lerner, A.P. (1959a), 'Consumption-loan interest and money', *Journal of Political Economy*, October, 512–18.

Lerner, A.P. (1959b), 'Rejoinder', *Journal of Political Economy*, October, 523–5.

Lerner, A.P. and D.C. Colander (1979), 'MAP: a cure for inflation', in D.C. Colander (ed.), *Solutions to Inflation*, New York: Harcourt Brace Jovanovich, pp. 210–20.

Lindbeck A. and D.J. Snower (1985), 'Explanations of unemployment', *Oxford Review of Economic Policy*, Spring.

Lindbeck A. and D.J. Snower (1986), 'Wage setting, unemployment, and insider–outsider relations', *American Economic Review*, May, 235–9.

Lindbeck A. and D.J. Snower (1988a), 'Cooperation, harassment and involuntary unemployment: an insider–outsider approach', *American Economic Review*, March.

Lindbeck A. and D.J. Snower (1988b), *The Insider–Outsider Theory of Employment and Unemployment*, Cambridge, MA: MIT Press.

Lloyd, C.L. (1960), 'The equivalence of the liquidity preference and loanable funds theories and the *new* stock-flow analysis', *Review of Economic Studies*, June, 206–209.

Loeb, H. (1946), *Full Production Without War*, Princeton, NJ: Princeton University Press.

Long, J.B. and C. Plosser (1983), 'Real business cycles', *Journal of Political Economy*, February, 1345–70.

Lucas, R. (1973), 'Some international evidence on output–inflation tradeoffs', *American Economic Review*, June, 326–34.

Lucas, R. (1976), 'Econometric policy evaluation: a critique', Carnegie-Rochester Conference Series, vol. 1, reprinted in R. Lucas (1981), *Studies in Business-Cycle Theory*, 6th printing (1987), Cambridge, MA: MIT Press, pp. 104–30.

Lucas, R. (1979), 'An equilibrium model of the business cycle', *Journal of Political Economy*, December, reprinted in R. Lucas (1981), *Studies in Business-Cycle Theory*, 6th printing (1987), Cambridge, MA: MIT Press, pp. 179–214.

Lucas, Robert (1984), 'Money in a theory of finance', in K. Brunner and A.H. Meltzer (eds), *Essays on Macroeconomic Implications of Financial and Labour Markets and Political Processes*, Carnegie-Rochester Conference Series on Public Policy, vol. 21, North-Holland.

Lucas, R.E. (1996), 'Nobel lecture: monetary neutrality', *Journal of Political Economy*, August.

Lutz, F. (1968), *The Theory of Interest*, Chicago: Aldine.

Maier, C.S. (1978), 'The politics of inflation in the twentieth century', in F. Hirsch and J.H. Goldthorpe (eds), *The Political Economy of Inflation*, Cambridge, MA: Harvard University Press.

Mankiw, N.G. (1985), 'Small menu costs and large business cycles: a macroeconomic model of monopoly', *Quarterly Journal of Economics*, May, 529–39.

Mankiw, N.G. (1992), 'The reincarnation of Keynesian economics', *European Economic Review*, April, reprinted in B. Snowdon and H.R. Vane (eds) (1997a), *A Macroeconomics Reader*, London and New York: Routledge, pp. 445–51.

Mankiw, N.G. (1993), 'Symposium on Keynesian economics today', *Journal of Economic Perspectives*, Winter, 3–4.

Mankiw, N.G. (1995), interview in B. Snowdon and H.R. Vane, 'New-Keynesian economics today: the empire strikes back', *American Economist*, Spring, reprinted in B. Snowdon and H.R. Vane (1997a) (eds), *A Macroeconomics Reader*, London: Routledge, pp. 452–77.

Mankiw, N.G. (2001a), *Principles of Economics*, 2nd edn, New York: Harcourt.

Mankiw, N.G. (2001b), 'The inexorable and mysterious tradeoff between inflation and unemployment', *Economic Journal*, May, c45–c61.

Mankiw, N.G. and D. Romer (eds) (1991), *New Kevnesian Economics*, Cambridge, MA: MIT Press.

Marshall, A. (1920), *Principles of Economics*, London: Macmillan.

Marshall, A. (1924), excerpt from *Money, Credit and Commerce*, reprinted in R. Clower (ed.) (1973), *Monetary Theory*, Baltimore, MD: Penguin Books, pp. 80–93.

Marty, A.L. and D.L. Thornton (1995), 'Is there a case for "moderate" inflation?', Federal Reserve Bank of St Louis *Review*, July/August, 27–37.

Masera, R.S. (1973), 'Deposit creation, multiplication and the euro-dollar market', in Ente per gli Studi Monetari, Bancari e Finanziari Luigi Einaudi, *Quaderni di Ricerche*, No. 11, Rome, pp. 123–89.

McCallum, B.T. (1983), 'The role of overlapping-generations models in monetary economics', in K. Brunner and A.H. Meltzer (eds), *Money, Monetary Policy and Financial Institutions*, Carnegie-Rochester Conference Series on Public Policy, vol. 18, pp. 9–44.

McCallum, B.T. (1999), 'Recent developments in the analysis of monetary policy rules', Federal Reserve Bank of St Louis *Review*, November/December, 3–11.

McCallum, B.T. (2001), 'Monetary policy analysis in models without money', Federal Reserve Bank of St Louis *Review*, July/August, 145–60.

McCallum, B.T. (2002), 'Recent developments in monetary policy analysis: the roles of theory and evidence', Federal Reserve Bank of Richmond *Economic Quarterly*, Winter, 67–90.

McCallum, B.T. and M. Goodfriend (1987), 'Demand for money: theoretical studies', in J. Eatwell, M. Milgate, and P. Newman (eds), *The New Palgrave; A Dictionary of Economics*, **1**, New York: Stockton Press, pp. 775–81.

Meckling, W.H. (1960a), 'An exact consumption-loan model of interest: a comment', *Journal of Political Economy*, February, 72–6.

Meckling, W.H. (1960b), 'Rejoinder', *Journal of Political Economy*, February, 83–4.

Mehra, Y.P. (2001), 'The wealth effect in empirical life-cycle aggregate consumption equations', Federal Reserve Bank of Richmond *Economic Quarterly*, Spring, 45–68.

Meier, G.M. (1954), 'Some questions about growth economics: comment', *American Economic Review*, December, 931–6.

Meinich, P. (1968), *A Monetary General Equilibrium Theory for an International Economy*, Oslo: Universitetsforlaget.

Meiselman, D. (1975), 'Worldwide inflation: a monetarist view', in D. Meiselman and A. Laffer (eds), *The Phenomenon of Worldwide Inflation*, Washington, DC: American Enterprise Institute.

Meltzer, A.H. (1963), 'The demand for money: the evidence from the time series', *Journal of Political Economy*, June, 219–46.

Meltzer, A.H. and K. Brunner (1963), 'The place of financial intermediaries in the transmission of monetary policy', *American Economic Review*, May.

Melvin, M. (1983), 'Vanishing liquidity effect of money on interest: analysis and implications for policy', *Economic Inquiry*, **21** (2), 188–202.

Menger, C. (1871), *Principles of Economics*, translated by J. Dingwall and B.F. Hoselitz (1981), New York: New York University Press.

Menger, C. (1892), 'On the origin of money', *Economic Journal*, June, 239–55.

Meyer, L.H. (2001), 'Does money matter?', Federal Reserve Bank of St Louis *Review*, September/October, 1–15.

Mill, John Stuart (1844 [1874]), *Essays on Some Unsettled Questions of Political Economy*, reprinted (1967), *Collected Works of John Stuart Mill*, vol. 4, Toronto: University of Toronto Press.

Mill, John Stuart (1848), *Principles of Political Economy*, reprinted (1965), *Collected Works of John Stuart Mill*, vol. 3, Toronto: University of Toronto Press.

Miller, M.H. and D. Orr (1966), 'A model of the demand for money by firms', *Quarterly Journal of Economics*, August, 413–35.

Miller, N.C. (2002), *Balance of Payments and Exchange Rate Theories*, Cheltenham, UK and Northampton, MA, USA: Edward Elgar.

Miller, P.J. (1980), 'Deficit policies, deficit fallacies', Federal Reserve Bank of Minneapolis *Quarterly Review*, Summer, 2–4.

Miller, P.J. and A. Struthers (1979), 'The tax-cut illusion', Federal Reserve Bank of Minneapolis *1979 Annual Report*, 1–9.

Mints, L.W. (1945), *A History of Banking Theory*, Chicago: University of Chicago Press.

Mises, L. von (1912), *The Theory of Money and Credit*, translation by H.E. Batson (1934), reprinted (1981), Indianapolis, IN: Liberty Classics.

Mishkin, F. (1982), 'Does anticipated monetary policy matter? An econometric investigation', *Journal of Political Economy*, February, 22–51.

Mishkin, F. (1995), 'Symposium on the monetary transmission mechanism', *Journal of Economic Perspectives*, Fall, 3–10.

Moini, M. (2001), 'Toward a general theory of credit and money', *Review of Austrian Economics*, December, 267–317.

Moore, B.J. (1988), *Horizontalists and Verticalists: The Macroeconomics of Credit Money*, Cambridge: Cambridge University Press.

Morgan, E.V. (1965), *A History of Money*, Baltimore, MD: Penguin Books.

Morgan, E.V. (1969), 'The essential qualities of money', *Manchester School*, September, 237–48.

Moss, L.S. (1976), 'The monetary economics of Ludwig von Mises', in L.S. Moss (ed.), *The Economics of Ludwig von Mises*, Kansas City, MO: Sheed and Ward, pp. 13–49.

Mundell, R.A. (1963), 'Inflation and real interest', *Journal of Political Economy*, June, 280–83.

Mundell, R.A. (1968), *International Economics*, New York: Macmillan.

Musgrave, A. (1981), '"Unreal assumptions" in economic theory: the f-twist untwisted', *Kyklos*, **34** (3), 377–87.

Neumann, M.J.M. and J. von Hagen (2002), 'Does inflation targeting matter?', Federal Reserve Bank of St Louis *Review*, July/August, 127–48.

Newton-Smith, W.H. (1981), *The Rationality of Science*, Boston and London: Routledge & Kegan Paul.

Okun, A.M. (1971), 'The mirage of steady inflation', *Brookings Papers on Economic Activity*, **2**, 485–98.

Okun, A.M. (1975), 'Inflation: its mechanics and welfare costs', *Brookings Papers on Economic Activity*, **2**, 351–90.

Okun, A.M. (1979), 'An efficient strategy to combat inflation', *The Brookings Bulletin*, Spring, 1–5.

Okun, A.M. (1980), 'Rational-expectations-with-misperceptions as a theory of the business cycle', *Journal of Money, Credit, and Banking*, November, part 2, 817–25.

Okun, A.M. (1981), *Prices and Quantities: A Macroeconomic Analysis*, Washington: Brookings Institution.

Olson, M. (1965), *The Logic of Collective Action*, Cambridge, MA: Harvard University Press.

Patinkin, D. (1949), 'Involuntary unemployment and the Keynesian supply function', *Economic Journal*, **59**, 360–83.

Patinkin, D. (1954), 'Keynesian economics and the quantity theory', in K. Kurihara (ed.), *Post Keynesian Economics*, New Brunswick, NJ: Rutgers University Press, pp. 123–52.

Patinkin, D. (1956, 1965), *Money, Interest, and Prices*, 1st and 2nd edns, New York: Harper and Row.

Patinkin, D. (1958), 'Liquidity preference and loanable funds: stock and flow analysis', *Economica*, n.s. 25, November, 300–18.

Patinkin, D. (1987), 'Walras's Law' in *The New Palgrave: A Dictionary of Economics*, **4**, pp. 863–8, New York: Stockton Press.

Patinkin, D. (1989), 'Introduction to second edition, abridged', in *Money, Interest, and Prices*, Cambridge: MIT Press.

Pazos, F. (1972), *Chronic Inflation in Latin America*, New York: Praeger.

Pesek, B.P. and T.R. Saving (1967), *Money, Wealth, and Economic Theory*, New York: Macmillan.

Pettengill, J. (1979), 'On the microfoundations of Keynesian unemployment', manuscript, University of Virginia, August.

Phelps, E.S. (1967), 'Phillips curves, expectations of inflation and optimal unemployment over time', *Economica*, August, 254–81.

Phelps, E.S. and J.B. Taylor (1977), 'Stabilizing powers of monetary policy under rational expectations', *Journal of Political Economy*, February, 163–90.

Phillips, A.W.H. (1958), 'The relation between unemployment and the rate of change of money wage rates in the United Kingdom, 1861–1957', *Economica*, November, 283–99.

Pigou, A.C. (1943), 'The classical stationary state', *Economic Journal*, December, 343–51.

Pigou, A.C. (1947), 'Economic progress in a stable environment', *Economica*, August, 180–88.

Plosser, C.I. (1989), 'Understanding real business cycles', *Journal of Economic Perspectives*, Summer, reprinted in B. Snowdon and H.R. Vane (eds) (1997a), *A Macroeconomics Reader*, London and New York: Routledge, pp. 396–424.

Poterba, J.M. (2000), 'Stock market wealth and consumption', *Journal of Economic Perspectives*, Spring, 99–118.

Rabin, A.A. (1977), 'A monetary view of the acceleration of world inflation, 1973–1974', Ph.D. dissertation, University of Virginia.

Rabin, A.A. (1993), 'A clarification of the excess demand for or excess supply of money', *Economic Inquiry*, July, 448–55.

Rabin, A.A. and L.B. Yeager (1982), *Monetary Approaches to the Balance of Payments and Exchange Rates*, essays in international finance no. 148, November, Princeton, NJ: International Finance Section of Princeton University.

Rabin, A.A. and L.B. Yeager (1997), 'The monetary transmission mechanism', *Eastern Economic Journal*, Summer, 293–9.

Radcliffe Committee (1959), *Report on the Working of the Monetary System*, London: Her Majesty's Stationery Office.

Radford, R.A. (1945), 'The economic organisation of a P.O.W. Camp', *Economica*, November, 189–201.

Ringer, F.K. (ed.) (1969), *The German Inflation of 1923*, New York: Oxford University Press.

Robertson, Sir D.H. (1963), *Lectures on Economic Principles*, London: Collins, The Fontana Library.

Rogoff, K. (1985), 'The optimal degree of commitment to an intermediate monetary target', *Quarterly Journal of Economics*, November, 1169–89.

Rotemberg, J.J. (1982), 'Monopolistic price adjustment and aggregate output', *Review of Economic Studies*, October, 517–31.

Salop, S.C. (1979), 'A model of the natural rate of unemployment', *American Economic Review*, March.

Samuelson, P.A. (1958), 'An exact consumption-loan model of interest with or without the social contrivance of money', *Journal of Political Economy*, December, 467–82.

Samuelson, P.A. (1959), 'Reply', *Journal of Political Economy*, October, 518–22.

Samuelson, P.A. (1960), 'Infinity, unanimity, and singularity: a reply', *Journal of Political Economy*, February, 76–83.

Samuelson, P.A. (1965), 'Equalization by trade of the interest rate along with the real wage', in R.E. Baldwin, et al., *Trade, Growth and the Balance of Payments*, Chicago: Rand McNally, pp. 35–52.

Sargent, T.J. (1986), *Rational Expectations and Inflation*, New York: Harper & Row.

Sargent, T.J. and N. Wallace (1975), '"Rational" expectations, the optimal monetary instrument, and the optimal money supply rule', *Journal of Political Economy*, April, 241–54.

Sargent, T.J. and N. Wallace (1976), 'Rational expectations and the theory of economic policy', *Journal of Monetary Economics*, May, 169–83.

Saving, T.R. (1971), 'Transactions costs and the demand for money', *American Economic Review*, June, 407–20.

Say, J.B. (1836), *A Treatise on Political Economy*, translated by C.R. Prinsep, Philadelphia: Grigg & Elliot.

Schelling, T.C. (1978), *Micromotives and Macrobehavior*, New York: Norton.

Schlicht, E. (1978), 'Labour turnover, wage structure, and natural unemployment', *Zeitschrift für die gesamte Staatswissenschaft*,134, 337–46.

Schultze, C.L. (1959), *Recent Inflation in the United States*, Joint Economic Committee study paper No. 1, Washington, DC: Government Printing Office, excerpted in R.J. Ball and P. Doyle (eds) (1969), *Inflation*, Baltimore, MD: Penguin Books, pp. 209–18.

Schultze, C.L. (1985), 'Microeconomic efficiency and nominal wage stickiness', *American Economic Review*, March, 1–15.

Schumpeter, J.A. (1917–18), 'Money and the social product', translated by A.W. Marget (1956), *International Economic Papers*, November, pp. 148–211.

Schumpeter, J.A. (1970), *Das Wesen des Geldes*, edited from manuscript by F.K. Mann, Göttingen: Vandenhoeck & Ruprecht.

Scrope, G.P. (1833), *Principles of Political Economy*, London: Longman, Rees, Orme, Brown, Green, and Longman.

Seater, J.J. (1993), 'Ricardian equivalence', *Journal of Economic Literature*, March, 142–90.

Selgin, G.A. (1987), 'The yield on money held revisited: lessons for today', *Market Process*, Fairfax, VA: George Mason University, Spring, 18–24.

Selgin, G.A. (1994), 'On ensuring the acceptability of a new fiat money', *Journal of Money, Credit, and Banking*, November, 808–26.

Shackle, G.L.S. (1961), 'Recent theories concerning the nature and role of interest', *Economic Journal*, June, 209–54.

Shah, P.J. and L.B. Yeager (1994), 'Schumpeter on monetary determinacy', *History of Political Economy*, Fall, 443–64.

Shapiro, C. and J. Stiglitz (1984), 'Equilibrium unemployment as a discipline device', *American Economic Review*, June, 433–44.

Silber, W.L. (1970), 'Fiscal policy in IS-LM analysis: a correction', *Journal of Money, Credit, and Banking*, November, 461–72.

Simpson, T. (1984), 'Changes in the financial system: implications for monetary policy', *Brookings Papers on Economic Activity* 1, 249–65.

Snowdon, B. and H.R. Vane (1997a), *A Macroeconomics Reader*, London and New York: Routledge.

Snowdon, B. and H.R. Vane (1997b), 'Politics and the macroeconomy: endogenous politicians and aggregate instability', in B. Snowdon and H.R. Vane (eds), *Reflections on the Development of Modern Macroeconomics*, Cheltenham, UK and Lyme, USA: Edward Elgar, pp. 204–40.

Snowdon, B., H. Vane and P. Wynarczyk (1994), *A Modern Guide to Macroeconomics*, Aldershot, UK and Brookfield, USA: Edward Elgar.

Solow, R.M. (1979), 'Another possible source of wage stickiness', *Journal of Macroeconomics*, Winter, 79–82.

Solow, R.M. (1980), 'On theories of unemployment', *American Economic Review*, March.

Sommer, A. (1929), 'Die makute, kin irrtum der geldlehre', *Jahrbucher für nationalokonomie und statistik*, **131** (2), 1–32.

Stanley, T.O. (1998), 'New wine in old bottles: a meta-analysis of Ricardian equivalence', *Southern Economic Journal*, January, 713–27.

Starr-McCluer, M. (2002), 'Stock market wealth and consumer spending', *Economic Inquiry*, January, 69–79.

Stiglitz, J.E. (1974), 'Alternative theories of wage determination and unemployment in LDC's: the labor turnover model', *Quarterly Journal of Economics*, 88, 194–227.

Stiglitz, J.E. (1979), 'Equilibrium in product markets with important information', *American Economic Review*, May, 339–45.

Stiglitz, J.E. (1987), 'The causes and consequences of the dependency of quality on prices', *Journal of Economic Literature*, March.

Swedberg, R. (1991), *Joseph A. Schumpeter: His Life and Work*, Cambridge: Polity.

Taylor, J.B. (1980), 'Aggregate dynamics and staggered contracts', *Journal of Political Economy*, February, 1–23.

Taylor, J.B. (1993), 'Discretion versus policy rules in practice', *Carnegie-Rochester Conference Series on Public Policy*, December, 195–214.

Taylor, M. (1995), 'The economics of exchange rates', *Journal of Economic Literature*, March, 13–47.

Thornton, D.L. (1994), 'Financial innovation, deregulation and the "credit view" of monetary policy', Federal Reserve Bank of St Louis *Review*, January/February, 31–49.

Thornton, D.L. (1999), 'Nominal interest rates less than zero?', Federal Reserve Bank of St Louis *Monetary Trends*, January, 1.

Thornton, H. (1802), *An Enquiry into the Nature and Effects of the Paper Credit of Great Britain*, reprinted (1978), Fairfield, NJ: Augustus M. Kelley.

Thurow, L.C. (1980), *The Zero-Sum Society*, New York: Basic Books.

Timberlake, R.H. (1964), 'The stock of money and money substitutes', *Southern Economic Journal*, January.

Tobin, J. (1952), 'Asset holdings and spending decisions', *American Economic Review*, May, 109–23.

Tobin, J. (1956), 'The interest elasticity of transactions demand for cash', *Review of Economics and Statistics*, August, 241–7.

Tobin, J. (1963), 'Commercial banks as creators of "money"', in Deane Carson (ed.), *Banking and Monetary Studies*, Homewood, IL: Irwin, pp. 408–19.

Tobin, J. (1965), 'Money and economic growth', *Econometrica*, **33**, reprinted in P.G. Korliras and R.S. Thorn (eds) (1979), *Modern Macroeconomics*, New York: Harper & Row, pp. 359–69.

Tobin, J. (1974), 'Friedman's theoretical framework', in R.J. Gordon (ed.), *Milton Friedman's Monetary Framework*, Chicago: University of Chicago Press, pp. 77–89.

Tobin, J. (1980a), 'Discussion', in J.H. Kareken and N. Wallace (eds), *Models of Monetary Economics*, Minneapolis, MN: Federal Reserve Bank of Minneapolis, pp. 83–90.

Tobin, J. (1980b), *Asset Accumulation and Economic Activity*, Chicago: University of Chicago Press.

Tobin, J. (1993), 'Price flexibility and output stability: an old Keynesian view', *Journal of Economic Perspectives*, Winter, 45–65.

Tolley, G. (1957), 'Providing for growth of the money supply', *Journal of Political Economy*, December, 465–85.

Trescott, P. (1989), 'Patinkin and the *real* real-balance effect', in D. Walker (ed.), *Perspectives on the History of Economic Thought, Volume II: Twentieth-Century Economic Thought*, Aldershot, UK and Brookfield, USA: Edward Elgar, pp. 199–216.

Trevithick, J.A. (1977), *Inflation*, New York: Penguin.

Triffin, R. (1966), *The World Money Maze*, New Haven, CT: Yale University Press.

Tsiang, S.C. (1966), 'Walras' Law, Say's Law and liquidity preference in general equilibrium analysis', *International Economic Review*, September, 329–45.

Tucker, D.P. (1971), 'Macroeconomic models and the demand for money under market disequilibrium', *Journal of Money, Credit, and Banking*, February, 57–83.

Turgot, A.R.J. (1766), *Sur la formation et la distribution des richesses*.

Valavanis, S. (1955), 'A denial of Patinkin's contradiction', *Kyklos*, **8** (4), 351–68.

van Ees, H. and H. Garretsen (1996), 'An annotated bibliography on the (macro)foundation of post Walrasian economics', in D. Colander (ed.), *Beyond Microfoundations: Post Walrasian Macroeconomics*, New York: Cambridge University Press, pp. 223–51.

Wallace, N. (1980), 'The overlapping generations model of fiat money', in J.H. Kareken and N. Wallace (eds), *Models of Monetary Economics*, Minneapolis, MN: Federal Reserve Bank of Minneapolis, pp. 49–82.

Wallace, N. (1983), 'A legal restrictions theory of the demand for "money" and the role of monetary policy', Federal Reserve Bank of Minneapolis *Quarterly Review*, **7**, 1–7.

Wallace, N. (1988), 'A suggestion for oversimplifying the theory of money', conference papers published as a supplement to the *Economic Journal*, March, 25–36.

Walras, L. (1954), *Elements of Pure Economics*, translated by W. Jaffe, Homewood, IL: Irwin.

Warburton, C. (1966), *Depression, Inflation, and Monetary Policy*, Baltimore, MD: Johns Hopkins Press.

Warburton, C. (1974), 'How to stop inflation and reduce interest rates, now and permanently', mimeograph, September.

Warburton, C. (1981), 'Monetary disequilibrium theory in the first half of the twentieth century', *History of Political Economy*, Summer, 285–99.

Warburton, C., book-length manuscript on the history of monetary-disequilibrium theory deposited in the library of George Mason University, Fairfax, VA.

Weiss, A. (1980), 'Job queues and layoffs in labor markets with flexible wages', *Journal of Political Economy*, June.

Weiss, A. (1990), *Efficiency Wages: Models of Unemployment, Layoffs, and Wage Dispersion*, Princeton, NJ: Princeton University Press.

Wheatley, J. (1807), *An Essay on the Theory of Money and Principles of Commerce*, vol 1, London: Cadell and Davies.

Wheatley, J. (1819), *Report on the Reports of the Bank Committees*, Shrewsbury: W. Eddowes.

Wicksell, K. (1898), *Interest and Prices*, translated by R.F. Kahn (1936), reprinted (1965), New York: Augustus M. Kelley.

Wicksell, K. (1934), *Lectures on Political Economy*, translated by E. Classen, London: Routledge & Kegan Paul, vols I and II, especially I, Part II.

Wilson, C.A. (1979), 'Equilibrium and adverse selection', *American Economic Review*, May, 313–17.

Wonnacott, P. (1958), 'Neutral money in Patinkin's money, interest, and prices', *Review of Economic Studies*, **26**, 70–71.

Yeager, L.B. (1956), 'A cash-balance interpretation of depression', *Southern Economic Journal*, April, 438–47.

Yeager, L.B. (1968) , 'Essential properties of the medium of exchange', *Kyklos*, **21** (1), 45–69.

Yeager, L.B. (1973), 'The Keynesian diversion', *Western Economic Journal*, June, 150–63.

Yeager, L.B. (1976a), 'Bootstrap inflation', *Journal of Finance*, March, 103–12.

Yeager, L.B. (1966, 1976b), *International Monetary Relations*, 1st and 2nd edns, New York: Harper & Row.

Yeager, L.B. (1976c), 'Toward understanding some paradoxes in capital theory', *Economic Inquiry*, September, 313–46.

Yeager, L.B. (1978), 'What are banks?', *Atlantic Economic Journal*, December, 1–14.

Yeager, L.B. (1979), 'Capital paradoxes and the concept of waiting', in M.J. Rizzo (ed.), *Time, Uncertainty and Disequilibrium: Exploration of Austrian Themes*, Lexington, MA: Lexington Books, pp. 187–214.

Yeager, L.B. (1981), 'Clark Warburton, 1896–1979', *History of Political Economy*, Summer, 279–84.

Yeager, L.B. (1982), 'Individual and overall viewpoints in monetary theory', in I.M. Kirzner (ed.), *Method, Process, and Austrian Economics: Essays in Honor of Ludwig von Mises*, Lexington, MA: Lexington Books, pp. 225–46.

Yeager, L.B. (1983), 'Stable money and free-market currencies', *Cato Journal*, Spring, 305–26.

Yeager, Leland B. (1985), 'The Keynesian heritage,' center symposia series No. CS-16, Center for Research in Government Policy and Business, University of Rochester, 4–11.

Yeager, L.B. (1986), 'The significance of monetary disequilibrium', *Cato Journal*, Fall, 369–99.

Yeager, L.B. (1988), 'On interpreting Keynes: reply to Leijonhufvud', *Cato Journal*, Spring/Summer, 205–8.

Yeager, L.B. (1991), 'New Keynesians and old monetarists', reprinted in (1997), *The Fluttering Veil Essays on Monetary Disequilibrium*, edited and with an introduction by G. Selgin, Indianapolis, IN: Liberty Fund, pp. 281–302.

Yeager, L.B. (1994a), 'Tautologies in economics and the natural sciences', *Eastern Economic Journal*, Spring, 157–69.

Yeager, L.B. (1994b), 'Eucken on capital and interest', *Journal of Economic Studies*, vol. 24, No. 4, 61–75.

Yeager, L.B. (1998), 'Are markets like language?', *Quarterly Journal of Austrian Economics*, Fall, 15–27.

Yeager, L.B. (2000), 'Against mistaken moralizing', *Quarterly Journal of Austrian Economics*, Spring, 49–54.

Yeager, L.B. (2001), 'The perils of base money', *Review of Austrian Economics*, December, 251–66.

Yeager, L.B. and associates. (1981), *Experiences with Stopping Inflation*, Washington, DC: American Enterprise Institute.

Yeager, L.B. and R.L. Greenfield (1989), 'Can monetary disequilibrium be eliminated?', *Cato Journal*, Fall, 405–21.

Yeager, L.B. and A.A. Rabin (1997), 'Monetary aspects of Walras's Law and the stock-flow problem', *Atlantic Economic Journal*, March, 18–36.

Yeager, L.B. and D.G. Tuerck (1966), *Trade Policy and the Price System*, Scranton: International Textbook Co.

Yeager, L.B. and D.G. Tuerck (1976), *Foreign Trade and U.S. Policy*, New York: Praeger.

Zecher, R. (1972), 'On the content and issues of current monetary economics', in D. Carson (ed.), *Money and Finance: Readings in Theory, Policy and Institutions*, 2nd edn, New York: Wiley, pp. 259–69.

Zincone, L. (1967), 'The real-balance effect: aspects and evidence', Ph.D. dissertation, University of Virginia.

Zincone, L. (1968), 'The real-balance effect: aspects and evidence', *Journal of Finance*, September, 693–94.

Index